Identity Transformation and Politicization in Africa

AFRICA: PAST, PRESENT & PROSPECTS

Series Editors

Toyin Falola, The University of Texas, Austin; and Olajumoke Yacob-Haliso, Babcock University, Nigeria

This series collates and curates studies of Africa in its multivalent local, regional, and global contexts. It aims fundamentally to capture in one series historical, contemporary and multidisciplinary studies which analyze the dynamics of the African predicament from deeply theoretical perspectives while marshalling empirical data to describe, explain, and predict trends in continuities and change in Africa and in African studies.

The books published in this series represents the multiplicity of voices, local and global in relation to African futures. It not only represents diversity, but also provides a platform for convergence of outstanding research that will enliven debates about the future of Africa, while also advancing theory and informing policy making. Preference is given to studies that deliberately link the past with the present and advances knowledge about various African nations by extending the range, breadth, depth, types and sources of data and information existing and emerging about these countries.

Recent and Forthcoming Titles

Identity Transformation and Politicization in Africa: Shifting Mobilization, edited by Toyin Falola and Céline A. Jacquemin

Guerrilla Radios in Southern Africa: Broadcasters, Technology, Propaganda Wars, and the Armed Struggle, edited by Sekibakiba Peter Lekgoathi; Tshepo Moloi, and Alda Romão Saúte Saíde

Copper King in Central Africa: Corporate Organization, Labor Relations, and Profitability of Zambia's Rhokana Corporation, by Hyden Munene

Rethinking Institutions, Processes and Development in Africa, edited by Ernest Toochi Aniche and Toyin Falola

Civil and Political Rights in Cameroon: A Theoretical and Contextual Appraisal, by Avitus Agbor

Decolonizing Interreligious Education: Developing Theologies of Accountability, by Shannon Frediani

Identity Transformation and Politicization in Africa

Shifting Mobilization

Edited by

Toyin Falola and Céline A. Jacquemin

LEXINGTON BOOKS
Lanham • Boulder • New York • London

Published by Lexington Books
An imprint of The Rowman & Littlefield Publishing Group, Inc.
4501 Forbes Boulevard, Suite 200, Lanham, Maryland 20706
www.rowman.com

86-90 Paul Street, London EC2A 4NE, United Kingdom

British Library Cataloguing in Publication Information Available

Library of Congress Cataloging-in-Publication Data Available

ISBN 9781666917925 (cloth) | ISBN 9781666917932 (epub) | ISBN 9781666917949 (paperback)

To all people of African descent who live on the continent or in diaspora and who struggle to transform, politicize, and mobilize for empowerment, positive change, and to secure the rights of people to nurture diverse, multilayered, and inclusive identities.

Toyin Falola and Céline A. Jacquemin

Contents

Introduction

Céline A. Jacquemin and Toyin Falola

Many stories of long-standing conflicts denounce immutable elements or dimensions of identities such as ethnicity, language, culture, or religion. Rather than remain constrained by the assumption of unchangeable dimensions of identities, this book interrogates the ways that identities are politicized, transformed, and used to mobilize by tracking examples throughout the African continent that demonstrate alternative choices for conflict resolution, examine philosophical and democratic ways of transforming identity, and provide some concrete options where institutions and technology mobilize for education and empowerment around issues of African identities.

The diverse research approaches integrated into the book chapters do not intend to provide a positivist exhaustive overview of identity themes for politicization, transformation, and mobilization on the African continent. Instead, the book seeks to bring together diverse methods and cases, with different perspectives to provide a wide array of ways to examine identity often assumed static even when acknowledged as socially constructed.[1] This volume questions whether identity is providing and sustaining power for elites, or fueling oppression and conflicts, being mobilized for exclusionary movements versus inclusive societal changes, or educating in ways that foster progress and development. Do aspects of African identities and the challenges they present also hold prospects for more inclusive and peaceful democratic and representative futures?

The authors cover a wide spectrum of expertise on different African countries. They come from diverse complementary disciplines (History, Political Science, Public Administration, Philosophy, Economics and Finance, Cultural Studies, Music, and International Relations), and use various methods and approaches in their research. Some contributors belong to the groups whose identity is being scrutinized and might even be participants in some of these efforts to politicize and mobilize, while others remain outside observers, who share some traits or interests with the African identities examined and provide different kinds of insights. Several chapters explore how studying African history and identity through innovative pedagogical projects, facilitated by the expansion of internet and new social media technologies, transform and connect identities to the African continent.

The genesis of this project came in 2019 when Professor Toyin Falola and Dr Céline Jacquemin sought participants whose research focused on identities to "critically examine the contested processes of identity formation, transformation, and politicization and the significance for African societies," past, present, and future. In the following section, we highlight the place where this book fits connected to several bodies of literature that address similar themes and concepts.

ETHNICITY AND AFRICAN IDENTITIES

Our volume expands further the systematic research conducted around the central themes of identity and adds to earlier scholarships that scrutinized concepts, histories, and trends surrounding African identities as part of studies centered on cultural, ethnic, religious, political, or developing issues.

Falola examined many dimensions of African identities in the context of *the Power of African Cultures* and provided an analysis of nationalism, religion, traditions, politics, the political economy of development and underdevelopment, and of language and gender, on both the African continent and within the diaspora. In the chapter on "Ethnic Nationalism," Falola explains:

> Ethnicity has served African politics as a bargaining device available to members of different groups to negotiate and compromise. [. . .] It is wishful thinking that cultural identities constructed by ethnicity will disappear with development. To the contrary, ethnicity is becoming stronger. Rather than seek the means to destroy loyalty to the group, it is much more effective to develop complementary identities that will enable the individual to seek a balance between the group and the nation. It should be possible to be a Yoruba, a Muslim, and a Nigerian at the same time. To give the individual the option of choosing one at the expense of the other is to set the modern nation on a dangerous path that will destroy it.[2]

This book, *Identity Transformation and Politicization in Africa: Shifting Mobilization,* provides its strongest contributions by following with Falola's recommendation of seeking examples and successes where African identities offer more inclusive, transformative, and multilayered dimensions for communities and individuals, and where technology and education can further improve possibilities for more constructive and inclusive futures.

Most often the literature that focuses on African identities has included the dimension of ethnicity. *Ethnicity & Democracy in Africa,* edited by Berman, Eyoh, and Kymlicka, questioned why ethnicity and religion created such tensions and political problems in communities in Africa and, therefore, sought examples of institutions that could support democratic nation-building.[3] In 2005, Posner published his seminal work in the field of African identities, *Institutions and Ethnic Politics in Africa,* where his theory grounded in the case study of Zambia explored how people at times chose to identify with their specific tribes versus prioritizing their larger language group and vice versa.[4] Posner's research demonstrated that the activation of specific dimensions of ethnicity was an important variable that could be researched and that institutional structural changes triggered the activation of ethnic dimension. As a central component of identities, ethnicity provides the space to look at ways that different dimensions of identities are politicized, transformed, or mobilized. Therefore, other groundbreaking scholarship integrated research from different parts of the African continent to examine these concepts further.

In 2008, Simpson and the contributors to their edited volume compiled an extensive study of *Language and National Identity in Africa* with examples from 19 countries throughout the continent to examine the relation of languages (and their status as majority or minority languages) with national, ethnic, and cultural identities.[5] In 2009 Falola and Usman edited a collection on *Movements, Borders, and Identities in Africa* that addressed issues of identity in the context of migration and within diasporas.[6] In their 2010 compilation about *Ethnic Diversity in Eastern Africa,* editors Njogu, Ngeta, and Wanjau surveyed cases of politicized inter-ethnic conflicts and mobilization that sought to get, maintain, or solidify power as the competition for resources intensifies.[7]

For detailed historic post-colonial African cases that investigate secessionist movements in Katanga, the Biafra, Eritrea, South Sudan, and Somaliland, we recommend the new edited volume published in 2020, by Thomas and Falola: *Secession and Separatist Conflicts in Postcolonial Africa.*[8] In a most extensive compilation of historical research from 2018, Falola and Shanguhyia, with many well-established contributing authors, provide a wide-ranging overview of many elements and themes connected to African identities in *The Palgrave Handbook of African Colonial and Postcolonial History.*[9]

In contrast, this book does not include several unfolding cases of ethnic conflicts that continue challenging identity politicization, transformation, and mobilization as these situations continue constantly evolving, and several recent publications shed specific valuable insights on the connections of identity in these unfolding struggles. For the very complex case of politization of identity interlaced with a strong linguistic dimension in Cameroon, we will direct our readers to a newly published book in 2019,

Nation Without Narration: History, Memory and Identity in Postcolonial Cameroon, by Ramon Fonkoué, where he provides a cross-disciplinary look in depth at Cameroon's currently volatile situation and investigates the roots of present conflicts through the continued relevance of post-colonial critical theory.[10] Fonkoué further reframes questions of modernity and development suggesting a method that draws from people's lived experiences that can also be applicable to other post-colonial contexts, in Africa and elsewhere. In the Horn of Africa, Ethiopia presents another current and most challenging fast-changing ethnic conflict that conflates a civil war with massive and egregious patterns of human rights violations while also bringing the country to the brink of a major famine. The recent conflict in the Tigray region in Ethiopia has produced several important pieces by Klosowizc, Raleigh et al., and Gavin.[11] In their 2021 report, Meester and Ezzedine more specifically examine the "Political Mobilization: The Ethnicization of Ethiopia's Informal Sector." They argue that nationalist cleavages are not new, but they have become more salient because of the changing mobilization over the past few years.[12] With the loss of its cohesion the ruling party turned to repression in a time of great economic upheaval that has increased the power of ethnically based mobilization in Ethiopia.[13]

Finally, the case of South Africa has attracted the interest of many scholars over time and particularly since the end of its Apartheid regime. The literature on South African identities provides many important examples where South African identity issues conjure a level of complexity different than in many other parts of the African continent because of the many intersections between identity and the implications from its Apartheid heritage. Early work on identity post-Apartheid includes the chapter on "Between Ethnicity and Nationhood: Shaka Day and the Struggle Over Zuluness in Post-Apartheid South Africa" by Susan Mathieson and David Attwell, and Kathryn Walker's work on "Resolving Debates Over the Status of Ethnic Identities During Transitional Justice" in 2012.[14] Some recent publications undertake investigations of identity, transformation, and mobilization, and include important new findings about the understandings of identities in South Africa. Klandermans concludes that group identification links social identity to collective identity and multiple or dual identities influence protest participation depending how collective identity can be politicized or radicalized.[15] Vorster examines in his article how values of transitional social justice compete with intergenerational conflicts, experiences, political interests, and group identities.[16] Voster argues for embracing justice as the principle to resolve land issues in South Africa. Instead, Lundren and Scheckle study in their work the transformation of identity in youth through experimental participatory research inviting youths to take pictures and asking them to express their experiences, feelings, and identities through language. Students' narratives share concepts of democracy, family, current situation, and culture to be most influential in their lives.[17] In his study "Engineered Zuluness: Language, Education, and Ethnic Identity in South Africa, 1835–1990," Arndt interrogates the actual overlap between speaking Zulu language versus being of Zulu ethnicity.[18] He explains that since American missionaries created the standard of Zulu literary language and imposed it through institutions and general socialization that Zulu functioned as a mandatory language between 1850 and 1990 and therefore does not necessarily identify Zulu ethnic roots but represents more of a modern identity different from its pre-colonial antecedents.[19] The scholarship on South African identities has also been broadening its focus to explore other dimensions of identities such as gender or gendered roles, sexual orientation, and other elements of recognized identities.

Recent scholarship by Kalemba examines gendered expectations and masculinity of Black male nurses, while Jackson explores how the African National Congress came to include the explicit protection against discrimination on grounds of sexual orientation.[20] Sauti argues in "The limitations of legalism and identity labels in post-apartheid South Africa [. . .] that the roots of the identity crisis in South Africa are embedded in systemic failures" that reproduced through birth certificate application, school enrollment forms, and other typical legal documents that require identification based on race, gender, and nationality, therefore automatically reproducing racial divisions anchored in the colonial past that posited Blackness against Whiteness and Nationalism against Otherness.[21] Sauti contends that as long as these forms are used South Africans will not be able to move away from these entrenched categories of identity.[22]

The next portion reviews research that examines similar concepts, themes, and specific elements of identity connected to politicization, transformation, and mobilization.

MOBILIZATION AT THE INTERSECTION OF ETHNICITY, RELIGION, AND LINGUISTIC MEMBERSHIP

The consequences of one's identity intersect with the research posited on ways to mobilize these identities. Klotz and Lynch reported from their survey of research approaches on identity that:

> framing meshes well with causal stories of mobilization, whereas social identity theory assesses individual status within a group. As a result, both incorporate an element of identity affirmation in their evaluations of success and failure.

Indeed, combining the two approaches would lead us to expect that framing would be most successful when its policy prescriptions reinforce in-group identities.[23]

Klotz and Lynch contend that "identities can be contradictory and overlapping and are certainly contested," and they see elements such as religion or class as just dimensions of complex, constructed, and changing identities.[24] Koltz and Lynch argue that:

> the use of language about ethnicity, for instance, tends to encourage the pursuit of collective goals based on race or religion while often devaluing those that stress gender or class distinctions. But religious beliefs and the boundaries of membership within ethnic groups do evolve over time. And neither gender nor class is a static category. These instabilities and ambiguities offer opportunities to redefine routine practices. For instance, women, embracing multiple identities, might mobilize for equal rights within a religious or ethnic group and, as an unintended consequence, improve their economic condition.[25]

Ethnicity is invoked as roots of intractable conflicts over resources.[26] However, extensive research on the African continent and around the world can show cases where diverse elements of ethnic identities can be invoked to build peaceful alliances rather only to sustain or reproduce conflicts. Ethnicity can be a very powerful tool for mobilizing people, enforcing boundaries, and/or building coalitions.[27] Religious affiliation represents the other dimension of identity often associated with oppression and bloodshed. The prevailing form of associational activities on the African continent has been participation in religious services and organizations.[28] Therefore, when looking at mobilization, we also need to assess the impact of religious affiliation. Riedl explains how religious organizations are mobilizing on multiple fronts in newly liberalizing pluralistic African environments.[29] Even when religious establishments' primary goals are to retain members and grow their membership, they have increasingly mobilized politically, at times invited by the ruling regimes (as in Zambia and Senegal) or in reactions to the government as with Kenya.[30] Political liberalization has fostered increasing religious pluralism which opens opportunities for religious mobilization in the political realm.[31] When religious mobilization also maps onto ethnicity, as Agbiboa and Okem describe in "Unholy Trinity: Assessing the Impact of Ethnicity and Religion on National Identity in Nigeria," how political mobilization anchored in ethnic and religious characteristics has been used to weaken the nation building component of a national Nigerian identity.[32]

For an in-depth review of the processes at play in Africa, a new publication by Green, "The Politics of Ethnic Identity in Sub-Saharan Africa," highlights that most often the question asked about politics and ethnicity is about how ethnicity influences politics.[33] Green wants instead to figure out "how politics can influence ethnic identity, especially in the short term."[34] To do so, Green examines how a newly elected president from a different ethnic group can create an incentive for citizens to switch their own ethnicity to belong to the ethnicity of the president in order to benefit from clientelism and other perks reserved for those with the favored ethnicity.[35] Green was able to trace that 'ethnic switching,' as he puts it, was more likely to occur as the level of autocracy increased. Therefore, Green reinforces the possibility for identity transformation.[36] His findings provide further openings to move away from the assumption that ethnicity is immutable. Green provides the example of motivation to change the prioritization of one's ethnic identities.

Another extensive study of mobilization was completed by Nasong'o in 2015 where he not only reviewed all previous works on mobilization (primordialism, internal colonialism theory, and modernization approaches) but more importantly proposed a new theory of Ethnic Mobilization and Violence, which he calls the 'Grievance Model.'[37] He applies this model systematically to the case of the Sudan to demonstrate that his 'Grievance Model' does explain that:

> deeply felt grievances on the part of an identity group coupled with political opportunity and resources result in the political mobilization of such a group in a quest for the redress of their grievances. Such political mobilization does not automatically lead to violence unless the state responds to the mobilized group with policies of denial. This is what happened in both the first civil war (1956–72) and the second civil war (1983–2005) [in Sudan].[38]

To address the politicization, transformation, and mobilization of African identities, the book is broken into three major sections. In the first section, we survey trends in identity politics, philosophical roots, and three of the major elements of identity, whether political (elites), or economic (monetary units), or cultural (music). The next section includes chapters that seek to overcome divisive dichotomies and move beyond exclusionary dimensions of identities to build more overarching inclusionary identities that foster democratization, development, and education. The third section of the book focuses on dimensions of identity transformation and mobilization through technology, and the opportunities that technology brings to educating about African identities and adds to the important lessons and pedagogical projects described in *Teaching Africa: A Guide for the 21st Century Classroom.*[39]

BOOK STRUCTURE

While no one volume can fully examine every aspect of identity transformation and politicization or mobilization on the African continent, this book provides three major sections that introduce many pressing issues that map onto identity transformation and politicization, and then turns to examining shifting mobilizing trends on the African continent. One of the positive attributes of this edited volume comes from looking at very different elements of identity whether ethical, political, elitist, economic, cultural, conflictual, transformative, or mobilizing found at the local, national, or even global levels. It also addresses dichotomies such as the prevalent conflicting priorities of farmers versus herders, as well as different elements often politicized to wedge a gap between ethnic groups. In addition, it examines other more civic-minded concepts for shared national identity from community service, restorative justice, performing arts, and music, to newly devised monetary units and redesigned political institutions for empowerment.

The book combines specific cases throughout the entire continent rather than solely focusing on Sub-Saharan African examples of identity politicization and transformation. The chapters bring detailed examples from Morocco, Tunisia, Libya, Senegal, Ghana, Nigeria, Kenya, Rwanda, and from outside the continent, from the United States by reviewing educational projects connected to African identities. While much of the research throughout the book focused on many traditional elements of identity, the third section of the book provides a look at the impact of technology on mobilization and enables us to investigate the pedagogy of building more inclusive identities, the activation of identity for democratization, and the mobilization of interest in African identity issues, even if at times used against the rights of oppressed groups.

Part I: Interrogating the Trends, Ethics, and Political, Economic, and Cultural Elements of Identity provides an overview of the politicization of African identities. It starts with the trends in the politicization of African identities, then an evaluation of the ethics of African identity issues within the Ubuntu philosophical context, next, an interrogation of the impact of political elites and institutions on the politicization of identity. It subsequently turns to an examination of how monetary identity as an economic element transformed sovereign identity, and finally, the section looks closely at music, so central to African cultures and identities, to highlight how musical performances encoded with oral traditions by communities assist in identity building and can facilitate sustained development.

Chapter 1, "Politics of Being and Its Contemporary Implications in Africa: Positive or Negative Trends?" written by Olanrewaju Atanda Orija, focuses on identity trends in general on the African continent and in particular in

Nigeria, not only one of the most populous countries in Africa, but also one that presents many of the patterns of ethnic diversity within its federal states that display characteristics similar to many other African countries, from having states with one dominant ethnic group, to states that have multiple conflicting ethnic groups, some states dominated by Muslims, while others have majorities of Christians or of animists. Orija explains how the politicization of identity intersected with regional cleavages threatens regional integration, collective interests, and broader nationalist inclinations, all foundations for a more inclusive national identity.

Olanrewaju Atanda Orija makes clear that the prevalent structural conditions in Africa, preserving particularism, resisting nationalism, and inducing ethnicism, reveal how the continent has been reconfigured by the process of modern globalization, modernization, and politicization of identity. The incidences of indigene-settler dichotomy, ethno-religious chauvinism, and politics of identity, seemingly deepening complexity of African identities thus significantly defining modern politics, have indeed precipitated conflicts rather than cooperation. This chapter examines how politicized identities have induced poor social mobilization, identity formation, and inequality in wealth and resources distribution, as well as the ways politics of being magnify fear of marginalization and exclusion, thus aggravating the implications of identity and ethnic politics. The study observes that the lack of holistic and inclusive African identities' mechanism exacerbates the tension between ethnic and religious when superimposed on regional cleavages for protection. These social practices evoke trending ethnic group formations that are becoming purveyors of identities. Ethnicism and tribalism propagate dastardly consequences for regional integration, inclusive collective interest, and weaken nationalism. The research adopts a qualitative framework of data collection and content analysis. Orija presents many of the central concepts for assessing African identities and introduces issues relevant to globalization, identity politics, the politicization of identity, politics of being, marginalization, and mobilization that run throughout several other chapters.

Chapter 2, "'Ubuntu' Dialogic Ethics: Towards a Liberal Theory of Virtue and Transformation of Identities in Africa," by Jude Chinwuba Asike and Patricia Ogugua Anwuluorah, examines how traditionally African Ubuntu philosophy has been eclipsed by many individualistic liberal concepts. The authors support recapturing Ubuntu elements to help transform identity and foster further development in Africa. Asike and Anwuluorah contend that contemporary debate about 'civil society' is in one measure, a debate about virtue and vice. It is a debate about the characterization of human existence for a cultivation of good or bad habits. This chapter is a renewal of African classical ethics anchored in the concept of *Ubuntu*, to explore a liberal theory of virtue for African development. The principles of Ubuntu as ethics of humanity, of a universal bond of sharing that connects all because it posits that "I am because we are" can propagate a dialectic of humanity caring towards others. It indicates goodness as a moral victory for self-actualization or achievement of higher moral goals for the entire community in which otherness can become a mirror or an intersubjective tool. This is expressed in the pursuit of common good, a quality we owe to each other or to otherness. This idealism suggests that African transformation is not just embedded in an individual; it is co-substantively bestowed upon the other for all. *Ubuntu* as a set of interrelated concepts invokes the spirit of reciprocity, collaboration, inclusiveness, and nationalism as central elements of cultural traditions in Africa. The chapter argues that Ubuntu is a moral philosophy of socio-political and economic virtue of knowledge, which would have transformed the developmental imperatives in Africa had it not been replaced with other paradigms (i.e., the Christian and Islamic traditional ideologies). It also suggests the exposition of African ethics in *Ubuntu* philosophy can be exhumed to rekindle the already forgotten virtues of our existential qualities and identities as Africans. It upholds the thesis that we can rekindle a language of virtue and vice in a culture that is fundamentally liberal. This creates a possibility of community, simultaneously altruistic and benevolent, by providing essential elements for examining a liberal theory of virtue and transformation of cultural, ethnic, and religious identities in Africa. Asike and Anwuluorah contribute to the volume in major ways by examining Ubuntu philosophy as it relates to identity transformation on the African continent.

In Chapter 3, "Interrogating Identity Politics in Nigeria," Soj Ojo explores how ethnic and cultural categories used to mobilize political behavior and allegiances are often manipulated by self-serving elites who politicize ethnicity for their own gains rather than truly advance the lives of the groups whose identity they politicize to mobilize support. Ojo offers an alternative perspective that interrogates the role of elites in the nature of identity politics in Nigeria and its impact on the creation of new national and local governing units that provide positions for more representation but also seem to divide further rather than unite the country. In this chapter, Ojo shifts the focus of discourse from scholarly orthodoxy on identity politics, which often emphasizes ethnic and cultural categories as distinct and boundary-defining. From such an orthodox perspective, it is often assumed that identity based on ethnic and cultural categories has great potential to inspire collective loyalties and passions to mobilize and energize political behavior. The chapter offers an alternative focus, which interrogates the nature and dynamics of identity politics. The central argument is that the ideological myths that have sustained orthodox identity politics are essentially self-serving and usually articulated by a dominant group of elite, religious fundamentalists, or by political entrepreneurs. The dominant group of elites is made up of persons who share a common personal identity, interest, norms, and practices that cut across ethnic boundaries. The chapter examines some theories of ethnic identity that have enriched scholarly discourse in the literature and provides insights into how groups are manipulated to perceive imagined and real threats to their tangible self-interests and characteristic traits as risks to the identity and interests of their ethnic group. The analysis shows how ethnicity becomes politicized and snowballs into identity politics when unsuspecting members of ethnic groups are manipulated and used by their political elite as partisan actors, involved in steps and activities intended to confront purported threats to their collective identity and interest. The research provides an alternative perspective for interrogating the nature of identity politics in Nigeria. Ojo's work considers how identity versus politics, in the way elites manipulate group interests, through myths and ideology, serve themselves rather than aspiring for the greater good. His research unveils possibilities for refocusing identity politics to better serve national unity, good governance, and sustainable development.

Next, Chapter 4, "Monetary Sovereignty, Sovereign Identities, and Monetary Identities in Ghana and Nigeria in the Late 1950s to early 1960s" by Bamidélé Aly explains how monetary sovereignty in the West African countries of Ghana and Nigeria became important elements of sovereign identity building. When Ghana and Nigeria moved away from the West African Sterling to their own money unit, creating their individual monetary identity became part of the nation building project where one national money provided a path that further empowered a distinct identity fostered by their newfound monetary independence. Bamidélé Aly recounts that before accessing their individual independence in 1957 and 1960, the Gold Coast and Nigeria, respectively, were part of the British Empire and as such their legal tender was the West African Sterling, which was pegged to the British Sterling but run by the West African Currency Board, headquartered in London. Ahead of the discussions about their independence, conversations were held to create their own monetary infrastructure to come off the West African Sterling and to operate their own affairs to gain not only their political independence but also their monetary sovereignty. The acquisition of their monetary sovereignty was important to shape the monetary identities in the nation-building process post-independence and also for their sovereignty identities. According to the Westphalian principles of "One Nation/ One Money," monetary sovereignty is inherent to sovereign ethnic identity. Aly's chapter compares Ghana and Nigeria to determine how their respective paths to political sovereignty intertwined with decisions for their monetary independence that transformed and empowered their identity.

The last chapter in the first section, Chapter 5, "Music as a Tool for Sustainable Development in Nigerian Society" by Maureen Ada Uche looks at how music has provided a very important and central cultural tool for identity building that can foster further sustainable development throughout each of the Nigerian regions irrespective of ethnic groups. Most African ethnic groups share the importance of music as a central element of one's identity. Uche explains that every society in Africa possesses cultural heritage that is distinct, yet familiar. Culture, including music, has therefore become an integral part for sustainable development in every society. The beliefs, practices, and cultural heritage of societies help to create avenues for an effective understanding of one's histories, culture, and social practices. This chapter presents music as a cultural indicator that portrays the beliefs, practices, and ideas—all elements of identity—of the society where it emerges. It highlights the various ways music can sustain the development of a society through exploration of cultural needs. This study outlines the indigenous music of communities in Nigeria (especially among the Igbo communities) as a culture and tool for sustainable development. Uche follows a historical design to enumerate songs, instrumentation, and dance as the basis for this study. The purpose is to showcase the rich cultural heritage and identities possessed by the economic, social, and cultural values inherent in the musical practices and performances of these indigenous groups. The chapter recommends the need to encourage the practice of music for sustained and sustainable development. Therefore, efforts should be made to enhance cultural musical heritage and reinforce musical roots of identities across boundaries.

Following the introduction of these main themes and elements of identity provided in the first section, the next segment of the book, Part II: Identity and Ethnic Conflict, Transformation, Reconciliation, and Empowerment, investigates three case studies within their extensive historical contexts to explore how major dichotomies of identity such as the herder/farmer categories, ethnic versus religious affiliations, or gender, were often used for oppression, yet identities, institutions, and structures can be transformed to empower all within these nations.

In Chapter 6, "Ethnicity, Peacebuilding, and Conflict Transformation in Nigeria: The Case of Herder–Farmer Conflict," Kialee Nyiayaana looks at ethnicity and the intersubjective understanding of conflicts between herders and farmers. Nationalism and the politicization of identity shape relations between social groups and produce competing political and ethnic claims that make peace building much more difficult. This chapter reflects on the impact of ethnicity on the resolution of the herder-farmer conflicts in Nigeria. It argues that although the conflict is historically rooted in resource competition between herders and farmers, ethnicity influences how the state and community politicizes policy responses to the conflict and their implementation in ways that act as barriers to building lasting peace between the two different occupational groups in Nigeria. Fulani pastoralist nomads predominantly practice Islam while people of the Hausa ethnic extraction in Nigeria tend to be settled Christian farmers. By the geographical configuration and ethnic diversity of Nigeria, ethnic and religious identities are intertwined in the struggle, by individuals and groups, for opportunities in Nigeria. The politicization of these different categories or layers of identities— occupational, religious, and ethnic identities—affects the construction of security threats posed by the herder-farmer conflict and the nature of the state and community responses to them. The chapter demonstrates, for example, how the policy actions of President Muhammadu Buhari, himself a Fulani, and his position on herdsmen killings have fueled perceptions that the Nigerian state has tended to condone armed attacks on farmers by herders in different parts of Nigeria. At the same time, to protect their source of livelihood from attacks from herdsmen, farmers, who in most cases are not Fulani-Hausa, have linked the protection of individual identities to the preservation of collective group identity. The logic of territorial nationalism and politics of identity, therefore, shape relations between both social groups (Igbo vs Fulani-Hausa) and generate competing ethnic and political claims such that designing and implementing effective peacebuilding interventions to resolve the herder-farmer conflict in Nigeria are made difficult because of the need to reconceptualize elements of individual and group identity.

The next chapter also starts with the very real and devastating impact that the politicization and implications of the farmer/herder dichotomy, instilled in Rwandans during colonial times that led to the devastation during the one hundred days of the 1994 Genocide Against Tutsi, and focuses on the way Rwandans have successfully transformed Rwandans' national identity to build an inclusive and welcoming open identity which has helped move the country forward. In Chapter 7, "How Rwanda Transformed Identity Post-Genocide," Céline A. Jacquemin explores how Rwandans transformed their individual identity since 1994. The Rwandan government built upon previous meaningful cultural traditions like Umuganda and the concept of community courts— Gacaca—to provide institutional ways of transforming identity and bringing all Rwandans to unite through national citizenship above and beyond any other differences that had divided them before. This new nation building project rather than resort to previous exclusionary kinds of identity elements (farmers Hutu vs. herders Tutsi) integrated many new elements to foster identity transformation. It also built upon the work from political and trauma psychologists, like Staub and Pearlman, who collaborated with international non-profit organizations and with governing officials and local citizen committees who are responsible for setting the priorities of the national days of Umuganda service. They even received support from non-profit organizations for the diffusion of a new radio program—Musekeweya—that provided many opportunities to learn about conflict resolution. National efforts to unite, rebuild, reconcile, and renew provided tools and processes for transforming

identity away from exclusionary or divisive ideology to strengthen democratic institutions and develop its economy.

In Chapter 8, "African Bureaucracies and the Implementation of Women
Empowerment Programs," Abidemi Abiola Isola, Tolulope Adeogun, and
Victor Adesiyan address gender equality, representation, and empowerment
by examining how Nigerian bureaucratic efforts for women representation
have not reached their goals of bringing meaningful representation of gender
throughout bureaucratic and political institutions. Gender equality, while
sought, has remained elusive. The authors make the case for the need for true
empowerment in order to make more headway in the area of administrative
female representation to yield true women empowerment. As African countries have taken the leadership in global rankings of women's parliamentary
representation, many studies have focused on the factors and dynamics
that have produced this result over the last twenty years. The twin puzzle
has been, first, that women's political ascension as executives and heads of
governments has not been commensurate with parliamentary progress on
this score. Second, the global leadership in parliamentary representation of
women has not trickled down to produce more gender-equitable societies,
despite decades of global activism to achieve this aim. This chapter's empirical research combines Maxine Molyneux's organizing theory with African
feminist theory to highlight how the presence of institutional and societal factors in Africa limit the efforts of women's organizations, both at the national
and international levels. These organizations are working towards increased
representation of women in political participation and decision making, both
in qualitative and quantitative ways. The study finds that there were challenges, as a cog in the wheel of the implementation of both national and
international laws and treaties, to empower women and encourage gender
mainstreaming in Africa. This chapter recommends that the patriarchal power
structure oppressing women should be transformed through African definitions of gender roles and identities, based in indigenous teachings of African
culture. This transformation should start in the homes, schools, and at social
gatherings, through the mobilizing and politicizing of meaningful gender representation, beyond simply teaching progenies the story of successful African
women, previously hidden by Eurocentric doctrines. The book then turns to
looking at ways in which social media and technology can be both beneficial
to learning about African identities and to claiming democratic and human
rights protections for Africans (and in one case can also be mobilized in a
detrimental way).

Part III: Internet and Social Media Foster Identity Change, Exploration,
and Mobilization turns to how technological developments have transformed
mobilization, as in the case of the Arab Spring in North Africa, but also how
they can improve the pedagogy of teaching about African history at the center

of African identity. The section ends with a case where social media and internet technology have helped to mobilize nationally to restrict democratic and human rights protections in Senegal, while providing international connections for targeted groups.

In Chapter 9, "Building Global Citizenship through the African Digital Public Humanities: The MaCleKi Collaborative," Meshack Owino and J. Mark Souther explain their pedagogical experiment with their project called MaCleKi that went beyond simply allowing students to explore another country through the internet, and helped students, in both the United States and in Kenya, build a much more global sense of citizenship rather than the local parochial sense of belonging they start with. Localized ethnic, religious, and regional-based identities can be transformed where technology provides the ability to share other groups' places and explore their geography, society, and stories to promote global consciousness and more inclusive categories of identity. The Owino and Souther chapter examines the possibilities and challenges of mobilizing digital public humanities to facilitate a new sense of global citizenship among the African public, especially among college students, and their counterparts in other places in the world. History faculty and students from Cleveland State University in Cleveland, Ohio, USA, and from Maseno University in Kisumu, Kenya, conducted a research project over the span of four years from 2014 to 2018. Sponsored by the National Endowment for the Humanities, their project examines the role of mobile devices in curating and disseminating stories about places, events, and people that might otherwise disappear from public memory, while at the same time facilitating learning among students from different parts of the world. Owino and Souther's experiment demonstrates that students who participated in the collaborative research and learning project not only did so successfully, but also developed a new sense of themselves as global citizens during and after their involvement. The students' experiences, attitudes, and worldviews increasingly changed during and after participating in the project. Their views of themselves and of the world changed as they worked with one another. Even though the students live in different parts of the world from one another, their collaborative interactions make them increasingly conscious of each other and of their places as citizens of the world. The students became proud of working with other students from other parts of the globe. Their consciousness as members of the global community increased. The chapter is therefore based on the role of mobile devices in facilitating learning and research among faculty and students across geographical spaces, and, more importantly, it reveals that such learning and research processes can be leveraged to promote global consciousness and citizenship in the modern world that transformed their self-identity. These are important questions for scholars to engage with given how the collapse of the Soviet Union, the end of the Cold War, and the subsequent downfall of governments across the African continent have led to the escalation during the past three decades of localized ethnic, religious, and regionally based identities now ubiquitous worldwide. Owino and Souther demonstrate how this case of transformed identity occurred for both students in the United States, as well as for the students in Kenya.

In Chapter 10, "Mobilizing Student Interest in African Identity: An Academic Project for the Real World," Bradford Whitener looks at the StMU Research Scholars project and how this enabled students to enlarge their interests, resonance, and mobilization beyond their own identities looking at African Americans and African history. This chapter looks at an experiment with university students that was designed to improve motivation and to maximize research and writing skills. The project changes students' motivation from seeing the tasks of researching and writing as mere assignments in a class to seeing themselves as doing something meaningful for the real world by collaborating to produce their own articles and improve them so they can be published on the internet. The project transformed the classroom into an organization and the assignments morphed from individual tasks to integrated collaboration requiring many ways of contributing to the organization to benefit each other. With online publications, students selected topics for research that mattered to them, often researching into facets of their own identities and cultural heritage. Many of the African and African American students engaged with topics that intersected with African diaspora issues, while students from other marginalized backgrounds sometimes also chose topics related to African and African American experiences because of the centrality of the issue of social justice and community. Over time, students involved in the collaborative publication project contributed research centered around their passion, which changed their motivation, both quantitatively and qualitatively. Grades improved and it enhanced their sense of belonging to a connected community of Research Scholars. This community of students published many articles that connected to African identities in a way that was completely unexpected. This high-impact, collaborative academic experiment significantly transformed the students and mobilized them to focus on ways they can shed light on social justice issues.

Aurora Nikkels, the author of the next chapter, is a veteran student of the StMU Research Scholars project described above by Whitener. Nikkels had already published several articles on Nelson Mandela when she chose a larger project looking at the impact of the internet on mobilization during the Arab Spring in three North African countries.[40] Her research was selected for inclusion in this volume because of the salience and relevance of her research that looks closely at several cases in North Africa at the beginning of the Arab Spring. In Chapter 11, "Institutional Change and Identity: Impact of the Arab Spring and Mobilization in North Africa," Aurora Nikkels looks at institutional change and identity to assess the impact of social media in several initial movements of the Arab Spring in North Africa. She investigates the role technology played in mobilizing different groups, as well as how the government responded with some policy shifts and new laws. Nikkels explains that Tunisia, Morocco, and Libya, part of the 22-nation League of Arab States, saw their populations mobilize during the beginning of the Arab Spring in 2011 demanding more democratic freedom and more economic opportunities. This chapter explores changes in government, constitutions, and laws, answering questions about how each government adapted to or fought back against the demands made by protesters. Nikkels tackles questions about the role played by technology, the internet, and social media in the mobilization and politicization of identity to further the claims of protesters. She also scrutinizes how governments responded to or resisted demands for change and democratization.

The last chapter of the book brings to the forefront disputed identities connected to sexual orientation or the rejection of binary categories of gender that remain much more contested than any of the others previously surveyed. While this makes these issues of mobilization for rights protection salient and current, the chapter also highlights the dangers brought by technology when manipulated to mobilize to further target and oppress minority groups. In Chapter 12, "Tracking Political and Religious Mobilization Against Queer Men in Senegal," Grayson Michael Posey takes a fresh look at how social media can be manipulated to mobilize not just for, but also against others, as was the case in Senegal against queer men. Posey links the creation of queer new visibility to the new technology of the internet and social media and proposes alternatives to alleviate the harm that is being brought upon these groups. Rising incidents of political and religious mobilization against queer and gender nonconforming male citizens in Senegal have been a growing concern in the study of minority rights on the African continent. This chapter investigates new queer identities born out of the misrepresentation of linguistic particularities and how contemporary political and religious movements have capitalized on homophobic sensibilities displayed by Senegalese citizens. Posey analyzes the shift in discourse about queer and gender nonconforming men following the 2008 publication of photos online for an alleged gay wedding. He tracks how collective retaliation following the publication ultimately led to violence and mobilization against queers, and anyone suspected as queer, in June 2021. This chapter definitively links the creation of the Senegalese queer identity with the newfound visibility of queer men in 2008, which intensified human rights violations and discrimination against queer men by increasing insecurity within Senegal. Posey proposes alternatives to alleviate immediate threats of physical harm for queer and gender nonconforming men of Senegal. This chapter wraps up an overview of issues connected to the politicization and transformation of identity with some of the newest salient identity elements of sexual orientation and gender non-conforming identities while also examining the central part that social media and the internet can play both in providing mobilization in support but can also rally resisting protecting the rights of oppressed minority groups.

NOTES

1. As explained by Audie Klotz and Cecelia Lynch, "Identities," in *Strategies for Research in Constructivist International Relations* (Armonk: M.E. Sharpe, Inc., 2007), 65–85.

2. Toyin Falola, *The Power of African Cultures* (Rochester: University of Rochester Press, 2003), 164.

3. Bruce Berman, Dickson Eyoh, and Will Kymlicka, *Ethnicity & Democracy in Africa* (Oxford: J. Currey, 2004).

4. Daniel N. Posner, *Institutions and Ethnic Politics in Africa* (Cambridge: Cambridge University Press, 2005).

5. Andrew Simpson, *Language and National Identity in Africa* (Oxford: Oxford University Press, 2008).

6. Toyin Falola and Aribidesi, *Movements, Borders, and Identities in Africa* (Rochester: University of Rochester Press, 2009).

7. Kimani Njogu, Kabiri Ngeta, and Mary Wanjau, *Ethnic Diversity in Eastern Africa: Opportunities and Challenges* (Nairobi: Twaweza Communications, 2010).

8. Charles Thomas and Toyin Falola, *Secession and Separatist Conflicts in Postcolonial Africa* (Calgary: University of Calgary Press, 2020).

9. Toyin Falola and Martin S. Shanguhyia, *The Palgrave handbook of African colonial and Postcolonial History* (New York: Palgrave Macmillan, 2018).

10. Ramon A. Fonkoué, *Nation without Narration: History, Memory and Identity in postcolonial Cameroon* (Amherst: Cambria Press, 2019).

11. For further reading, please see Robert Klosowicz, "Identity, Ethnic Conflict, and Communal Conflict in Sub-Saharan Africa," *Politeja* 17, no. 5 (2020): 171–90; Clionadh Raleigh et al., *Ethiopia: At risk of Multiplying Conflicts Stretching the Capacity of the State* (Armed Conflict Location & Event Data Project, 2021); Michelle Gavin, *The Conflict in Ethiopia's Tigray Region: What to Know* (Council on Foreign Relations, February 10, 2021), 1–7.

12. Jos Meester and Nancy Ezzeddine, *A Transition at Work? The Ethnicization of Ethiopia's Informal Sector* (The Hague: Clingendael, February 2021).

13. Ibid., 37.

14. Susan Mathieson and David Attwell, "Between Ethnicity and Nationhood: Shaka Day and the Struggle over Zuluness in Post-Apartheid South Africa," in *Multicultural States: Rethinking Difference and Identity*, ed. David Bennett (London: Routledge, 1998); Kathryn Walker, "Resolving Debates over the Status of Ethnic Identities during Transitional Justice," *Contemporary Political Theory* 11, no. 1 (2012): 68–87.

15. P. G. Klandermans, "Identity Politics and Politicized Identities: Identity Processes and the Dynamics of Protest," *Political Psychology* 35, no. 1 (2014): 1–22.

16. Nico Vorster, "Land, Group Identities and Competing Justice Values in South Africa: Reformed Perspectives on Embracive Justice and Permeable Identity Formation," *In die Skriflig/In Luce Verbi* 53, no. 1 (January 2019): 1–7.

17. Bert Lundgren and Eileen Scheckle, "Hope and Future: Youth Identity Shaping in Post-Apartheid South Africa," *International Journal of Adolescence and Youth* 24, no. 1 (January 2019): 51–61.

18. Jochen S. Arndt, "Engineered 'Zuluness': Language, Education, and Ethnic Identity in South Africa, 1835–1990," *The Journal of the Middle East and Africa* 10, no. 3 (July 2019): 211–35.

19. Ibid.

20. Joshua Kalemba, "'Being Called Sisters': Masculinities and Black Male Nurses in South Africa," *Gender, Work, & Organization* 27, no. 4 (July 2020): 647–63; Joseph Jackson, "Roots of Revolution: The African National Congress and Gay Liberation in South Africa," *SSRN Electronic Journal* 44, no. 2 (2019): 613–70.

21. Gloria Sauti, "The Limitations of Legalism and Identity Labels in Post-Apartheid South Africa," *Africanus* 49, no. 2 (November 2019): 1–17.

22. Ibid., 15.

23. Klotz and Lynch, *Strategies for Research*, 76.

24. Ibid., 70.

25. Ibid., 7.

26. James Habyarimana et al., "Why Does Ethnic Diversity Undermine Public Goods Provision," *American Political Science Review* 101, no. 4 (November 2007): 709–25.

27. Benn Eifert, Edward Miguel, and Daniel N. Posner, "Political Competition and Ethnic Identification in Africa," *American Journal of Political Science* 54, no. 2 (2010): 494.

28. Naomi Chazan et al., *Politics and Society in Contemporary Africa* (Boulder: Lynne Rienner Publishers, 1992).

29. RB Reidel, "Transforming Politics, Dynamic Religion: Religion's Political Impact in Contemporary Africa," *African Conflict and Peacebuilding Review* 2, no. 2 (2012): 47.

30. Ibid., 48.

31. Ibid., 48.

32. Daniel Egiegba Agbiboa and Andrew Emmanuel Okem, "Unholy Trinity: Assessing the Impact of Ethnicity and Religion on National Identity in Nigeria," *Peace Research* 43, no. 2 (2011): 98–125.

33. Elliot Green "The Politics of Ethnic Identity in Sub-Saharan Africa," *Comparative Political Studies* 54, no. 7 (June 2021): 1197–226, p. 1198. See also Kate Baldwin and John D. Huber, "Economic versus Cultural Differences: Forms of Ethnic Diversity and Public Goods Provision," *American Political Science Review* 104, no. 4 (November 2010): 644–62; Raphaël Franck and Ilia Rainer, "Does the Leader's Ethnicity Matter? Ethnic Favoritism, Education, and Health in Sub-Saharan Africa," *American Political Science Review* 106, no. 2 (May 2012): 294–325; James P. Habyarimana et

al., *Coethnicity: Diversity and the Dilemmas of Collective Action* (New York: Russel Sage Foundation, 2009); José G. Montalvo and Marta Reynal-Querol, "Ethnic Polarization, Potential Conflict, and Civil Wars," *American Economic Review* 95, no. 3 (June 2005): 796–816; Daniel N. Posner, "The Political Salience of Cultural Difference: Why Chewas and Tumbukas Are Allies in Zambia and Adversaries in Malawi." *The American Political Science Review* 98, no. 4 (2004): 529–45.

34. Green, "The Politics of Ethnic Identity in Sub-Saharan Africa," p. 1198.

35. Ibid., p. 1200.

36. Ibid., pp. 1219–20.

37. Wanjala S. Nasong'o, "Explaining Ethnic Conflicts: Theoretical and Conceptual Perspectives," in *The Roots of Ethnic Conflict in Africa: From Grievance to Violence* (New York: Palgrave Macmillan, 2015), 17–20.

38. Wanjala S. Nasong'o, "Deep-Seated Historical and Socioeconomic Grievances: The North-South Conflict in Sudan," in *The roots of ethnic conflict in Africa: from grievance to violence* (New York: Palgrave Macmillan, 2015), 34.

39. Brandon D. Lundy and Solomon Negash, *Teaching Africa: A Guide for the 21st-Century Classroom* (Bloomington: Indiana University Press, 2013).

40. Aurora Nikkels, "Sticks & Stones May Break My Bones, but My Words Will Build an Army Against Apartheid," StMU Research Scholars, April 7, 2019, https://stmuscholars.org/sticks-and-stones-may-break-my-bones-but-words-will-build-an-army-apartheid/.

PART I

Interrogating the Trends, Ethics, and Political, Economic, and Cultural Elements of Identity

1

Politics of Being and Its Contemporary Implications in Africa

Positive or Negative Trends?

Olanrewaju Atanda Orija

The African continent is blessed with a rich history, heritage, and incredible civilization. African identity remains vast as the continent of Africa whose boundaries—geographical, historical, cultural, and representational—have changed, according to prevalent ideas and formations of global racial identities and power. This indicates that Africa is reconfigured by both the process of modern globalization and the project of African integration. Her identities, therefore, suffer from prehistoric documentation, because the process and practices in the continent strip off primordial authenticity and essentialism. Identities are complex inventions, mutually constitutive, existential, and epistemic constructions.[1] Africans as a people should be understood within their own self-constructed status and identity, and as creators of their own nations.[2] Africa and African identities are in states of being and of becoming, while identity remains a crucial and basic need because it is a potent tool and strong catalyst for driving social mobilization.

The concerns over prehistoric authenticity and essentialism require weapons of history, provoke intellectual reflections on the 'essence' of Africa by African philosophers and resolutions to advance movements, mobilize Africans to reframe how we think about African identities, with ideological and mental commitments to recover African values and prevent foreign degrading perceptions, cultural denigration, and non-African standards.[3]

The discourse on ethnic identities requires probing into the intersectional nature of identities—Hausa, Yoruba, Igbo and Zulu—how the people constructed and invented categories of a shared sense of being, that is, collective identities, expressed in ethnicity: a product of colonial happenstances. Its consequences are that the formation of identities has been reconstructed with its dynamic character, shifting, constructed, and reconfigured. Before race was fundamental to identity formation, European domination provoked a racial response among Africans and diaspora, particularly, relying on Western philosophy and ideological conjecture that Africans do not have a culture of their own, thereby indicating negative presumptions that Africans are primitive and barbaric.[4]

The European construct distorts African identity and her cultural perspectives considering how foreign paradigms and value-judgments negatively defined Africa's civilization and cultures. Eurocentric historiography and Western historical documentations seem to be informed by the lack of doxographic traditions among Africans, yet it is inadequate ground for denying the existence of traditional African philosophy, comparable to Western philosophy. This lack of recorded opinion termed lack of writing and literacy, by Hountoundji, is conterminous to Derrida's deconstruction of authoritarian structure: 'logocentrism.'[5] There is, perhaps, the need to unmask logic of supplementary to transcend metaphysics of presence.[6]

Others identified oral tradition as a source of African traditional philosophy constructed out of proverbs; folklore among other collective wisdom indicates that African cultural values thrive in their traditional thought. Yet, the prevalent historiography relied on Eurocentric and Western historical documentations to assert identity domination; this in particular requires African intellectuals to upscale weapons of history, doxographic in modern African philosophy, compared to traditional philosophy, which seems to permit Western philosophy dominations, distortions, and battered African identity, culture, and histories, to the extent that any genuine African philosophy must be rooted in postcolonial society.[7]

The aforementioned reversal impacts of the Eurocentric constructions and history of negation is a denial to African identity.[8] This engenders fear of future extinction. Restoring Africa with its ancient intellectual heritage, as the European paradigm and their value judgment seems to define Africa's civilization and cultures as somehow intellectually secondary to foreign and Eurocentric historiography. Their assumed intellectual superiority, cultural domination; and conquest have devalued African histories and her identity. History reveals that people cannot separate themselves of culture; either they participate in their own culture or foreign culture, though African cultures and the cultural diversity indicate commonality of cultures in Africa.[9]

Experiences of Africans and of Blacks are undeniably negative in world-views, and this is traceable to Western historical documentations of negation in Adeleke's narration damaging African identity and cultures.[10] Africans and Blacks confronted a formidable and combative historical tradition legitimizing negative worldview as "barbarians," "the dark continent," and "heathens" are nicknames "enlightened" Europeans mobilized to justify Africans' subordination. This tragic historical consciousness, according to Dubois Cook (1960), revealed that Africans and diaspora Blacks need historical and cultural rebirth, weapons of history to reclaim and combat the prevalent racism permeating the intellectual culture ever since the nineteenth century.[11]

Identity diversity, among other dynamics, informed growing intellectual reflections on the 'essence' of Africa and the crave for the recovery, required seeking historical knowledge, which seemingly suffered dearth, among African's essentials to determine the future with Africa's destiny as well as the need for balance between particularity and universality.[12] Thus, identity discourse, significant to Africa's postcolonial era and the need for the weapon of history, is due to past misrepresentations on identity and divisions of Africans by foreigners and colonial rulers. As Europeans and colonial powers widened differences along ethnic fault lines, reconstructed African identity, and termed it ethnicity in Africa, to invent tribalism and worsen existing divisions among Africans.[13]

The broader notion of identity emerged in favor of particular identities through its colonial past: policy of divide and rule.[14] For instance, during the colonial rule, political orders, policy actions, representation organizations and agendas, favored ethnic lines, engendered politicization of ethnicity and other tendencies; religion, cultural beliefs, languages, origin cum space led to rivalry, ethnic conflicts, and other forms of social mobilizations in Africa.[15] Thus, fixed ethnic fault lines prompt favoritism, marginalize certain social groups, and these issues reconstruct African life, politically, culturally, and economically, fueling identities difference among Africans. Identities in Africa were reconfigured in relation to one another.

The practice of politics of difference provides foundation for contemporary structural conditions and pattern of distribution of rewards, perhaps, favor particular identity.[16] This nature of particularity contaminates universality, whereas universality remains the only positive condition for politics. Since no identity in the world ought to be asserted ahead of other identities, without referring to the universal dimension that governs its horizon.[17]

The implications of politics of being, in particular, induces incidences of indigene-settler dichotomy, ethno-religious crisis and deepens the complexity of identity, ethnicity, and religion, among others. Perhaps, reconstructed Africans' social practices, their values, and in the process, seemingly battered the distinctive shared traits with others and brotherhood traditional values that Africans' philosophy is known for, during precolonial days in Africa to marginalization and exclusion, opposes their known practices of communalism, egalitarianism, kinship and respect for the humanism of the individuals, among other values that African systems espouse. By implication, their value systems detest class or mass struggles or social group exclusions. Thus, the nexus between ethnic groups and the state in search for security (welfare) identity and recognition is to ensure that minorities are protected and respected, and to ensure their grievances are adequately addressed. This will reduce opportunity for ethnic mobilization, with equitable access to various services the state provides. These creative measures will shift cultural and political norms of identity.

Relying on the aforesaid, there is need for the weapon of history, to urge African scholars towards advancing mental commitments on how to recover their values.[18] It suggests Africans should constantly promote their values through history. As the fear of Africa's future extinction indicates, the continent needs to survive sufferings from prehistoric authenticity and essentialism, denial, conquest, and cultural domination, as well as the trauma caused by the Europeans. The devaluation of African histories and the importance of their identity revealed that African culture and histories have been seen as primitive, barbaric, and not worth knowing about. Since there is a gap between one's inner identity and one's behavior, vis-à-vis surrounding societies as a result fix together of these two cultures in modern times. Fukuyama notes that multiculturalism today is "a game at the end of history" that should not interfere with or influence decision making in the public sphere.[19] Thus, feeling of evolving beyond identities or tendencies defined by language, color, religion, ethnic nationalities, or invented tribalism by colonial masters, gave up the brotherhood notion in Africa, and citizenship in multicultural societies, exemplified with cases of terror attacks in Nigeria, rights populist movement in Egypt, and trending xenophobia in South Africa.

It is against this backdrop that it is imperative to examine social mobilization, from the lens of identity politics, and identify its implications in Africa with a view to providing a systematic reflection on identities. It equally reflects on the implications of politics of being in Africa as a mobilization tool in complex terrain.

POLITICS AND POLITICIZATION OF IDENTITY

According to communitarians, individuals cooperate, therefore political community is the arena of mutual cooperation and not of conflict. Thus, the essence of being lies in the spirit of cooperation and aid which constitutes the foundation of political organization, an individual being develops his identity, talents, and pursuits in life only from his place in the community. Community is a social relationship based on sharing common characteristics, common values, and interest. Since, it is the natural characteristic of each community, it can be discovered that when people see their common interest, they naturally tend to co-operate in its pursuit, relying on social solidarity, fraternity based on common culture and values to achieve a social goal. Politics of being is activity concerned with the identification and pursuit of common interest and good of the community.

Politicization of identity on the other hand, is a subjective application of identity for a cause. It is the most crucial and the only means by which groups can be mobilized for a particular reason or purpose.[20] It is a process by which elite manipulate, propagate, through the dynamics of group identities, and associate to a certain extent, issue, or instrument of disagreement. Thus, this practice influences the group formation and cohesion with the use of symbols, narratives, and myths, to engineer and fabricate the boundaries of identity to specify who "we" and "they" are. The practice of construction of the out-group (them) as enemy and anti-in-group (us) is a potent process of politicizing an issue to drive a cause. In modern times, politicization of identity is increasingly experiencing changes in local and global spheres, preserving particularity, resisting universality, and promoting difference as it affects social cohesion and integration.[21] This nature of politics reconfigured group relations, broke down social bonds, deprived some, and marginalized vulnerable identities.[22]

IDENTITY AND IDENTITIES

Identity is a multidimensional concept that has both objective and subjective meaning. Identity is experienced as a characteristic that is objective and that distinguishes the self, even if subjectively felt. Identity filters individual experience and promotes a collective sense of solidarity.[23] When a group of people identify themselves with particular ethnic, religious, occupational, or national traits of the respective groups, it becomes a social practice. Identity draws from ideology, values, traditions, language, and collective goals. It is universal, the idea linked to state identity, national identity, transnational identity, ethnic identity, tribal identity, social identity, individual or personal identity. It can also have subnational focus, like ethnic, religious, and transnational, with sexual identity or gender identification.[24]

Erikson provides that identity describes the intersection between group and individual. It is an attribute of group that provides recognition, definition, meaning, affinity, and reference for each member of that group to act individually or collectively.[25] It refers to the way people see themselves—the groups in which they belong. It is simply the aspects of themselves that they use to describe themselves. It is part of culture and nationalism, and not irreducible since the nationalist sentiments change while ethnicity persists. Identity is a question of "who am I," and with "what do I" stressing identification, which implies "I/we." It is the feeling of individuals and collectivities that stems from the mutual recognition of the interaction of like and unlike units.[26]

Identity represents the essence of self versus other and is often determined externally by each societal group. It is based on social identity theory and symbolic interactions of sociology, particularly from social psychology.[27] To the social psychologist, individuality is socially constructed by the interactions with the group in which they belong and they construct common identities supported through their actions. Identity differentiates between groups (like in- and out-groups), where the collective selves identify themselves with other members, yet are viewed by the others as different. In view of this, the self is socially constructed and always "being" (reproducing) and "becoming" (changing).[28]

Plessis quoting Placide observes that most contemporary conceptions of identity denote a move from bounded or fixed object, where identity is essential, fundamental, unitary, and unchanging, if it is conceived in a singular term.[29] However, identities are plural, if constructed and reconstructed, through social-historical action. Constructed identities, are contested and constantly evolving.[30] Different identities (ethnic, regional, religious, and class, etc.) overlap with, or crosscut, each other.[31] Identity of collectivities stems from categorizing as 'selves' characteristics such as ethnicities, states, nations, civilizations, among others. These forms of identification systematically revealed that separating, or singling, concept of identity seemingly misleading; rather, identity is an overlapping concept. Its historical and local context should be identified, as marker of distinctiveness.[32]

Relying on the foregoing, identity is a social construction, and identification premised on identity, draws from psychological sources, in which there are feelings of loss (exclusion, deprival) or belonging; a feeling of fear (insecurity) or safety (security); and provides the perception instrumentalizing material and concrete interests and abstract and symbolic ones.[33]

IDENTITY POLITICS

The fusion of identity and politics gives sense to politics of identity, politicization, or identity politics, alluding to politics of difference.[34] It is a social construct emphasizing state of being or being identical. Therefore, being, belonging, and believing in a group of persons binds 'being' together, termed identities. These are markers and pillars of identity and sociability, to distinguish a group from other groups, widening sense of belonging, in which believing finds expression within the context of the group's identifiable interest. It is quality of being identical with a section or ethnic group and relying on the sense of belonging. The pillars of identity, like being, with a strong sense of belonging matter, as belief affects politics. These markers shape the way being understood mobilizes and affects participation in politics. Thus, politics of being and that of belonging raise questions of the politics of non-belonging (stranger), which is acute in Africa due to multiple and conflicted political and cultural referents promoted fear, competition for resources and power, that continuously engender different forms of conflict, and has triggered xenophobic violence against those who defined as strangers who rob natives from opportunities to work, earn status, or access resources.[35]

AFRICAN IDENTITY: MYTH OR REALITY?

The continent of Africa is known with multiple and conflicted spatial, political, and cultural referents, though, there is little agreement on the sources and meanings of the word "Africa." Its usage evolved in Roman times, while referring initially to North Africa, then, before it was extended to the whole continent, from the first era. By implication, Africa was a European imperial construct confined to the space and regions conceptually mapped as 'sub-Saharan Africa' seen as the pristine locus of the real Africa. Therefore, Africa and her identities are both states of being and of becoming.[36]

Africa is a place and in reality, a Black continent on the globe with large concentration of Black people. Impliedly, Black color typifies sub-Saharan African physical identity. This element informed Dukor to stress that there is a particular continent in the globe, with large concentration of Black people, indicating that color is a registered identity, while the African continent is known as the "Land of the Blacks." These distinguished Africa's race from Whites. Thus, Blackness is the primary identity of Africans. Ethically, Dukor while exploring generosity and hospitality of African people notes that Africans, generally, welcome others into their communities, even strangers.[37]

African identity is multifaceted, as self-hood is core to Africans, and they are easily identifiable ontologically. The self, in African metaphysics, means being-with-others. They are essentially a being-with race, as individuals in relationships with others within an African community have distinctive traits, which according to Nyerere, is African brotherhood. Thus, the essence of self in Africa is 'being-with-others,' sharing with others, and stressed brotherhood.[38] Cueing by this, the African continent is known as the land of the Black, thus, Black race, is distinguished from Whites on both color and ethnicity.

Consequently, Africans are known for "WE," as contemporary "I" in African states, borrowed from Whites, and by implication, individual being in Africa is not 'autonomous self,' but the social, communal, and relational self.[39] The concept of 'being-with,' in African identity, means that Africans are known for "WE" and not "I." This ontological relationship among individuals in Africa is not a force existing by itself rather, such being has an ontological relationship with other living beings.[40] African social practices, during precolonial days, emphasize communalism, egalitarianism, the values of brotherhood and kinship, and respect for the humanism of the individuals; these are values that the African system espouses. It detests class struggle, exclusions, marginalization, or disempowerment of certain social groups, which opposes increasing and reverberating xenophobia practices of identity differences in Africa in modern times.

AFRICA AND POLITICS OF BEING

The place and role of individuals in African politics is the distinct way of being, common to African societies making distinctions between individuals within each society, ethnic groups, and between different communities, relying on shades of origin, identity, locality, and their different invested political meanings, its understanding of the workings of politics at the local, regional, and national levels, as well as its political uses in Africa.[41] Put differently, the identity of a person, and that person's place in society, is an indication that a human 'being' and their sense of 'belonging' cannot be disentangled and separated. Thus, a sense of belonging in practice is that inhabitants, particularly in Africa, cherish their origin and ethnic identity.

Anthropologists thrived on systematically studying origins. This reciprocal influence of political life in Africa, indicates how origin and locality stimulate politics of being. Though in Western societies, the French have values for a sense of origin, while Americans stress who they are. Thus, the idea of a sense of belonging, origin, and identity come together, and origin and locality cannot be separated in the analysis of identity formation. Politicization of identity is a mobilization tool in a multicultural terrain, such as Africa. It remains a significant factor to social and political behavior. Thus, issues of identity seemingly subsumed under the vague rubric of tribalism, since anthropologists often equate identity with tribes in reminiscence of how people viewed themselves, but in limited frequency.[42]

In sum, the politics of being focuses on issues of identity and locality by not neglecting or taking for granted forms of identification, such as ethnicity. Therefore, issues of individuals and import of origin, among others, are significant markers of identity, as well as core to the systematic study of identities in Africa today, as far as discourse of politicization of identity is concerned.

IDENTITIES, ETHNICITY, RELIGIONS, AND REGIONS

Identities differentiate and recognize being and define personalities, along fault lines, or give meaning to personalities along tendencies, such as ethnicity, religions, regions, place of birth, and languages, particularly among multiethnic nationalities. The African continent typifies a continent with multiple identities, such as ethnicity, religions, color, languages, and regions. Multiple identities give meaning to individuals and draw diversity lines with others. By implication, diversity contributes to identity formation in which identities are politically salient. This informed Osaghae and Suberu, who defined identity as any group attribute that provides recognition or definition, reference, affinity, coherence, and meaning for individual members of a group, acting individually or collectively.[43] Identities, therefore, serve political purposes and are implicated in the day-to-day struggles for recognition, competition for opportunities, resources, political power, or privileges in contemporary Africa.

Ethnicity is a universal human attribute.[44] Ethnic groups are commonly defined by external markers such as language, region of origin, culture of tradition, and heritage.[45] Ethnicity constitutes the most basic and politically salient element of identity. Regardless of the competitiveness of the situation, Nigerians are more likely to define themselves along their ethnic affinities than along any other group identity characteristic.

Relying on that knowledge, Lewis and Bratton conducted an empirical study to determine the percentage of ethnic identity factor, and the study revealed that 48.2 percent of Nigerians identify along ethnic fault lines, or label themselves with an ethnic (including linguistic, regional, or religious) group, indicating how salient ethnicity is among Nigerians at home and in the diaspora.[46] Despite this, the numbers of ethnic groups in Nigeria still require proper documentation.

Several studies, such as Odetola, count ethnic groups in Nigeria to be 250, while Otite documented 374.[47] Akinyemi alludes that to some it is as high as 450, while others estimated only 360.[48] The diversity of African ethnicities was recently projected at 825.[49] As a result, Africa is being regarded as the most variegated continent.[50] However, in Nigeria, the ethnic majorities who have significantly shaped politics and the polity are the Hausa/Fulani, Yoruba, and Igbo groups. The minority side includes Efiks, Ijaws, Itsekiri, Igala, Idoma, Tiv, Jukun, and Birom, among many others. The struggle among ethnic groups has historically been framed along these ethnic lines;

thus the structures of institutions in contemporary Nigeria are not insulated from the potency of ethnicism.[51] It is a strong catalyst that drives social mobilization. Often, politicization reinforces differences between groups, in different regions, including in Nigeria.[52]

African societies are often portrayed as very religious, grounded in the presence of the vast number of faith-based groups (Christians, Muslims, Animists, and others) that exist in most African countries, including Nigeria. Religious identity, like all other elements of identity, is socially constructed, but nonetheless real and very salient.[53] For instance, in Nigeria, in the Northern region of the country, Hausa-Fulani predominantly identify as Muslims. The Yoruba in the Southwestern region are comprised of both Muslims and Christians, while the Igbo in the Southeastern region are predominantly Christians. The religious label ascribed to each ethnic group, though not problematic, has become politicized and its deployment assures for privileges, power, and resources for some ethnic groups while depriving others.

In the observation of Ijere, under worst structural conditions and intense political competition, religion becomes an instrument of mobilization by actors and interest groups.[54] Toyin Falola notes that no one can aspire or agitate without pretending to be religious.[55] The political class in Nigeria has a way of exploiting religion as a mobilization tool to achieve their social ambitions with political mobilization based on religious attachment.[56] The contributions of Africans to ethnic problems began during the colonial period. Ipso facto, ethnic divisions and their political implications were internalized. After independence, the ethnic cleavages were consolidated, leading to civil wars in Nigeria and in many other countries.[57]

Identities and regional cleavages evolved from the colonial past structures during the state formation process in Africa. In Nigeria, for instance, the most fundamental issue the country had to contend with was the issue of the North and South divide. The successive structure after 1914 tied to the other cleavages (North, East, and West) emerged in 1946 by the introduction of the three regions. Before the fourth, the Mid-West was created in 1963. Historically, ethnicism (majority and minority syndrome) rooted within these structures, and the domination and marginalization that followed.

Akinyemi validates the foregoing observation that pattern of politics of being has dragged us to the challenge of domination and exclusion.[58] This existential threat among elite common to the Nigerian actor, shows that the majority continuously deploys strategies of ethnic mobilization and exclusionary politics to gain access to privileges of offices. These social practices have indeed promoted regionalism, that is, the North for Northerners, East for Easterners, and West for South Westerners. Ijere stressed that this discriminatory and mobilization process increases struggles among ethnic groups in Nigeria, as the pattern was entrenched.[59] He further asserts that this did not only broaden fault lines but also widened the indigene and non-indigene distinction among Nigerians, therefore making fault lines even more acute in Africa.[60]

By implication, regional cleavages and ethnicism provide the basis for mass and fierce struggles for power and exclusionary politics in Nigeria and in Africa at large. For instance, in contemporary Nigeria, the six geopolitical zones, which typify dominant or contemporary regionalism, remain significant in politics of being in Nigeria. To a large extent, regional cleavages reinforce old regional and ethnic cleavages, thus prompting struggles among ethnic groups in Africa.

NATIONS, TRIBES, AND ETHNIC GROUPING: RECONSTRUCTION DISCOURSE

A "nation" or "people" comprises the group of human beings who identify as a nation or people and determine its common destiny as such and is bound by its common heritage, which can be historical, racial, ethnic, linguistic, cultural, religious, or territorial.[61] Here the words "nation" and "people" are used interchangeably. A nation, nationality, or people is a group of people who share a common culture or customs, intersubjective meanings, or language, beliefs in common, or related identities, and who inhabit an identifiable and predominantly contiguous territory.[62]

The historical literature on early African attempts at forming nation states usually lacks any comparison with processes that went on in the other parts of the world. Europe, from 1815 till around 1870, after several wars came together in 1919. While the process that went on in the 19th century in Africa was akin to that of Europe, the power relationship and the resulting patterns of domination or resistance remain quite different. The major issue in reference to Africa is pejoratively referring to the large degree of conflicting ethnic diversity as balkanization. Even with that, people of the Balkans are from areas of Europe; thus, ethnicity is then equated to language and culture which morphs the concept of tribes into polities and then into ethnic groups that cut across linguistic or cultural units.

In his analysis, Van Pixteren reports on Doornbos and Van Bisbergen's work:

> Doornbos and Van Binsbergen (who I would place in the "Africa is a country" camp) give a good overview of the problems associated with studying tribal and ethnic identity in Africa. They point out how the "ethnic distinctions non-African scholars imposed in their early twentieth-century pioneering analyses of African ethnicity were often subsequently appropriated as objective truth by African actors (. . .)"—the process known as ethnicization. They take issue

with the image of Africa as a patchwork of a large number of 'tribes,' each with
their own territory, culture and language. They also question the absoluteness
with which ethnicity is seen, feeling that it is situational in nature. "An increasing number of situations are constructed (. . .) primarily in terms of identities
other than ethnic, notably in terms of religion, gender, class, professional group
and national state." These points may have some validity, but Doornbos and
Van Binsbergen risk throwing away the child with the bathwater here. Indeed,
in chapter 5 in the same book, Van Binsbergen analyzes the emergence of
Nkoya ethnic feeling as a form of false consciousness. Further on, in chapter 8
he discusses the Kazanga festival—there, he seems to accept the legitimacy of
the Nkoya approach.[63]

Osaghae and Suberu explain that an increasing number of situations are "constructed in terms of identities, other than ethnic notably in terms of religion,
gender, class, professional group and national state."[64]

MODERN POLITICS OF DIFFERENCE AND IDENTITIES
CRISIS IN AFRICA: INSIGHT FROM NIGERIA

The entire African continent, inclusive of Nigeria, contains multiethnic
states. Thus, the multinationalities are not peculiar to the African continent.
Although it is not a negative phenomenon, each African state shapes its own
response to multiethnic politics. For instance Europe, often assumed as an
undifferentiated continent, was a variegated continent with each country
being a rainbow of nationalities.[65] This indicates that descriptions and applications of Africa and Nigeria were the colonialists' artificial creation, in reference to the 1915 amalgamation in Nigeria by Lord Lugard, informed negative
perceptions and the mistaken beliefs that before the colonial intrusion, groups
in Nigeria lived in splendid isolation.[66] It is mistaken because, to use Lagos
as an example, long before British colonization, the Nupe settled in Oshodi,
the Epe settled in Epetedo, and the Ijesas settled in Ijesatedo.[67] But the question is how did they get here? Is it neglect of rational subject and morality?
In simple terms, politics dragged *African state* into application of pernicious
term, along ethnic fault lines. Thus, identity crisis prevails, and reinforces
political differences in different climes.[68]

Recently, Torffing alluded that the postmodern condition is significantly
associated with neglect of the rational subject, acting as a self-willed instrument in the political circle.[69] This prevalent condition indicates that there can
be no separation between the subjects and the objective sphere, rationality
and morality no longer serve as the absolute foundations for the subject's
political, ethical judgment and decision making. A sort of breakdown of sites

of collective decision making, and a universal division of the political and social field that engender a mass of incommensurable identities and ideological perspectives, due to regularity of identity politics, impacts with the incidence of social movements like ethnicity, gender, religion, sexual identity, and traditional cleavages.[70]

Consequently, identity politics returns with ethnicity, religious fundamentalism, indicating 'postmòdern' racism in which the logic of difference and incommensurability is used to justify ethnic group separation, and to displace ideology.[71] Showing how individuals and groups in political fields are held together by the struggles, driven by differences and divisions, signifying pattern, and dominated by political subjectivity: 'The common denominator of all of them would be their differentiation from workers' struggles, termed "class" struggles, then to mass movements, along tendencies, indicating 'whole field of differences.'[72]

This struggle differs from class to mass tendencies, with incidences of 'new social movements' as a struggle against exclusion and marginalization. Thus, politics of pure opposition today characterize identity politics. They struggle against state power and oppression but differ from the struggles between workers and artisans of the industrialization period. Their struggles against relations of subordination, the destruction of their organic and communal way of life by factory systems and industrial technology, or proletarian fights against capitalism in Marx's radicalized notion, that reduce workers to the Marxist vision.[73] Proletarian struggle against capitalism with characters of heterogeneity or its antiauthoritarian character of subaltern struggles and identities—peasants. Intellectuals déclassés, and the crucial revolutionary role of the proletariat which had been dismissed by Marx.[74] Thus, Bakunin offered 'mass' to 'class' to characterize this heterogeneous revolutionary identity, 'class' implying hierarchy and exclusiveness.[75]

The politics of identity systematically exclude by this social practice and identification process that reconstruct identities, reconfigure social relations, as well, denude other major ethnic groups, in favor of the Hausa in Nigeria. This politics of difference via ethnicity is a replica, and contemporary character of structural conditions in Africa, indicating how postcolonial Africa preserves particularity and resists universality, which detests African values of brotherhood. This situation prompts concern of the author to raise the question: What are the implications of identity politics in African social formations? It is evident that Africa is a diverse continent, despite its diversity and long list of African ethnicities: 825 in total as well as spreading of African groups over many continents and more than one country—266 in total shows that diversities along boundaries, race, ethnic, and other identities requires managing a complex continent that calls for compromises, while Nigeria is a complex country to manage as well.[76]

In Nigeria, for instance, there are three major ethnic groups: Igbo, Yoruba, and Hausa. Hausa consistently assert their identity against other identities. The problem attracted Akinyemi to note that asserting identity to the detriment of other ethnic identities is the problem.[77] It is an existential threat, by implication, assertion of an ethnic identity that is negative is not acceptable. Nigeria just like other states in Africa is heterogeneous. It is a state of nationalities, with many nationalities. Some have suggested that ethnic groups in Nigeria are comprised of about 360 nationalities. Others have suggested 450 nationalities—typical Nigerian hyperboles—to the point that any tiny locality or village becomes categorized as a nationality or ethnicity. Managing such a complex polity requires compromises, thus the need to adopt historical perspective.[78]

Nigeria is a multiethnic state is a fact that cannot be denied. The following are the most populous and politically influential according to the *CIA World Factbook* ": Hausa and Fulani 29%, Yoruba 21%, Igbo (Ibo) 18%, Ijaw 10%, Kanuri 4%, Ibibio 3.5%, Tiv 2.5%."[79] The experience is counterproductive for anyone to deny his or her ethnic identity, while asserting one identity over other identities is an existential threat. Thus, the recognition of one's ethnic identity is essential, but asserting that identity to the detriment of other ethnicities is the problem. In Akinyemi's explanation, a behavior based on an assertion of one's identity as if that is the only identity in a multiethnic state is ethnicism which is negative, unacceptable, and prevents nurturing feelings that support universal humanity, integration, and challenges national unity.[80] By implication, if a nation state is not capable of nurturing community and intensifies the politics of difference, identity conflicts may debilitate the state's essence and its affairs.

According to Newman the politics of difference explains how different identities along ethnic, regional, religious, class, etc., often overlap with, or cut across each other.[81] The intervening variable of deep ethnic division, dangerously invented as tribalism by colonialists, further reconstructed and reconfigured identity in Africa.[82] This constituted a dangerous invention in Africa that provided the foundation for how primordial ties in Africa are being reconstructed and negotiated in the contemporary world.[83] It indicates that different identities in Africa have become tools for mobilization. Politics of difference in contemporary Africa marginalize, exclude, and indeed disempower certain social groups.

Theoretical Discourse on Identity Politics

This study is anchored in conceptual frameworks that determine and define race and their people's identity; hence, identities like culture are constructionist. Identities are always changing and fundamentally constructed, broadly through external relations of language in the structuralism; thus, identities are socially and historically constructed.[84] Different conceptions from Rorty, Bennett, Bailey, Castells, Deleon and Naff, and Osaghae and Suberu point to poststructuralist reconstructions and explore the identification process, through which collectives create distinctions, establish hierarchies, and renegotiate rules of inclusion.[85] Others are Derrida's focus on difference, Foucault's genealogy of epistomes, among other contemporaries' offered theoretical works significant to identity politics.[86] Despite their differences, the issues raised by social constructionists' and postmodernists' direct scholarly attention to a collective's struggle to self-name, self-characterize, and other critical concerns underscore the politics of identity, identification processes, and identities analysis.[87]

Postculturalism reveals how politics of pure opposition characterizes much of today's identity politics emphasizes difference over universality, and suggests their preoccupation with multicultural politics of difference.[88] By implication, salient political and active identities, civil and primordial ties, intricately connect and mutually reinforce each other.[89] The concept of collective identity and the political movements spur and constitute an important concern for identity scholars, as issues of politics are upstretched.[90]

Identity politics provides the focus on the formation and experience of social class.[91] However, concerns on identity politics move scholars beyond this "holy trinity" of the discursive field. In recent times, identity-based movements mobilize rather than respond; they fight to expand rights, no longer to reach freedom as during independence struggles; they organize for greater opportunities rather than for ultimate liberation. Corroborating this, Melucci Alberto notes that,

> The freedom to have which characterized . . . industrial society has been replaced by the freedom to be. The right to property has been, and remains, the basis of both industrial capitalism and its competitor model, "real socialism." In post–material society, there emerges a further type of right, the right to existence, or rather, to a more meaningful existence.[92]

Cueing into the above, identity politics creates "new social movements," collective initiatives that are self-reflexive and sharply focused on the expressive actions of collective members.[93] These new social movements suggest a special form of agency—a self-conscious "collective agency." Identities emerge and movements ensue because collectives consciously coordinate action and mobilize ethnic group members, consciously develop offenses and defences, deliberately insulate, differentiate, mark, cooperate, persuade, and coerce. In such a context, agency encompasses more than the control and transformation of one's social environment.[94]

The social construction of identity always takes place in a context marked by power relationship.[95] Manuel Castells avers that identity discusses social actors as "the process of construction of meaning on the basis of cultural attribute, or related set of cultural attributes, that is/are given priority over other sources of meaning."[96] He points out that identities organize the meaning of the individuals in the society. According to him, identities (e.g., ethnic, religious, place, boundaries, race, religion, gay, Latino, feminist, class, regional, and gender identities), are sources of the meaning for actors themselves, and constructed through a process of individuation.[97]

Bailey alludes and encourages readers to ponder about the "problematic of identity" rather than focus on "identity" itself in political analysis.[98] He explains the problematic of identity on the changing individuals (or self) and the continuity of the collective identity as a signifier of social meaning, with their different invested political meanings, and the workings of politics, at the local, regional, and national levels, as well as its political uses in Africa.[99]

Bennett emphasizes the need to manage and express complex identities in fragmented societies, such as in Africa, that are fast replacing the energy once devoted to grand political projects, like national-building, political and economic integration.[100] In Rorty's idea, the role that identity plays in an individual's life varies within the context.[101] This informed Bailey to offer "identity multiplexing" while explaining how different individuals can be layered and ranked to describe the "layering and ranking of individuals by individuals based on their different identities in different arenas."[102] For example, this practice of politics of difference among different ethnic groups, race, or a person may express the identity of Africa . . . or that of African-American when pursuing goals of racial equality, of "feminist" when joining other women to combat sex discrimination in hiring, and of "lesbian" when writing a legislator in support of same-sex marriage. Such gender identities define and give meaning to group identity, based on sex or gender affinity. Therefore, an individual's affinity with an identity group that formed a social movement might be taken to define his or her identity as a person. Young contends that "every individual necessarily has affinities with many social groups, and that lives of different individuals are structured by differing constellations of groups. If each group defines a person's identity, then identity groups exist and are important."[103]

Academics have therefore called for the redesign of political institutions to compensate for the lack of representation and social inequality reproduced by these institutions and experienced by some groups. The distinction drawn on identities, its role between identity of individual persons, or group identities among social theorists on identity, tied to "rational self-interest" is "objective," is an underlying variable factor. But Naff contends that identity cannot be collapsed satisfactorily into interest, or to reflect it, except as part of a personal and/or political project.[104]

On the economic plane, Bailey writes that identity boundaries tend to be "softer," and more fluid than the "hard lines of economic interest."[105] He adds that identity should be distinguished and not fused with an individual viewpoint. While identity group politics in which "the individual 'identifies' with the group is primarily for psychological or cultural reasons," interest group politics "is largely about coming together to advance collective economic . . . or regulatory interest, when dealing with public policy in an economic framework is usually for economic gain or protection."[106]

Castells distinguishes three forms and origins of identity building.[107] Legitimizing identity is "introduced by the dominant institutions of society to extend and rationalize their domination vis-à-vis social factors."[108] An example is the identity of citizens confined to political factions within the limits established state power. Resistance identity formation is "generated by those actors that are in positions/conditions devalued and/or stigmatized by the logic of domination, thus building trenches of resistance and survival on the basis of principles different from, or opposed to, those permeating the institutions of society."[109] Examples includes religious fundamentalism and queer culture enclaves that involve the "exclusion of the excluders by the excluded."[110]

Castells believes that project identity "may be the most important type of identity-building in our society."[111] This shows that formation occurs "when social actors, on the basis of whichever cultural materials are available to them, build a new identity that redefines their position in society, and, by so doing, seek the transformation of overall social structure."[112] For example, feminists move beyond the defensive stance on women's identity and women's rights to "challenge patriarchalism, thus, the patriarchal family, and the entire structure of production, reproduction, sexually, and personality on which societies have been historically based."[113]

Poststructuralists develop as a response to postmodernity condition through the movement known as structuralism. The essential idea is that experience or 'reality' is structured primarily through relations of language: that is, we understand ourselves and the world around us only through an external linguistic structure that determines meaning, indicating signifier in relation to differences, termed "symbolic dimension," through which identities were fixed or overdetermined.[114] In political terms, the postmodern condition significantly associated with neglect of the rational subject, acting as the self-willed instrument in the political circle. As prevalent conditions of the postmodern era indicate, there can be no separation between the subject and the objective sphere. Consequently, identity politics return with the re-emergence of ethnicity, religious fundamentalism, as new forms of 'postmodern' racism in which the logic of difference and incommensurability is used to justify ethnic group separation and displaced ideology.[115]

But social constructionists contend that identities are constructed by sociocultural environments, and that there is no fixed essence shared by all Africans. African people are the product of their social environment, and identities are constructed through everyday social interaction.[116] The dynamic character of identity formation, mobilization processes, shifts identity diversity in Africa.[117] For instance, African and other postcolonial states are often categorized as deeply divided states in which political issues often engender imaginary lines, leading to contest along fault lines of the complex ethnic, religious, race, regional, religious, class and regional cleavages on the continent.[118]

In the global context, the contemporary political field is held together by the struggles, particularly those of the masses. For some time, it has been dominated by division, and by a whole series of different and competing identities and struggles of the 'new social movements' such as Blacks, feminists, gays, ethnic minorities, students, environmentalists, consumers, antiwar activists, and so on. The trending, dominant "political subjectivity is defined: the common denominator of all of them would be their differentiation."[119] These new antagonistic struggles point to a contemporary anarchist political moment. Incidences of 'new social movements' are primarily struggles against exclusion, marginalization, and *domination* rather than economic exploitation, as the Marxist paradigm contends.[120] Though they also contest capitalist exploitation where struggles against economic exploitation are the broader-aspect relations of the domination experienced.

In sum, "identities are self-defined psycho-cultural constructs that give meaning and purpose to an individual's life," in all places.[121] They are constructed through a process of internal dialogue and social interactions. Individuals have complex and multiple identities that are selectively expressed and mobilized in different arenas at different times. Identities are less rigid and more fluid than the many roles individuals play in life, although there is some overlap between these.[122] Human power relations combined with their social status limit the choice of identities they have. In that sense, a person's identity integrates many elements, such as social status, dominant ethnicity, group membership, and so much more.[123] DeLeon and Naff explain that individual involvement in new social movements that politicize identity can be mobilized by many reasons from psychological to cultural or religious often prioritized above economic self-interest.[124] Identity building through collective and political action or politicization can produce the forms of legitimizing identity, that is, supporting the state and the established social order.

CONCLUSION

This chapter explains that African identities are as complex as the continent of Africa itself. Africans and their identities are both in state of being and of becoming. This geographical space has changed, to prevalent ideas, formations of global racial or ethnic identities through the process of modern globalization. African identities are inventions, mutually constitutive, existential, and epistemic constructions. Identity impacts the world in cooperative-building since it is transformative, and contends that it will be counterproductive if all multicultural societies, nationalities, or the regions in the world deny ethno-religious and other dominant identity cleavage characteristics. Europe, despite being a multicolored continent, is made of states each composed of a rainbow of nationalities, with seemingly lower practices of marginalization.

For that reason, admitting ethnic identity is essential, but politicizing identities against others can be detrimental to others' identities and can thwart integrative efforts. Politicization can fuel religious fervor in battles for recognition, in control of resources, and in disputes over power sharing, while continuing to neglect historical grievances, further ingraining prejudices, and throwing merit overboard while igniting destructive mobilization. Hence, the need to uncover positive virtues, and requisite values to be a member of the wider society, to grow people who are conscious of their identity. When identities turn all human spheres to endeavor into identities of difference and ethnic chauvinism, problems remain and can seldom be overcome.

Finally, identity represents a fundamental need, because it is a potent tool and strong catalyst for social mobilization. Its spread and movements built around identities can increase marginalization and exclusion, and this worsens social identity formations which continuously describe economic, political, and cultural issues thus significantly defining modern politics. Hence, the place of recognition for identities needs to be adjusted to meet different identities' demands. To achieve this requires holistic and inclusive mechanisms for citizens' inclusion in governance and equality in wealth and resources distribution.

NOTES

1. Paul Tiyambe Zeleza, "The Inventions of African Identities and Languages: The Discursive and Developmental Implications," *36th Annual Conference on African Linguistics* (Somerville: Cascadilla Proceedings Project, 2006), 19.

2. Amadiume, cited in Barry Hallen, *A Short History of African Philosophy* (Bloomington, Indiana University Press, 2002), 64.

3. For information regarding the history, please see Earl E. Thorpe, *Black Historians: A Critique* (New York: William Morrow, 1970); William D. Wright, *Black History and Black Identity: A Call for a New Historiography* (Westport: Praeger, 2002); John Ernest, *Liberation Historiography: African American Writers and the Challenge of History, 1794–1861* (Chapel Hill: University of North Carolina Press, 2004); and Stephen G. Hall, *A Faithful Account of the Race: African American Historical Writing in Nineteenth-Century America* (Chapel Hill: University of North Carolina Press, 2009). For information on African values, please see Philani Jili, "African Identity and an African Renaissance" (Master's thesis, University of Natal, 2000); and Hallen, *A Short History of African Philosophy*.

4. Jili, "African Identity."

5. Paulin J. Hountondji, *African Philosophy: Myth and Reality* (Bloomington: Indiana University Press, 1996), 69.

6. Derrida, cited in Saul Newman, *Power and Politics in Poststructuralist Thought: New Theories of the Political* (London: Routledge, 2005).

7. Jili, "African Identity."

8. Tunde Adeleke, "Africa and Afrocentric Historicism: A Critique," *Advances in Historical Studies* 4, no. 15 (2015): 200–15.

9. Jili, "African Identity."

10. Adeleke, "Africa and Afrocentric Historicism," 200.

11. A. E. Afigbo, *The Poverty of African Historiography* (Lagos: Afrografika, 1977).; O. Uya, *Perspectives and Methods of Studying African History: Papers Presented at the History Week, University of Calabar, 1976–1979* (Enugu: Fourth Dimension Publishers, 1984); Thorpe, *Black Historians*; Wright, *Black History and Black Identity*; Ernest, *Liberation Historiography*; Hall, *A Faithful Account of the Race.*

12. Eghosa E. Osaghae, and Rotimi T. Suberu, *A History of Identities, Violence, and Stability in Nigeria,* CRISE Working Paper no. 6 (Oxford: University of Oxford: Centre for Research on Inequality, Human Security and Ethnicity, 2005).

13. Jili, "African Identity"; Hallen, *A Short History of African Philosophy*.

14. Jili, "African Identity," 2.

15. Frank Okenna Ndubisi, "The Philosophical Paradigm of African Identity and Development," *Open Journal of Philosophy* 3, no. 1 (February 2013): 222–30.

16. Derrida, cited in Newman, *Power and Politics*.

17. Ibid.

18. Jili, "African Identity"; Hallen, *A Short History of African Philosophy*; Ernest, *Liberation Historiography*; Hall, *A Faithful Account of the Race*; Thorpe, *Black Historians*; Wright, *Black History and Black Identity*.

19. Francis Fukuyama, "Identity, Immigration, and Liberal Democracy," *Journal of Democracy* 17, no. 2 (2006): 7.

20. Marium Ahktar, "Role of Identity Crisis and Relative Deprivation as Catalysts of Political Violence and Terrorism: Case Study of Kurd Fighters in Turkey," *RAIS Journal for Social Sciences* 2, no. 1 (2018): 49–66.

21. Newman, *Power and Politics.*

22. Ahktar, "Role of Identity Crisis."

23. Oogh Alubo, "Citizenship and Identity Politics," in *Conference Proceeding on Citizenship and Identity Politics in Nigeria* (Lagos: CLEEN Foundation, 2009); Ahktar, "Role of Identity Crisis."

24. Anton Du Plessis, "Exploring the Concept of Identity in World Politics," in *Politics of Identity and Exclusion in Africa: From Violent Confrontation to Peaceful Cooperation* (Pretoria: University of Pretoria, 2001), 13–25.

25. Erikson, cited in Osaghae and Suberu, *A History of Identities*, 5.

26. Plessis, "Exploring the Concept of Identity."

27. Bruce Cronin, *Community Under Anarchy: Transnational Identity and the Evolution of Cooperation* (New York: Columbia University Press, 1999).

28. Richard Deleon and Katherine Naff, "Identity Politics and Local Political Culture: The Politics of Gender, Race, Class, and Religion in Comparative Perspective," conference paper (Philadelphia: American Political Science Association, 2003).

29. Placide, quoted in Plessis, "Exploring the Concept of Identity,"

30. Audie Klotz and Cecelia Lynch, *Strategies for Research in Constructivist International Relations* (Armonk, New York: M.E. Sharpe, Inc., 2007).

31. For more information, please see Donald L. Horowitz, *Ethnic Groups in Conflict* (Berkeley: University of California Press, 1985); James D. Fearon and David D. Laitin, "Explaining Interethnic Cooperation," *The American Political Science Review* 90, no. 4 (1996): 715–35; Barry R. Weingast, "The Political Foundations of Democracy and the Rule of Law," *The American Political Science Review* 91, no. 2 (1997): 245–63; Daniel N. Posner, "The Political Salience of Cultural Difference: Why Chewas and Tumbukas Are Allies in Zambia and Adversaries in Malawi," *The American Political Science Review* 98, no. 4 (2004): 529–45.

32. Patrick Chabal, *Africa: The Politics of Suffering and Smiling* (New York: New Zed, 2009), 31.

33. Vendulka Kubalkova, Nicholas Onuf, and Paul Kowert, eds., *International Relations in a Constructed World* (Armonk: Routledge, 1998); Zaki Laïdi, *A World without Meaning: The Crisis of Meaning in International Politics* (London: Routledge, 1998), 53–60.

34. Deleon and Naff, "Identity Politics and Local Popular Culture"; Newman, *Power and Politics*.

35. Chabal, *Africa: The Politics of Suffering and Smiling*, 57.; Paul Tiyambe Zeleza, "The Inventions of African Identities and Languages: The Discursive and Developmental Implications," conference paper (Somerville: 36th Annual Conference on African Linguistics, 2006), 14–26; Osaghae and Suberu, *A History of Identities*, 2005 working paper; Ebenezer Oni and Samuel Okunade, "The Context of Xenophobia in Africa: Nigeria and South Africa in Comparison," in *The Political Economy of Xenophobia in Africa,* ed. Adeoye O. Akinola (New York: Springer Cham, 2018), 37–51.

36. Zeleza, "In Inventions of African Identities and Languages," 19.

37. Maduabuchi Dukor, *African Freedom: The Freedom of Philosophy* (Saarbrücken: LAP LAMBERT Academic Publishing, 2010), 157.

38. Julius K. Nyerere, *Ujamaa. English Ujamaa-essays on Socialism* (Dar-es-Salaam: Oxford University Press, 1968).

39. Pantaleon Iroegbu, *Metaphysics, the Kpịm of Philosophy* (Owerri: International Universities Press, 1995), 75.

40. Placide Tempels, *Bantu Philosophy* (Paris: Presence Africaine, 1959), 60.

41. Chabal, *Africa: The Politics of Suffering and Smiling.*

42. Ibid.

43. Osaghae and Suberu, *A History of Identities.*

44. Patrick Chabal and Jean-Pascal Daloz, *Africa Works: Disorder as Political Instrument* (Oxford: James Currey, 1999); Londale, cited in Thomas Chukwuma Ijere "Political Parties, Identities and Violent Conflict in Nigeria," *International Journal of African and Asian Studies* 13 (2015): 111.

45. Daniel N. Posner, "Regime Change and Ethnic Cleavages in Africa," *Comparative Political Studies* 40, no. 11 (November 2007): 1302–27.

46. Peter Lewis and Michael Bratton, *Attitudes toward Democracy and Markets in Nigeria: Report of a National Opinion Survey, January–February 2000* (Washington, D.C.: International Foundation for Election Systems, 2000).

47. Theophilus Olatunde Odetola, *Military politics in Nigeria: Economic Development and Political Stability* (New Brunswick: Transaction Books, 1978); Onigu Otite, *Ethnic Pluralism and Ethnicity in Nigeria: With Comparative Materials* (Ibadan: Shaneson, 1990).

48. Bolaji Akinyemi, "The New Country We Need," *Vanguard News*, December 20, 2015, https://www.vanguardngr.com/2015/12/the-new-country-we-need-by-prof -bolaji-akinyemi/.

49. Bert van Pinxteren "African Identities: N New Perspective" (Thesis, African Studies Centre, Leiden University, 2018).

50. Akinyemi, "The New Country We Need."

51. Ijere, "Political Parties,"

52. Ahktar, "Role of Identity Crisis."

53. Laakso and Olukoshi cited in Ijere, "Political Parties," 111.

54. Ijere, "Political Parties," 111.

55. Falola, cited in M. H. Kukah, *Religion, Politics and Power in Northern Nigeria* (Ibadan: Spectrum Books, 1993).

56. Ijere, "Political Parties," 111.

57. Toyin Falola, *The Toyin Falola Reader on African Culture, Nationalism, Development and Epistemologies* (Austin: Pan-African University Press, 2018).

58. Akinyemi, "The new country we need."

59. Ijere, "Political Parties."

60. Chabal, *Africa: The Politics of Suffering and Smiling.*

61. UNPO cited in van Pinxteren, "African Identities."

62. Van Pinxteren, "African Identities."

63. Martin Doornbos and Wim van Binsbergen, *Researching Power and Identity in African State Formation: Comparative Perspectives* (Pretoria: Unisa Press, 2017), 71–72, cited in Bert van Pinxteren, "African Identities: a New Perspective" (Thesis, African Studies Centre, Leiden University, 2018), 13.

64. Eghosa E. Osaghae and Rotimi T. Suberu, *A History of Identities, Violence, and Stability in Nigeria,* CRISE Working Paper no. 6 (Oxford: University of Oxford: Centre for Research on Inequality, Human Security and Ethnicity, 2005).

65. Akinyemi, "The Mew Country We Need."; Van Pinxteren, "African Identities."

66. Van Pinxteren, "African Identities."

67. Akinyemi, "The New Country We Need."

68. Ahktar, "Role of Identity Crisis."

69. Torffing, cited in Newman, *Politics and Power*, 4.

70. Newman, *Politics and Power.*

71. Akinyemi, "The New Country We Need"; Fukuyama, "Identity"; Newman, *Politics and Power.*

72. Ernesto Laclau and Chantal Mouffe, *Hegemony and Socialist Strategy: Towards a Radical Democratic Politics* (London: Verso, 2001), 59, 111.

73. Laclau and Mouffe, *Hegemony and Socialist Strategy*, 156; see also Newman, *Politics and Power.*

74. Ibid.

75. Michail Aleksandrovič Bakunin, *Marxism, Freedom and the State*, trans. K.J. Kenafick (London: Freedom Press, 1950), 47.

76. Van Pinxteren, "African Identities."

77. Akinyemi, "The New Country We Need."

78. Ibid.

79. "Nigeria" *The World Factbook* (Washington D.C.: Central Intelligence Agency, continuously updated), https://www.cia.gov/the-world-factbook/countries/nigeria/#people-and-society.

80. Akinyemi, "The new country we need."

81. Newman, *Politics and Power.* See also Fearon and Laitin, "Explaining Interethnic Cooperation"; Horowitz, *Ethnic Groups in Conflict*; Posner, "Political Salience of Cultural Difference"; Weingast, "Political Foundations."

82. Van Pinxteren, "African Identities."

83. Gyeke, cited in Hallen, *A Short History of African Philosophy*, 31.

84. Jili, "African Identity"; Hallen, *A Short History of African Philosophy*; Newman, *Politics and Power*; Van Pinxteren, "African Identities."

85. Rorty, cited in Martin F. Asiegbu, "Contemporary African Philosophy: Emergent Issues and Challenges," In *A New Journal of African Studies* vol. 12 (2016):1–24; W. Lance Bennet, "The Uncivic Culture: Communication, Identity, and the Rise of Lifestyle Politics," *PS: Political Science and Politics* 31, no. 4 (1998): 741–61; Robert W. Bailey, *Gay Politics, urban Politics: Identity and Economics in the Urban Setting* (New York: Columbia University Press, 1999); Manuel Castells, *The Power of Identity* (Malden: Wiley-Blackwell, 2010); Deleon and Naff, "Identity Politics and Local Popular Culture"; Osaghae and Suberu, *A History of Identities.*

86. J. Derrida, *Margins of Philosophy*, trans. A. Bass (Brighton: Harvester Press, 1982); Michel Foucault, "Nietzsche, Genealogy, History," in *The Foucault Reader*, ed. P. Rabinow (New York: Pantheon, 1984a), 76, 1–399.

87. Karen A. Cerulo, "Identity Construction: New Issues, New Directions," *Annual Review of Sociology* 23, no. 1 (August 1997): 392–93.

88. Deleuze and Guattari cited in Newman, *Politics and Power*, 141.

89. Osaghae and Suberu, *A History of Identities*.

90. Cerulo, "Identity Construction."

91. Stuart Mack Blumin, *The Emergence of the Middle Class: Social Experience in the American City, 1760–1900* (Cambridge: Cambridge University Press, 1989).

92. Alberto Melucci, *Nomads of the Present: Social Movements and Individual Needs in Contemporary Society* (Philadelphia: Temple University Press, 1989), 177–78.

93. Melucci cited in Cerulo, "Identity Construction," 393.

94. Ibid.

95. Deleon and Naff, "Identity Politics and Local Popular Culture."

96. Castells, *The Power of Identity*, 6.

97. Ibid.

98. Bailey, *Gay Politics, Urban Politics*, 10; and Deleon and Naff, "Identity Politics and Local Popular Culture."

99. Bailey, *Gay Politics, Urban Politics*, 10–11; see also Chabal, *Africa: The Politics of Suffering and Smiling*.

100. Bennet, "The UnCivic Culture," 755.

101. Rorty, R. (1993), 'Stories of Difference: A Conversation with Richard Rorty,' Bulletin: (V) 2–3:23–45 and Rorty, cited in Martin F. Asiegbu "Contemporary African Philosophy: Emergent Issues and Challenges," In *A New Journal of African Studies* vol. 12 (2016): 1–24.

102. Bailey, *Gay Politics, Urban Politics*, 31.

103. Iris Marion Young, *Inclusion and Democracy* (Oxford: Oxford University Press, 2000),

104. Deleon and Naff, "Identity Politics and Local Popular Culture."

105. Bailey, *Gay Politics, Urban Politics*, 32.

106. Ibid., 13.

107. Castells, *The Power of Identity*, 6–12.

108. Ibid., 6.

109. Ibid., 8.

110. Ibid., 8.

111. Ibid., 8.

112. Ibid., 9.

113. Ibid., 12.

114. Newman, *Politics and Power*, 3–5.

115. Newman, *Politics and Power*; Fukuyama, "Identity,"

116. Jili, "African Identity," 7.

117. Osaghae and Suberu, *A History of Identities*.

118. Ibid.

119. Laclau and Mouffe, *Hegemony and Socialist Strategy*, 59.

120. Ibid.

121. Richard Deleon and Katherine Naff, "Identity Politics and Local Political Culture: The Politics of Gender, Race, Class, and Religion in Comparative Perspective," conference paper (Philadelphia: American Political Science Association, 2003).

122. Ibid.
123. Ibid.
124. Ibid.

2

'Ubuntu' Dialogic Ethics

Towards a Liberal Theory of Virtue and Transformation of Identities in Africa

Jude Chinwuba Asike and Patricia Ogugua Anwuluorah

It is not clear at all, how we can rekindle a language of 'virtue' and 'vice' in cultural identities that have embraced individualistic and liberal norms in Africa today. The contemporary debate about 'civil society' is in one measure, a debate about virtue and vice. It is a debate about formation of human character or identity—the kind needed by citizens to sustain liberal democracy and other institutions that form and nurture human personality either for good or evil. The chapter provides a broad-ranging consideration about the nature of civility in contemporary Africa. Modern moral philosophy is uncomfortable with the concept of vice. It is not entirely at ease with the virtues either. In fact, both virtue and vice have some characterizations in their interpretations. To characterize a person's dispositions as vices is not friendly, because it is likely to be a prelude to hostilities. Old-fashioned reprobation speaks in the language of vice, but modern moral criticism prefers to talk of rights and their violation. By a right, is meant a morally weighty claim entailing duties with which others must comply (it is hypothetically normative rather than causal or epistemological). The issue of individual 'right' is meant morally for the concept of entitlements, because the doctrine of 'rights' establishes for each individual, property in the life that is one's own.

Within this fundamentally liberal framework, it is tempting to see vice and virtue as either otiose or dysfunctional. If a vicious act is one that violates the rights of someone else, then it is out to be condemned forthrightly as such; we do not need a separate vocabulary of vices to express our disapproval.

Perhaps, there is a considerable gulf separating the concept of Western philosophical thought with that of African philosophical thought. The gulf is between the subjectivity and objectivity of individual ethos towards the concept of rights where one connects to the character of one's ethnic identity, norms, and values. *Ubuntu* is the evaluation of 'rights' as an individual observance of virtue or vice within the context of the community ethos; a utilitarian consideration of common good of the community and the acceptability of all individual identity in the society.

The chapter is concerned with the conceptual reorientation of virtue and vice within the framework of identity formation that is anchored in demonstrably liberal values. Thus, within this dimension, *Ubuntu* as an African philosophical ethics, no doubt avails the genuine standard of justifications in the epistemic framework of vice and virtue. *Ubuntu* invokes a sense of duty and responsibility to a communal democratic process of reciprocity and collaboration of the people in the political community; helpful in transforming identity in ways that retrieve the roots that are fundamental to the way Africans approach life. It exhibits principles of virtue in a sense of collaboration with others. "I think therefore we are."[1] It is not in the same manner of Descartes, in which he opined thus: "I think therefore I am."[2] *Ubuntu* provides a common element for diverse group identities to overcome ethnic, religious, socioeconomic, linguistic, and cultural dimensions for inclusive communal focus of the purpose of the individual.

In keeping with the African practices and culture(s), life is usually seen as a duty towards the maximization of love of the community, and not just on the individual autonomy. It is like the Heideggerian existential phenomenology of 'being for others'; a *throwness* into a world that they have not made but that consists of potentially useful things, including cultural as well as natural objects and because these objects come to humanity from the past and are used in the present for the sake of future goals, *Ubuntu* posited a fundamental relation between the mode of being of objects, of humanity, and of the formation of human identity in time.

CONCEPTUAL CLARIFICATIONS

Ubuntu: *Ubuntu* is a word derived from the Bantu language and it literally means love, brotherhood, and oneness. It symbolizes oneness in Africa, an existence *towards others*; and does not require cultural homogeneity which must be nuanced for its effective actualization. It is a way of life, and it provided the ground for renewal of African identity through the dialogic interaction of love for others in the society.[3] It is a 'humanity towards others' often translated as "I am because we are." To the Africans, *Ubuntu* symbolizes peace, a harmonious living together as a people.

Dialogic: This is a word that is derived from the English word *dialogue*, a conversational agreement to reach a consensus between two or more different people/groups.[4] In the dimension of African ontology, *Ubuntu* provides a dialogic framework for peace among the diverse states and cultures in Africa. It means an exchange of truth, freedom, and political participation amongst member communities by providing fair opportunities for resolving issues amicably for the common good of its people.

Ethics: The term is derived from the Greek word *ethos*, meaning 'character' or 'custom,' and refers to the principles or standards of human conduct.[5] It sometimes relates to our moral standard of life, about the 'ought' and 'ought not' of our conducts.

Dialogic Ethic

Dialogic ethic is the only common ground on which people can get together. It is an agreement to bridge the hiatus or lacuna between people in areas of politics, economic, and social fragmentations of ideas within a community. Dialogic ethic is an ethical convergence which reveals that different civilizations have made moral progress and have determined to live together harmoniously in their lives. It signifies the importance of a cross-cultural judgment in our societies.[6]

Ubuntu **Dialogic Ethic:** This relates to the networks of civic engagement that foster the study of norms of generalized reciprocity. It encourages the emergence of social trust among members of the community. It is an epistemic structure of spiritual, economic, and political order in the society, which allows dilemmas of collective action to be resolved peacefully. It embodies the spirit of collaboration with others, which serves as a cultural unity and political democratization of the people. Principally it does not allow the building of the social capital for individual interest only. Thus, it is based on this eschatological structure of virtue, that *Ubuntu* retains its potential for critical dialogic amidst the pressures to enlarge the dominion of logics of administration and control in African society. The advanced moral virtues within the bounds of *Ubuntu* make it possible for human dialogic arrangements which ensure that all members in the community are in existential relationships.[7]

Virtue: The term is of Latin origin *virtus,* which means 'valor, merit, moral perfection,' and *vir,* 'man.'[8] It connotes the quality of goodness, knowledge, love, peace, etc. It wholly means ethically good habits in which we orient ourselves into the civility of good behaviors. It is antithetical to the concept of "vice" as a base for ethically bad habits.

Liberal Theory of Virtues: This is a state or quality of being a vital source of 'social capital,' those "feature of social life networks, norms, and trust—that enable participants to act together more effectively to pursue shared objectives."[9] It is a view that life is or can be just and humane, that it can be appropriate to humankind only on the ground of intersubjective rationalism. Reason enables a person or group into a deliberative rationality. Thus, it is for this reason that *Ubuntu* is recapitulating on the paradigmatic examples of virtue of liberalism towards the networks of social interactions, in generalized reciprocity. Hence, a liberal theory of virtue in the same sense of *Ubuntu* broadens the participants' sense of self identity, by "developing the 'I,' in the 'We,' or (in the language of rational-choice theorists) enhancing the participants' 'taste' for collective benefits."[10] It is on a related note, that the singular individuals with distinctive values, desires, habits, activities, creations, and ideas are within the community interest. It is a necessary and sufficient condition for political legitimacy and/ or authority than to be for defense of individual interest.

Identity: Identity can be referred to as the characteristics, feeling, or beliefs that distinguish people from others, a sense of national, cultural, personal, and group identity. The identity of a people lies in the way of life of such people. This way of life helps them find meaning in themselves and in what they do.[11] According to Esimone and Umezinwa:

> Identity can be seen as a means through which an individual or group of persons is recognized as being different due to its prevailing character. It is a display of behavior or personal character through which an individual or group of persons is being recognized. Identity is also seen as person's conception of his group affiliation and individuality.[12]

Azide also described identity as: "loyalty to a group in a society who share common cultural traits which they find difficult to subordinate to the general or universal culture. The members use those traits as distinctive features for social identification."[13]

VIRTUE: ITS SCOPE AND LIMITS

Virtue as a quality of being morally good is of great value in the formation of identity of an individual in a community because of its intimate connection with human dignity and self-respect. Virtue in accordance with moral principles is an element of human identity in conformity of behavior or thought on the nature of human conduct. Originally, the word "virtue" is from the Latin word "*vir*," meant manliness, and the Greek "*aperri*" had a similar sense.[14]

The word 'virtue' wholly means an ethically good habit which orients people to the civility of good behaviors. It is antithetical to the concept of "vice" as a base for an ethically bad habit. Kadankavil, as Socrates opined, "Virtue is knowledge and vice is ignorance."[15]

Subsequently, this concept runs throughout the history of Western philosophy in a passionate search for knowledge. Since virtue is knowledge, it can be taught. It is the right act of true wisdom which individuals must attain and learn to adopt as a habit. In a virtuous person, the emotions and appetites are habitually illumined by right reason like the free citizens of a well-governed state, but in the vicious person they are an unruly mob. Thus, the subliminal tendency in this is on the control of human appetite. Appetite and emotion are the motives or sources of action towards the acquisition of virtues or vicious.

The goal of this chapter, as earlier mentioned, is the reorientation of the true concept of vice and virtue within a framework of identity formation that is anchored in demonstrably liberal values which suggest that African transformation is not just embedded in an individual; but rather, it is co-substantively bestowed upon the other for all-*Ubuntu*. As a set of ethical principles in African identity transformation, *Ubuntu* invokes the spirit of genuine goodness amongst the African people. As a moral principle, it assigns a prominent place to virtue without incivility within the African cultural identity, and recognizes a baseline of minimum acceptable conduct. These are the prescriptions impacting on the rights of others. One may not transgress or trespass against the rights of others in the community. The individual is always conscious to act in accordance with the norms of the society. The norm is a stipulation of the right reason to be democratic and to exist virtuously well in the community. The sublimity of the individual thought is illuminated by right reason to reciprocate love, and to be in collaboration with others in the community. Virtue is therefore the result of the cultural inquisition or orientation in the community; the moral guideline for socio-political and economic virtue of knowledge that creates a possibility of community which is simultaneously altruistic and benevolent by providing essential elements for examining a liberal theory of *virtue* and transformation of identities in Africa.

It also follows that most matters of moral salience occur within the community discretion. This discretionary spectrum extends from the baseline upward of the communities' virtues and not heroism or sainthood as it is in Western philosophical thought. It is at these strata rather than at the level of individual acceptability that virtue occurs. Thus, the individual at this juncture is encapsulated by the community and is constrained in conduct by the rights of others as a matter of urgency not only to himself or herself but to all those with whom he or she interacts. The baseline of communities' virtues observance is the logic of *Ubuntu* ethics in Africa. The selection of appropriate mode of life is the intention of every person's desire. The systematic decentralization of judgments of value underpins the foreign cultural innuendos that come into the African culture. Modernity with its reorganization of institutions and social conditions of states in Africa has accultured the people into a system of division and systematic decentralization of judgment of value, which underpins the liberal toleration of the atomistic values in Africa. "This concept of toleration is consequentially pluralistic, not simply in the negative sense of countenancing different modes of life—that would merely reprise toleration—but as positive affirmation of multiple varieties of value."[16] Pluralism, here, celebrates sociality in the sense of inclusivity of people with different cultural backgrounds and institutions. The issue of virtue at this point of inclusivity of cultures becomes the rationale of individual judgment, and hermeneutics. To put it in another way, this conception of morality invariably becomes the avalanche of individual subjectivism that rejects the African communitarian's standard to personal appraisals. The account is individualistic, and holds that values are individuated by reference to the persons whose goods and evils they are. Entities more comprehensive than the individual such as classes, races, nations, or species are not recognized as having claims or responsibilities of their own; rather, whatever moral standing they may possess is reducible without reminder to that which attaches to distinct persons. Furthermore, in labeling the account of individuality are also constraints on ethical justifications, for not specifically consenting it to individuals' particular interest. What is within it, is on the essence of moral latitude in the dialogic ethics of the organizations of institutions in Africa (for example the community relationships and personal responsibility) interchange from that realm of African moral philosophy of *Ubuntu* to the concept of individualistic rationality of personal appraisals. This is the rationale for the harmonious existentialism in Africa. The challenge then is to find a common ground of unity towards the acceptability on its epistemic framework of rationality in dialogic ethics. The answer, therefore, stands on the hermeneutic understanding of the concept of virtues through practice, conducive to the identification and securing of that which is worth believing, having, making, or doing. Vices, correspondingly, are habitual traits that direct one away from these goods. Within the dimension of *Ubuntu*, in African ontology, the adverbial qualifier of virtue is centralized in collaborative stance of purpose. The individuals are implored innately to acquire the norms of the society which is the epistemic understanding of their ontology. The ontic or despotic proverbial circumstances of existentialism are not within the language game of epistemic culture in Africa. Thus, the issue of dispensational value of justice as with the occurrence of vices, do not really matter most, because individual existence is holistic, and beings are in ontological relationships with each other revolving in reciprocity.

The practical and theoretical leap from this 'structural irrepresentability' to the standard of principles of virtue enunciated in *Ubuntu* would either be justified in theory of utilitarianism or Kantian ethics. Utilitarianism and Kantian ethics are essentially theories of justice writ large, and justice is seen as the most universal of the virtues in so far as it involves a disposition to give to all persons their due. Justice is to be extended to all; it is at least a common denominator. Thus, within the spheres of moral philosophies, Kantian ethics is by standard presented as the polar opposite of utilitarianism: while for utilitarianism, it is the consequences of people's actions that carry all moral weight; for the Kantians, consequences do not matter— rather, moral value is solely a function of the motives brought to action. The only thing good without qualification, insists Kant, is the will that directs itself by the signal of duty. Duty, in turn, is understood as that which pure reason commands and the voice of reason in practice is the categorical imperative, bidding us to act only in accord with precepts that are universalizable. Kantianism, therefore, rejects the utilitarian criterion of consequentialist maximization. To phrase the contrast spatially, utilitarianism peers outward in businesslike fashion at the effects in the world that one's actions can engender, while the Kantian gazes inward at the maxims that guide choice.

Despite the considerable gulf separating the two theories, both have some elements of binary beat in comparison with the concept of *Ubuntu*, which acts conspicuously above and beyond the call for duty. It is as a result of the call for duty as well as for the matter of consequences, the right action for duty which yields the desired amount of utility. Through punctilious observance of conventional form, one indicates one's continued allegiance to norms of interpersonal civility, including the most fundamental precepts of individual autonomy. Manners in the sense of reciprocity, collaboration, inclusivity, and brotherhood determine the attentiveness to boundaries between self and others. This affords the visible indicators rather than being controlled by them. Manners are part of the orientation of culture in the community. It is an act of national or communitarian integration of existentialism rather than an act of individualistic calculation.

UBUNTU DIALOGIC ETHICS: TOWARDS A LIBERAL THEORY OF VIRTUE

The normative understanding of the concept of *Ubuntu* refers to the fact that the Africans have some forms of dialogic ethics which have a formative influence on the moral dispositions of members, towards the civilities of virtue in Bantu language that refer to the interrelational reciprocity and collaborations among members of African communities. It connotes love, peace, humanistic, holistic building of the society, positive peace building, justice, and showing of remorse and repentance. It is the main arms of the theoretical virtues in African ontology, which occurs through the modeling of good citizens and benevolence in the society. 'I am because we are,' and 'we are because I am': this is the spirit of *Ubuntu*, as an African social ethics. This is the concept of virtue as disposition of body and mind acquired through practice of love and reciprocity to others.

It is also a philosophical concept of vital force which morally pervades in everyone's life to be human.[17] *Ubuntu* is a bond of unity amongst the people of Africa. A person belongs to his/her community by participating and sharing with others in and outside his community. Every single human being only becomes a truly human being by means of relationship with others in the society. The emphasis here is to establish the imperatives of human existence in the political communities of Africa. It is a vital force for peace in African ontology, which signifies the principles of reconciliations, reciprocity, inclusivity, democracy, and humanism. It is a holistic way of unifying everybody in the community. Thus, for one to live effectively in the community, he/she must imbibe the principles of *Ubuntu* in his/her lives.

It is useful to note that Africans had formal modes of existence that gave them the status of political communities before the arrival of Euro-Christian tradition and Arabic-Islamic tradition in Africa. The African transformation agenda prior to the modernization period was rejuvenated with the philosophical concept of *Ubuntu*. Perhaps, *Ubuntu* philosophy is the first in a series of intellectual and political responses to the expansion of Western philosophical thought and Arabic traditions in Africa. The Western philosophical thought more than any other brand developed a flourishing mythology and ideology. However, according to Vanden-Berger, the Westernization process resulted from:

(1) The prevailing forms of capitalist exploitation, notably illustrated by slavery in the New World and incipient colonial expansion in Africa. (2) Social Darwinism which dovetailed with economic liberalism of the late 19th century. Liberal utilization like John Stuart Mill's legitimized laissez-faire, which in turn was reinterpreted as a mandate not to interfere with any form of human inequality and suffering. It literally reflected the platonic idea which would have supported the view that Negroes were slaves as a result of natural selection.[18]

The essence of *Ubuntu* is to promote a culture of peace, tolerance, peaceful co-existence, and mutual development. It is a systematic entrenchment of the people's ideology within the society in which they live. Only in community with others has each individual the means of cultivating his or her gifts in all directions; only in the community, therefore, is personal freedom possible.

The alienation of individuals is negations of the lives of the communities. On a related note, Tutu declared that:

> *Ubuntu* is very difficult to render in a western language. It speaks to every essence of being human. When you want to give high praise to someone we say, 'Yu U nobuntu'; he or she has Ubuntu. This means that they are generous, hospitable, friendly, caring and compassionate. They share what they have. It also means that my humanity is caught up, is inextricably bound up, in theirs, we belong to a bundle of life. We say 'a person is a person through other people' ("in Xhosa Ubuntu ungamntun gabanyeabant and in Zulu Urnuntungumuntun gumuntungabanye"). I am human being because I belong, I participate, I share. A person with ubuntu is open and available to others, affirming of others, does not feel threatened that others are able and good.[19]

Thus, to draw an inference with *Ubuntu* would mean to become a point of reference with Marxism. Marx's philosophy, therefore, is like the philosophical ideas of *Ubuntu* striving to rationalize society through the individual participation and activities in the societies. Corroborating this, Soccio in his opinion of Marx observes that:

> Society will at least be able to provide decent, meaningful lives to virtually everyone. As a result, no one will need private property or wealth. Instead of having to compete for a good life, we will live harmoniously, doing creative, satisfying work that benefits us individually at the same time it benefits society collectively. There will be only one class, hence no class conflict. The economy will reach a state of balance and history as such, class struggle will end.[20]

Thus, it is from the virtue of the above, that one considers the political and ideological tendency underlying in *Ubuntu* and Marxism. Historical materialism, for Marx, represents the basic theory and method which he used in the study of history to demonstrate the truth of his prediction of an inevitable class war between the proletariats and the capitalists. With this, therefore, the classical point of divergence with *Ubuntu* is that Marxism, as a Western ethical value, is based on a single social context for contemporary cultures and enrichment purposes. On the other hand, *Ubuntu* is considered to be more fundamental to the life of everyone in the political community. Relating to this, Ortega in the "Revolt of the Masses" argues that:

> The fundamental radical truth is the co-existence of myself with the world. Existing is first and foremost co-existing-it is I, myself, seeing something which is not myself, it is I loving another being, it is I suffering from things.[21]

It may surely not be wrong to synchronize Ortega's existentialism with that of *Ubuntu's* African existential analytics. Both have the cognitive vision of the world as one entity. In view of Ortega, both the subject and object are united in nature, but they are relatively independent from the other. Hence, for *Ubuntu* and as well as Ortega, to have a cognitive vision of the world is to exist for the world. Every existence is entirely not without the subject and object; both are complements of the other, which means that they are in constant conjunction. It is within these philosophical trajectories that we see *Ubuntu* as a philosophical transformation of the political communities in Africa. Life is a subjective striving of the individual in society, and the vocation of self is mainly meant for the self-realization in the community of self-shared understanding and diversity.

This situation is consequently paradoxical—that is, while we are nursing the ambitions of African hegemony with the ideal of *Ubuntu* as a sign of African imperative for institutional development, the problems now lie with the defects in African hegemony as a result of modernity with its reorganization of institutions in Africa, which realigned the people(s) into different modes of cultures. How then should the people reorganize the differences or fragmentations created as a result of modernity in Africa? Green argues thus:

> Cultural differences reflect not only a history but also fundamental variations in what people hold to be worthwhile. As long as variations persist they will invite comparison and questioning of the practices and preferences of others. It may be disconcerting to have to acknowledge that members of historically stigmatized racial and ethnic groups often do things their way not just because they have been excluded from mainstream institutions by prejudice and discrimination, but because they find the values and institutions of the larger society inferior to their own.[22]

> By articulating the pressure of racialized subordination or tribal sentiments, the preferences for cultural homogeneity of dialogic ethic relations are really needed for harmonious living in Africa. For this reason, *Ubuntu* would be sought after to provide the bases for cultural unity among cultures in Africa. The conceptualization of *Ubuntu* as a peace building process in Africa, is not only in the absence of war, conflict, violence, fear, destruction and human sufferings, but also in the absence of unequal and unjust structures, with cultural practices about security, democratic participation, respect for human rights, developments, social progress and justice.[23]

However, some critical issues that emerged with this concept of *Ubuntu* are its justifications with the Western philosophical thought. The ideological and culturally specific conception of human rights is from the point of view of communication relations. The Western approach to human rights stresses on 'individualism,' but Africa is 'universalistic' in its approach to human rights. A very explicit argument here is that in Africa, the clash is obvious between the specificity of rights of the Western philosophical thought and the universalistic rights of the African philosophical thought which are in juxtaposition to each other. It is useful to remember that cultural and racial variations are among the most enduring characteristics in the age of modernity. Hence, diversity is certainly a fact to build within a dialogic ethic transformation for development in African states.

UBUNTU DIALOGIC ETHICS TRANSFORMATION OF IDENTITIES IN AFRICA

The African continent comprises of people with different cultures, religions, ethnicities, ideologies, and nationalities otherwise known as identities. On a daily basis, men are being confronted with various types of identity-related issues. A closer look at the root of conflicts that do arise could be traced down to the principles of ethnocentrism—the belief that one's culture is superior to others. According to Francis:

> The conceptualization of 'Ubuntu' as a peace building process in Africa, is not only in the absence of war, conflicts, violence, fear, destruction and human sufferings, but also in recapitulation of the absence of unequal and unjust structures, and cultural practices about security, democratic participation, respect for human rights, development, social progress and justice.[24]

UBUNTU DIALOGIC ETHICS TRANSFORMATION OF CULTURAL AND ETHNIC IDENTITIES

Culture is an exclusive preserve of human beings that is learnt and transmitted from one person to another. It includes knowledge, beliefs, arts, morals, laws, customs, and other capabilities and habits required by individual as members of society.[25] Identity refers to the whole culture of people with which the people are known or identified. People who share the same culture usually identify with the same things. They speak the same language; share the same beliefs, laws, and customs. An individual identifies with various groups throughout life from family to national level. Thus, cultural identity endears the members of the group to one another, and fosters oneness, friendship, mutual trust, and love. Cultural identity teaches us to recognize that cultures of others are important to their members as ours is to us, and there is no superiority/right or inferior/wrong culture. Therefore, fanatical attachment or identification with a culture generates ethnocentrism.

Ethnicity refers to cultural factors such as nationality, culture, ancestry, language, and belief. Ekweariri and Mbara argue that although ethnicity has centrality of purpose, ethnicity emerges when it is relevant as means of furthering emergent collective interests and changes according to political changes in the society.[26] Recently, ethnic sentimentality has been of great concern across the continent because of divisive elements in the unity and progress of Africa.

Ubuntu invokes a sense of duty and responsibility to a communal democratic process of reciprocity and collaboration of the people in the political community—helpful in transforming identity in ways that retrieve the roots that are fundamental to the way Africans approach life. An example of African social ethics as a model of *Ubuntu* dialogic method of cultural integration is the Igbo indigenous concept of human rights and justice. As Okere averred:

> In the indigenous setting, one cannot claim the same distinguished pedigree or trajectory of development of rights as in the Western world; but there are native precursors or faint undeveloped versions of the same western concept and that they have sprouted on other lands is perhaps the best justification to call human rights. In Igbo indigenous thought the expression that most aptly enunciates the principle of the human rights of every human is the saying: *"Egbe bere Ugo bere nke si ibe ya ebela nkukwaa ya"* Translated as: "Let the Kites [common birds of prey] have the right to perch, let the Eagles have the right to perch, whoever denies the other the right to perch, let it have its wings broken—let it be 'anathema.'"[27]

This is the curse that morality visits on the bird that would push its fellow bird to that extremity. But this is the way of speaking of birds, yet it enunciates a cardinal philosophy of human co-existence. 'Live and let live.' You have rights and entitlements, but every other human being has them too. It is a plea for justice and equity, but it is a statement demanding respect for rights.[28] The right to perch is every bird's inalienable right; otherwise it could fly itself to exhaustion and death if it had no landing rights. It is the minimum it needs to survive, to sustain itself, to get rest, to have living space. If it lost that right perhaps to a bigger, more powerful bird or to any other bird, it would be condemned to fly till kingdom come, perhaps breaking its wings in endless flight.

According to Obiefuna and Izuegbu the picture of *Ugo* (Eagle) represents the noble or the high class of the society, while the picture of *Egbe* (Kite) represents the mean/poor of the society.[29] In this regard, no matter whose position in life, justice among the Igbo promotes equality of rights and privileges. This is corroborated by Nzomiwu thus:

> Igbo sense of justice entails that in a community both the strong and the weak, the poor and the rich, the noble and the mean, the least and the greatest, should live in perfect harmony and one who attempts to deprive the other of this right to harmonious co-existence should be greatly penalized.[30]

Indeed, Okere lamented that:

Among the Igbo the question of ultimate right has sanctions way above human reach. The gods using death as avenger impose a sanction beyond man. Here is the germ of a spirit that should have been allowed to evolve into part of our political culture. All this, however, has been truncated by the interloping colonial Leviathan.[31]

Thus, any attempt at denying any person this opportunity to equal right is injustice. Justice is done if each of the members of the society is allowed to co-exist with others and at the same time enjoys equal opportunity with all. The picture shown in the above proverb which the Igbo commonly refer to reveals the Igbo concept of the value of justice. It demands that everyone should accommodate another. This idea of justice among the Igbo may account for the reason they easily relax in any part of the world trying to take the place as their home. The belief in the equality of right has seen many Igbo contributing in development across the globe with a particular notion of living in harmony.

UBUNTU DIALOGIC ETHICS TRANSFORMATION OF RELIGIOUS IDENTITIES

Religion is one of the social change dynamics which necessitates the rise of conflict. Religious conflict is part of the sociological malaise that destroys the human existential ontology. The thesis that emerges from the sociological and philosophical impacts of religion makes it a veritable tool for the growth and development of man; yet it has enormous negative effects on humanity. The variability and vicissitudes of membership in religions breed conflict to the point that there is need for the moral use of dialogue. Indeed, what is paramount at this point is the cultural relationship which is within the ambiances of humanity. For this, Keller and Iyob assert that:

The role of religion in the 21st century Africa and its impact on transitions to democracy have been obscured and distorted by flawed assumptions that the realm of faith in its infinite varieties of norms and rules governing humanity's relations to the 'divine' constituted impediments to democracy.[32]

This morally complied with the panoply of statehood in postcolonial Africa which was confronted immediately with the challenges of governing diverse multitudes lacking both coherence and consensus on the precepts of just/ righteous rule. It is in this perspective that the hegemonic elite(s) project of secular modernity has been distorted with incessant religious conflicts. There are so many more cases of conflicts in Africa to the point that we require a profound dialogic interpretation as an avalanche for the genuine goal of arriving at accepted secularism.

In order to avoid the collapse of the state hegemonic institutions, thereby supplanting anarchism, war, and destruction of life and property due to religious conflicts, there may be need to regulate the political institutions through a dialogic process of a consensus that will harmonize the existence of pluralism in the state. It is the most effective means of honoring this obligation; it is by creating institutional frameworks which widen the boundaries of the dialogic community. The new policies of change through dialogue become the new ethical commitment for the society's stability. Most members of such a society may share many of their cultural traits and traditions, but the bond which unites them can owe as much on ethical commitment to open dialogue as to a sense of primordial achievement.

It is under this trajectory that the transformation of political community would constitute a revolution in the areas affected because societies would no longer confront each other as geopolitical rivals in the condition of anarchy. More dialogic relations would spell the end of ethnocentrism with religions and ethnic sentiments. The *Ubuntu* dialogic principles will enhance co-operation to engineer a wider process of change that will secure higher levels of respect for pluralism, and thereby counter the ideological blindness of religious identities, which results in the incessant religious conflict. Profusely, it is on the ground that the global resurgence of religious identities and institutions require more nuanced debates questioning the linear assumptions linking separation of religion and state to democratization of societies. *Ubuntu* dialogic consciousness will bring much attention to be paid to the dynamic relations between religion and politics. Such dialogue acknowledges the endurance of religion as a source of just/righteous rule and the impact of faith-based institutions on the polity. The attainment of consensus through public dialogue on what constitutes just/righteous rule in multiethnic and multireligious nations will guarantee neutral arbitration of conflict. It will be to make the state the interpreter of religious cum state laws in a condition of mutual existentialism. Thus, it is in this time of thought that the exogenesis of religious fanaticism, fundamentalism, and terrorism would be stopped. Religion, therefore, in this circumstance, becomes the harbinger of individual moral transformation on the character formations and socialization. Abdullahi corroborated this by shifting the emphasis from state to the civic sphere where dialogue would nurture a "process of negotiation . . . promoting the spirit of independent inquiry and supporting personal responsibility for . . . moral and religious choices. . . . "[33] Here, it proves that a just citizen is a just society and that the practice of democracy extols the virtue of individual character in the conformity with the moral and legal norms of the state.

CONCLUSION

There is, of course, lots of debate about this matter, on the genuine principles of virtue, but the chapter accepts the view espoused in the concept of *Ubuntu* as the organ principles of virtue in Africa. It is the dialogic ethic transformation of communities' relation in Africa. "As it was relegated to the background due to the wide range of influences in modernity, perhaps, more importantly, the structures of the postmodern thinking are entirely new structures of dialogue which require new sets of metaphysical thinking in restructuring the world's communities."[34] "The outcome of the dialogic ethic relations among [diverse] cultures in the world today, have not yet resulted in positive [peace building]. It is still very contestable in reaching the desired goal."[35]

However, *Ubuntu* as a formidable structure of peace building in Africa can be equally utilized in global peace building. This will enhance the global essence of living together, harmoniously in our age. It will also remove all the atavistic tendencies or vicious ethically bad habits in the world communities. We have pointed out salient points and aspects of the moral principles of *Ubuntu* which would have transformed the developmental imperatives in Africa had it not been replaced with other ideologues (i.e., the Christian and Islamic traditional ideologies). The chapter also suggested the expositions of African ethics in *Ubuntu* philosophy to be exhumed to rekindle the already forgotten virtues of our existential qualities as Africans. It has corroborated the thesis that we can rekindle a language of virtue and vice in a culture that is fundamentally liberal.

RECOMMENDATIONS

The status of moral universals is a more central question in contemporary social and political theory. It is on the right set of virtue. Of course, from time of history, there have been opposing and irreconcilable positions on the need for and status of moral universals. Habermas is frequently associated with the claim that postmodernist and related perspectives lack the moral resources for criticizing the structures of power which they oppose. However, it is on the basis of this shaking foundation of universal moral virtues that the following recommendations are made:

- *Ubuntu* as a liberal theory of virtue in Africa should be given an effective legitimization in transforming group identity for nation building in the interest of the common good.

- The idea of inclusivity is central to democracy; but it must be transcended and moderated by a deeper sense of common citizenship with the principle of enculturation of *Ubuntu*.[36]
- For the genuineness of the transcultural unit to occur, the balanced view of the past must be encouraged. Thus, within this dimension, *Ubuntu* can be utilized in our peace-building process, for the resolution of conflict, convergence, and coexistence of cultures in Africa.
- It could be of relevance for the sustenance of the global peace, as it does not require the cultural homogeneity, which puts it in the right epistemic framework of 'dialogic ethic.'

NOTES

1. Jude C. Asike, "The interplay between philosophy and religion: The perspectives of the Igbos, South-East, Nigeria," *Journal of Religion and Culture* 16, no. 2 (2016): 177–80.

2. Louis P. Pojman, *Philosophy: The Pursuit of Wisdom* (Belmont: Wadsworth, 2001), 141.

3. David J. Francis, "Peace and Conflict Studies: An African Overview of Basic Concepts," in *Introduction to Peace and Conflict Studies in West Africa: A Reader*, ed. Shedrack Gaya Best (Ibadan: Spectrum Books, 2006).

4. Albert Sydney Hornby and Michael Ashby, *Oxford Advanced Learner's Dictionary of Current English* (Oxford: Oxford University Press, 2000).

5. Akpenpuun Dzurgba, *Principles of Ethics* (Ibadan: Agape Publications, 2000), 78.

6. Jude C. Asike, "The Philosophical Concept of 'Ubuntu' as Dialogic Ethic and the Transformation of Political Community in Africa," *OGIRISI: a New Journal of African Studies* 12, no. 1 (2016): 1–16.

7. Jude C. Asike and Ogugua Patricia Anwuluorah, "Ubuntu Dialogic Ethics: Towards a Liberal Theory of Virtue for Development of Common Good," *Oracle of Wisdom Journal of Philosophy and Public Affairs* 2, no. 2 (2018): 1–7, http://owijoppa.com/journals/V2N2_2018/V2N2P1-2018_OWIJOPPA.pdf.

8. Albert Sydney Hornby, *Oxford Advanced Learner's Dictionary* (Oxford: Oxford University Press, 2010).

9. Robert D. Putnam, "Bowling Alone: America's Declining Social Capital," *Journal of Democracy* 6, no. 1 (1995): 67.

10. Ibid., 76.

11. M. Maha, "Italo Festival of the Igala as Panacea for Fostering National Identity," in *The Humanities and National Identity*, eds. P.A. Uchechukwu et al. (Awka: Fab Anieh, 2013), 82.

12. C. C. Esimone and E.C. Umezinwa, "Music: An Instrument of Identity and Social Security," in *The Humanities and National Identity*, eds. P. A. Uchechukwu et al. (Awka: Fab Anieh, 2013), 34.

13. J. Azide, "Culture and National Identity," in *Basic Foundations in Arts and Social Sciences* eds. M. E. Onuora and C. O. N. Oguji (Enugu: Frefabag, 2007), 493.

14. Austin Fagothey, *Right and Reason: Ethics in Theory and Practice* (St. Louis: Mosby, 1981), 201.

15. Thomas Kadankavil, *Ethical World: A Study on the Ethical Thought in the East and the West* (Bangalore: Dharmaram Publications, 1995), 8.

16. Loren E. Lomasky, "Towards a Liberal Theory of Vice (and Virtue)," in *Civil Society, Democracy, and Civic Renewal*, ed. Robert K. Fullinwider (Lanham: Rowman & Littlefield Publishers, 1999), 278.

17. The remaining paragraphs of this section 'Ubuntu Dialogic Ethics: Towards a Liberal Theory of Virtue' are reprinted from the article by Jude C. Asike, "The Philosophical Concept of 'Ubuntu' as Dialogic Ethic and the Transformation of Political Community in Africa," *OGIRISI: a New Journal of African Studies* 12, no. 1 (2016): 7–13. Reprinted with permission.

18. Pierre L. Vanden-Berger, *Race and Racism: A Comparative Perspective* (New York: John Willey, 1967), 57.

19. Desmond Tutu, *No Future Without Forgiveness* (London: Rider, 1999), 10.

20. Douglas J. Soccio, *Archetypes of Wisdom: an Introduction to Philosophy* (Belmont: Wadsworth, 2001), 399.

21.José Ortega y Gasset and Howard Lee Nostrand, *Mission of the University* (New York: The Norton Library, 1966), 231–32.

22. James W. Green, *Cultural Awareness in the Human Services: A Multi-Ethnic Approach* (Boston: Allyn & Bacon, 1999), 5.

23. David J. Francis, "Peace and Conflict Studies: An African Overview of Basic cCncepts," in *Introduction to Peace and Conflict Studies in West Africa: A Reader*, ed. Shedrack Gaya Best (Ibadan: Spectrum Books, 2006), 27.

24. Ibid.

25. T.J. Okeke, "Cultural Diplomacy and Ethnic Tension in a Multi-Religious Society: An Example of Nigeria," in *The Humanities and Globalization in the Third Millennium*, eds. A. B. C. Chiegboka, T. . Utoh-Ezeajgh, and G. I. Udechukwu (Nimo: Rex Charles and Patrick, 2010), 248–54.

26. C. S. Ekweariri and N. Mbara, "Ethnic Sentimentality and the Search for Social Stability in Nigeria. A Reading of Kinsley Agubom's 'The Bitter Truth,'" in *The Humanities and National Identity*, eds. P. A. Uchechukwu et al. (Awka: Fab Anieh, 2013), 62–66.

27. T. Okere, "Addressing Multi-Cultural and Human Rights Issues in the Formation of Priests and Religious in Africa," in *The Hermeneutics of Culture Religion and Society*, ed. I. O. Oguejiofor (Onitsha: Wisdom Technologies Entertainment, 2015), 77–78.

28. Ibid., 78.

29. B. A. C. Obiefuna and S. C. Izuegbu, "The Igbo Value of Justice: A Tool for Good Governance in Nigeria," in *Humanities and African Values*, eds. E. C. Umezinwa, K. L. Nwadialor, and I. L. Umeanolue (Awka: Fab Anieh, 2016), 145.

30. John Paul C. Nzomiwu, *The Concept of Justice among the Traditional Igbo: An Ethical Inquiry* (Awka: Fides Publications, 1999), 53.

31. Okere, "Addressing," 78.

32. Edmond J. Keller and Ruth Iyob, *Religious Ideas and Institutions: Transitions to Democracy in Africa* (Pretoria: Unisa Press, 2012), 169.

33. Abdullahi Ahmed An-Na'im, *Islam and the Secular State: Negotiating the Future of Shari'a* (Cambridge: Harvard University Press, 2010), 2–3.

34. Jude C. Asike, "The Philosophical Concept of 'Ubuntu' as Dialogic Ethic and the Transformation of Political Community in Africa," *OGIRISI: a New Journal of African Studies* 12, no. 1 (2016): 14.

35. Ibid.

36. Ibid., 15.

3

Interrogating Identity Politics in Nigeria

Soj Ojo

In its general contextual usage in political anthropology, identity politics often conveys notions of political organization, activities, behavior, or orientation driven by some underlying conditions, experiences, and interests of individuals or designated groups, defined by ethno-geographical origin, membership of which is generally by ascription. The concept of ethnic group is the most basic, from which other related concepts such as ethnicity, ethnic identity and identity politics are derived. A common feature often associated with ethnic politics is the tendency to distinguish various sociocultural and geopolitical categories from each other as different and distinct, in which members also see themselves as different rather than members of one collective universe. The most fundamental aspect of identity politics in this orthodox sense is that it reflects a primordialist perspective, described by Isawji as the oldest in the sociological and anthropological literature.[1] As alluded to by its mainstream proponents, the primordialist analytical model presents ethnicity as ascribed, in which at birth, a person "becomes" a member of a particular group and ethnic identification is based on deep, "primordial" attachments to that group.[2] Notable protagonists whose exposition specifically on ethnic identity and politics in Nigeria fit clearly into the orthodox primordial perspective are Nnoli and Otite.[3] Also belonging to the orthodox tradition, but whose writing is described as a "soft" form of primordialism, is Anthony D. Smith, who at the time of his death, was Professor Emeritus of Nationalism and Ethnicity at the London School of Economics.[4] Central to the primordialist perspective as reflected in Stack and Warren is what its proponents interchangeably refer to as ethno-symbolism or myth-symbol.[5] Ethno-symbolism as a core element of ethnicity thrives on traditional myths rooted in ideologically couched narratives of historical experiences, especially past and present socio-political and economic injustice, deprivation, and marginalization, suggestive of specific courses of action for remediation.

Until recently, mainstream ideas and analytical perspectives provided by scholars to explain the problems of ethnicity and politics relied mainly on scholarly orthodoxy rooted in primodialist theoretical perspective. A common feature of such orthodox narratives was that they often alluded to the inevitable consequences of conflicts resulting from sociocultural diversity and societal heterogeneity. Though outside the focus of this chapter, other perspectives from which orthodox narratives on ethnic identity have benefited as reflected in Wan and Vanderwerf include instrumentalist approach, social constructivist approach, and psycho-cultural interpretation theory.[6] This is the basis of the common assumption that ethnic politics is unavoidable in a society characterized by sociocultural heterogeneity. When conceptualized from this perspective, ethnic politics refers to the form assumed by politics when its processes, structures, operative rules, practices, competitions, and struggles for power, resources, and other public goods, conflicts, and other associated problems are defined mainly along ethnic lines.

It is from this consideration that Ugbana Okpu argued that in the most usual approach, key national issues and Nigeria's history in general, have been viewed from the perspective of the difference between the Hausa, Fulani, Igbo, and Yoruba or their political parties and their struggles for political domination.[7] To the foregoing perspective also belong presentations and narratives authored by Post and Vickers in which reference was made to the 'stress-producing' elements in the Nigerian political system.[8] The sources of conflict in Nigeria were accordingly identified as "Conglomerate Society, the System of Rewards and the Structural Frame."[9] Earlier scholarly endorsements and applications of the primodalist theoretical perspective to the analysis of ethnic identity from which studies on Nigeria have benefited include those of Leo Kuper and M. G. Smith.[10] Underlying this theoretical perspective is the idea that in a culturally divided society each cultural section has its own way of life, with its own distinctive action systems. Also included are common interests, cultural norms, practices, and social relations that are relatively exclusive to each ethno-cultural section. Thus, pluralism is perceived as coexistence of incompatible social and institutional formations. This is mainly because in a culturally divided country, the relationship between nationalism and cultural sectionalism is invariably problematic in response to the forces of heterogeneity within the political system. From the standpoint of nationalism, it is taken as axiomatic that the nation and political system are coterminous. This implies that every nation will have its own state. In the context of Nigeria, aptly described by Peter Ekeh, using the notion of 'the two publics,' the possibility of nationalist consciousness growing into a movement and evolving as a political force has historically always been whittled down by primordial interests and demands of cultural sections.[11] Alluding to the effect of sectional and sociocultural diversity on politics and identity in Nigeria, Post and Vickers noted that "at certain times and in certain situations, it meant something fundamental and overriding to individuals that they were Yoruba, Hausa, Tiv, or whatever."[12] In relation to issues of majority/minority ethnic identity and party politics in Nigeria, Okpu remarked that in a situation where the interests of the major ethnic groups were jealously protected by their political parties, the ethnic minority groups were obliged to organize themselves politically.[13] Thus, it is argued that the growing number of ethnically based political bodies formed by sectional group that felt hitherto marginalized by majority groups in Nigeria came out of political exigency. It could not have been otherwise, given the existence of diverse sociocultural groups in the country driven by the desire to achieve competitive progress through organized bodies. This is the explanation usually given to the preponderance of political parties founded and organized along ethno-cultural and geopolitical lines in Nigeria during the immediate years after independence. Also, a great deal of the narratives and explanations that dominated the literature on the crises and conflicts that culminated in the collapse of Nigeria's First Republic drew mainly on the paradigm of inevitability of crisis and conflict within the context of the country's heterogeneity. Accordingly, descriptive and interpretive analysis provided by scholars to explain military involvement in Nigerian politics, and key government policies such as appointments to top government positions, creation of more states, and local governments in Nigeria before the end of military rule in 1999 were rooted largely in primordial theoretical perspective on ethnicity and politics.

ALTERNATIVE CRITIQUE ON ETHNIC IDENTITY DISCOURSE

This chapter represents a paradigm shift from scholarly orthodoxy on identity politics, predicated on ethnic and cultural categories, perceived as distinct and boundary-defining, with great potential to inspire collective affinities, loyalties, and passions in people to mobilize them into action, and energize them politically. This entails an interrogation of the scholarly discourse on identity politics often couched in the ideological myths of sociocultural diversity and primordial passion. Specifically, we examine some of the tangible and intangible elements of ethnic identity that characterized identity politics in Nigeria. The analysis provides insight into how individuals and groups are manipulated to perceive imagined and real threats to their tangible and intangible characteristics as dangers to their interests. This exposition attempts to show how ethnicity becomes politicized and snowballs into an instrument of political identity when groups become political actors, involved in activities intended to confront threats to their identity and interest.

The framework adopted in this chapter provides an alternative perspective for interrogating identity politics in Nigeria with two main objectives in view. First, to show that the sociocultural myths that have sustained identity politics in Nigeria have historically been articulated by a dominant group of elites and political entrepreneurs who project themselves as spokespersons and defenders of the interests of their people. These are persons who ultimately use such activities to construct platforms for the pursuit of their personal interest and political ambition. Second, it is also intended to demonstrate that this dominant group of elites and political entrepreneurs share common personal identity traits, interest, and practices that cut across ethnic boundaries. In other words, a member of the Nigerian political elite may by origin belong to any of the ethnic groups in the southern geopolitical zones of the country, but it is instructive that essentially, he or she shares common elements of personal identity with their counterpart elite from any of the other ethnic groups or geopolitical zones of Nigeria. This is mainly the case when the pursuit of their personal political interest is at stake. Some elements of personal identity that members of Nigerian political elites share irrespective of their ethnic origin include the following six elements.

ELEMENTS OF PERSONAL IDENTITY OF MEMBERS OF THE NIGERIAN POLITICAL ELITE

- They are persons historically linked with politics and governance by virtue of political positions they occupied and who benefited greatly from opportunities for self-enrichment that exist at various levels of government in Nigeria through perquisites of office or corruption and in most cases both. As reflected in Paul Okorie's interview with Nigeria News Agency published in *The Sun* of 7 February 2020, Nigeria ranks among the highest in the world's list of highest paid political office holders including senators and others.[14] He expressed the view that Nigerians will not accept any review that will lead to increase in the monthly salaries and emoluments of political office holders. Also, in an interview with BBC News Africa, a Nigerian politician and former senator, Shehu Sani, revealed that Nigerian senators are entitled to monthly expense allowances of 13.5 million Naira (£27,000; $37,500), in addition to their monthly salaries of more than $2,000.[15]
- They are persons placed in position of advantage socially and economically over and above most other members of their communities and the

society at large as a result of the stupendous wealth they acquired from previous or current positions held in government.

- Their advantageous position confers such great influence that makes them the most influential members within their ethnic identity group as their counterparts from other ethnic identities.
- They are persons who have evolved as the most visible members of the society, with a history of political office they may have occupied in the past. Today in all parts of the country, we find on the Nigerian political landscape persons who since independence have been part of virtually every governing administration, occupying various positions of political relevance. This explains why in various parts of the country, there are what appear as political dynasties with generations of family members who at different times held one prominent political position or another and still remain dominant in the current power relations. The influence members of such families enjoy within their ethnic group make it possible for them both to build up political support and also to manipulate political recruitment processes in pursuit of their selfish political interest.
- An element of personal identity common to members of the Nigerian political elite is that they are largely self-serving; primarily concerned with personal interests; and ready and willing to sacrifice the common interest and undermine existing rules, globally acknowledged moral standards, and principles of democracy and good governance such as free, fair, and credible elections, transparency, and political accountability in the pursuit of their personal, political, and economic interests.
- Finally, Nigerian political elite irrespective of their ethnic origin appeal to the myths of ethnic affinity, perceived injuries of past and present socio-political and economic injustices and inequities as a strategy to inspire the people, mobilize, and ignite political action. Therefore, ethnic identity fuels elite manipulation of the society for elite self-serving interests.

ELITE OPPORTUNISM AND MANIPULATION OF ETHNIC IDENTITY

The Nigeria experience provides a good example that divisive narratives, ethno-sectional antagonism, and hostility often associated with the struggle and competition for the control of national power and resources are largely orchestrated by the political elite. This has resulted in the use of *ethnic politics* as a common appellation to describe the nature and character of politics in Nigeria. In effect, the Nigerian political elite are usually at the forefront of this divisive narrative used to express perceived frustration and misgivings of people within their own ethnic group over the country's socio-political structure and access to national power and resources. This is because there is a correlation between socio-political structure of Nigeria and access to national power and resources, which elite political opportunists often purport to place their ethnic group at great disadvantage within the country's body politic. Though they often present themselves as persons defending the interests of their ethnic group, as a result of the self-seeking tendencies perpetrated by the Nigerian political elite, genuine inclusion in politics remains a remote possibility and democratic development remains stalled. Abundant evidence exists how the Nigerian political elite has historically manipulated ethnic identity within the country in furtherance of interests and agenda that are self-serving to them. This is often in relation to the pursuit of ambition for political office or to influence the dynamics of the national polity with some personal benefit in view. It has thus become difficult, if not impossible, to speak in any concrete terms of, say, the Yoruba, the Igbo, the Hausa, the Fulani, or the Ijaw as an ethnic group with a clearly definable interest without inviting some critical question. Such critical questions may be in the form of: Whose Hausa? Whose Fulani? Whose Yoruba? Or whose Ijaw? Such questions are pertinent as there are past politicians who claimed they spoke for or represented the interests of their ethnic groups but merely served their personal interest. This is the context in which members of the Nigerian political elite have always been at the forefront of agitations and campaign over perceived geopolitical imbalance and fear of domination and marginalization of minority ethnic groups by the majority ethnic groups within the Nigeria heterogeneous political community. To justify the need for collective action in response to perceived threat to their common interest, the Nigerian political elite often appeal to principles of self-determination, justice, equity, and political equality as strategy to get the people to support the perceived objective. The perceived objective in this regard is to ensure that no one ethnic group dominates or is dominated, monopolizes, or is marginalized in respect of access to the country's political power because of advantage or disadvantage arising from size, language, or geographical location. A typical manifestation of this tendency is when the people are mobilized to agitate for creation of new states and local government areas. Such agitations are used to put pressure on those at the helm of federal level political affairs to initiate political reform programs to serve as mediating and countervailing forces to deal with dissatisfaction and demands emanating from perceived problems, especially that of noninclusion inherent in the Nigeria heterogeneous political space. The perceived problems are supposedly addressed through creation of new states and local government areas to mitigate perceived ethno-structural imbalance and to achieve parity or some form of balance in the federation. Two specific problems that state creation is supposed to solve or mitigate are participation crisis and distribution crisis. These crises are part of Nigeria's postindependence challenges often metaphorically referred to as 'unresolved national question.' The problem is really that of determining how far further federal division should go to provide a final answer to the problem of the quest for autonomous units in Nigeria. This is because newly created states and local government areas are potential beneficiaries from allocation of oil revenue accruing to the federation account based on the existing sharing formula of 52.68%, 26.72% and 20.60%, to the federal, state, and local governments respectively.[16] Ultimately, the immediate beneficiaries are members of the political elite. They are the ones who seize the opportunity so created to seek political offices as governors, commissioners, ministers, local government chairs and other key political offices through Nigeria's noninclusive and self-serving political recruitment processes. By constitutional provision, local government areas serve as the constituency for election into the House of Representatives and states are also delineated into three senatorial districts each, as constituencies for election into the Nigerian senate. Creation of new states and local government areas, therefore, offers members of the political elite opportunity to actualize their personal interests and political ambition of membership of the National Assembly. Members of the political elite usually initiate agitation campaigns for the creation of new states and local government areas. Elites benefit from the influence and resources they need to mobilize the needed organizational and logistic support. To this extent, across ethnic boundaries, members of the political elite employ such opportunistic and manipulative strategies in pursuit of their personal and selfish interests. The stupendous wealth resulting from perquisites of office and exploitation of political office for self-enrichment obviously often far outweighs concern for ethnic identity and interest in the quest for new political positions to further grow the Nigerian political elite. This exemplifies the relevance of the age-long epistemological perspective provided by Harold Laswell that perceived politics as activities relating to the shaping and sharing of power to determine "who gets what, when and how."[17] It also provides a practical illustration that politics extends beyond the realm of state affairs when interrogating the question of whether power, which is the main object of politics, is sought and obtained as an end in itself or as a means to an end.

The persistent reference to structural imbalance and perceived ethno-sectional domination and marginalization as an unresolved national question in Nigeria remains one of the dysfunctional effects of the opportunistic use of ethnic diversities by the Nigerian political elite for their selfish political interests in the competitive quest for access to national power and resources. Creation of more states has thus created more problems than it has solved. For example, no sooner is a new state created than other groups emerge as new minorities who are marginalized. Nigeria's geopolitical structure is made up of four regions as at the country's First Republic in 1963.[18] The map in Figure 3.1 clearly shows that the northern region alone was bigger than the other three regions put together. The problem of federal imbalance inherent in this geopolitical structure is at the root of identity crisis that has characterized politics in Nigeria.

This has also been the basis for unending agitations for more states as well as recent demands for restructuring of the Nigerian federation. As a result, through states creation exercises at various times, several states have been created out of these four regions. Creation of 12 states under the Yakubu Gowon military regime in May 1967 was aimed at reconciling North and South parity by having six states in the North and six states in the South. However, it does not appear if till this date, this parity has been achieved as demands for the creation of more states have continued unabated.

Table 3.1 shows the evolution of Nigeria from its political structure of four regions in 1963 to its present 36 states. The table shows that western region as it was in 1963, had by 1996 evolved into eight different states as a result of various states creation exercises. Table 3.1 also shows a replication of this trend in the parts of Nigeria that were northern and eastern regions up to

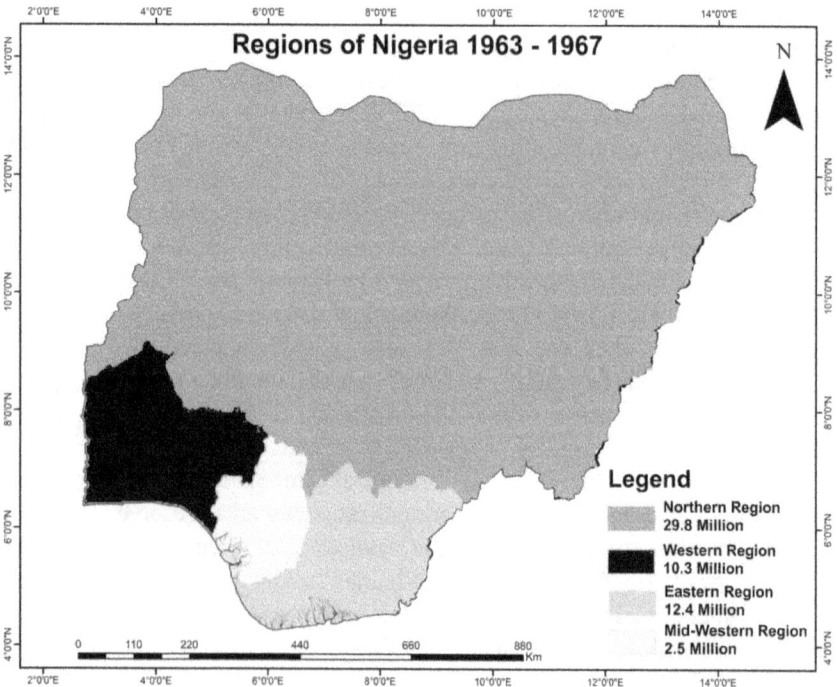

Figure 3.1

Table 3.1 States Created from the Nigerian Geo-Political Structure from 1960 to 1996

Source: This table was created by the author using various sources.[20]

1960	1963	1967	1976	1987	1991	1996
Eastern Region From 1960 to 1963		South-Eastern State (Carved out of Eastern Region in 1967)	Cross-River State (Carved out of South-East in 1967)	Akwa-Ibom (Carved out of Cross River in 1987)	Akwa-Ibom	Akwa-Ibom
			Rivers State (Carved out of Eastern Region in 1967)	Cross-River / Rivers	Cross-River / Rivers	Cross-River / Rivers / Balyesa (Carved out of Rivers State in 1996)
		East-Central	Imo State (Carved out of East-Central State in 1976)	Imo	Imo / Abia (Carved out of Imo State in 1991)	Imo / Abia / Ebonyi (Carved out of Enugu and Abia State)
		Rivers	Anambra State (Carved out of East-Central State)	Anambra	Anambra / Enugu State (Carved out of Anambra State)	Enugu / Anambra
Western Region from 1960 to 1963	Western	Lagos State (Carved out of Western Region in 1967)	Bendel (Mid-West Renamed Bendel State)	Bendel	Delta State (Carved out of Bendel State in 1991)	Delta
					Edo State (Carved out of Bendel State in 1991)	Edo

1960	1963	1967	1976	1987	1991	1996
		Western	**Ogun State** (Carved out of Western State in 1976)	Ogun	Ogun	**Osun State** (Carved out of Ogun State)
	Mid-West Region (Carved out of Western Region in 1963)		Lagos	Lagos	Lagos	Lagos
					Osun (Carved out Oyo State in 1991)	Ogun
		Mid-Western	**Ondo State** (Carved out of Western State in 1976)	Ondo	Ondo	Ondo
						Ekiti (Carved out of Ondo State in 1996)
			Oyo (Carved out of Western State in 1976)	Oyo	Oyo	Oyo
Northern Region		Benue Plateau (Carved out of Northern Region in 1967)	**Plateau State** (Carved out from Benue-Plateau in 1976)	Benue	Benue	Benue
			Bauchi (Carved out of North-East in 1976)	Bauchi	Bauchi	Bauchi
				Borno	Borno	Borno
		North Central State (Carved out of Northern Region in 1967)	**Borno State** (Carved out of North-East in 1976)	**Kebbi State** (Carved out of Sokoto State in 1991)	Kebbi	Kebbi

1960	1963	1967	1976	1987	1991	1996
			Kaduna	Kaduna	Kaduna	Kaduna
		Kadun (Carved out of Northern Region in 1967)			Jigawa (Carved out of Kano State in 1991)	Jigawa
					Adamawa (Carved out of Gongola State in 1991)	Adamawa
		North Western	Kano (Carved out of Northern Region in 1967)	Kano	Kano	Kano
			Niger (Carved out of Northwest in 1996)	Kwara (Carved out of Northern Region in 1967)	Kwara	Kwara
		North Eastern	Kwara	Katsina (Carved out of Kaduna State in 1987)	Katsina	Gombe (Carved out of Bauchi in 1996)
						Katsina
					Yobe (Carved out of Borno State in 1991)	Nasarawa (Carved out of Plateau State in 1996)
			Gongola (Carved out of Northeast)			Yobe
				Niger	Niger	Kogi
						Niger
			Sokoto (Carved out of North-Western in 1976)	Sokoto	Sokoto	Sokoto
					Kogi (Carved out of Kwara and Benue States in 1991)	Plateau

1960	1963	1967	1976	1987	1991	1996
		Kano	Plateau (Carved out of Benue-Plateau in 1976)	Plateau	Plateau	Taraba
					Taraba (Carved out of Gongola State in 1991)	Zamfara (Carved out of Sokoto State in 1996)

1963, which by 1996 had evolved into 19 and nine states respectively through various states creation exercises.[19]

These have combined to give Nigeria its present 36 states geopolitical structure. The immediate consequence of the creation of new states and local government areas as earlier noted is that they become new centers of power, politics, and governance that offer members of the political elite opportunities for political positions. This is so because every state in Nigeria is represented in both chambers of the National Assembly as provided by the constitution. The new states also provide platforms for political recruitment to key political positions such as state governors, state legislators, and important positions in the executive arm of government that members of the political elite usually occupy. This is clearly reflected in Table 3.2 that shows the distribution of members of the National Assembly by states. While it could be said that creation of states allows for more inclusive political participation, this is precisely what the political elite opportunistically exploit in furtherance of their personal and selfish interest. This explains why they are often in the forefront of agitations for creation of new states. Members of the political elite who feel their interests were not met under previous engagements often initiate a new platform to demand a new state of their own in pursuit of their personal agenda and interests. A new circle of agitation therefore begins, based on perceived marginalization, which sets in motion demand for the creation of yet another new state. A case in point was the political elite of Igbo extraction that championed the agitation of the Igbo "ethnic nationality" group for more states. They argued that it was unjust and unacceptable for the Yoruba and Hausa/Fulani ethnic groups to have had five states each from the 1976 state creation exercise while they got only two (Anambra and Imo states).

One consequence of this for Nigeria as a country is its deconstructive effect for national citizenship. This is discernible in the impression it creates of an evolving form of new nationalism based on ethno-sectional identity. This view has also been alluded to with sufficiently elaborate insight provided by Eghosa Osaghae and perspectives provided by Kymlicka and Norman.[22] A further interrogation of this dimension of identity politics in Nigeria reveals that the country is inevitably contending with the problem of the clash between

Table 3.2 Distribution of members of the Nigerian National Assembly per States, Local Government Areas and Abuja Federal Capital Territory (FCT)

Source: This table was created by the author using various sources.[21]

S/N	States	Number of Local Govt Areas	Senate Members per State	House of Representatives Members per State	Total National Assembly Members per State
1.	Akwa-Ibom	31	3	10	13
2.	Cross-River	18	3	8	11
3.	Rivers	23	3	13	16
4.	Balyesa	8	3	5	8
5.	Imo	27	3	10	13
6.	Abia	17	3	8	11
7.	Ebonyi	13	3	6	9
8.	Enugu	17	3	8	11
9.	Anambra	21	3	11	14
10.	Delta	25	3	10	13
11.	Edo	18	3	9	12
12.	Osun	30	3	9	12
13.	Lagos	20	3	24	27
14.	Ogun	20	3	9	12
15.	Ondo	18	3	9	12
16.	Ekiti	16	3	6	9
17.	Oyo	33	3	14	17
18.	Benue	23	3	11	14
19.	Bauchi	20	3	12	15
20.	Borno	27	3	10	13
21.	Kebbi	23	3	8	11
22.	Kaduna	23	3	16	19
23.	Jigawa	27	3	11	14
24.	Adamawa	21	3	8	11
25.	Kano	44	3	24	27
26.	Kwara	16	3	6	9
27.	Gombe	11	3	6	9
28.	Katsina	34	3	15	18
29.	Nasarawa	16	3	5	8
30.	Yobe	17	3	6	9
31.	Kogi	21	3	9	12
32.	Niger	25	3	10	13
33.	Sokoto	23	3	11	14
34.	Plateau	17	3	8	11
35.	Taraba	16	3	6	9
36	Zamfara	23	3	7	10
Abuja FCT	Abuja FCT	6	1	2	3
FCT	**TOTAL**	**774**	**109**	**360**	**469**

ethnic identity and citizenship. Nigeria's nation building efforts have thus been plagued by the debilitating effects of denationalization of politics and deconstruction of citizenship in the same sense as reflected in Sassen Saskia and Oommen T. K.[23] As at the end of the Nigerian First Republic, Lagos state had four local government council areas while old Kano state had two. Lagos today has 20 local government areas as enshrined in the 1999 constitution of Nigeria (as amended). The present Jigawa state was created out of the old Kano state. The present Kano state now has 44 local government areas while Jigawa has 27. In the First Republic, Lagos doubled that of old kano, which now has 71 while Lagos has 20. Also, the former Bendel state had 19 local government council areas in the Second Republic. In 1991, Bendel state was split into Edo and Delta states. Upon the creation of these two states, the then military regime created 25 local government areas in Delta state and 19 in Edo state. This pattern was also replicated in several other states across the country. Ever since, there has been no end to the demand for creation of more states to redress perceived or alleged ethnic imbalance, domination, and marginalization. The same can also be said for the progressive alteration of the geopolitical landscape of Nigeria from a federation of four regions in 1963 to its present 36 states structure and a Federal Capital Territory as well as the division of the country into six geopolitical zones in 1993. The military regime under Sani Abacha introduced the system of geopolitical zones in 1993 with designated states under each of the six geopolitical zones. The geopolitical zones have now evolved as a prominent factor in Nigeria for the purpose of allocation of public goods, be they political, economic, or social across the zones. Made up of three in the north and three in the south, the six geopolitical zones are North-West, North-Central, North-East, South-West, South-East, and South-South. Invariably, creation of these new centers of power has come with the concomitant result of increased elite opportunism in their quest for positions of power. It is a central argument of this chapter that the Nigerian political elite has always capitalized on creation of states and local governments as opportunity to pursue their personal political interest.

It also raises issues that have been a substantive part of the lingering challenges of politics and governance in Nigeria, relating to problems of inclusion, distribution, and participation crises, often metaphorically referred to as the national question. As alluded to by Adeyemi, how to determine the number of desirable states that will satisfy all shades of interest in the country has remained problematic.[24] Also, it is unlikely if it will ever be possible to find an appropriate threshold to determine the minimum and maximum number of constituent units for an acceptable and workable federalism in Nigeria. The situation is not helped by the fact that there is continuing clamor and agitation for the creation of more states coming from different parts of the country. When the National Assembly called for memoranda for state creation from interested nationality groups and people, the House of Representatives committee received more than 35 requests for creation of states. Different groups from different states across the country besieged the National Assembly with records, facts, and figures to show how and why they deserve to benefit from creation of new states. At the end, the committee rejected all the proposals and demand for the creation of new states because the committee found that most of the states being agitated for reflected lack of financial and economic viability. This is an inherent defect that has hitherto plagued more than 85 percent of the states in Nigeria, where governments are unable to provide basic social services and infrastructure, as well as socioeconomic needs for the people such as employment, education, and health care. In most states of the federation, several months' arrears of unpaid salaries and other entitlements are being owed by government to workers and retirees, with the adverse consequences of rendering state governments increasingly dependent on the central government within an otherwise federal polity. Though outside the immediate concern of this chapter, the issue of state creation and especially how it has continued to impact adversely on the country's national polity, democratic process, and electoral system are all important enough to be mentioned and noted.

In the light of the foregoing, it is apparent that we can learn so much about the nature of identity politics in Nigeria by moving away from narratives woven around ideological myths of primordial theorizing to adopt a framework that critically interrogates the role of the political elites in manipulating sociocultural diversity and ethno-sectional heterogeneity issues for the sole purpose of personal political gains. The quest for new insight and alternative approach to the analysis of the substantive issues involved in ethnic identity discourse has inevitably entailed some critical interrogation of the primordial theoretical perspective of ethnic identity problems in plural societies. There is a growing inclination towards an alternative perspective, which represents a deconstruction of mainstream ideas and assumptions of orthodox theoretical perspectives on ethnic identity discourse. The views canvassed in this chapter subscribe to this emerging perspective. In so doing, it represents an alternative framework that looks beyond the confines of ethnic identity and primordial ideological persuasion as the most plausible and relevant focus in the quest for insights and explanations for problems of identity politics in plural societies as exemplified by Nigeria.

NON-ETHNIC ELEMENTS OF COLLECTIVE IDENTITY

An important point to note is that apart from ethnicity, other variables relating to identity also come into relevance in politics. Thus, assuming or suggesting that identity politics is limited to ethnicity or sociocultural diversity leaves many other factors of identity and political interest out of consideration. For example, although competition and conflict are germane to politics, ethnicity is not necessarily at the root of all competition or conflict in politics. Competitions often center on issues of power, resources, representation, and access to public goods (often perceived as scarce). Winning these competitions necessitates appealing to other elements of collective identity. This explains why identity politics is increasingly becoming a preferable term to ethnic politics in referring to the wide range of variables that define the complexity of contemporary Nigerian society. This brings into relevance elements of identity such as socioeconomic background, class, gender, age, and varied physical inability when examining various issues relating to political inclusiveness. Not only does this require a reconceptualization of the ethnic identity problematic, it signals a timely need to discard old tendencies of explaining problems of political identity, competition, and conflict based entirely on sociocultural diversity and perceived deep moral commitment engendered by notions of cultural affinity and ethnic loyalty. There may be more that people have in common that will elicit a sense of collective identity and action than ethno-cultural affinity and loyalty ever could. This line of thought is generally endorsed by scholars committed to models of society and politics based on democratic values. Prominent scholarly endorsements of this emerging subfield are well reflected in the contributions of Apter and Rosberg, Atkinson, and Young among others.[25] When situated in a context such as this, identity politics takes on a meaning that holds some ideological connotation relating to activities and organizational engagements of designated groups who have certain characteristics in common. Such shared experience or interests quite often cut across ethnic boundaries. Examples include persons who belong to groups easily designated by their occupation, socioeconomic status, age, education levels, income, unemployment, gender, physical disability, or property ownership. Other relevant elements are family roles such as father, mother, son, and daughter. Based on such characteristics, members identify themselves as distinct from others and participate openly in organizational activities in support or representation of their common interest. Members of such groups appeal to the characteristics and interest, which they have in common to inspire collective loyalty and a sense of oneness among them. Also, no ideological myths are constructed by any dominant or privileged members of such groups to obtain the moral commitment of other members to mobilize them for collective action against any perceived threat or deprivation in order to elicit support for their common interest. In a sense, mobilizing under a seemingly more inclusive platform could be of potential benefit to the entire community and thereby no less reflective of self-interest for some than of personal gain. However, the main concern here is the underlying personal interest and political ambition served for the leader who mobilizes the more inclusive group. Good examples are political activists and youths that exist in virtually all parts of Nigeria, with membership that cut across ethnic boundaries. They are found mainly within those already of voting age or even younger, but who perceive themselves as politically excluded. Also, members have certain shared experiences or characteristics that give them a sense of collective identity and commitment to collective action. A typical example is the youth organization that emerged under the name *"Not too young to run,"* in the buildup towards the 2019 Nigerian general elections. The *Not Too Young to Run* movement emerged as a platform for youths, who perceived themselves as excluded from meaningful participation in the country's political recruitment process and therefore took to vigorous campaign for expansion of the political space. The movement got the massive support of youth across ethno-sectional boundaries within the country in pressing for constitutional amendment to remedy the situation. The agitation of this group culminated in the presentation of a bill to the National Assembly. The bill sought amendment to certain sections of the constitution of the Federal Republic of Nigeria with a view to reducing the age qualification for election to key political positions. The positions are those of President of Nigeria, state governors, Senate, House of Representatives, and state Houses of Assembly. The specific sections for which they sought amendments were 65, 106, 131, and 177 of the 1999 Constitution of the Federal Republic of Nigeria (as amended).[26] The bill was passed by the National Assembly, and it subsequently assented to by the President. As part of the campaign, the movement hosted a town hall meeting in December 2018 with speakers and members of the state Houses of Assembly. This extracted further commitments from the states and as a result, the bill was subsequently passed in 33 of the 36 states of the federation. This attested to the strength of support the Nigerian youths mobilized for the *Not Too Young to Run* political project that cut across ethnic boundaries. It also bears an eloquent testimony to the fact that the reality of competition, conflict, and the imperative of collective interest, group affinity, and identity politics are not limited to issues of ethnicity and sociocultural diversity in society. Also, the ideological undertone in the objective provided the main drive for the *Not Too Young to Run* movement. It had nothing to do with the personal or selfish interest or political ambition of any particular individual. This made it different from ethnic political groups rooted in primordial cultural narratives and ethnic elite opportunism. Surajujul Olanrewaju explained that the protagonists of the *Not Too Young to Run* movement, like young people all over the world, are not propelled by the mere desire for opportunity to occupy leadership positions and impact the lives of fellow young people.[27] Their commitment is borne out of their tiredness with promises of a better tomorrow that never comes. Thus, youths gave membership and strength to the *Not Too Young to Run* group and could rightly be identified as a movement ideologically significant as an advocacy platform for advancing the course of a more inclusive political recruitment process in Nigeria. A key moment for the *Not Too Young to Run* movement for its campaign for a more inclusive political recruitment process to allow for increased participation of young people in politics and government was its July 2018 National Day of Action. On that day young Nigerians marched on the National Assembly at Abuja to demand that their elected representatives pass the *Not Too Young to Run* bill. Placards displayed by young Nigerians to express the motives behind their campaign contained such slogans as: "Champions and Change-Makers," "Not Too Young to Run Promotes Intergenerational Dialogue," "Invest In Youth," "If Young People Can Vote Why Can't They Be Voted For," "Remove Age Limit For Running For Offices," "We Are Capable To Lead," "Inclusion For All," among others. The movement demonstrated great promise and potential to crystallise into a new political paradigm and to end a trajectory of noninclusive leadership. The *Not Too Young to Run* movement has gone on to inspire similar actions in other African countries, and a global *Not Too Young to Run* campaign sponsored by the Office of the UN Secretary-General's Envoy on Youth. This is evident in reports contained in Champions and Change-Makers Representative Democracies.[28]

GENDER AND IDENTITY POLITICS

Orthodox theoretical perspectives on identity politics fail to consider gender, more particularly in reference to women and the problem of noninclusive political participation. The perspective of women exclusion from mainstream political leadership recruitment processes requires interrogation to critically expose issues of identity politics in Nigeria. Since politics posits game of numbers, and women constitute more than half of Nigeria's population; women express outrage that in spite of their numeric dominance, they have perpetually been the worst victim of noninclusive political leadership recruitment processes in Nigeria. As shown in the report of the National Bureau of Statistics, the population of Nigeria in 2017 was estimated at 199 million people compared to about 193 million in 2016.[29] Of this population, women and men constituted 97,908,000 and 101,092,000 respectively. In effect, men and women constituted approximately 49.2 and 50.8 percent of the country's population. The report also showed that the proportion of men in the national labor force participation rate was 82.6 percent, while women accounted for 17.4 percent. Thus, men constituted the bulk of employment in the federal and state Ministries, Departments, and Agencies. As reflected in the report, on the average, 72.3 percent of senior positions in State Civil Service were occupied by men compared to 27.7 percent occupied by women.[30] As a result of their shared experience of alienation from political leadership roles in Nigeria, women have in recent times been vigorously engaged in building platforms and alliances in pursuit of agenda of equality and affirmative action to remedy discrimination against women and historical exclusion from political leadership positions. Scholars in more recent times have examined the relevance of gender to issues of identity politics in Nigeria. Dickson, Enim, and Egbe Inyang acknowledged that constraining and discriminating factors continue to perpetuate gender inequalities in Nigeria, resulting in continued exclusion of women from recruitment into positions of power.[31] Also lending credence to the issue of women exclusion from political leadership as a lingering problem germane to the analysis of identity politics in Nigeria, Omonubi-McDonnel noted that politically, Nigerian women exist as a 'negligible and undermined force, with little political involvement.'[32] Thus, political engagements and alliance formation that have historically drawn women to support and participate in collective activities to demand more open political space and more inclusive processes of political leadership recruitment are not driven by forces of ethnic identity. Rather, mass involvement of women in such activities has been propelled by a common desire to ensure mitigation of their shared experience of political marginalization. The widespread culture of patriarchy and male chauvinism in Nigeria has for a very long time undermined the rights of women and exposed them to exploitation and marginalization on issues relating to leadership and development. The existence of unequal power relation resulting in disproportionate distribution of rights and privileges, which disadvantage women repeatedly, remains a great concern. Women formed diverse advocacy groups in the quest to enhance their status and to increase access for women. Dating back to the pre-independence era of Nigeria, as evidenced in a report published by *Nawey*, there emerged a couple of women who were in the forefront of the activities and fierce struggle of women for their social, economic and political emancipation.[33] They include Mrs. Margaret Ekpo, Mrs. Janet Mokelu, Ms. Young, and the late Mrs. Funmilayo Ransome-Kuti and Hajia Gambo Sawaba.[34] Adamu also provided useful insight into the historical trajectory of women struggle for political emancipation in Nigeria.[35] The Aba Women's Riots of 1929, when market women of Igbo extraction protested British exploitation through taxation policy, highlights how women capitalized on their traditional power to fight against oppressive policies of the colonial rulers. Women have their very effective traditional power they exercise when expressing anger through protest. This could degenerate into more serious mass action such as women going around nude. To avert the consequences such action could result in, immediate steps are often taken to resolve the issue at stake. A good example was the Aba women riot of 1929 that lasted two months, during which the rebellion waged by local market women was triggered by the imposition of what was perceived as exploitative taxes, targeting women, who in Igbo tradition, had always been tax-exempt.[36] Another example was the protest of Abeokuta market women and some educated women in 1948 to denounce colonial taxes and failure of the traditional rulers to object to the colonial taxation policies. They openly criticized the *"Alake"* of Abeokuta (the traditional ruler) for not protecting his subjects from what they perceived as an unnecessary burden of colonial tax but accepted to be used for tax collection by the colonialists. Also worthy of note was the role of Mrs. Funmilayo Ransome-Kuti, who upon learning of the struggle of the market women, formed a new body by name Abeokuta Women's Union (AWU), a body made up of educated Abeokuta ladies who joined in solidarity with the Egba market women in their struggle to end the colonial policy of arbitrary and excessive taxation. Mrs. Fumilayo Ransome-Kuti led this group that grew and later became a platform that brought the character of colonial governance and policies, the status of women, and their absence from public affairs under interrogation, creating pressure for reform. Women activism became a powerful component of the independence movement. Other women's organizations that emerged on the Nigeria political landscape in the quest for women's emancipation, equality, and empowerment were built on the foundation laid by these earlier anticolonial resistance struggles. They include the National Women's Union (NWU) founded in 1947. Others are Women in Nigeria (WIN), Federation of Nigerian Women's Societies (FNWS), Kudirat Initiative for Democracy (KIND), and National Council of Women Societies (NCWS). It is neither forces of ethnic affinity, sectional interest, nor primordial loyalties that drove these women's movements. Okeke and Franschet explain that the National Women's Union (NWU) was the first women organization in Nigeria with a national outlook, based on nationwide representation that cut across ethnic, religious, and socioeconomic class boundaries.[37] The National Council of Women's Societies (NCWS) formed in 1959 as an umbrella for women's organizations across Nigeria emerged later and provided a platform for identity, engagement, and struggle for socioeconomic and political emancipation of women. The activities of these women organizations have assisted greatly in inspiring women to develop more self-confidence, assert their rights, and to fully embrace activities in support of total sociopolitical and economic emancipation of women.

The exclusion of women from political roles presents obvious hurdles to the representations of women's interests that so easily can cut across ethnic identity. For example, equal participation in politics for women in terms of percentage has still not been realized in Nigeria. Also, despite Nigeria being a signatory to a number of international instruments that permit and require women's access to political and economic leadership, these have not been fully implemented, and existing laws made to protect and promote women's rights or prevent injustices against women are flagrantly flouted. Although a number of other prodemocracy and civil society groups are also involved in pushing for these inclusive roles, nevertheless women's efforts ensured more inclusive roles for women and their socio-political and economic emancipation have yielded tangible results. For example, within Nigeria's recent political history, especially since the 1999 democratic dispensation, issues of women representation in top political offices are now accorded prominent consideration in policy formulation and campaigns of political parties. The result is that women now occupy important positions in politics and government more than ever before. At least six women, among several others, could be named who have held high-ranking political positions. Ipalibo Banigo, the first female Deputy Governor of Rivers State, Kofoworola Bucknor served as Lagos State Deputy Governor from 1999–2003, Pauline Tallen, the current Women Affairs Minister, and Valerie Ebe, the first female Deputy Governor of Akwa Ibom State and served from 2012–2015. Cecilia Ezeilo and Yetunde Onanuga work as the current deputy governors of Enugu state and Ogun state respectively. For a very long time, a key issue at stake was the highly visible inequity between men and women in public governance positions. A limited number of females participated in structures of governance where key policy decisions and resource allocation were decided. The political space for more women aspirants and political actors to assume key political positions in government has thus been opened through increased advocacy and engagements for more inclusive roles for women in governance and politics. As an expression of increasing prominence being accorded the role of women in politics and governance, a Federal Ministry of Women Affairs and Social Development was established in 1999, with the mandate to periodically review substantive and procedural laws that affect women. As Table 3.3 shows, women have served as minister of this ministry since its inception.

CONCLUSION AND RECOMMENDATION

One obvious result of the long reliance on the myths of ethno-cultural diversity and primordial theoretical persuasions for explanation and analysis of identity politics problems in Nigeria is that it blurs the true nature of the problem and consequences of identity politics in Nigeria and thus limits the scope of possible solutions open for consideration. It also diverts attention from the interrogation of critical factors in the quest for solutions to the lingering problems associated with politics and development in Nigeria.

Table 3.3 List of Ministers of the Ministry of Women Affairs and Social Development since 2007

Source: This table was created by the author using various sources.[38]

S/No	Name	Term
1	Saudatu Bungudu	2007–2008
2	Salamatu Hussain Suleiman	2008–2010
3	Salamatu Hussain Suleiman	2008–2010
4	Zainab Maina	2011–2015
5	Aisha Jummai Alhassan	2015–2018
6	Aisha Abubakar	2018–2019
7	Paulen Tallen	2019–present

This chapter examines perspectives from dominant ideas and mainstream contributions to the vast literature on issues of ethnicity and identity politics. The exposition in this chapter supports recent growing inclination towards an alternative perspective on identity politics discourse that moves beyond ethnicity and integrates other elements. In the quest for new insight, the chapter identifies and interrogates substantive issues that have for so long blurred proper understanding of the nature, purpose, and consequences of ethnic politics in Nigeria. The deconstruction of mainstream ideas and assumptions of orthodox scholarly perspectives on identity and ethnic politics discourse inevitably suggests a redirection of focus to other critical variables. Prominent among such variables are non-ethnic elements and characteristics central to an individual's identity that could as well be mobilized in further-ance of purposes that go beyond parochially, geographically, and ethnically confined interests. In effect, besides ethnicity, other elements of identity sometimes become of equal relevance in the pursuit of common interests and contestation for political power and access to national resources. This chapter identifies opportunism and manipulation of Nigeria's ethno-cultural diversity by members of the political elite in pursuit of their selfish interests and personal political ambition as problems at the root of identity politics in Nigeria. Members of the Nigerian political elite share a common tendency to capitalize on primordial ethnic identity as essential strategy to obfuscate any other option for mobilization and power. This frantic quest for politi-cal power employs the same opportunistic and manipulative strategies in pursuit of interests and ambition that are personal at the expense of the Common Good. These ethnically based strategies often appeal to principles of self-determination, justice, equity, and political equality in the bid to justify the need for collective action in response to perceived threat to the common interest of their sole ethnic group. Political agitations for the continued cre-ation of more states and local government Areas have thus been mostly initi-ated and spearheaded by members of athe political elite. A central argument of this chapter examines how elite opportunism and manipulation of Nigeria's ethnic diversity reproduces cultural hostilities and ethnic conflicts resulting from contestation for political power within and between various ethnic groups in Nigeria. In the process, the collective interest of various ethnic groups and the overall interest of national development remain both compromised and hindered. Members of the political class who use ethnic identity issues to attain positions of power hardly make the interest of such ethnic groups their priority. The stupendous wealth they acquire while in office, and their vast material possessions are not held on behalf of their constituents, whose interest they claim to represent. The main interest they serve in office is their personal interest. This explains why they rely more on desperate and irregular methods that subvert the prescribed rules and procedures rather than promote goodwill and freely expressed mandate of the people when seeking election or re-election into positions of power. When they resort to such desperate methods to mobilize votes, they care neither for their ethnic groups nor for the collective interest but rather only intend to consolidate their position. The enormous resources they deploy towards their re-election bid come from their personal fortunes derived from previous opportunities of political offices held. In effect, they represent themselves while in office to serve their personal interests and do not see themselves under any obligation to make any other interest their priority. The result is that ordinary citizens, who constitute the various ethnic groups manipulated and mobilized by the political elites, have not witnessed any widespread improvements under various political dispensations since independence. Yet, members of the political class have continued to intensify their grip on national power and resources. Ending or curbing self-serving elite opportunism and manipulation of ethnic identity represents a positive step towards more inclusive political leadership and new possibilities for development in service of the Common Good. To end the country's problem of self-serving elite and manipulation of ethnic identity issues, which have for so long thwarted political accountability, good governance, and development in Nigeria, requires a genuine commitment to democratic practice that is grounded in more inclusive identity traits than exclusionary ethnic boundaries allow. In this regard, the enthronement and practice of true democracy is imperative as a matter of utmost national priority. Towards this end, strengthening democratic institutions and processes, and allowing them to function and flourish unhampered requires a national commitment grounded in more encompassing democratic ideals. Meeting this irreducible condition can guarantee inclusive power relations, increased development, and more equally shared prosperity. This is the way to go in a country where ethnic challenges have persisted with no mechanism to ensure viable platforms for ensuring political inclusiveness, accountability, responsiveness, and good governance. The argument in support of prescribing the democratic alternative is that identity politics is not necessarily limited to ethnicity and sociocultural diversity. Youth and women's exclusion, germane to competition and conflicts in politics, signpost other interests outside ethnicity often used to win competition over power, resources, or public goods, and necessitate, instead, appeals to other elements of collective identity, some of which have been identified in this chapter.

NOTES

1. Wsevolod W Isajiw, "Definition and Dimensions of Ethnicity: A Theoretical Framework," in *Joint Canada–United States Conference on the Measurement of Ethnicity* (Ontario, April 2, 1992).

2. Clifford Geertz, *Old Societies and New States* (New York: Free Press, 1963); Harold Isaacs, "Basic Group Identity: The Idols of the Tribe," in *Ethnicity: Theory and Experience*, eds. Nathan Glazer, Daniel Patrick Moynihan, and Corinne Saposs Schelling (Cambridge: Harvard University Press, 1975), 29–52; John F. Stack, *Ethnic Mobilization in World Politics: The Primordial Perspective* (Greenwood Press, 1986).

3. Okwudiba Nnoli, *Ethnic Politics in Nigeria* (Enugu: Fourth Dimension Publishers, 1978); Onigu Otite, *Ethnic Pluralism and Ethnicity in Nigeria* (Ibadan: Shaneson, 2000).

4. Isajiw, "Definition and Dimensions."

5. John F. Stack and Christopher L. Warren, "Ethnicity and the Politics of Symbolism in Miami's Cuban Community," *Cuban Studies* 20 (1990): 11–28.

6. Enoch Wan and Mark Vanderwerf, "A Review of the Literature on Ethnicity, National Identity and Related Missiological Studies," *Global Missiology* (2009).

7.Ugbana Okpu, *Ethnic Minority Problems in Nigerian Politics, 1960–1965* (Stockholm: Libertrck, 1977), 1.

8. Ken Post and Michael Vickers, *Structure and Conflict in Nigeria, 1960–1965* (London: Heinemann, 1973), 11–17.

9. Ibid.

10. Leo Kuper and Michael G. Smith, *Pluralism in Africa* (Berkeley: University of California Press, 1969).

11. Peter P. Ekeh, "Colonialism and the Two Publics in Africa: A Theoretical Statement," *Comparative Studies in Society and History* 17, no 1 (1975): 91–112.

12. Ken Post and Michael Vickers, *Structure and Conflict in Nigeria: 1960–1965.* (London: Heinemann, 1973), 1–2.

13.Okpu, *Ethnic Minority.*

14. "Ex-Commissioner, Don Kick against Pay Rise for Political Office Holders," *The Sun Nigeria*, February 7, 2020, https://www.sunnewsonline.com/ex -commissioner-don-kick-against-pay-rise-for-political-office-holders/.

15. "Nigerian Senator 'Busts Open' $37,500 Expenses Payments," *BBC News*, March 12, 2018, https://www.bbc.com/news/world-africa-43377690.

16. Richard Amaechi Onuigbo and Eme Okechukwu, "State Governors and Revenue Allocation Formula in Nigeria: A Case of the Fourth Republic," *International Journal of Accounting Research* 2, no. 7 (2015): 14–36.

17. Harold Laswell, *Politics: Who Gets What, When, and How* (New York: World Publishing Company, 1930).

18. Office of the Surveyor General of the Federation, *Map of Nigeria*, Abuja, Nigeria.

19. The author created this table using information obtained from Ejitu N. Ota, Chinyere Ecoma, and Chiemela Godwin Wambu, "Creation of States in Nigeria, 1967–1996: Deconstructing the History and Politics," *American Research Journal of Humanities and Social Sciences* Volume 6, Issue 1, 1–8; from "List of Nigeria States by Date of Statehood" accessed on 11 February 2022 https://en.wikipedia.org /wiki/List_of_Nigerian_states_by_date_of_statehood as well as "States of Nigeria" accessed 11 February 2022 from https://en.wikipedia.org/wiki/States_of_Nigeria.

20. Ejitu N. Ota, Chinyere Ecoma, and Chiemela Godwin Wambu, "Creation of States in Nigeria, 1967–1996: Deconstructing the history and Politics," *American Research Journal of Humanities and Social Sciences* Volume 6, Issue 1, 1–8; from "List of Nigeria States by date of statehood" accessed on 11February 2022 https://en .wikipedia.org/wiki/List_of_Nigerian_states_by_date_of_statehood as well as "States of Nigeria" accessed 11 February 2022 from https://en.wikipedia.org/wiki/States_of _Nigeria

21. National Assembly, Federal Republic of Nigeria, Members of the House of Representatives and list of Senators from https://nass.gov.ng/mps/members accessed on 10/27/2021 and National Assembly, Federal Republic of Nigeria, https: //nass.gov.ng/mps/senators accessed on 10/27/2021 and from the "Nigerian Senators of the 9th National Assembly," Wikipedia, last modified November 18, 2021, https://en.wikipedia.org/w/index.php?title=Nigerian_Senators_of_the_9th_National _Assembly&oldid=1055944035; "House of Representatives (Nigeria)," Wikipedia, last modified November 22, 2021, https://en.wikipedia.org/w/index.php?title=House _of_Representatives_(Nigeria)&oldid=1056495534; "Local government areas of Nigeria," Wikipedia, last modified November 30, 2021, https://en.wikipedia.org/w/ index.php?title=Local_government_areas_of_Nigeria&oldid=1057983074.

22. Eghosa Osaghae, "Ethnicity and Contested Citizenship in Africa" In Emma Hunter (Ed) *Citizenship, Belonging, and Political Community in Africa.* Cambridge centre o f African Studies series 2016 Ohio University Press *(2016)* 256-281SeealsoWill Kymlicka and Wayne Norman, "Return of the Citizen: A Survey of Recent Work on Citizenship Theory," *Ethics* 104, no. 2 (1994) 352–81.

23. Saskia Sassen, "Towards Post-National and Denationalized Citizenship," in *Handbook of Citizenship Studies*, (eds) Engin F. Isin, and Bryan S. Turner (London: SAGE Publications Ltd, 2003), 278. See also Saskia Sassen, "Denationalization" in *The Blackwell Encyclopedia of Sociology* (American Cancer Society, 2007), https: //doi.org/10.1002/9781405165518.wbeosd028 (Accessed on 20 October 2021). Of additional value is the insight provided by T. K. Oommen, *Citizenship, Nationality, and Ethnicity: Reconciling Competing Identities* (Cambridge: Polity Press, 1997).

24.O. Oluwatobi Adeyemi, "The Politics of States and Local Governments Creation in Nigeria: An Appraisal," *European Journal of Sustainable Development* 2, no. 3 (2013): 155–74.

25. David E. Apter and Carl Gustav Rosberg, eds., *Political Development and the New Realism in Sub-Saharan Africa* (Charlottesville: University Press of Virginia, 1994); Ronald R. Atkinson, "The (Re)Construction of Ethnicity in Africa: Extending the Chronology, Conceptualization and Discourse," in *Ethnicity and Nationalism in Africa: Constructivist Reflections and Contemporary Politics*, ed. P. Yeros (London: Palgrave Macmillan UK, 1999), 15–44; Crawford Young, "Evolving Models of Consciousness and Ideology: Nationalism and Ethnicity," in *Political Development and the nNew Realism in Sub-Saharan Africa*, eds. David E. Apter and Carl Gustav Rosberg (Charlottesville: University Press of Virginia, 1994), 61–86.

26. Constitution of the Federal Republic of Nigeria (1999): 32–70, https://wipolex.wipo.int/en/text/179202.

27. Surajujul Olanrewaju, "Pursuing Its Self-Serving Agenda, National Assembly Kills 'Not Too Young to Run' Bill," *Sahara Reporters*, July 16, 2017, http://saharareporters.com/2017/07/16/pursuing-its-self-serving-agenda-national-assembly-kills-not-too-young-run-bill.

28. "Publications," Action Aid International, accessed August 9, 2021, https://actionaid.org/publications.

29. *Statistical Report on Women and Men in Nigeria,* National Bureau of Statistics, accessed August 26, 2021, https://nigerianstat.gov.ng.

30. Ibid.

31. E. Ekpe Dickson, Eja Eni, and John Egbe Inyang, "Women, Gender Equality in Nigeria: A Critical Analysis of Socio-economic and Political (Gender Issues),"*Journal Research in Peace, Gender and Development (JRPGD)* 4, no. 1 (2014): 11–20.

32. Morolake Omonubi-McDonnell, *Gender Inequality in Nigeria* (Ibadan: Spectrum Books, 2003).

33. Olushola Ojikutu, "Yoruba Women in the Pre-Independence Era," 2011, http://234next.com/csp/cms/sites/Next/ArtsandCulture/5594609-147/story.csp, cited in Mariam Marwa Abdul et al., *Analysis of the History, Organisations and Challenges of Feminism in Nigeria* (Nigerian Group, 2011), 8, http://www.nawey.net/wp-.

34. See 1. Funmilayo Ransome-Kuti, https://en.wikipedia.org/wiki/Funmilayo_Ransome-Kuti2. Remembering Funmilayo Ransome-Kuti: Nigeria's 'Lioness of Lisabi' Could be found in https://www.aljazeera.com/features/2020/10/1/ Retrieved 23 October 2021. 3. To this category also belong "Remembering Margaret Ekpo and the Enugu strike massacre" https://www.aljazeera.com/features/2020/12/12/ Retrieved 23 October 2021 and 4. Hajiya Gambo Sawaba: 'The most jailed Nigerian female politician' by Tayo Agunbiade https://www.aljazeera.com/features/2021/2/15/hajiya-gambo-sawaba-the-most-jailed-nigerian-female-politician Retrieved 23 October 2021.

35. Fatima L. Adamu, "Woman's Struggle and the Politics of Difference in Nigeria," gender politik online, Freie Universität Berlin (2006), http://web.fu-berlin.de/gpo/pdf/tagungen/fatima_l_adamu.pdf (accessed October 25, 2021).

36. Mariam Marwa Abdul, et al. *Analysis of the History, Organisations and Challenges of Feminism in Nigeria* (Nigerian Group, October 2011).

37. Philomina E. Okeke–Ihejirik and Susan Franceschet, "Democratization and State Feminism: Gender Politics in Africa and Latin America," *Development and Change* 33, no. 3 (2002): 439–466.

38. Federal Republic of Nigeria, Federal Ministry of Women Affairs, https://nigeria.gov.ng/executive/federal-ministry-of-women-affairs/, accessed on 2–12–2022 and earlier Ministers from "Federal Ministry of Women Affairs and Social Development," Wikipedia, last updated September 17, 2021, https://en.wikipedia.org/w/index.php?title=Federal_Ministry_of_Women_Affairs_and_Social_Development&oldid=1044879918.

4

Monetary Sovereignty, Sovereign Identities, and Monetary Identities in Ghana and Nigeria in the Late 1950s to Early 1960s

Bamidélé Aly

Before accessing their individual independence in 1957 and 1960, respectively, the Gold Coast (now Ghana) and Nigeria were part of the British Empire and as such their legal tender was the West African Sterling, which was pegged to the British Sterling but run by the West African Currency Board, headquartered in London. Ahead of the discussions to their independence, conversations were held to create their own monetary and financial infrastructure to come off the West African Sterling and to run their own affairs and to gain not only their political independence but also their monetary sovereignty. The acquisition of their monetary sovereignty was important to shape not only the monetary identities in the nation-building process postindependence but also their sovereign ethnic identities. It is relevant to compare the Gold Coast/Ghana and Nigeria because they were both operating in the same legal and administrative environments, using the same currency, the same official language, and the same British (Imperial) weights and measures.[1] However, as analyzed by Aluko, Ghana was stronger than Nigeria in terms of economic development: many Nigerians moved to Ghana in search of better wages but Ghanaians did not migrate *en masse* to Nigeria.[2] Hence, comparing these two countries provides compelling cases in terms of state colonial legacy, state formation, postcolonial monetary institutions and infrastructure, sovereign identities, monetary sovereignty, and identities.

According to the Westphalia principles of "One Nation/One Money," the monetary sovereignty is inherent to sovereign identity. Indeed, the Treaty of Westphalia introduced the concept of territorialization and the right of a nation to impose any form of coercion.[3] However, the newly independent nation-states of Ghana and Nigeria were not treated pari passu in the Sterling Area system, were too ethnically diverse to form a "traditional," equal, and sovereign state from a monetary (and political perspective) on the international stage.

This chapter compares Ghana and Nigeria over the years 1955 to 1967 and how their respective paths to political independence and sovereignty were intertwined with their monetary independence and identity. To which extent could the establishment of their own individual central bank along with the demise of the West African Currency Board be perceived as an outward symbol of attaining 'monetary independence' but not real monetary sovereignty and identity?[4]

First, the theoretical framework will outline the implications of monetary sovereignty in monetary creation and the legal tender in the Gold Coast and in Nigeria prior to their independence. Second, we will analyze the situation of Ghana in terms of monetary sovereignty and identity. Third, we will view the case of Nigeria. Finally, this paper aims at identifying if the Westphalian principles worked for both nation-states or were merely a myth and the credibility of their monetary policies.

MONETARY CREATION ON THE EVE
OF THE INDEPENDENCE

In the history of the political units and within their international boundaries of the Gold Coast and Nigeria, monetary creation in these British dominions was centralized by the British government and the Bank of England. This section will cover first monetary sovereignty from a legal perspective. Second, we will explore the framework of monetary creation prior to the political independence of both countries.

DEFINITION OF MONETARY SOVEREIGNTY

To understand the purpose of this chapter it is first important to anchor it in a theoretical framework. The right to coin and mint money has always been the preserve of the Emperor or the King, as we are reminded by Arthur Nussbaum—*jus cudendae monetea*—and belongs to the supreme power in every state.[5] It belongs to the public sphere and is linked to the concept of legal tender, which is a new concept in the history of money.[6] And the citizens use this legal form of money as *bona fide* holders.[7] Legal tender means that a creditor cannot refuse if tendered by a debtor in payment of his debt and thus a legal tender is a lawful medium of payment and implies public receivability.[8] However, the harmonization and the centralization of printing money is a modern concept which dates back to the 19th century at the time of the Industrial Revolution. The Industrial Revolution allowed the standardization of minting and thus the centralization of monetary innovation. Eric Helleiner developed this theory in his book *The Making of National Money Territorial Currencies in Historical Perspective.*[9]

Claus Zimmerman proposed an interesting definition of monetary sovereignty driven by law and economics in that it confers a right to i) create money as a legal tender or *ius cudendae monetae*, ii) conduct a monetary policy and an exchange rate policy, thus iii) control the circulation and use of its legal tender within and outside its borders, and iv) introduce some governance rules to underpin domestic financial integrity and stability.[10]

In that respect, the money creates a social contract between the central government and monetary authorities and the citizens, whereby the citizens entrust the issuance and the preservation of the value of money as unit measure and account within the national boundaries of the country. The public has faith in the national monetary authority when cash is sufficiently available to secure payments nationally and internationally. In other words, the monetary authorities must identify themselves and act as the lender of last resort so that citizens accept the social contract of trust and shape the identification in the national money.

Stephen D. Krasner in *Power, the State and Sovereignty* has a multifaceted approach to sovereignty such as international legal sovereignty, Westphalian sovereignty, domestic sovereignty, and interdependent sovereignty.[11] All these concepts and definitions cover i) the territorial aspect of a legal tender controlled by a political and central authority and infrastructure, and ii) an international recognition.

Andreas Osiander considers that the monetary sovereignty is driven by the premise that the acceptability of money is dependent on social conventions, namely "a claim" agreed by domestic and international stakeholders, and the relationship between the central bank and the Treasury.[12] On the other hand, Tymoigne argues that monetary sovereignty is not reliant on the foreign acceptance of the domestic money.[13]

However, since the creation of the international borders of the Gold Coast and Nigeria, the monetary creation was neither centralized nor monitored nor organized by the West African Currency Board.

West African Currency Board

With the establishment of the West African Currency Board on November 12, 1912, the Gold Coast and Nigeria shared a common currency, the West African Sterling, following the Lord Emmott Committee.[14] Silver coins were introduced in 1912 followed by banknotes in 1916 with the engagement of the Royal Mint.[15]

The West African Currency Board was not operating as a central bank. Interestingly, as demonstrated by Aluko and seen in the colonial sources, although these countries shared a common currency, they were tied to the colonial commercial systems.[16] Intro-colonial commercial exchanges were not particularly encouraged, and their respective main trading partner remained the United Kingdom.

The West African Currency Board guaranteed trade flows and tax collection in a legal tender currency recognized by the British authorities.

The article, "Central Banks for New Dominions," published in *The Economist* in August 1956, discusses the creation of the National Bank of the Gold Coast.[17] However, interestingly, in simple words, it explains the function of the West African Currency Board, whose currency is interchangeable with sterling not only at fixed rate but automatically. The authority has discretion neither to decide the rate of exchange nor to expand or contract the volume of currency. It simply issues coins or notes locally against a deposit of sterling in London. It holds the sterling so received in cash or in gilt-edged investments and this sterling is paid out again on demand whenever local currency is paid in. The system is a faithful reflection of the political dependence that goes with it. In the matter of interest rates and credit control the pace is set in London. The supply of currency in a colonial territory fluctuates almost automatically with the vagaries of the colony's balance of payments and the volume of its London funds. This may be right and acceptable when the territory concerned has little or no indigenous credit system and its economy is dependent on comparatively few exportable primary products. In those circumstances the balance of payments should indeed govern the supply of money. But when a domestic capital market emerges in such an economy and when its output becomes more diversified, the need for an independent mechanism of credit control arises. There should then be a central institution that will help to smooth out fluctuations in the supply of money by absorbing foreign exchange arising from a favorable balance of payments and sterilising the resultant increase in the cash reserve of the commercial banks or reversing the operation in times of depression.

Due to this peg and strong links to the British Sterling, the destinies of the West African Sterling were aligned with those of the British Sterling. Indeed, due to i) gold and silver shortage during the Great War, and ii) the promulgation of the Currency and Bank Notes Act, 1914 led to the introduction of bank notes, first in Nigeria in July 1916 and thereafter in Ghana in September 1916.[18] The convertibility with gold was also stopped as the Gold Standard system was suspended. Nigeria was the largest economy of British West Africa, hence the banknotes were introduced in this colony. The value of the West African Sterling was backed by liquid assets denominated in British Sterling.[19] During the the preparations for the political independence for both countries, discussions took place to create a central bank and a currency. In 1952, the West African Currency Board under Mr. J.L. Fisher organized a Commission to analyze the potentials of creating a Central Bank at the request of the Nigerian government.

An article of *The Economist* dated March 5, 1960 indicates that Ghana and Nigeria stressed the advantages in creating confidence in their new fiat currencies by remaining members of the Sterling Area and are each in favor of remaining members of the Sterling Area.[20]

We thus understand that the monetary sovereignty is intertwined with the state formation and national identity, whereby a free nation, as it was thought in the 1950 and 1960s, should be able to issue and monitor its own fiat currency so that its own citizens can identify themselves and accept the social contract between this authoritative power and its citizens. This social contract implies trust, as it is implicit in the Latin meaning of *fiat*. As we have seen above, the West African Currency Board did not set the former Gold Coast and Nigeria at an economic advantage, as all excess of liquidity was not ploughed back in the local economies but placed in the form of cash or bonds in the UK to support the British economy. Notwithstanding, the West African Currency Board was the precursor for demanding the establishment of central banks in Ghana and subsequently in Nigeria.

THE CASE OF GHANA

Ghana presents a compelling case since it was the first of the British Sub-Saharan territories to access independence. In the process of state-building, Sarah Stockwell analyzes and describes how the British authorities assisted the Gold Coast in building key infrastructures such as financial institutions to support a real economy financing completely independent from the United Kingdom's influence, *prima facie*.[21] Having said that, we learn in an article titled "Banks and Self-Government" published in February 1957 that when the Gold Coast Legislative Assembly was preparing the "Bank of the Gold Coast Ordinance, 1957," it was already decided the Ordinance had a specific provision for the new currency, whereby the parity of the new with the British would be maintained and be backed by specific assets and fully redeemable with the British Sterling. This made the case for a highly desirable tradeable currency for a country whose economic structure was depending on exporting agricultural products such as cocoa and minerals for cash generation. Nevertheless, this new monetary infrastructure was mirroring the status and the structure of the Bank of England.

On another note, Nkrumah had planned to move Ghana out of the colonial economic and political framework to a modern sovereign state.[22]

Political Process to Independence

On August 3, 1956, the Gold Coast Legislative Assembly passed a motion by 72 votes to nil asking for independence from the Commonwealth.[23] Ghana promulgated on February 22, 1957, a constitution for its independence. It provided for a Governor-General representing the Queen, a Cabinet of Ministers collectively responsible to Parliament, a Legislative Assembly of 104 members plus the Speaker, election of all members including the Speaker, election of all members of Parliament by universal adult suffrage and by secret ballot, a public service commission to advise the Governor-General of the Gold Coast, a judicial service commission to advise the Governor-General on judicial appointments, a regional assembly in each of the five regions to which any bill affecting the traditional functions and privileges of a chief must be referred before it is introduced into the National Assembly.[24] On March 6, 1957, Ghana became an independent and sovereign state of Ghana bringing Ghana to full membership of the Commonwealth, in July 1960 a unitary Republic.[25]

Ghana had a strong financial position thanks to i) its world's leading position as a producer and exporter of cocoa, and ii) its gold deposits, and iii) a budget surplus and strong fiscal balances.[26] Kwame Nkrumah planned to move Ghana out of the colonial capitalistic, economic, and political framework to a modern sovereign state.[27]

New Monetary and Financial Infrastructures

In the article "Central Bank for Ghana" published by The Economist in February 1957, we can discover that Mr. J. B. Loynes was involved in the creation of a new financial and monetary infrastructure on par with those existing in the United Kingdom and *in fine* on par with the rest of the developed world.[28] In other words, the new Ghanaian currency was deemed as strong as the British Sterling with the same purchasing power.

Indeed, the new financial and monetary system was to be doted of a central bank, namely the Central Bank of Ghana, with the functions of currency issue, the sole banker of the government to smooth over marked seasonal fluctuations in revenues driven by coca exports and facilitate all commercial banks. This central bank was *designed to form ultimately the focal point for the country's financial machinery* and adopt the prudential rules such as imposing on other banks the maintenance of a minimum holding of liquid assets and their uncommitted capital.[29] Furthermore, the new currency was during a transitional period fully guaranteed by British Pound Sterlings with the aim of maintaining it in the Sterling Area.[30] For the UK, as explained by Catherine Shenck and Sarah Stockwell, the UK was protecting the Sterling Area against non-sterling currencies, given that Ghana and Nigeria were net contributors in the Sterling Area and kept significant sterling-denominated liquid assets placed and managed in the UK financial system, which in turn protected the British balance of payments.[31] Looked at in a different angle, it was a way to maintain the prominence of the sterling vis-à-vis many of the hard and soft commodities denominated in the rise of the American dollar.

The new Ghanaian central bank started its operations on August 1, 1957, and was a split from the Ghana Commercial Bank.[32] The assets were divided between the central bank, named Bank of Ghana, and a commercial concern.[33] The first governor of the Bank of Ghana, Mr. Alfred Eggleston, served a term of five years; his Deputy Governor was D. F. Stone.[34]

The issue of the new Ghanaian currency, named the Ghanaian Pound, was introduced to the general public by the Bank of Ghana on 14 July 1958.[35] The currency replaced the West African Currency Board's notes and coins formerly in circulation. Ghanaian currency was on par with the British Sterling and consisted of the denominations listed in Table 4.1

Mr. K. A. Gbedemah, Gold Coast Minister of Finance, contracted a British company, Thomas De LA Rue and Co. in London, with a total amount £125,000 to print the domestic banknotes.[36]

The Central Bank of Ghana is the Bank of Ghana established by the government by the Bank of Ghana Ordinance in March 1957.[37] It has a Banking Department and an Issue Department. Its headquarter is in Accra while the Ghana Commercial Bank serves as its currency agents in Kumasi and Takoradi. Commercial Banking is done by four banks, two of which have their head offices in London. They are the Bank of West Africa Limited with 40 branches, and the Barclays Bank, D.C.O. with 63 branches. The other

Table 4.1 New Ghanaian Currency

Source: This table was author-created.

Medium	Denominations
Notes	£G5, £G1, 10/-
Cupro-nickel coins	2/-, 1/-, 6d, 3d
Bronze coins	1d, ½d

two are the government-owned Ghana Commercial Bank with a capital of £500,000 and the Ghana Co-operative Bank with concentrates particularly on short-term financing of local and district co-operative societies. There is also a Post Office Savings Bank to encourage retention of local liquidity and the local funding of the real economy by the Ghanaian citizens and taxpayers. In that respect, it is worth noting the adoption of a bill for the establishment of building societies with the aim of working closely with the Government Housing Corporation to build or acquire housing.[38]

Apart from commercial banks, for the development of a local money market and to attract foreign investors to underpin the economic development plans of the country post-independence, the only other financial institution operating in Ghana is the Accra Clearing House, which was established in April 1958.[39] A total of 333,000 cheques at a value of £G130.5m were cleared in 1959. In February, March, and April 1960, £G6m of Treasury bills were issued by the Bank of Ghana. The operation was renewed in May 1961 with the issuance of 4m government debt with 5% maturing in 1965–66.[40] This issuance aided to inject liquidity in the real economy and the coca trade between the producers and the Cocoa Marketing Board.[41]

The government intended to issue them monthly, thus giving a nucleus of short-term chapter suitable for bank portfolios, which may lead to the beginning of money markets.

In 1957, Ghana disposed of sufficient liquid assets to underpin its second five-year development plan (1959–1964) and to invest in its infrastructure thanks to cocoa export. Nevertheless, the seven-year plan (1969–1970) could not meet its ambitions due to i) the sharp drop in cocoa price in the world markets in 1961, ii) the fall in commodities prices reducing revenue streams, and iii) the rise in imported inflation for capital and physical assets. The initial refusal to devalue led to an increase in inflation and a deterioration in trade balances. The cocoa prices collapsed further in 1965 and the government still refused to devalue to improve the economic situation.

In 1966, the one-party state—Convention People's Party, instituted by Nkruma—was deposed by a military coup to be replaced by the National Liberation Council under the helm of Lt. General Joe Ankrah, leading to a change in economic direction, as we will see in the next subsection.

Towards the Crisis of 1967

Whilst the new Republic of Ghana had full membership in the British Commonwealth to access preferential commercial relationships with the other members and its national currency was deemed strong and exchangeable thanks to its peg to the British Sterling, the Nkrumah government decided to impose an exchange control in 1961 with serious repercussions on the wider domestic economy.[42] Although it seems that the Ghanaian government of that time resolved to protect their domestic market and at the end assert their economic and sovereign authority, given that the balance of payments was in deficit and the country was importing more than it was exporting, and that UK liquid assets in Ghana were small.[43] The markets perceived this action as a future devaluation of the national currency, which was the perfect logic when a government was to reduce the deficit of its balance of payments and current account.

When Nkrumah was deposed, Ghana devalued its currency in July 1967 due to forex shortage and also in order to boost cocoa output. On July 8, 1967, the devaluation of the cedi from 10 shillings to 7 shillings took effect following the announcement by Brigadier Akwasi Amankwa, a member of the National Liberation Council and Commissioner for Finance driven by the inflationary policies of the Nkrumah regime due to cheap imports and increasing costs of exports and the black market.[44] The new government aimed at offering a 30% pay rise to cocoa producers for their crops by reducing or eliminating import duties for them and sale taxation for the agricultural sector.[45] Nevertheless, on July 11, 1967, the FT reported a drop in cocoa prices in spite of a record turnover.[46] These measures i) led to further growing living costs, and ii) made smuggling with the neighboring Ivory Coast more profitable on the back of i) declining consumption of cocoa in Western countries, and ii) a general negative market sentiment for cocoa.

On November 21, 1967, the British monetary authorities devalued the British Sterling by 14% from USD2.80 to USD2.40. This event overvalued *de facto* the currencies of the Sterling Area. Following the devaluation of the British Sterling without informing the members of the Sterling Area, the Bank of Ghana devalued its own currency to neutralize the effects of the British Sterling devaluation, as i) its main revenues were driven by the cocoa export, ii) its main trading partner was the United Kingdom, and iii) the country has large sterling assets held by the Bank of England.[47] The main issue at stake was to protect the purchasing power of its national currency pegged to the British sterling.

Ghana, formerly known as the Gold Coast, was the trailblazer for being the first country in British West Africa to become independent. Thus, it is equally compelling to review and analyze how Nigeria fared in the context of the monetary transitions from the West African Sterling to the Nigerian Sterling and its political independence from the United Kingdom.

Despite the political independence of Ghana, the United Kingdom was involved in shaping the monetary infrastructures by linking them to those under British control by providing technical assistance in the sense that the first Governor of the Central of Bank and first Deputy-Governor were British experienced bankers.

Second, by pegging the Ghanaian Sterling to the British Sterling, the national currency did not acquire true monetary independence and was kept under a form of monetary coercion imposed by currency bloc as Jonathan Krishner theorized in his seminal work.[48] In order not to lose its economic development advances, Ghana decided to devalue its currency immediately following the British move revealing a sign that it had not acquired complete monetary sovereignty.

THE CASE OF NIGERIA

Nigeria was the second country in West Africa among the British dominions and the members of the West African Currency Board to gain access to independence. In spite of the existing of a number of indigenous banks operating in Nigeria coexisting with the Bank of West Africa, Barclays Bank D.C.O, two American banks of which Chase Manhattan Bank, the Banque de l'Afrique Occidentale, a French bank, *inter alia*, monetary creation was not only driven by local companies but also by the framework around the West African Currency Board.[49]

In the early 1950s, demands arose from the Nigerian House of Representatives to set up a domestic and centralized central bank.[50] These requests were rejected. Following a study trip and a feasibility study, JB Loynes agreed that a central bank in Nigeria should be established.[51] The Central Bank of Nigeria started its operation on July 1, 1959.

After looking shortly at the process to political independence of Nigeria, we will analyze the crisis of 1967.

The Path to Political Independence

On October 1, 1960, Nigeria became independent. The Union Jack was brought down, and the white green National Flag of Independent Nigeria was unfurled at midnight on September 30.[52] The new Prime Minister was Sir Abubakar Tafawa Balewa. The Governor-General was Sir James Robertson. The Federation of Nigeria became a Federal Republic on October 1, 1963. The Nigeria (Constitution) Order in Council, 1960, was replaced with a Republican Constitution by Parliament with the concurrence of the Regional Legislatures.[53]

New Monetary and Financial Infrastructures

The advisor of the Bank of England, Mr. J. B. Loynes, produced a report, in 1957, on the establishment a new central bank for Nigeria.

With effect from July 1, 1959, a new Nigerian currency has been in circulation issued by the newly established Central Bank of Nigeria.[54] It replaces the currency formerly being issued by the West African Currency Board and which was currently being accepted as legal tender until it goes out of circulation. Nigerian currency was at par with the British Sterling.

Paper money consists of 100/-, 200/-, 10/-, and 5/-notes. There are coins to the value of 2/-, 1/-, 6d., 3d., 1d. and (in Northern Nigeria only) one-tenth of a penny. The new coins are smaller in size than the West African currency. Nigerian currency is minted in London, and represents the largest single order so far handled by the Royal Mint. One thousand million coins were ordered, and the minting was expected to be completed by the middle of 1961. Indeed, in May 1958, the FT reports that the Central Bank of Nigeria (CBN) signed a contract with a British firm, Bradbury Wilkinson and Co., in the amount of £200,000 to print bank notes issued by the CBN in four denominations, namely 5s, 10s, £1, and £5.[55]

A Stock Exchange was established in Lagos, the federal capital in 1961. The foundation members were Senator T. A. Doherty, Sir Odumegwu Ojukwu, Malam Yardua, Mr. Akintola Williams, John Holt (Nigeria) Ltd., and Investment Company of Nigeria.

The banking system of the Nigerian Federation is regulated by the Banking Ordinance, the latest edition of which came into effect in 1959.[56] The Ordinance prescribes procedures and standards for the conduct of banking business, defines permissible capital and reserve structures, and authorizes the central bank to prescribe the minimum liquid assets that must be held by commercial banks. The central bank fixed the liquidity ratio at 25% of gross demand and time liabilities in November 1959. A bank must obtain a license before it operates and the federal government may order the closure of any bank which does not fulfill the requirements of the Banking Ordinance. There is a Banking Examiner in the Federal Ministry of Finance empowered to conduct regular examination of all licensed banks and to help and advise them wherever possible.

On July 1, 1959, the Central Bank of Nigeria was established by the federal government. It is a bank of issue and holds accounts both for the Government of the Federation and for other banks. The same year, the local issuance of government bills by the Central Bank of Nigeria was an additional tool to showcase the monetary independence and to increase the liquidity of the local market with a domestic currency away from the West African Currency Board and the patronage of the Bank of England, and most likely to attract foreign investors to support its economic development plan.[57]

As disclosed in various banking and political science publications such as *West Africa Annual*, apart from the central bank there were at the end of 1960 13 banks in Nigeria, namely: Bank of West Africa, Bank of the North,

Barclays Bank C.C.O., Banque de l'Afrique Occidentale, National Bank of
Nigeria, Muslim Bank, Agbon Magbe Bank, Chase Manhattan Bank, British
and French Bank, Co-operative Bank, Bank of Lagos, African Continental
Bank, and Bank of America.

The new Nigerian currency appeared to be as strong as the British Sterling
and a strong international currency. As of July, the Nigerian note circulation
stood at £66,071,391 with external reserves of £64,131,462 as backing.[58]

The Pound Crisis of 1967

According to an article published by the FT "Nigerian Pound Still Strong,"
the Central Bank of Nigeria restricted the repatriation of Nigerian currency
abroad to ease foreign exchange difficulties.[59] The level of total external
reserves (£51m) including gold (£7m) remained strong. However, the
Governor of the Central Bank, Dr. Isong, declared the Nigerian Sterling
remained strong, although it was said that the Nigerian currency was trading
below its face value in the UK. This decision happened when Nigeria was
enmeshed into a costly civil war.

Until the civil war in 1967, Nigeria was one of the largest contributors to
the sterling system due to the quota of reserves sterling assets it was bound to
keep after the WACB was demised. In the sterling zone, all currencies were
pegged to the British Sterling thus widening the national commercial and
public of the United Kingdom.

Due to the sudden devaluation of the British Sterling in 1967, Nigeria
saw its foreign exchange reserves fall rapidly. The devaluation occurred on
November 21, 1967. The *Daily Times* reports that the sterling had gone down
by 2s 10d against the Nigerian Sterling. The Commonwealth Relations Office
Yearbook of 1967 published in its section on Commonwealth Currency that
the value of the British Sterling moved from US$2.80 to US$2.40 and from
parity against the Nigerian Sterling to £1 3s 5d.[60]

Nigeria under the economic guidance of Chief Awolowo decided not to
devalue the Nigerian Sterling unlike most members of the Sterling Area had
done, in particular as Ghana did. The effects of the British Pound devaluation were not immediate. It is only at the last weekend of February 1968 that
the Governor of the CBN, Dr. Clement Isong, announced at the Institute of
Bankers in Lagos that the country had a loss of £8m as the UK was its main
export country; the loss was driven by the facts that: i) the Nigerian Sterling
was weakened by speculators in the international market, ii) its exports did
not become cheaper as a result of the devaluation as it did not factor in the
operation costs, iii) there was a reduction in petroleum and other products,
and iv) the import bills for military equipment as a result of the civil war
had increased. Finally, the CBN asked the International Monetary Fund the

permission to increase its quote in the fund. In this chapter, we also learned the devaluation of the sterling and the domestic economic slowdown had a negative impact of the foreign currency reserves for Nigeria: they stood at £93m in 1965 and fell to £84m at the end of 1966 to reach about £45m at the end of 1967.

The devaluation of British Sterling had a contagious adverse effect to most sterling area's economies, which slowly cleared the way for an alternative system to this so- called "optimum currency area."

CONCLUSION

By pegging its new currency, Nigeria akin to Ghana found an easy way to automatically internationalize their respective national currency and to reduce any form of volatility at a crucial time when foreign and domestic investments were needed to build up their nations' economic development.

The United Kingdom during this period was suffering economic hardships and globally gold reserves were put under pressure, which led to a forced devaluation of the British pound. Most of the members of the Sterling Area refused to devalue. However, the artificial maintenance of their exchange rates against the British Sterling resulted into monetary losses for the Nigerian authorities to manage. Their purchasing power of their foreign currency reserves were depreciated. Thus, it was time to take initiatives to avoid any form of correlation with the British Pound, the currency of the former colonial master.

Independent and centralized monetary creation is key in state-building. The populations of Ghana and Nigeria welcomed the political and monetary transition to a political independence and the creation of new currencies away from the West African Sterling.

Going through the archives of the time, it is difficult to affirm that these nations acquired their monetary sovereignty given that the United Kingdom had its best interests at heart to keep the prominence of the City of London as a financial center, to channel funds and liquidity. In other words, the main issue was to remain "*the financial centre of the world, the banker of all nations.*"[61] On the other hand, the peg to the British Sterling brought a strong hedge against inflation for the members of the sterling bloc.

The Sterling Area was based on preferential payments system, whereby all exchanges rates with the national currency were quoted in sterling, payments and private assets were centralized or kept in London, members were free to make payments with the sterling zone but were imposed restrictions for payments made outside the sterling zone.[62] Catherine Shenck described the mechanisms of the colonial sterling, in that the former Gold Coast and Nigeria held significant amounts of sterling assets.[63]

The unilateral devaluation of the sterling in 1967 resulted into a stronger national cohesion and identity in both countries and reinforced the willingness to strengthen their monetary sovereignty.

NOTES

1. Olajide Aluko, *Ghana and Nigeria, 1957–70: A Study in Inter-African Discord* (London: Rex Collins, 1976), 40; L.K. Jakande, *West Africa Annual, 1964–1965* (Lagos: John West Publications Ltd., 1964), 22, 75.

2. Aluko, *Ghana and Nigeria*, 47–48.

3. For information on territorialization, please see Eric Helleiner, *The Making of National Money: Territorial Currencies in Historical Perspective* (Ithaca: Cornell University Press, 2002). For information regarding coercion, please see Joann Chirico, "Setting the Stage" in *Globalization: Prospects and Problems*, ed. Joann Chirico (Thousand Oaks: Sage Publications, 2014), 60–84, https://us.sagepub.com/sites/default/files/upm-assets/56780_book_item_56780.pdf.

4. This expression is borrowed from Erin E. Jucker-Fleetwood, *Money and Finance in Africa* (New York: Frederick A. Praeger Publishers, 1964), 21.

5. Arthur Nussbaum, *Money in the Law* (Chicago: Foundation Press, 1939), 25, 5.

6. Ibid., 37.

7. Ibid., 55.

8. Ibid., 37, 40, 42.

9. Helleiner, *The Making of National Money*, 296.

10. In Latin, *ius cudendae monetae* means "The right to coin." See also Claus Zimmerman, *A Contemporary Concept of Monetary Sovereignty* (Oxford: Oxford University Press, 2014), 3–4.

11. Stephen D. Krasner, *Power, the State, and Sovereignty: Essays on International Relations* (London: Routledge, 2009), 179–80.

12. Andreas Osiander, "Sovereignty, International Relations, and the Westphalian Myth," *International Organization* 55, no. 2 (2001): 251-87.

13. Eric Tymoigne, "Monetary Sovereignty: Nature, Implementation, and Implications," *Public Budgeting & Finance* 40, no. 3 (2020): 49–71.

14. CO 964; The other countries of dominions using the West African Sterling as their legal tender were Sierra Leone and The Gambia.

15. Aluko, *Ghana and Nigeria*, 55; Bamidele Aly, "The Status of the West African Sterling in Southern Nigeria in 1916," in *There Came a Time: Essays on the Great War in Africa—Edited Collection* eds., Anne Samson, Ana Paula Pires, and Dan Gilfoyle (Rickmansworth: The Great War in Africa Association/TSL Publications, 2018), 327–41; Sarah Stockwell, *The British End of the British Empire* (Cambridge: Cambridge University Press, 2018), 24.

16. Aluko, *Ghana and Nigeria*, 56.

17. "Central Banks for new Dominions," *Economist* (August 11, 1956), 507+, The Economist Historical Archive.

18. Jakande, *West Africa Annual*, 319. The Pound Sterling: Under this Act, the Bank of England might, with the consent of the Treasury, temporarily issue notes in excess of the legal limit, provided that Parliament was informed immediately of such excess issue. See also The UK National Archives—CO984/2.

19. In Accounting terms and broadly speaking, liquid assets consist of cash, debt securities (bonds), and equity securities (stocks). See also Stockwell, *The British End*, 55.

20. "They like the Sterling Area," *The Economist* (March 5, 1960), 929, The Economist Historical Archive.

21. Stockwell, *The British End, 335.*

22. A. D. Amarquaye Laryea and Bernardin Senadza, "Trade and Exchange Rate Policies since Independence and Prospects for the Future," in *The Economy of Ghana Sixty Years after Independence*, eds. Ernest Aryeetey and Ravi Kanbur (Oxford: Oxford University Press, 2017), 106.

23. Jakande, *West Africa Annual*, 67.

24. Colonial Office—The Proposed Constitution of Ghana presented by the Secretary of State for the Colonies to Parliament by Command her Majesty, February 1957; The Ghana Independence Bill presented by Mr Secretary Lennox-Boyd, supported by R. A. Buttler, Mr Chancellor of the Exchequer, Lord John Hope, ordered by the House of Commons to be printed 28 Nov 1956; Ghana Independence Bill, Order for 2nd Reading read [Queen's Consent on behalf of the Crown, signified] pp. 229–326 in Official Report of Fifth Series Parliamentary Debates—Commons 1956–1957, volume 562, Dec 10–Dec 21; and Queen's Speech Debate on Address, pp. 764–766, volume 560, Nov 6 to Nov 23.

25. "Bank of British West Africa," *Financial Times* (May 22, 1957), 7, Financial Times Historical Archive; "Bank of West Africa," *Financial Times* (May 21, 1958), 13, Financial Times Historical Archive.

26. Ernest Aryeetey and Ama Pokuaa Fenny, "Economic Growth in Ghana: Trends and Structure, 1960–2014," in *The Economy of Ghana Sixty Years after Independence*, eds. Ernest Aryeetey and Ravi Kanbur (Oxford: Oxford University Press, 2017), 45; See also Robert Darko Osei and Henry Telli, "Sixty Years of Fiscal Policy in Ghana: Outcomes and Lessons," in *The Economy of Ghana Sixty Years after Independence*, eds. Ernest Aryeetey and Ravi Kanbur (Oxford: Oxford University Press, 2017), 68, 71.

27. Ibid., 71–72; Amarquaye Laryea and Senadza, "Trade and Exchange Rate Policies," 106.

28. "Central Bank for Ghana," *Financial Times*, (February 20, 1957), 9, Financial Times Historical Archive.

"Central Bank for Ghana," *Economist*, (February 23, 1957), 670, The Economist Historical Archive.

29. Commonwealth Central Banks," *Financial Times* (August 29, 1957), 3. Financial Times Historical Archive; "Tighter Exchange Controls," *Economist* (July 15, 1961), 275. The Economist Historical Archive.

30. Ghana Bank Note Circulation," *Financial Times*, (July 23, 1958), 5, Financial Times Historical Archive. As of close of business July 15 1958, on the second day of the new Ghana currency, the total of Ghana notes and coins issued was £8,894,670. This was backed by £3,893,150 of West African Board notes and coins withdrawn from circulation on July 14 and 15, and £5,001,520 sterling balances and Treasury bills.

31. Stockwell, *The British End*, 145; Catherine R. Schenk, *The Decline of Sterling: Managing the Retreat of an International Currency, 1945–1992* (Cambridge: Cambridge University Press, 2010).

32. "New Bank for Ghana," *Financial Times* (June 17, 1957), 7, Financial Times Historical Archive.

33. "Ghana Bank Report," *Financial Times*, (August 28, 1958), 5, Financial Times Historical Archive.

34. Alfred Eggleston was at his nomination connected for nearly 40 years, having served in the National Bank of Scotland, the Standard Bank of South Africa, the Imperial Bank of India, and the Reserve Bank of India. "Governor for New Bank of Ghana," *Financial Times*,(May 6, 1957), Financial Times Historical Archive.; "£2m. Ghana Treasury Bill Issue," *Financial Times*, (February 6, 1960), 7, Financial Times Historical Archive.

35. Jakande, *West Africa Annual*, 74; "Central Bank for Ghana," *Financial Times*, (February 20, 1957), 9, Financial Times Historical Archive.

36. "Our History," De La Rue, accessed December 8, 2020, https://www.delarue .com/about-us/our-history-orig; "De La Rue," British Museum, accessed December 8, 2020, https://www.britishmuseum.org/collection/term/BIOG147804; see also "Gold Coast Currency," *Financial Times*, (September 20, 1955), 9, Financial Times Historical Archive.

37. Jakande, *West Africa Annual*, 75.

38. "Bank of British West Africa Limited," *Financial Times* (May 22, 1957), 7, Financial Times Historical Archive.

39. Jakande, *West Africa Annual*, 75.

40. "Ghana Issues 5% Stock," *Financial Times* (May 30, 1961), 11, Financial Times Historical Archive.

41. "Ghana Cocoa Financing." *Financial Times* (October 16, 1961), 1, Financial Times Historical Archive.

42. "The Implications of Exchange Control," *Financial Times* (July 7, 1961), 5, Financial Times Historical Archives.

43. Ibid.

44. Our Own Correspondent, "Ghana Announces 30% Devaluation," *Financial Times*, (July 10, 1967), 2, Financial Times Historical Archive.

45. Our Accra Correspondent, "Adroit Move to Build Up Home Industries?" *Financial Times* (July 26, 1967), 7. Financial Times Historical Archive.

46. John Edwards, "Record Turnover as Cocoa Slumps," *Financial Times*, (July 11, 1967), 2, Financial Times Historical Archive; "Commodity Market Reports and Prices," *Financial Times* (July 11, 1967), 2, Financial Times Historical Archive.

47. "Ghana Remains Undecided." *Financial Times*, (November 21, 1967), 29, Financial Times Historical Archive.

48. Jonathan Kirshner, *Currency and Coercion: The Political Economy of International Monetary Powers* (Princeton: Princeton University Press, 1995), 289.

49. For information on indigenous banks of Nigeria, please see Eyo, *Nigeria and the Evolution of Money*, 91–100; Saroj Kumar Basu, *Central Banking in the Emerging Countries* (New York: Asia Pub. House, 1967), 19, 21.

50. Eyo, *Nigeria and the Evolution of Money*, 101.

51. Ibid., 102.

52. Jakande, *West Africa Annual*, 200.

53. Nigerian Independence Act, 1960.

54. "Bank of West Africa Limited," *Financial Times*, (June 3, 1959), 7, Financial Times Historical Archive; Jakande, *West Africa Annual*, 222; JS Badger, "The Central Bank," *Financial Times* (October 30, 1962), IV, Financial Times Historical Archive; "Bank of the Gold Coast," February 2, 1957.

55. "Nigerian Bank Note Order," *Financial Times*, (May 16, 1958), 1, Financial Times Historical Archives.

56. Jakande, *West Africa Annual*, 223.

57. "Bank of West Africa Limited," *Financial Times* (May 25, 1960), 6, Financial Times Historical Archive.

58. "Nigerian Note Circulation," *Financial Times* (August 9, 1961), 6, Financial Times Historical Archive.

59. "Nigerian Pound Still Strong," *Financial Times* (September 14, 1967), Financial Times Historical Archive.

60. "Sterling Devalued Against the Nigerian Sterling," *Daily Times of Nigeria*, November 21, 1967.

61. Albert E. Feavearyear, *The Pound Sterling: A History of English Money* (London: Oxford University Press, 1931), 299.

62. Paul R. Mason and Catherine Pattillo, *The Monetary Geography of Africa* (Washington, DC: Brookings Institution Press, 2005), 19.

63. Schenk, *The Decline of Sterling*.

5

Music as a Tool for Sustainable Development in Nigerian Society

Maureen Ada Uche

Culture as a phenomenon has played its role in the life of people, bringing them together to form groups of believers and practitioners of shared belief systems. Cultural heritage provides a central component of one's identity. Culture, therefore, portrays its meaning in the life, values, and practices of people who act as performers of the shared tradition in a belief system.

Nigerian society projects its identities based on the cultural belief systems and practices of societies or communities that make up the country. Their intentions are mainly to showcase their cultural behaviors, beliefs, and values in a diversified society and to the outside world. The richness of these cultural practices in their various activities can be seen in their economic, political, social, and even religious performances which have formed part of their cultural heritage. Every facet of human development among these groups is culturally oriented and culture centered. It is therefore imperative that the cultural values be upheld for a sustained development and for future documentation. One of the means of disseminating, transmitting, reproducing, and upholding cultural values of a society is through its music. The musical traditions of every society therefore speak of its cultural package and give that community an identity. Its music portrays its language, behavior, economic practices, and political status, etc. An indigenous music system in every society plays its roles in the development of that society as a media for information to communicate its ideas and ideals within and outside cultural boundaries.

Development enhances the building of each nation. Every nation depends on its cultural heritage and other accomplishments which they have to develop further and to sustain continued progress. Development is a gradual process towards achievement in various areas that will enhance nation building and create positive changes in a society.[1] Every society experiences changes and as such should be prepared for these shifts, bearing in mind that their cultural heritage is foundational to their identity, hence, it should be rooted and upheld while these constant adjustments occur from one generation to another. Innovations bring in changes which may positively be welcomed and utilized in nation building and development but the identifying features of a nation such as their culture, specifically indigenous music types, must be included as intrinsic parts of the national cultural heritage. The diverse music of each Nigerian group portrays the cultural heritage of its communities.[2] Despite the diversity of cultures, there are similarities in their musical art performances and shared artistic ideas. This is especially common among communities that share boundaries with each other and seem to meet on musical grounds during a performance that necessitates their coming together for the purpose of the performance.

TRADITIONAL AFRICAN MUSIC AND CULTURE

As an art, music has helped to keep homo sapiens in a communicative state whereby there has always been room for people to share their feelings, exchange ideas, and portray their shared beliefs as individuals, communities, and as nations. Music is integrated into the indigenous activities of communities in Nigeria, from birth to death. Music's artistic and communicative roles in the lives of individuals cannot be overemphasized since it creates avenues for communities to interact socially. It also educates them regarding their historic and cultural states, creating an avenue for shared knowledge of their musical legacy. Music is therefore a part of people's culture that has been used as a tool to understand the social potentialities of communities. Indigenous musical arts came into existence right from the origin of the community where they emerged.[3] Music was and is still used to communicate and express the nature of the activities going on in communities. Music serves as a tool of expression in various ways and at different times of performances, hence there is music for leisure, traditional marriages, naming ceremonies, burial/funeral ceremonies, festivals, and traditional worship, etc. There are also special songs meant strictly for these living milestone events, as well as dances and traditional musical instruments associated with each special role.

The traditional music of a society to an extent mirrors the cultural heritage of that society. This is because the traditional music explains the beliefs as well as the behaviors and attitudes of a community in a clearly defined way that is easily shared and therefore not unfamiliar to other societies. Culture is of humans; and for humans to understand one's environment, one must first appreciate its cultural resources positively and appreciate water developmental projects that can sustain future consumption.

Music and culture go hand in hand to portray the existence of a society and its potentialities in its historic stance, economic achievements and possessions, social states, and development processes.[4] African traditional music and culture are therefore inseparable since music follows each African in almost every stage of life, reflecting through both the events that occur at each stage. Meki Nzewi points out that "music makes human; it supervises, explains and illuminates the human society."[5] The inseparable nature of music and culture is being defined here by the aforementioned. Culture makes human in a society; it molds each person, hence these elements are reflected in the knowledgeable practices of norms and values that govern them and when these norms and values are adhered to and practiced, that society is identified and recognized through its cultural practices.

Each society practices its culture which distinguishes each from the others. In this vein, humans have therefore made systematic attempts to produce the totality of a way of life, which can generally be described as the culture of a group. People here means members of a community who have come together to live in the same environment, develop the environment, and engage in the same occupation for their livelihood. Rules and regulations therefore abound among the communities in order to make them identifiable and distinguishable to other communities outside theirs. These rules and regulations which are part of their cultural pattern are adhered to as they engage in their communal activities that enhance the development of their society.

Adedeji and Omosilade report Vidal, who notes that:

> Musicians in African society are the custodians of their culture. The history of a particular people is kept from generation to generation through oral medium by professional musicians. The history of important events in the society, and the personalities involved in these events are recorded for posterity through songs.[6]

Folk songs among the *Igbo* community of Nigeria, as is the case also with other ethnic groups, aim to educate, entertain, worship, and communicate events and feelings. They are sung in their local/native dialect and transmit messages directly and indirectly. Songs are functional in the enactment of sociocultural and political events that occur in the society. Musicians in the society contribute to the development of the community through songs which are basically meant to provide information about the community and the activities going on and reflect beliefs and central elements of the group identity, its cultural heritage, the history of the community, and its politics as well. There are songs for leisure, didactic songs, festival songs, and burial songs. There are also slay songs which are apparent during special celebrations like festivals; all these are meant to communicate, correct, educate, inform, and entertain. Song texts communicate clearly to its audience for proper understanding and total acceptance by the community since its popularity and acceptance depend on the community, hence proper communication encourages active participation. In the past, therefore, folk songs belonged to the community, and not to any individual. Folk songs come in different ways among the *Igbos* of Nigeria; they are sung, recited, and chanted, depending on the occasion. Singing is a natural means of expression among the *Igbos* of Nigeria who express every one of their feelings and thoughts through songs. The birth of a baby is welcomed and announced through songs, the crying baby is entertained by its mother or member of the family with lullabies:

> Onye mulu nwa n'ebe kwa? / Who gave birth to this crying baby?
> Egbe mulu nwa n'ebe akwa / The vulture's child is crying
> Wete euziza wetee ose bring / Some spice and pepper
> Weta amuma wege ji tee / Bring the stone to grind them all
> Ka umu nnunu lacha aka / Let the birds eat and lick their fingers.[7]

The melody in the above song is meant to calm the baby and probably send the baby to sleep. The text teaches the little ones their dialect, names of spices used for cooking which are found in their area and are used by their mothers at home as well. Lullabies to the *Igbos* are meant to educate the girls in the community on how to take care of their own children when they become mothers.

Okafor and Lawrence point out that "the arts may be a manifestation of culture and so will traditions, beliefs, customs and practices."[8] The music of the *Igbo* communities of Nigeria presents its cultural beliefs in their various activities which involve members of the community who maybe direct or indirect performers. In the burial ceremonies, their music reflects on the cultural beliefs of life after death. Burial ceremonies are organized in such a way that every member of the community is involved no matter one's age. The youths have their roles to play as instrumentalists and mourners, the women and older men also play their roles and have their songs as well. Music for burial ceremonies therefore has their special songs and instrumental sessions.

As an aspect of culture, music therefore portrays the belief, practices, and identities as well as interests and occupation of communities. Isaac Udoh contends that "the cultural values and norms of a society are embedded in their traditional music."[9] He stresses that "traditional music is the society's cultural matrix/culture indicator and a common identity."[10] Dan Agu also reports that "traditional music is rooted and perpetuated by the people. It is the spontaneous music of a people, race, region, or nation. It is more directly associated with traditional, religious and political system."[11] The importance of traditional music in the development of societies is not farfetched. Traditional music reflects on the lives of individuals and prepares them for every stage of their life in and outside their cultural ground. An in-depth knowledge of their traditional music gives an insight into the cultural, economic, and political system of their society. Festival celebrations among the *Igbo* of Nigeria portray their occupational interests and practices as well as their religious inclination towards the belief and worship of their deity. Festival songs praise their gods/goddesses who contribute to the successful and rich produce from their farm annually. This period also creates an opportunity for talented musicians to showcase their talents and creativity as singers, dancers, and instrumentalists. Festival celebrations create an informal school for the community to render, learn, and accept new songs, which provides an avenue for new songs to be rendered, learnt, and accepted by the community.

Igbo communities, through their festival celebrations, are not restricted from citing the political instability of the community. Slay songs are highly recommended to expose individuals or groups that have committed crimes. These slay songs (*Igba-abu*) are meant to educate members of the community as well as correct the offenders. Through this information, decisions may be reached later to decide the fate of the offenders. They are either ostracized or made to pay fines. Slay songs are only allowed during festival celebrations. If sung outside its expected event, the singer(s) will be punished.

> Ewoo obi kadioo ewoo (exclamation) obi kadioo
> Ewoo ehh o kisi eme-o? / Is this how you act/behave?
> Obikadi igbu si-obodo / If you kill everyone in the community
> Ngi n'onye g'ebi-o? / Who will you live with?
> Og'ekwei mee-oo? / Will you succeed?[12]

The above song is an example of a slay song which portrays inhumanity meted on man and its effect, exposing the evil deeds of a man who believes in taking the laws into his hands. The song not only exposes the evil action but condemns it; hence the community has adopted the song. The above song also talks of justice and peace which is highly welcomed and appreciated in the community for sustained development. The functionality of traditional songs is therefore apparent in the roles they play in human activities. They are either sung a capella (i.e., without instrumental accompaniment) or with instrumental accompaniment and clapping.

Traditional dances of the *Igbo* communities come in different ways and on various occasions. Festival dances, for example, are performed with dance drama portraying their occupation and means of livelihood. Every age group has their dances and each play very special roles in the development of their musical culture. Traditional dances are organized for recreation amongst children and even adults in the communities as well as other occasions such as festival performances, or marriage ceremonies. There are special dances meant for special occasions which are symbolic and meant strictly for the particular occasion in which the dance appears. One of such dances among the delta *Igbo* of Nigeria is called *Egwu Ota* and is meant for a particular portion of the burial ceremony. This, however, is accompanied with special drums and other musical instruments played by professional musicians.

TRADITIONAL MUSIC FOR
SUSTAINED DEVELOPMENT

Nigerian society is very rich in culture. Languages, dressing, economic practices, and other beliefs, values, and indigenous practices identify various cultural heritage. One can therefore identify an ethnic group/community through its cultural heritage and practices. The shared culture (ideas, ideals, and beliefs) of a group of persons who live together is demonstrated through musical performances. Cultural beliefs emanate from musical practices, religious inclinations, economic involvement, and political practices. These shared practices and beliefs sustain and reproduce the strength of Nigerian society. The organization of music for cultural activities has always been part of the cultural practices of every community in Nigerian society; take away their indigenous music and these communities would become unidentifiable.

Music classifies the ethnic groups in Nigeria since it is an avenue used to communicate their cultural ideas, entertain their audiences, express their feelings, project their economic and political situations, and even worship their gods/goddesses. Every musical presentation serves a function, hence music performances or songs raised by individuals or groups are not ignored. They draw attention, welcoming responses by those with whom they communicate. Music forms part of the cultural practices—it portrays the society's way of life in an aesthetic and artistic form. This is reflected in their indigenous songs, dances, and traditional religious worship. Music is, therefore, not an isolated art, but a performing art form which a society uses as an explanatory forum of who they are, what they do, what they believe in, and how they live. Music and culture therefore explain and illuminate the society, Blacking contends that "music is not an isolated art," but describes it as "a humanly organized sound."[13] Richard Okafor explains that,

> the implications here (i.e., Blackings statements), is that though there are many sounds in creation, some natured, others made by living things, only sounds which have been deliberately organized by man to specific ends—expressions of emotion, communication of ideas, touching the senses and the emotions,

calming the nerves or turning the minds to certain plains of communication and worship—only these sounds deliberately organized by man qualify to be called music.[14]

In all totality, music shapes humans and societies, and in return people create new songs, music, and performances. Music brings out the hidden creative nature in humans portraying the aesthetic and artistic qualities that man possesses and finally reflecting the society man lives in as well as the norms and values of that society that shapes and forms the character of man. Agu summarizes this by pointing out that, "Music serves not only as a medium for entertainment and social relationships but as an intricate part of development of the mind, body and soul."[15] To buttress the aforementioned fact, Onyeji gives a general philosophy of indigenous music where he states that, "Indigenous music in Nigeria and Africa is a human centered art."[16] He concludes his view where he quotes Nzewi, who maintained that "indigenous music is feeling and communal therapy, a humanizing communion, a sharing in human-being-ness."[17] The *Igbo* musical activities encourage active participation in their performances which may be singing, dancing, and instrumental pieces. Although, women are not allowed to play certain musical instruments, the *Igbo* women play the maracas and bells which they use to accompany their songs during occasions that call for social gatherings. Today, women use these instruments and other Western instruments in their churches to accompany their songs. There are traditional instruments which are used for certain occasions of worship and other symbolic purposes. To understand the sounds and usages of these instruments, one must be an active participant in the musical performances and activities of the community.

Active participation in the cultural practices of these communities will bring about a sustained development that will merge with changes that are meant to continually occur due to global changes as a result of intercultural relationships and interactions. Meki Nzewi reiterates that "In indigenous Africa, music is closely interwoven with how the society or community conducts its political, religious, health, economic, educational and social affairs."[18] He further stresses that "everybody in an indigenous African community grows up with basic musicality acquired through obligatory participation, in any capacity, in appropriate musical arts performances from childhood."[19] He concludes that "exceptional expertise is recognized even at a tender age."[20] The concept of development is recognized and appreciated when the cultural heritage of a society forms the basis for the growth of that society irrespective of other intrusions from others outside the cultural boundaries. Intrusions may be positive but should not eradicate the existing ideas and behaviors which are identifiable values to the community. Intrusions should be welcomed and added to enhance the cultural values of the community for a sustained and effective development.

Obligatory and active participation in musical performances prepare the individual for changes that may occur from within and outside the communal boundaries. With these, cultural values are upheld and maintained, and new ideas are welcomed to form part of the existing ones. As a tool for sustained development, music therefore serves its purpose in regard to encouraging informal and formal music training where the trainees indulge in learning music to understand their culture through the knowledge and study of their traditional music and that of other societies. Music remains an intrinsic means of socialization and identity formation within one's community.

As a tool for sustained development also, involvement in musical performances and training will help individuals acquire musical skills that will promote self-reliance and eradicate poverty. Bearing in mind that one of the things that thwarts development in any nation is unemployment among its citizens, skill acquisition through music can reduce poverty and create jobs for talented musicians of all types—singers, dancers, and instrumentalists, as well as music educationists, studio producers, etc. Ogurinade states that "an agreement to trim down the level of poverty in any society is the provision of skills to allow people participate in the production of goods and services as individuals or as members of groups."[21] He concludes that "music is an extremely cost effective and powerful language that all culture relate with, a direct and potent tool that sustain urban and rural community building as well as the healing process of individuals and communities."[22] Music cuts across every barrier in its entertainment and communication to unify individuals of different cultures and with different talents to share their musical experiences and innate creativity. These are achieved through spontaneous and organized musical exchanges both formal and informal.

RECOMMENDATION

Music is an important part of any program being carried out in African (Nigerian) societies which host a lot of rural areas who still see music as educational and motivational means of acquiring knowledge as well as for entertainment. Jaime Booth Cundy affirms that:

> [T]he potential for music to have a positive impact on development and peace extends as far as a radio wave. Beyond the impact on individuals creating and performing the music, the passive experience of listening to music either live or recorded can also be significant . . . The ability of music to travel to the farthest corners of the world means it can reach people that have previously

been neglected due to their remoteness . . . Music has the ability to bring people together; it bridges social, cultural, and economic divides. It teaches principles of co-operation, respect and understanding. Music builds resilience; self esteem and self efficacy which are all invaluable to the sustainability of any program.[23]

Here, music is portrayed as a powerful weapon of communication, expression, and as an instrument for knowledge and self-improvement.

African societies have used music as a medium of entertainment, education, self-reliance, and communication, as well as documentation. Music, among other arts, has formed the basis for information of all types despite their language differences. Understanding the intention in a musical performance was not difficult for individuals because of their involvement and active participation in their musical activities.

Today, the above seems farfetched because of cultural intrusions which have almost taken over the rich cultural heritage of Nigerian society, affecting every structural aspect of the country. Therefore, active participation in the musical performances that take place in the various communities will help the present generation understand and appreciate their cultural heritage. Active participation not only exposes individual members of a community to the musical and cultural ideas of their community, but it also helps to understand and uphold the norms and values of their culture, teaches them how to properly manage their goods and services, and further contribute to the political state of the community and the nation as well.

Musical expertise brings about self-reliance in societies where it is difficult for one to get good jobs. A professional musician becomes self-employed and an employer of labor in the society. Informal musical training should be further encouraged as this will help to eradicate poverty and promote self-reliance in Nigerian society.

One of the positive effects of a sustained development in any society is the ability to maintain the positive elements of life before continuous global changes unsettle everything they knew about the world. To maintain the existing culture of any society, the cultural heritage of the people must be properly passed on through documentation and archival settings that provide a reference center for the younger generation to seek and cite. Formal education should therefore encourage the need for the study of the cultural heritage of communities instead of concentrating more on Western culture. Traditional African music should be part of the curriculum. In music learning, for example, traditional African instruments and their features should be studied alongside the Western musical instruments. This will help the learner to be conversant with traditional instruments of his community, its sound and material production as well as symbolic representations to the cultural norms and values of the community. Today, traditional instrumentalists are highly sought after to perform during burial occasions, either in churches or for traditional burial ceremonies. These are avenues for job creation and self-reliance for a sustained development of the community and the nation.

CONCLUSION

This chapter projects the traditional musical arts as a tool for sustained development that reinforces one's cultural heritage and group identity. It discusses and maintains the need to rely on the musical culture of the *Igbo* communities and the Nigerian society in exploring the creativity that each possesses in order to help in maintaining and promoting the cultural heritage inherent in each as well as giving the opportunity for self-reliance for an effective and sustained development. This chapter also highlights the fact that the exploration and practices of musical culture will not only create room for talent discovery among artists, but it will also showcase the various talents that the performers have and further encourage interactions among them. This will foster intercultural exchange of musical ideas and nurture creativity.

Musical organizations among societies in Nigeria such as the World Black and African Festivals of Arts and Culture, known as FESTAC, have in the past encouraged social interactions and cultural ideas, giving opportunities for informal learning situations where people learn and share or acquire knowledge of the culture and musical practices with each other. Music has therefore created a forum for learning both in formal and informal settings; in politics, music plays many roles in popularizing the political candidates, praising them, unseating unwanted political leaders, and installing others to their desired positions. Music also plays its important role in traditional festivals and worship which portrays the historic stories and achievements of ancestors and their contributions, as well as worship of various gods and goddesses, and transmitting knowledge of the cultural origins and boundaries of the communities. These mediums of entertainment, identity reinforcement, and knowledge transmission have and will help generations to understand their environment and enjoy the norms and values of their traditions. Music interactions among the present generation will not only create room for talent discovery, it will encourage unity in diversity where people of various cultural backgrounds will come together for peaceful social interactions. Gatherings of this nature will encourage peaceful co-existence among the Nigerian society. As a tool and culture for sustained development, music has also helped to restore confidence to individuals who have in one way or the other battled with psychological problems. Musical settings make rooms for talent discovery and to display each artist's gift. These performances helped mold the characters of cultural groups, traditions, and communities in Nigerian and African societies.

NOTES

1. Chinyere Ukpokolo, *Being and becoming: Gender, Culture and Shifting Identity in Sub-Saharan Africa* (Denver: Spears Media Press, 2016).
2. Ikenna Emmanuel Onwuegbuna, "Music as an Embodiment of Culture and Philosophy: a Survey of Nigerian Folk Songs," in *Astride Memory and Desire Peoples, Cultures, and Development in Nigeria,* ed. C. Krydz Ikwuemesi (Eugu: ABIC Books, 2012), 291–309.
3. G. N. Devy, Geoffrey V. Davis, K. K. Chakravarty, *Performing Identities: Celebrating Indigeneity in the Arts* (New Delhi: Routledge, 2015).
4. Toyin Falola and Augustine Agwuele, *Africans and the Politics of Popular Culture* (Rochester: University of Rochester Press, 2009).
5. Meki Nzewi, *Learning the Musical Arts in Contemporary Africa: Derived from Indigenous Knowledge Systems* (Pretoria: Centre for Indigenous Instrumental African Music and Dance, 2005).
6. A. O. Vidal quoted in Femi Adedeji and Tayo Omosilade, "'I Say No': The Rebuff of Anti-Democratic Forces in Orlando Owo's Music," *Nsukka Journal of Musical Arts Research* 1 (2012): 69.
7. Centuries- old traditional song to welcome the birth of a child from the oral traditions of the Igbo people, written from memory and translated into English by the author, professor of music and traditional singer.
8. Richard Okafor and Lawrence Emeke, *Nigerian Peoples and Culture* (Enugu: New Generation Ventures LTD, 2013), 15.
9. Isaac Udoh, "The Integrity of Traditional Music in the Nigerian Society': a case study of Annang music," *Nsukka Journal of Musical Arts Research* 1 (2012): 119.
10. Ibid.
11. Dan C.C. Agu, "Traditional African Music: Contributions to Contemporary Music Creation and Performance Techniques," in *Humanities and All of Us,* ed. E. Oguegbu (Ontisha: Watch Word Publications, 1990), 80–86.
12. Centuries old traditional slay song from the oral traditions of the Igbo people, written from memory and translated into English by the author, professor of music and traditional singer.
13. John Blacking, *How Musical Is Man?* (London: Faber & Faber, 1976), 6.
14. Richard Okafor, *Music in Nigeria Society* (Enugu: New Generation Books, 2005), 1.
15. Agu, "Traditional African Music," 49.
16. Christian Onyeji, "Towards Nigerian Social and Cultural Integrity: The Contributions of the Nigerian Indigenous Musicians (with Particular Reference to Abigbo Music of Mbaise)," *Nsukka Journal of Musical Arts Research* 1 (2012): 51.
17. Meki Nzewi, quoted in Christian Onyeji, "Towards Nigerian Social and Cultural Integrity,"

18. Meki Nzewi, *Musical Practice and Creativity: An African Traditional Perspective* (Bayreuth, Germany: IWALEWA-Haus, Univ. of Bayreuth, 1991), 6.

19. Ibid.

20. Ibid.

21. D.O.A. Ogunrinade, "Music Education as a Pillar to Sustainable Development in Nigeria," *Journal of Economics and Sustainable Development* 6, no. 3 (2015): 85.

22. Ibid.

23. Jamie Booth Cundy, *Music and the Millennium Development Goals* (Canadian Artists for African Aid, 2019), 8.

PART II

Identity and Ethnic Conflict, Transformation, Reconciliation, and Empowerment

6

Ethnicity, Peacebuilding, and Conflict Transformation in Nigeria

The Case of Herder–Farmer Conflict

Kialee Nyiayaana

The violent attack in Benue state on New Year's Day, 2018, by herdsmen, which claimed 80 lives, reminded us of the growing intensity of herder–farmer conflicts in Nigeria. Prior to the Benue attack, about 40 people were killed in Ukpabi-Nimbo, a farming community in Enugu state on April 25, 2016, by herdsmen in what was described as an invasion on the community.[1] The invasion was a reprisal attack for the killing of a Fulani cattle owner by youth of the Ukpabi-Nimbo community.[2] The Ukpabi-Nimbo community in the southeast of Igboland as in several parts of Nigeria has experienced an escalation of herder–farmer tensions consistently for over three years before the attack of April 25, 2016. Even in the southern belt of Nigeria's oil-rich Niger Delta, clashes between herders and farmers are emerging themes in scholarly investigation. This has moved the focus of research in the Niger Delta beyond the traditional concerns of militancy, oil rebellion, cultism, armed politics, and electoral violence.[3]

Indeed, since the early 2000s, the herder–farmer conflict has spread to almost every part of Nigeria. Between 2016 and 2018, there were at least 310 recorded cases of deadly clashes involving herders and farmers in 26 of Nigeria's 36 states.[4] In 2018 alone, no fewer than 2,073 people were killed, a casualty figure that doubled the Correlate of War Project, which argues that a war situation exists when there are 1,000 recorded battlefield deaths in a year.[5]

Besides the death toll, the conflict has had devastating economic consequences. A study by Mercy Corps estimated that the federal government was losing about $13.7 billion in revenue annually because of herder–farmer conflicts in the Benue, Kaduna, Nasarawa, and Plateau states.[6] This cost does not include the economic and social impact of the conflict on local communities and households. Overall, the herder–farmer conflict has become a serious source of concern in Nigeria, not necessarily because of its destructive impact, but also because of its increasing ethnicization that affects the construction of its related security threats and policy responses.[7] For example, the categorization and ranking of Nigeria's Fulani herdsmen as the fourth terrorist group in the world in 2015 by the Global Terrorism Index has contributed to the complexities of essentialization and securitization of the herder–farmer conflict in Nigeria.[8] Such Fulanization of herdsmen killings, it is argued, may engender ethnic hatred, and trigger violent interethnic confrontations with potential to escalate into another civil war in Nigeria. The concept of Fulanization as used here reflects the proclivity towards the essentialization of herdsmen killing that is centered on the Fulanis. More broadly, Fulanization is used to describe the ideology and strategy of establishing and consolidating Fulani political, economic and cultural domination in Nigeria which further politicizes ethnicity. As popularly conceived in the southern part of Nigeria, the argument about Fulanization is that armed attacks on farming communities by herdsmen constitute part of the strategic goals of land grabbing, displacement, and colonization by the Fulani people that are consistent with the Jihadist struggle of 1804.

Maiangwa explains in his analysis of the context that the dynamics of the herder–farmer conflicts in Nigeria revolve "around issues of land ownership, grazing rights, climate change, settlement and movement, de-territorialization, and resource competition."[9]

This chapter aligns with the deterritorialization argument to contribute to the literature on the impact of ethnicity on the escalation and durability of internal conflicts.[10] It asks two key questions: How does ethnic identification affect how the state and community politicize responses to the herder–farmer conflicts in Nigeria and influence its escalation? How does ethnicity affect peacebuilding outcomes and transform the nature of the conflicts and violence between herders and farmers in Nigeria?

The main argument is that ethnicity influences how the state and local communities politicize policy responses to the conflict and their implementation in ways that constrain effective peacebuilding between herders and farmers in Nigeria. In an attempt to secure their livelihoods, both farmers and herders in Nigeria link the protection of their individual identities to the preservation of collective group identity. To put it differently, when farmers are attacked by herdsmen or vice versa, those attacked perceive that their ethnic, religious identities, and livelihood are collectively attacked. Constructing the conflict in ethnic terms thus shapes relations between both herders and farmers and generates competing identity claims over access to scarce resources such as farming or grazing lands to the extent that designing and implementing effective peacebuilding interventions to resolve the conflict remain difficult. Identity becomes a mobilization tool to fight for each group's interests.

The foregoing argument is structured into five sections. The introduction underscores the destabilizing impact of the herder–farmer conflict on the social development, peace, stability, and security of Nigeria, followed by the theoretical exploration of existing explanations of the causes and course of the conflicts. The next section deals with the conceptual analysis of who is a herder and who is a farmer and relates the question of identity formation and identity protection to the politicization and reconfiguration of the conflict. The rest of the chapter examines the relationship between ethnicity and the nature of state response to the conflict and how the state response contributes to the ethnicization of the conflict in terms of mobilizing each respective group in Nigeria. Finally, an explanation of how local resistance to the conflict results in an ethnic security dilemma due to the resort to the ethnicization of protection by both farmers and herders.

WHAT DOES THE LITERATURE SAY ABOUT THE DYNAMICS OF HERDER–FARMER CONFLICTS IN NIGERIA?

A significant body of literature suggests that in precolonial West Africa, relations between herders and farmers were characterized by reciprocity and mutual benefits, and these interactions remained largely peaceful. Davidheiser and Luna note that through emergent processes of exchange, migrant Fulani pastoralists developed and built interdependent relationships with sedentary farmers, a kind of host–stranger relationship.[11] A key defining characteristic of these relationships was the practice where pastoralists graze their cattle on farmlands that have already been harvested, and the dung of the cattle provided manure for the farmer.[12] Specifically, pastoralists graze farmlands after each harvest and before the next planting season with the mutual benefits with the pastures feeding livestock who leave behind manure that enriches the soil for farmers. These exchanges also transcend dairy and agricultural produce to include, for example, gifts of money, sugar, and tea to herders by farmers to entice them to enrich the farms with cattle manure in post-harvest periods.[13] These various forms of reciprocal exchanges promoted complementarity and long-term symbiotic relationships, which were generally conducive to reconciliation and peaceful coexistence between both social groups of commodity producers.[14] Over the years, particularly from the colonial era and postcolonial periods of the 1960s onwards, relations between herders and farmers across West Africa had become increasingly conflictual and violent.[15]

The change from complementary to conflicting relationships has been explained from different theoretical perspectives. Some scholars draw attention to the intersections of climate change, population pressure, and migration in the contentious evolution of herder–farmer relationships. Drought, desertification, and fast- disappearing green pastures caused by climate change and environmental degradation influence and intensify migration of herdsmen in search of new grazing opportunities that often lead them into conflict with sedentary farmers. In fact, since the latter part of the 20th century, particularly from the 1960s on, there has been a progressive movement of herders from the northern belt of Nigeria, who increasingly suffer from drought and desert encroachment, into the south for much greener pastures where water resources remain more abundant. According to Maiangwa, the "patterns of Fulani nomadic migration into Nigeria intensified from the 1960s onward as many of them fled the drought stricken Sahelian belt to Nigeria's Middle Belt Region."[16] Some interrogate the scarcity of grazing land from the point of view of the collapse of government policy on grazing reserves in northern Nigeria as a major structural cause of the herder–farmer conflict. The argument is that as part of a broader strategy by the Nigerian government to promote sustainable development of livestock production in the country, it enacted the Grazing Reserve Act of 1965, which made lands available to herders in Northern Nigeria.[17] The implementation of the law led to the establishment of about 417 grazing reserves across the northern region in the 1960s.[18] However, the government could not continue with the land reserve policy, ending in its eventual collapse. The failure by the government to retain and enforce the grazing reserves policy has been attributed to the structural shift from an agriculture-based economy to oil in the 1970s as a result of the discovery and commercial exploitation of oil resources in the Niger Delta region of Nigeria.[19] There is also the issue of encroachment on the designated lands due to population growth, urbanization, and physical development, which together reduced herders' access to and usage of the grazing reserves.[20]

Consequently, the ineffectiveness of the grazing reserve policy has meant that herders increasingly depended on, or resorted to open grazing on, farm lands with implications for clashes between herders and farmers.[21] Indeed, policies that have emanated in Nigeria since the Grazing Land Law of 1965 have failed to produce the desired result of promoting sustainable and long-term development of the pastoral system in the country.[22] The point, therefore, is that the lack of ability to secure regular access to grazing lands by herders has become a constant obstacle to pastoral production in Nigeria, creating perpetual conditions of competitive struggles between farmers and herders for scarce land resources as herders move into the southern part of the country in search of greener pastures and encroach on farmlands. Generally, this push factor theory, hinged on environmental scarcity and competition for land, is very important. Nevertheless, the scarcity argument tends to present herder–farmer conflicts as necessarily inevitable, suggesting a new Malthusian theorization of the relationship between resource scarcity and violent conflict.[23] Moritz, for example, points out that some areas suffering increasingly from ecological scarcity in Sudan have not been particularly prone to conflict and violence, drawing attention to other causal factors.[24] Akov supports Moritz's view, arguing that we must look beyond the resource-scarcity debate, noting that herder–farmer conflict in Nigeria is complex and relates to larger issues of "elite land grabbing, ethno-religious identity construction, weak state capabilities, the citizenship question, corrupt traditional institutions, the lack of an effective land tenure system, and a widespread culture of impunity."[25] For example, the inability of the state to effectively guarantee security for both farmers and herders, and the whole question of open grazing and unrestricted movement of cattle on roads including the highways in the 21st century in search of greener pastures by herders underscore the failure of government to provide the conditions for both food production systems to thrive in the country.

Contributing to the state capability debate, Okoli and Ogayi identify the Nigerian state security crisis as the main structural determinant of the escalation versus diffusion of herder–farmer conflicts throughout Nigeria.[26] The analysis underscores a broken social contract between the Nigerian state and its citizenry in the provision of adequate security and physical protection.[27] This is well illustrated, for instance, by the increasing acquisition and use of sophisticated weaponry such as AK-47 rifles by Fulani herders in Nigeria.[28] Yet, small arms proliferation and cattle rustling correlate and exacerbate the intensity and incidence of herder–farmer conflicts in Nigeria.[29] Consequently, the lack of protection for both farmers and herders increases the need for both sides to mobilize support and arm themselves for self-protection which in turn makes the lethal outcome of the disputes more frequent.

Taken together, the existing theoretical perspectives are relevant in understanding recent trends in the herder–farmer confrontations in Nigeria. However, what is relatively understudied is the extant role and impact of ethnicity on the transformation of the conflict. Generally, the literature on the relationship between ethnicity and violent conflicts in Africa argues that mobilized by elite and/or conflict entrepreneurs, or rooted in the struggle against perceived and real marginalization, attachment to ethnic identities, whether such identities are socially or primordially constructed, do generate grievances, ethnic fears, or reignite ethnic animosity in ways that lead to the outbreak and prolongation of interethnic violence including civil wars.[30]

Accordingly, ethnicity is considered inherently conflictual also because it has been politicized and made divisive.[31]

In Nigeria, armed attacks of Fulani herdsmen on farming communities and villages have been largely framed as ethnic violence directed against sedentary farmers, most of whom are Christians and Yoruba, the Tiv amongst others. Similarly, Fulani herders contextualize a sense of victimhood in relation to "their perceived treatment as non-indigenes and second-class citizens to sedentary farmers."[32] Shared perceptions of victimhood linked to notions of identity contestations have, therefore, mobilized, fueled, and reinforced reprisal attacks by both farmers and herders, respectively, thereby creating ethnic rivalry that presents a security dilemma in the country. In this sense, the herder–farmer conflict contributes to ethnic hatred between ethnic groups in Nigeria within the context of what Ali Mazrui calls retribalization of politics.[33] Ethnic identity politics underlined by cultural agency has emerged and remains a critical variable in understanding both the onset and intensity of the herder–farmer conflict in Nigeria.[34]

WHO ARE THE HERDERS AND FARMERS? THE CRISIS OF CITIZENSHIP, IDENTITY POLITICS, AND THE RECONFIGURATION OF HERDER–FARMER VIOLENCE

Herders and farmers have been distinguished based on their ethnic and social origins. A conceptual distinction, some have argued, is difficult to sustain in reality and practice—not the least, because the dialectic of long-term economic sustainability strategy adopted by both herders and farmers has sometimes underlined transitions from pastoralism to farming and vice versa, transitions that sometimes lead to conflict over resource competition amongst individual herders or farmers.[35] At the household level, some farmers keep goat, sheep, and cattle while some pastoralists also practice farming. Beyond the household level, seasonal variations in weather and environmental conditions, and underscored by economic survivability motivations, herders and farmers do switch occupations.[36] Thus, defining herders as strictly Fulani, for example, is conceptually misleading. Indeed, agropastoral adaptation strategy is important and remains a regular practice across West Africa.[37] Therefore, "it would be misleading to think of agriculture and pastoralism as two mutually exclusive systems; many pastoralists practice agriculture and as many agriculturalists keep livestock in West Africa."[38] Besides, many who rear cattle are not necessarily Fulani people. For example, "Fulbe who identify as pastoralists may have no animals and make a living by farming, while young men from agricultural groups may work as salaried herders for Fulbe pastoralists."[39] Nevertheless, nomadic pastoralism is historically and strongly associated generally and overarchingly with the Fulani people across West Africa. Farmers, whose occupation requires settling in one place, generally consider the Fulani as having a unique culture, not only because they are pastoralists who concentrate on herding livestock, but also because they consider their language, dressing, and eating habits to be different from those of the sedentary farming population. Again, herders tend to be almost exclusively Muslims in their religious beliefs and are of the Hausa-Fulani ethnic group, while many sedentary farmers tend to be traditional animist worshipers and Christians, the majority of whom belong to other ethnicities. By the geographical and cultural configurations of Nigeria, the Hausa-Fulani, who are mainly Muslims, and also practice nomadic pastoralism, dominate the northern part of the country while in the south, ethnic groups such as the Yoruba, Igbo, and other ethnic minorities primarily share Christianity as their religion and tend to be sedentary farmers. This geographical division of Nigeria reinforces the link between religion, ethnic nationalism, and identity-based conflicts in the country.

Furthermore, the mobile nature of herders constitutes a form of identity in itself. Constantly moving from one place to the other in search of greener pastures for their livestock, herders are conceived as a 'landless' group of people in their relationship to the sedentary farmers who claim indigeneity to, and ownership of lands.[40]

In Nigeria, when interpretations of the indigenous versus migrant dichotomy interact with wider religious, social, and political issues, such as having access to state resources and opportunities, they underscore ethnic cleavages further and reinforce the saliency of identity politics and identity contestations. These contestations form an enduring source of controversy and conflict between herders and farmers in Nigeria. This has been further complicated by the fact that the Nigerian state is an underdeveloped and multiethnic society, one that has not, for example, practically resolved the question of who is a citizen and an indigene. In fact, for Maiangwa, the whole problem of herder–farmer conflicts can be reduced to struggles over indigeneity claims linked to the larger unresolved issue of citizenship in Nigeria.[41]

The roots of the indigeneity and citizenship contestations in Nigeria, as in much of Africa, lie in the legacy of European colonialism. Mammood Mamdani points specifically to how European colonial "policy of indirect rule underpinned the institutionalization of ethnic difference and the reproduction of ethnic identity into particular forms of political identities."[42] In a broader sense, Mamdani argues that the nature of colonial state making in Africa, profoundly grounded in indirect rule sets in motion, processes of politicization and evolution of cultural ethnic identities into complex political identities such as the indigene/settler dichotomy, religious, and regional identity. In the context of Nigeria, British imperialism helped to deepen ethnic distinctions between the Fulani people and other ethnic groups, a process that evolved first with Fulani migration into northern Nigeria in the 14th century as a result of the Trans Saharan trade and later consolidated by the Fulani Jihadist war of the 19th century. How both processes contributed to a wave of Fulani migration into northern Nigeria, the evolution of indigenous and non-indigenous identity, and ultimately constituted major conflict cleavages between herders and farmers since then to-date deserves a brief interrogation.

As early as the 11th century, Islam has been practiced as a religion in northern Nigeria even though it had few adherents or followers because the Bori cult was still prevalent amongst the people. Bori cult worship was a pre-Islamic religious practice amongst the ancient Hausa people in which the belief in spirits dominated, influenced, and regulated social, cultural, economic, and political life in northern Nigeria. Adherents believe that performing Bori rituals provide healing for the sick and protect the people from danger and these benefits amongst others endeared the Bori cult to the people.[43] However, between the 14th and 16th centuries, Islam gained significant visibility and a foothold in the region. The Trans Saharan trade was significant in the history of the growth and spread of Islam across West Africa and, in particular, in the formation and construction of ethno-religious Fulani identity in northern Nigeria. In fact, trade and Islam were intricately linked. Falola and Heaton, for example, argue that "as trade spread to savannas and Sahel, Islam spread with it."[44] Fulani traders from Sudan and Songhay were the major agents in the spread of Islam in established Hausa states in Northern region, as in Kanem Bornu. Articles of trade between the Fulani traders and indigenous Hausa people initially involved gold and slaves but later expanded to include other goods such as weapons, salt, pepper, and kola nut.[45] A remarkable feature of the spread of Islam during the era of the Trans Saharan trade was that it was largely peaceful. The trade also contributed to the gradual establishment of Fulani settlements and Fulani identity in the north.

The second wave of Fulani migration into northern Nigeria resulted from a Jihadist expedition in the 19th century. Led by Usman dan Fodio, the Jihad was motivated by the desire to spread puritanical Islam. It was claimed that Islam worshippers in the north were not deeply rooted in the teaching and practices of the Prophet Mohammed. This claim was contradicted by the situation in Kanem Bornu, where the practice of Islam was very strong and well established before the attacks of Usman dan Fodio. To some, therefore, the Jihadist war was fundamentally driven by political objectives: the establishment of Fulani supremacy and political control over Hausaland by the Fulani. The establishment of the Sokoto Caliphate in 1804 and the imposition of a theocratic state in the whole of the northern region founded on Islamic traditions and values spoke to this fundamental political objective of the Islamization agenda of Usman dan Fodio. As Falola and Heaton have observed, " . . . in the space of just over five years, the religious movement of Usman dan Fodio had united all of previously fragmented Hausaland under one Islamic state, and within 30 years this became one of the largest states ever established in west Africa."[46] The Islamization and expansionist motives of Usman dan Fodio were extended to the Middle Belt and Yorubaland. Importantly, as Islam spread to other parts of Nigeria, especially into the Middle Belt region or to central Nigeria, and later into Yorubaland and other parts of the south, Fulani settlements and Fulani identity were established, formed, and consolidated. According to Moritz, in northern Nigeria, for example, Fulani pastoralists participated in jihads to rule over and enslave non-Muslim people at the beginning of the 19th century when they established the Sokoto Caliphate.[47] Per Moritz, "the resentment between these groups remains strong today and when conflicts occur the idioms of war and slavery are often used to describe the other group."[48]

ETHNICITY AND THE NATURE OF STATE REPONSES TO HERDER–FARMER CONFLICT AND IMPLICATIONS FOR ESCALATION

Ethnicity entrenches perceptions of incompatibility of goals between the pastoralists and farmers in Nigeria and thus shapes the nature of state responses and the evolving dynamics of the escalation of the herder–farmer conflict. In Nigeria, struggles over state resources and representation in national institutions are more often made "on the grounds of ethnic, communal, religious, indigenous, regional and geopolitical (zonal) identities than on the basis of state recognized subnational units.[49] Consequently, typical of most African states, the Nigerian state and its bureaucracy are composed of political elites and people from most of the different ethnic groups of the country, who more or less represent the state and "play the part of 'delegates' of their kin groups or ethnic groups."[50] Given this character of ethnic organization of the Nigerian state, social cultural forces play an important role in shaping the nature of state responses in an attempt to resolve the herder–farmer conflict in Nigeria. In order to effectively explore the impact of ethnicity on the nature of state response and its implications for violent escalation of this conflict, we must further clarify the concepts of ethnicity and ethnic groups.

According to Nnoli, ethnicity refers to "a social phenomenon associated with interactions among members of different ethnic groups."[51] Osaghea adds that these interactions are characterized by competition, conflict, or cooperation and more importantly, whether the interaction is competitive, cooperative, or conflictual, there is always the tendency by ethnic groups to employ or mobilize ethnic identity and ethnic difference to gain advantage.[52]

This process is often characterized as ethnic politics. The centrality of ethnic politics rests on the fundamental belief in a common identity and corporate consciousness that tend to underlie the basis for differentiating one social group from the other, raising issues of 'othering' and discrimination. For Oyovbaire, therefore, ethnicity means a state of affairs whereby, in the process of a country's modernization, ethnic groups tend to develop corporate consciousness and to define this consciousness in terms that are based not on a common language, religion, culture or history per se, but based significantly on a sense of socioeconomic exclusiveness towards other ethnic groups.[53]

The definition of an ethnic group, on the other hand, lays emphasis on important distinctive linguistic, cultural, and territorial markers that form the basis for identification and differentiation of one ethnic group from another. These attributes include common language, culture, myth of origin, and territory. Accordingly, ethnic groups have been defined as "social formations distinguished by the communal character of their boundaries, which include language and culture."[54] Similarly, Osaghae defines an ethnic group as "a group whose members share a common identity and affinity based on common language and culture, myth of origin and territorial homeland, which have become basis for differentiating 'us' from 'them,' and upon which people act."[55]

Drawing on the above cultural conceptualizations of an ethnic group, what is very clear is that ethnicity is a social categorization where a group is ascribed with common identity that distinguishes it from others.[56] Nevertheless, ethnicity has no permanent boundary as it can be subjected to changing group characteristics.[57] At the individual level, constructivist interpretations of ethnicity would argue that ethnic identity can be constructed, reconstructed, and reconfirmed. For example, it is not uncommon to observe that those seeking employment in Nigeria, especially in national institutions located outside of their ethnic states of origin, do falsify their certificates of indigeneship in order to get jobs. In this way, economic considerations and the desire to take material advantage trump rigidly held ethnic and communal identity, thus contradicting the strong corporate character that tends to underline ethnic belonging. In this regard, perception of economic insecurity plays a key role and shapes how people make use of ethnicity as a livelihood and coping strategy in Nigeria. This is because preferences and self-interests of individual members of an ethnic group vary with the social environments, circumstances, and contexts. Similarly, from an instrumentalist perspective, it is argued that ethnicity has been a tool for political control and manipulation by elites for personal rather than a group's gains. In fact, the very idea of ethnic identity has been contested. Anderson argues that ethnic groups are social constructions and could be described as imagined political communities invented by a figment of human imagination.[58] To the extent of this artificiality of an ethnic group, ethnic conflict speaks more to private rather than group interests. But others would contend that "since ethnic conflict takes place between groups, it is important to take into account the possibility that people are not only motivated by self-interest, but also care about their group."[59] Moreover, "identity is often very durable, creating lasting attachments and strongly affecting individual behavior."[60]

Clearly, ethnicity and political elitism interact in such a way that Nigerians, irrespective of the ethnic origins, are victims of state elites in one way or the other. For example, during electoral campaigns, political elites appeal to ethnic sentiments to win elections and get access to state power ostensibly for primitive accumulation of wealth.[61] Nevertheless, primordialism, the assumption that identities are fixed, remains a powerful political force in Nigeria. It responds to the historicity of communalism in Africa as well as the legacies of British colonial state making.

The British colonial powers cobbled diverse ethnic groups together and engendered regional separateness to the extent that non-material aspects of statehood in Nigeria remain largely underdeveloped as its institutionalization. There is no common national identity that has been forged amongst the diverse ethnic groups in Nigeria as a rallying point for state building. Ethnicity presents such a strong element of identity that it determines access to state services and other economic opportunities. This is further complicated by the fact that the state is not objectively neutral and cannot be treated as an abstract entity denuded itself of ethnic identity or with a single overriding interest. At present, the Nigerian state is more or less a federation of ethnic groups and as Azam has observed, this is a typical African organization of society where the state bureaucracy and the political elites are composed of people from most of the different ethnic groups of the country.[62] The Federal Character Principle, which is enshrined in the Nigerian constitution, supports Azam's argument. Premised on the logic of promoting ethnic balancing and political unity, the Federal Character Principle provides that the appointment and promotion of civil servants in Nigeria's bureaucracy including admission of students into tertiary institutions must take into consideration the ethnic origins and ethnic spread of the candidates. What this suggests is that ethnicity is not only legally institutionalized and enforced, but it also shapes relationship of the people to the state and to one another through the state.[63] It is within this institutional, structural, and historic context that an understanding of how ethnicity shapes the nature of state responses to the herder–farmer conflicts can be meaningfully appreciated.

The first tenure of the Mohammadu Buhari's regime as a democratic president, 2015–2019, significantly highlights how strong primordial attachment to ethnic group sentiments impacted negatively the role of the state in responding to the crisis of herder–farmer conflicts and contributed to its escalation in

Nigeria. The emergence of Buhari as the President of Nigeria saw a new wave of deadly attacks by herdsmen on farmers and villagers across the Nigerian federation for a variety of motivations including to secure grazing fields and wider questions of land ownership, territorial, and identity contestations.[64] This is not to argue that armed attacks by herdsmen and herder–farmer conflicts are entirely new in postcolonial Nigerian history or to say the state has been more effective in responding to it. No. The conflict has been there since the 1980s, but was mainly confined to northern Nigeria, especially in the Middle-Belt region. However, the point of emphasis is that the recent escalation of attacks of the herdsmen across Nigeria, and the response particularly in southern Nigeria during the current administration, have been predicated on the arguments that when Buhari, a Fulani from Katsina state, assumed the presidency, the herdsmen appeared to have been emboldened by the politics of ethnicity. This correlation is hinged on the response gap between the rising incidence of herdsmen attacks and the apparent demonstration of lack of political will on the part of the Nigerian state under the leadership of Buhari to contain the rampaging herdsmen.[65]

The dominant perception in Nigeria, especially amongst Nigerians in affected communities, is that President Buhari has unfairly favored the herdsmen, who are perceived to be his Fulani kinsmen in Nigeria's hyper-ethnicized politics. Buhari is a life patron of the Miyetti Allah Cattle Breeders Association of Nigeria. Buhari's ethnic connections to the Fulani ethnic group and background in pastoralism tend to undermine the will to act decisively, hence "the nature of the security response of his administration to herdsmen violence has been particularly questionable."[66] For example, when President Buhari ordered a military crackdown on the rampaging herdsmen, it was not backed by any concrete action to show a commitment to protecting vulnerable Nigerians' lives. Some specific instances are illustrative. "In February 2016, following public outcry over attacks by herders that killed scores of people in 10 farming villages in the Agatu local area of north-central Benue state, Buhari ordered an investigation, but nothing came out of it."[67] In fact, the Benue killings on New Year's Day 2018 and other subsequent attacks are indications of the ferocity of the herdsmen versus weak and deficient verbal condemnations by the President without practical actions to stop the carnage. Similarly, on July 15, 2016, the Chief of Defense, General Gabriel Olonisakin, announced "Operation Accord" to stop the violence. Again, nothing more came of that campaign.[68] Beyond the security lapses, the Buhari government on March 3, 2016, announced through Audu Ogbeh, the Minister of Agriculture, that it was sending a bill to the National Assembly to prohibit cattle from roaming in cities and villages in Nigeria. To date, the cattle banning bill remains a promise cruelly betrayed. This is the case because herdsmen continue to act with impunity. In fact, they are recently considered more deadly and more dangerous than the Boko Haram sect. In 2018, the Global Terrorism Index reported that herders killed more Nigerians than Boko Haram, noting that killings by herdsmen were responsible for the majority of terror-related deaths in Nigeria, 1,158 fatalities.[69] Regrettably, the federal government under the leadership of Buhari had failed to demonstrate strong political will to contain the violent activities of the herdsmen across the country, thereby fueling perceptions, especially in much of southern Nigeria, that the "President has deliberately turned a blind eye to the herdsmen security crisis because he comes from the same Fulani ethnic group."[70]

These ethnic sentiments compelled attention and were further given credence when the same President Buhari swiftly declared the Indigenous People of Biafra (IPOB) a terrorist group and authorised the militarisation of the southeast. These actions of President Buhari have been viewed as "political suppression of legitimate dissent,"[71] which had been led by the IPOB in their struggle for an independent state for the Igbo people in the southeast. It will be recalled that the IPOB has since 2012 embarked on several protests against the federal government for what they perceived as deliberate political marginalization of the Igbo people in the leadership of Nigeria. One of the claims of marginalization is that since political independence in 1960, the Igbo people as a major ethnic group in Nigeria had been denied the opportunity of producing a president for the country and have been deliberately skewed against in the provision of infrastructural development projects by the federal government. It is on this perceived marginalization that the IPOB predicates its struggle for a Biafran state, which the Buhari regime had responded to, basically through military repression strategies in ways that did not apply equally to the activities of herdsmen and the security threats they pose to the nation. For example, it was only in November 2021 that bandits were declared terrorists by the Buhari-led federal government.

The support of double standards in the response of Buhari to the Indigenous People of Biafra and the herdsmen's security dilemmas are explained by Weaver as grounded in political ethnicity.[72] "The declaration of the IPOB as a terrorist organisation and discursive constructions of security threats posed by the group raised questions of securitisation within the context of politics of protection and national security."[73] Nigeria's Senate denounced the deployment of Operation Python Dance and set up a committee "to probe the alleged violations of human rights committed by the soldiers. Similarly, the United States' government promptly rejected claims that the IPOB was a terrorist group. Beyond the issue of IPOB and herdsmen security crisis, Buhari has also been accused of making political appointments and recruitments into the civil service that highlight ethnic patronizing."[74] Appointments favored the northern region so much that it was in violation of Nigeria's federal character principle that emphasizes ethnic integration as noted earlier. Currently, about

80% of the security chiefs appointed by Buhari are northerners. Apart from outright violations of the Federal Character Principle, Buhari's alleged political indifference to herdsmen killings of farmers has fueled perceptions that the Nigerian state is implicated in condoning Fulani armed attacks on farming communities in Nigeria.

The policy of cattle colony initiated by the Buhari government in 2017 to address the rising incidence of herder–farmer conflicts in Nigeria also draws attention to how group identification and ethnic cleavages shape responses to peacebuilding efforts and increase the risks of ethnic violence. At the center of the cattle colony proposal was that state governments would donate lands for grazing by herders and as of 2018, 16 states presumably from the north had agreed to the policy as reported by Audu Ogbeh, the Minister of Agriculture.[75] The cattle colony policy was conceived in the context of a joint venture between the federal and state governments. Apart from contributing to ending the incessant conflicts between herders and farmers, the participating state governments would benefit from social facilities associated with the colonies such as improved roads, a school for nomads' children, and health facilities, all of which was to be funded by the federal government.

The cattle colony proposal was, however, rejected by the states, especially the southern states, for two reasons rooted primarily in ethnicity. First, the rationale behind donating public lands for private businesses of cattle rearing that excluded the farmers was questioned. The predominant argument is that Fulani herders were singled out for favor by the federal government because the President is Fulani. He was rewarding the herdsmen who had demonstrated high propensity to violence and armed intimidation in Nigeria. Second and more fundamental, the cattle policy presented a cattle colonization project aimed at planting Fulani herdsmen across the country and the subtle but strategic implementation of the Islamization agenda of the Hausa-Fulani group in Nigeria. In other words, the cattle policy proposal was interpreted as a disguise for recolonization and the extension of the Jihadist experience of the 19th century. On the whole, the political climate engendered by ethnicity frustrated the cattle colony proposal as those in the south drew on idioms and memories of Jihadist war of the 19th century and it associated enslavement and territorial conquest to describe and reject the cattle policy. The change of name of the cattle colony proposal to the Rural Grazing Area (RUGA) by the Buhari government did not convince the people in the south that it was not a grand strategy for Islamization, Fulanization, and land grabbing. Beyond the Buhari era, ethnicity has historically shaped responses to the herder–farmer conflict even at the level of the state governments in ways that resolving the conflict and building lasting peace between herders and farmers have been problematic. In the Plateau state, Higazi shows that claims and counterclaims over indigenous rights and exclusion have influenced local narratives and perceptions of threat, security, and identity implications of the lingering crisis of herder–farmer conflicts due to the political and material benefits indigenous status provides by giving access to the Plateau State government and its administrative and patrimonial structures.[76] The main finding is that "the ways in which the violence is understood—as a direct physical experience and socially and historically—shapes both the Plateau State government's involvement in the conflicts, and local responses."[77] Higazi rationalizes that "with the influx of outsiders over the past century, predominantly Christian indigenes seek to control local access to the state and avoid political domination by non-Plateau groups, especially Hausa-Fulani Muslims."[78] Interestingly, "access to the state varies significantly through time and between indigenous groups, as it depends on their size and level of representation within any particular administration."[79] The case of the Benue state is not radically different from the Plateau in terms of contestations between indigenes versus migrant Fulani herdsmen strangers. A key contentious provision of the 2017 Benue State Open Grazing Prohibition and Ranches Establishment Law is that it imposes stringent conditions upon potential ranchers based on their indigene status. Ranching is the practice of raising herds of animals or cattle on a large farm and ranchers are people who own or operate on the ranch.

According to the 2017 Benue State Law, prospective ranchers who are not categorized as native in the Benue State must access at the same time they apply for permission. This process necessitates an environmental impact assessment with many levels of assessment and seeking approval from the landowner, head of the family, and the designated heads of family.[80] The important issue here is that the creation and reinforcement of social and ethnic distinctions between native and non-native in the application process by the law in an environment that is already volatile is both a source of discrimination and potential source for conflicts. In fact, rejecting the law, *Miyetti Allah Kautal Hore,* went to court to challenge its legality on the grounds that it contradicts the Nigerian constitution.[81]

ETHNICITY, ETHNIC SECURITY DILEMMA, AND THE ESCALATION OF HERDER–FARMER CONFLICTS

One of the consequences of the rising incidence of herder–farmer conflicts is the growing ethnic security dilemma. In an attempt to secure their livelihood from the threats and violence associated with the conflict, both herders and farmers tend to retreat into the ethnicization of protection with ramifications for the escalation of the conflict. The point is that the patterns of social identification shape conflict risks between herders and farmers. The conflict itself also shapes patterns of social identification. Both ways, the result is an increasing ethnic security dilemma that leads to the further ethnicization of protection in a context where the institutionalization of the state remains weak.

On the part of the herders, there is increasing militarization evident in the acquisition and use of deadly weapons such as the AK-47 to protect cattle. One major argument advanced is that pastoralists in Nigeria have militarized because they are confronted by new realities of large-scale cattle-rustling processes similar to the experience of Kenya. While this reason can explain the transition from sticks-wielding herders to AK-47 holders, organized but frequent armed attacks on farming communities by herders suggest other motives. His analysis explains that the proliferation of weapons has become a defining feature of herdsmen activities in Nigeria which put farming communities under constant intimidation and threat.

The farming communities have responded to these emerging security challenges posed by armed confrontations of herdsmen in two major ways. First, increasingly resorting to community vigilantism takes on the character of ethnic protection against Fulani invaders. The second approach is community arming. By arming the community, local communities as political collectivities distinct from militant or militia groups acquire sophisticated weapons and build community armories for purposes of self-protection that map onto ethnic identity preservation. Both community vigilantism and community arming processes are not new in Nigeria. For example, prior to the incursion of herdsmen aggression, Bisina's research in the Niger Delta shows that "most communities in the region have local armories that are located outside of the communities and so, a mere raid on a community could be an exercise in futility as arms in private hands are less than 10% of the total arms stockpiled by the communities in secret armories."[82] Community arming is a prevalent phenomenon in regions or areas associated with violent conflicts in Nigeria, especially because in most cases the Nigerian state has not been effective in upholding its security functions. In 2016, Theophilus Danjuma, a former defense minister of Nigeria, called on local communities to arm themselves in self-defense against the rampaging by militarized herdsmen who have been described as local versions of the Boko Haram terrorist groups. Danjuma's call was interpreted by some as the legitimization of community arming process that questions the institutional legitimate role of the Nigerian state as a security provider. However, as local communities fashion their own security infrastructure, it argued its own internal logic for insecurity and peacebuilding. This internal logic expresses itself in the competitive struggle amongst local communities for acquisitions of superior armament, a competition sustained by the need to promote both collective security and protect local identity. According to Moritz, the former governor of Ekiti state, Ayo Fayose, for example, recommended communities in Ekiti state to spray poisonous herbicides on their farmlands in order to keep Fulani herders away while vigilante groups cheered them for defending their territories.[83] In this sense, the political logic of deterrence results in a sort of local arms race that intensifies the ethnic security dilemma. Whether within the context of herders of farmers, the politicization of cultural differences and the construction of identity form crucial elements in reinforcing the ethnic security dilemma and the escalation of the conflict. The support by Myatti Alalah for the herdsmen, for example, goes beyond the protection of its professional members to include protection of ethno-religious identities that are believed to be at stake in the conflict. So, it is with the framing of the conflict by sedentary farming communities. The entire ethnic community is threatened and should be protected from the Fulani invaders who often attack the farming communities at night. More recently, almost all the states in southern Nigeria had enacted laws, banning open grazing of cattle as a response to violent atrocities of herdsmen while those in the north refused to do so. The northern governors perceive such laws as targeting the Hausa-Fulani people.

CONCLUSION

The structural issue of ethnic identity contestation and politics of belonging in Nigeria is a major trigger of the herder–farmer conflict which fuels its escalation. Ethnic identification shapes the nature of responses to the conflict such that reconciliation between herders and farmers and the effective resolution of the conflict have become increasingly difficult. For example, President Buhari's alleged political indifference to herdsmen killings has fueled perceptions that the Nigerian state is implicated in sustaining Fulani armed aggression against farmers and farming communities due to his being Fulani with a personal deep cultural experience of and attachment to pastoralism. Furthermore, the chapter argues that there is an interaction between ethnicity politicization and mobilization, and the ethnic security dilemma and the escalation of herder–farmer conflicts. This manifests in responses by both farmers and herders to security threat implications of the conflict that take on the character of the ethnicization of protection. As herdsmen acquire and deploy sophisticated weaponry to protect cattle including launching attacks on farming communities, so the latter resort to community vigilantism and community arming processes to secure their livelihood and local communities. Both ways, the political logic of deterrence results in a sort of local arms race that increases violence rather than security. Both politicize cultural differences built on the construction of identity, which reinforces mobilization along ethnic lines and produces greater insecurity. What all this suggests is that any meaningful attempt to resolve the herder–farmer conflicts must respond to and address the sociocultural dynamics interconnected with ethnic identities and interests within the context of how identity becomes politicized to mobilize to sustain conflicts rather than to overcome them.

NOTES

1. Anastasia Sandra Akerjiir, "Increasing Farmer-Herder Conflict in Nigeria: An Assessment of the Clashes Between The Fulani Herdsmen and Indigenous Farmers in Ukpabi-Nimbo Community Enugu State" (M.Sc diss., Wageningen University, 2018), 46.

2. Ibid.

3. Blessing Nonye Onyima and Victor Chidubem Iwuoha, "New Dimensions to Pastoralists–Farmers Conflicts and Sustainable Agricultural Development in Agadama and Uwheru Communities, Niger Delta," *African Security* 8, no. 3 (2015): 166.

4. Amnesty International, *Harvest of Death: Three Years of Bloody Clashes between Farmers and Herders in Nigeria* (Abuja: Amnesty International Ltd, 2018), 6.

5. Ibid.; Melvin Small and David J. Singer, *Resort to Arms: International and Civil Wars, 1816–1980* (Beverly Hills: Sage Publications, Inc, 1982), 213.

6. Mercy Corps, *The Economic Costs of Conflict in Nigeria* (Mercy Corps, 2015), 3.

7. Kodili Henry Chukwuma, "Constructing the Herder–Farmer Conflict as (in) Security in Nigeria," *African Security* 13, no. 1 (January 2020): 55.

8. Ibid.

9. Benjamin Maiangwa, "'Conflicting Indigeneity' and Farmer–Herder Conflicts in Postcolonial Africa," *Peace Review* 29, no. 3 (July 2017): 283.

10. Stephen Van Evera, "Primordialism Lives!," *APSA-CP: Newsletter of the Organized Section in Comparative Politics of the American Political Science Association* 12, no. 1 (2001): 20–22; Huma Baqai, "The Role of Ethnicity in the Conflict Spectrum of South Asia," *Pakistan Horizon* 57, no. 4 (October 2004): 57–68; Laura Thaut Vinson, "Disaggregating Ethnicity and Conflict Patterns: Evidence from Religious and Tribal Violence in Nigeria," *Ethnopolitics* 19, no. 1 (2018): 19–44.

11. Mark Davidheiser and Aniuska Luna, "From Complementarity to Conflict: A Historical Analysis of Farmer–Fulbe Relations in West Africa," *African Journal on Conflict Resolution* 8, no. 1 (July 2008): 78.

12. Ibid., 80–81.

13. Michael M. Horowitz, and Peter D. Little "African Pastoralism and Poverty: Some implications for Drought and Famine," in *Drought and Hunger in Africa: Denying Famine a Future*, ed. Michael H. Glantz (Cambridge: Cambridge University Press, 1987) 62; Kaderi Noagah Bukari, Papa Sow, and Jurgen Scheffran, "Cooperation and Co-Existence Between Farmers and Herders in the Midst of Violent Farmer-Herder Conflicts in Ghana," *African Studies Review* 61, no. 2 (July 2018): 80.

14. Bukari, Sow, and Scheffran, "Cooperation," 80.

15. Davidheiser and Luna, "Complementarity," 82; Mark Moritz, "Changing Contexts and Dynamics of Farmer-Herder Conflicts across West Africa," *Canadian Journal of African Studies* 40, no. 1 (2006): 2–3.

16. Maiangwa, "Conflicting Indigeneity," 283.

17. S. A. Ingawa, G. Tarawali, and R. von Kaufmann, *Grazing Reserves in Nigeria: Problems, Prospects and Policy Implication* (Addis Ababa: International Livestock Centre for Africa, 1989): 4–5.

18. Ugwumba Egbuta, "Understanding the Herder–Farmer Conflict in Nigeria," *Conflict Trends* 3 (2018), 42; U. S. Abdullahi, H. N. Daneyel, and Y. H. Aliyara, "Grazing Reserves and Pastoralism in Nigeria: A Review," *Vom Journal of Veterinary Science* 10 (2015): 138.

19. Egbuta, "Understanding," 42.

20. Chris M A Kwaja, and Bukola I Ademola-Adelehin, *Responses to Conflicts Between Farmers and Herders in Middle-Belt, Nigeria: Mapping Past Efforts and Opportunities for Violence Prevention* (Washington, D.C.: Search for Common Ground, 2018), 7; Akachi Odoemene, "Whither Peacebuilding Initiatives? The Escalation of Herder–Farmer Conflicts in Nigeria," Kujenga Amani, accessed February 18, 2019, https://kujenga-amani.ssrc.org/2017/04/07/whither-peacebuilding-initiatives-the-escalation-of-herder-farmer-conflicts-in-nigeria/.

21. Odoemene, "Whither."

22. E. Fabusoro and C. I. Sodiya, "Institutions for Collective Action among Settled Fulani Agro-Pastoralists in Southwest Nigeria," *The Journal of Agricultural Education and Extension* 17, no. 1 (February 2011): 55.

23. Val Percival, and Thomas Homer-Dixon, "Environmental Scarcity and Violent Conflict: The Case of South Africa," *Journal of Peace Research* 35, no. 3 (1998): 279–80.

24. Moritz, "Changing Contexts," 13.

25. Emmanuel Akov, "The Resource-Conflict Debate Revisited: Untangling the Case of Farmer–Herdsman Clashes in the North Central Region of Nigeria," *African Security Review* 26, no. 3 (July 2017): 289.

26. Al Chukwuma Okoli, and Cornelius O. Ogayi, "Herdsmen Militancy and Humanitarian Crisis in Nigeria: A Theoretical Briefing," *African Security Review* 27, no. 2 (April 2018): 138.

27. Ibid., 138–39; Adam Higazi, "Farmer-Pastoralist Conflicts on the Jos Plateau, Central Nigeria: Security Responses of Local Vigilantes and the Nigerian State," *Conflict, Security, & Development* 16, no. 4 (July 2016): 381–82.

28. Egbuta, "Understanding," 41; Tope Shola Akinyetun, "Staff to Gun: Fulani Herdsmen in Nigeria," *Asian Journal of Multidisciplinary Studies* 4, no. 8 (July 2016): 39–41; Azeez Olaniyan and Aliyu Yahaya, "Cows, Bandits, and Violent Conflicts: Understanding Cattle Rustling in Northern Nigeria," *Africa Spectrum* 51, no. 3 (2016): 95.

29. Olaniyan and Yahaya, "Cows," 95; Suleiman Abdullahi, Victor E., and Binta M., "The Menace of Cattle Rustling and Banditry in North-West Nigeria: A Case Study of Katsina State," *Journal of Research & Method in Education* 7, no. 6 (2017): 45–6.

30. Nicholas Sambanis, "Do Ethnic and Nonethnic Civil Wars Have the Same Causes?: A Theoretical and Empirical Inquiry," *Journal of Conflict Resolution* 43, no. 3 (2001): 263.

31. Claude Ake, "What Is the Problem of Ethnicity in Africa?" *Transformations,* 22 (1993): 1–14; Okwudiba Nnoli, *Ethnic Politics in Nigeria* (Enugu: Fourth Dimension Publishers, 1978), 5.

32. Maiangwa, "Conflicting Indigeneity," 284.

33. Ali Mazrui, "Violent Contiguity and the Politics of Retribalization in Africa," *Journal of International Affairs* 23, no. 1 (1969): 89.

34. Maiangwa, "Conflicting Indigeneity," 283.

35. Mark Breusers, Suzanne Nederlof, and Teunis van Rheenen, "Conflict or Symbiosis? Disentangling Farmer-Herdsman Relations: The Mossi and Fulbe of the Central Plateau, Burkina Faso," *The Journal of Modern African Studies* 36, no. 3 (1998): 361.

36. Ruth Mace et al., "Transitions Between Cultivation and Pastoralism in Sub-Saharan Africa," *Current Anthropology* 34, no. 4 (1993): 363, 371.

37. Ann Waters-Bayer and Wolfgang Bayer, "Coming to Terms: Interactions between Immigrant Fulani Cattle-Keepers and Indigenous Farmers in Nigeria's Sub-humid Zone," *Cahiers d'Études Africaines* 34, nos. 133, 135 (1994): 216.

38. Moritz, "Changing Contexts," 9.

39. Ibid., 23.

40. Maiangwa, "Conflicting Indigeneity," 283.

41. Ibid., 283–84.

42. Mahmood Mamdani, "Beyond Settler and Native as Political Identities: Overcoming the Political Legacy of Colonialism," *Comparative Studies in Society and History* 43, no. 4 (2001): 653–61; Mahmood Mamdani, "Making Sense of Political Violence in Postcolonial Africa," *Identity, Culture, and Politics* 32, no. 2 (2002): 6–11.

43. Umar Habila Dadem Danfulani, "Factors Contributing to the Survival of the Bori Cult in Northern Nigeria," *Numen* 46, no. 4 (1999): 412.

44. Toyin Falola and Matthew M. Heaton, *A History of Nigeria* (Cambridge: Cambridge University Press, 2008), 32.

45. Ibid., 33.

46. Ibid., 65.

47. Moritz, "Changing Contexts," 9–10.

48. Moritz, "Changing Contexts," 10.

49. Eghosa E. Osaghae, "Foreword: Nigerian Federalism—A Project in Crisis," in *Nigerian Federalism in Crisis: Critical Perspectives and Political Options*, eds. Ebere Onwudiwe and Rotimi T. Suberu (Ibadan: John Archers, 2005), vii.

50. Jean-Paul Azam, "The Redistributive State and Conflicts in Africa," *Journal of Peace Research* 38, no. 4 (2001): 437.

51. Nnoli, *Ethnic Politics,* 5.

52. Eghosa E. Osaghae, *Structural Adjustment and Ethnicity in Nigeria* (Uppsala: Nordiska Afrikaninstiutet, 1995), 11.

53. S. Egite Oyoybaire, "On the Concept of Ethnicity and African Politics," *Présence Africaine*, no. 92 (1974): 180.

54. Nnoli, *Ethnic Politics*, 5.

55. Osaghae, *Structural Adjustment*, 1.

56. Noah Echa Attah, "Contesting Exclusion in a Multiethnic State: Rethinking Ethnic Nationalism in Nigeria," *Social Identities* 19, no. 5 (September 2013): 608.

57. Fredrik Barth, *Ethnic Groups and Boundaries: The Social Organization of Culture Difference* (Long Grove: Waveland Press, 1998): 17–18.

58. Benedict Anderson, *Imagined Communities: Reflections on the Origin and Spread of Nationalism* (London: Versp, 1983), 48–58.

59. Nicholas Sambanis and Moses Shayo, "Social Identities and Ethnic Conflict," *American Political Science Review* 107, no. 2 (2013): 295.

60. Ibid.

61. *Editor's note:* For more information, please see Chapter 3 of this volume.

62. Azam, "Redistributive," 437.

63. Mamdani, "Making Sense," 11.

64. Emmanuel Terngu Vanger and Bernard Ugochukwu Nwosu, "Institutional parameters that condition farmer–herder conflicts in Tivland of Benue State, Nigeria," *African Security Review* 29, no. 1 (January 2020): 20.

65. Kialee Nyiayaana, "Voting without Choosing? Ethnic Voting Behavior and Voting Patterns in Nigeria's 2015 Presidential Election and Implications for Institutionalization of Social Conflicts," NOKOKO Institute of African Studies, vol. 7, 2019, 104.

66. International Crisis Group, *Herders against Farmers: Nigeria's Expanding Deadly Conflict* (Brussels: International Crisis Group, September 19, 2017), 11.

67. Ibid.

68. Ibid.

69. Cletus Ukpong, "Herders Killed More Nigerians in 2018 Than Boko Haram—Report," *Premium Times*, November 21, 2019, https://www.premiumtimesng.com/news/headlines/364355-herders-killed-more-nigerians-in-2018-than-boko-haram-report.html.

70. Kialee Nyiayaana, "Voting without Choosing? Ethnic Voting Behavior and Voting Patterns in Nigeria's 2015 Presidential Election and Implications for Institutionalization of Social Conflicts," NOKOKO Institute of African Studies, vol. 7, 2019, 105.

71. Ibid., 105.

72. Ole Wæver, "Aberystwyth, Paris, Copenhagen: New Schools in Security Theory and the Origins between Core and Periphery," (paper presented at Montreal International Security Association Conference, Montreal, March 2004), 13.

73. Ibid.; Barry Buzan, Ole Wæver, and Jaap De Wilde, *Security: A New Framework for Analysis* (Boulder: Lynne Rienner Publishers, 1997), 29.

74. Ibid.

75. Emeka Omeihe, "Cattle Colonisation!," *The Nation*, January 22, 2018, https://thenationonlineng.net/cattle-colonisation/.

76. Higazi, "Farmer-Pastoralist Conflicts," 370.

77. Ibid., 365.

78. Ibid., 370.

79. Ibid.

80. Chris M. A. Kwaja, and Bukola I. Ademola-Adelehin, *The Implications of the Open Grazing Prohibition and Ranches Establishment Law on Farmer-Herder Relations in the Middle Belt of Nigeria* (Washington, DC: Search for Common Ground, December 2017), 8.

81. Ibid.

82. Joel Bisina, "Reducing Small Arms, Increasing Safety and Security and Minimizing Conflicts in the Niger Delta Region," (paper presented at a Roundtable organized by African Strategic and Peace Research Group, Benin City, Nigeria, June 2003), 8.

83. Chukwuma, "Constructing the Herder–Farmer Conflict," 65.

7

How Rwanda Transformed
Identity Post-Genocide

Céline A. Jacquemin

The topic of ethnic identity and transformation in Rwanda was first examined in the seminal works by Catherine Newbury in her 1975 dissertation and then published in her 1988 book.[1] Another study had looked at Rwandan ethnicity or Hutu and Tutsi identity previously, Maquet published in 1967, where he suggested that tribalism and identity were immutable and failed to see how the politicization of identity had helped the oppressed majority Hutu mobilize against both the local Tutsi monarchy and against Belgian colonial power. Armed with an exclusionary nationalist ideology that originated in Hutu Power (PARMEHUTU) to carry out a revolution for independence, Hutu carried out large-scale massacres of Tutsi during their struggle for Rwanda's independence from Belgium and forced out even larger numbers of Tutsi into exile into Uganda.[2] By the early 1990s, the civil war in Rwanda and the 1988 massacres in Burundi drew attention to Newbury's work that provided a much richer understanding of the political and economic implications of being Hutu or Tutsi in Rwanda.[3] My own research examined Rwanda since the mid-1990s and questioned particularly how the international community had framed these massive human rights violations and how in turn it had impacted their response.[4] The 1994 Rwandan genocide against Tutsi validated what Newbury's work explained about how group identity of previously socioeconomic categories of Hutu and Tutsi had been politicized. Her original works from 1975 and 1988 provided a more contextualized assessment of the implications of how being Hutu or Tutsi had changed over time and mobilized Hutu against Tutsi to the egregious events that accompanied the struggle for independence from 1959 to 1963.

My first research sought to understand what had pushed over 1.5 million Rwandans to walk across into Goma, Zaire, in June 1994.[5] This inquiry led me directly to examine the 4 years prior with the civil war and the short-lived peace agreement that led to the 1994 Rwandan Genocide. To understand these events required looking into the background of the 1994 Genocide against Tutsi which led me to delve deeper into the questions of ethnic identity and its politicization.[6] My work explored the transformation of the country over the past two decades for which I investigated the consolidation of Rwandan national identity and the efforts even throughout the diaspora to support the country's development as a whole and the open invitation to return or visit the homeland for any and all Rwandans.[7] More recently, I started questioning the motivation that drove some Rwandans I knew well, to sacrifice for their country in often unexpected ways. There was the professor in California who gave up her tenure and US citizenship to go serve the current government as Rwandan Ambassador, the former cultural attaché at the Embassy who decided after 3 years in the US to return and start a business in Kigali, and many youths I met at the Rwanda Days or during Kwibuka Commemorations who yearn to go home, after years in the US, aspiring to make a difference for their country. These youths were completing their university education in the US or in Canada and they fully intended to return to Rwanda after graduation to serve their country. These trends have made Rwanda an African country with a brain gain while so many of its neighbors are hard pressed to hold on to their talent.[8] What is it that Rwandans see as the imperative to serve their country despite already realized opportunities for wealth and success abroad? How is it that so many Rwandans, inside and outside Rwanda, have a level of commitment to their nation's development project that defies most conventional wisdom? These questions led to the close examination of the elements of identity transformation the Rwandan government undertook alongside its mobilized population. I investigated the ways in which the government supports citizens' initiatives to build an inclusive and unifying Rwandan citizenship identity. The government brought back the cultural tradition of community work, known as Umuganda, the monthly required day of service within one's community to build schools, hospitals, or clean and repair streets, dig new water wells, or establish new community centers, etc. Several types of national efforts have anchored the identity transformation campaign integrated in the nation building project where all Rwandans are called upon to participate.

This chapter surveys some of the central elements and processes for identity transformation. First, it examines closely the practice of Umuganda that was brought back a few years after the genocide. How has Umuganda helped to consolidate the mobilization, commitment, and realization of both identity transformation and development at the same time? Then, we look at other ways that Rwandans have engaged entire communities in healing and rec-onciliation processes with the Gacaca courts. Even if these were not perfect in bringing justice, these community-based traditional tribunals provided the means to include victims, perpetrators, and community members in forging practical and inclusive forward- looking solutions. Next, the chapter turns to Rwanda's radio project *Musekeweya,* intended to support the transformation of identity by promoting community-based and inclusive, peaceful ways of resolving conflicts and ethical dilemmas. The analysis looks for how these approaches to identity transformation in the context of community proj-ects, community justice, and culturally relevant media programs prevented the reconstruction of ethnic categorizations that would have perpetuated genocide ideology and instead replaced it with a more inclusionary national Rwandan identity.

Over time, many have come to hear, read, or watch accounts of the 1994 Rwandan Genocide Against Tutsi. However, few have invested the time and energy needed to understand and know the extent to which this resulted from the Hutu extremists in the government who planned and orchestrated the geno-cide in 1994 in Rwanda to avoid sharing power with Tutsi that was dictated by the terms President Habyarimana agreed to in the Arusha Peace Accord signed in August 1993.[9] Hutu extremists had used all means at their disposi-tion to instill fear in people relying on nonstop radio broadcasts that called for killing all Tutsi (even giving names and locations of people to kill) and months of planning attacks in order to engage the larger population in mass killings of Tutsi in 1994 following the assassination of General Habyarimana, himself a Hutu.[10] Hutu extremists and genocidaires commanded the Army who was being forced to integrate the military with Rwandan Patriotic Front troops (RPF) against whom they had fought during the 3-year civil war that preceded. The Arusha Peace Accord required that 50% of commanding posts and 40% of enlisted personnel be from the RPF, a deal the Rwandan Army preferred to ignore, partaking instead in the genocide against Tutsi hoping all would be eradicated.[11] Rwandan civilians who remained in Rwanda following the genocide and those who returned understood and believed that the country had to overcome its greatest challenge yet in the face of the destruction of the physical infrastructure, of the devastation of its institutions, of the tearing apart of the social fabric of its communities, in addition to the debilitating damage, physical and emotional, done to families and to individual survivors. The country also had to deal with those who perpetrated acts of genocide in the first place, many of whom were still present in the country. The Rwandan Patriotic Front swept through the country to halt the genocide and bring Liberation in July 1994, which set in motion the largest and fasted exodus of Rwandans into Goma, Zaire. This meant the RPF, and moderate Hutu had to engage all those living in the country to participate in a massive effort to rebuild the country and reimagine a national identity for a peaceful future that could foster inclusivity.

The first section of this chapter explains how identity transformation in Rwanda became part of the nation building project, as Purdekova argues, rather than a simple nationalist project for civic inclusion.[12] Reinstating Umuganda followed its earlier tradition of regular participation by the community in volunteer work for public projects.

HISTORIC LEGACY

The Rwandan government undertook the project of transforming the identity of its people following the genocide because it could not rebuild the country after having lost so much of its population in 1994, first to the genocide, and then to the massive exodus of refugees. Therefore, any provision to move forward required providing space for inclusion of all, whether Hutu, Tutsi, or Twa. Over time the Rwandan government designed, built, and strengthened its democratic institutions.[13] The government along with its citizens, bureaucrats, and elected officials, developed a strong network of institutions that have become efficient and professionalized. The country set its vision on becoming fully independent and favored ways that aid could foster future self-reliance rather than pin it in a continuous cycle of dependency. To this end, the government created the Rwanda Development Board in 2009—the agency that oversees Rwanda's business regulations, foreign investments, tourism promotion, environmental conservation, and broader economic and development planning.[14] In 2020 the Rwanda Development Board had set its goal for foreign direct investments to reach 20% of its GDP.[15] This vision matched the desire of Rwandans to find ways to thrive economically, live in peace, and avoid any return to the dominance of genocide ideology, or to the previous exclusionary patterns of functioning. Most Rwandans want to focus on education, business, development, opportunities for their children, and therefore most supported measures that outlawed the expression of genocide ideologies and they also wanted to preserve all Rwandan lives (like abolishing the death penalty in 2007).[16] Rwandans embarked on an ambitious project of identity transformation to value each Rwandan as essential for the larger community, their nation, to thrive.

Pottier describes the process as a 'reimagined' identity to bring all its people under the unifying concept of Rwandan citizenship.[17] This communitarian unifying vision promoted a new sense of inclusive belonging with a higher purpose to serve the nation rather than the divisive ethnic markers previously politicized, both during colonial times and further entrenched after independence, and then again promoted in the early 1990s to plan and carry out the

Genocide Against Tutsi.[18] The nation building project in Rwanda included many important pieces. First, the government imposed the overarching concept of Rwandan citizenship as an essential pillar to providing Rwandans with ways to conceive of a future inclusive of all people, no matter their role during the genocide or their place of birth, or residence. Second, the government brought back the practice of Umuganda to reinstate community works that created an avenue for sharing one's community needs with the government's vision and increasing participation in community service. The process of identity transformation in Rwanda was originally primarily imposed top-down. However, administrative edicts would not have succeeded had the population not been involved in the building of the symbols for this new identity. Therefore, the government called on the population for genuine involvement inviting Rwandans to submit entries for a new flag and for a new national anthem.[19] Community engagement fostered decentralizing decision-making processes eventually enabling each community to select future projects for Umuganda. Addressing the legacy of the 1994 Genocide Against Tutsi also required bringing to justice over 150,000 alleged perpetrators. Therefore, the government also brought back traditional community tribunals: Gacaca.

Critics pointed out that this identity transformation was driven entirely by the state and that the state forbidding through legislation the use of certain ethnic terms in public discourse, even to prevent the reproduction of divisive politics and dangerous genocide denial accounts, amounted to the suppression of free speech. However, the goal of helping all citizens see themselves as belonging to this broader group with an overarching inclusive "Rwandan" identity could not succeed without some clear individual grassroot mobilization to make this identity resonate with most citizens while promoting unity. The regular participation in locally sponsored activities helped to further mobilize Rwandans for development through Umuganda. These regular activities in groups helped them all develop their sense of self and belonging and provided them ways to grieve and deal with the trauma experienced. It gave them positive goals and support systems within their own communities that organized at the smallest local levels of neighborhoods in Kigali and other larger cities and at the village level in the more rural parts of the country.

Umuganda, a form of national community service, requires individual Rwandans participate in substantive ways in the overarching nation building project. Rwandans take pride in the level of cleanliness of their entire country which they attribute to their required community service the last Saturday of every month from 8 to 11 am when all must participate in either local, regional, or national Umuganda projects.[20] Umuganda is not only a way to require community service from all Rwandans or to keep a small densely populated country clean, but my research also shows that it includes several other essential elements of identity transformation that are relevant to one's education in acquiring and sharpening leadership skills, and for fostering motivation and mobilization around the message of Rwandan unity.

While identity remains constructed, changing, and contested, identity also provides more than just ways one describes oneself.[21] Identity has very serious cultural, political, economic, and even deadly consequences for many around the world. This is especially true of the 1994 Rwandan Genocide Against Tutsi. The way people were identified sealed their fate. Rwandans previously identified by the 1930 Belgian- conducted census when they issued ID cards that categorized people as either Hutu or Tutsi or Twa, in unchangeable ways. Moderate Hutu, who supported the plans for democratization and the integration of Tutsi in the country as specified in the Arusha Accords, often described as Hutu Moderates, were also ruthlessly targeted for extermination during the events that took place between April and July 1994.[22] This sent a very clear message to all: Tutsi would be slaughtered and anyone, even Hutu, who dared protecting them risked meeting a similar fate.[23] The Rwandan Army under Habyarimana had fought for 3 years against the RPF who, as a part of the Arusha Accord, were given 50% of officer positions in the integrated Rwandan military. The Accord also set up a transitional government dominated by Tutsi since RPF troops were about to cease the capital Kigali when the French and Belgians put pressure to halt the fighting.[24] All Tutsi found themselves as targets of a planned and systematic genocide that also affected Hutu who protected Tutsi or who openly supported the transition to power sharing. In 100 days, the Rwandan Army with Hutu Paramilitary troops and the Hutu extremists in government called the previously trained youth militias to the streets and recruited by broadcasting over the radio any civilians willing to kill, reading lists of names and places where to find them to "exterminate them."[25] The toll of the 100 days reached over 1 million people dead— primarily Tutsi—and left behind over 600,000 young orphans, and over 1.5 million refugees, and countless internally displaced.[26]

Therefore, can we understand how: "Ethnic identities can acquire political salience" when they are manipulated to divide.[27] This is in opposition to conventional wisdom that often generalizes that all ethnic tensions are intrinsically grounded in ancient tribal hatred as was first argued and reported by Newbury.[28] Instead, even when there can be elements entrenched in identities that are immutable and unavoidable in their essence, mobilization determines whether these will result in ethnic violence.[29] It is the politicization and the benefits or denial of grievances assigned to specific ethnic identities that make the difference.[30] Presidential rhetoric and elite narratives exacerbated the implications of ethnicity.[31] So, to successfully transition away from genocide politics and prevent iterated violence, Rwanda's nation building had to include identity transformation. The Rwandan economy had been decimated during the genocide, the little infrastructure it had prior was destroyed, and worse: Rwandans who were educated or who were of working age were either killed or attempted to seek refuge abroad. For this transformation of identity to take place, it meant moving away from the previously constructed categories of Hutu, Tutsi, and Twa that carried such deep meaning in Rwandan society and in its language, Kinyarwanda, in order to overcome the colonial legacy of politicization and exclusionary consequences for the terms, herders or Tutsi and farmers or Hutu.[32]

Rwanda constructed a new overarching identity primarily based on more inclusive concepts of citizenship, community, and national symbols rather than the exclusive socioeconomic and ethnic identities used in the previous centuries. German and Belgian colonial powers promoted ethnic division by privileging Tutsi (herders) to levy heavy taxes against the majority Hutu farmers.[33] The independence movement was principally a backlash against the ethnic privilege enjoyed during colonial times and saw a centralization of power in the hands of Hutu.[34] Therefore, the devastation from the genocide could have engendered decades of further violence, as was the case in the neighboring state of Burundi.[35] Instead, this nation building project supported by the reimagined unifying Rwandan national citizenship identity led to deep transformations, development, and stability within Rwanda.

Once the genocide had been stopped by the Rwandan Patriotic Front (RPF) in July 1994, the new RPF led the Rwandan government and implemented a campaign to include all people of Rwandan origins, no matter their role during the genocide, and no matter their previous ethnic identity, the transformation was not without its discontents who saw it solely as an imposition by the state to control people.[36] The project to transform identity grew and within a few years saw the reinstituted practice of Umuganda or community work provide it with a great venue and vehicle to promote inclusion and foster development on a much larger scale. The practice of Umuganda has provided essential free labor to assist in development projects needed locally for nation building. This element of relying on mobilization and adherence to a common purpose underscored the way in which calls for unity resonated with most of the population and mobilized Rwandan citizens in the long haul. The next section looks more closely at the concept and practice of Umuganda and its ramifications.

BEYOND IDENTITY: UMUGANDA, UNIFICATION, POVERTY REDUCTION, AND BEYOND

In Rwanda in the wake of the genocide and the utter devastation of the country, the government understood the urgency in addressing the ethnic divide and the need to give all Rwandans a unifying message to turn the country around.

Within a decade after the genocide, this "new Rwanda" where previous ethnic categories had been officially banned and replaced with a discourse about a more inclusive concept of Rwandan citizenship became more widespread but criticized by some like Ingelaere as imposed by Rwandan elite leaders.[37] The government used different ways to communicate the reimagined identities such as theatre where actors came to perform nationhood.[38] Due to the ambition of this identity transformation project, it required several approaches for officials to promote narratives of altruism, of inclusion, and of national unity. The newly reinstated Umuganda requirement also provided the ability for government officials to hear from the local communities. Following the 3 hours of required service on the last Saturday of each month, officials sit down with community members and discuss issues and answer questions about options to plan and address urgent community needs. All government officials at the highest levels, including ministers, the President, and their families when physically in country, are also required to participate in their own community or in the community where they are on that Saturday. Traveling around Rwanda does not provide an exemption. Umuganda was brought back as a nationally required practice in 2001.[39] Umuganda became a vehicle for unity both in bringing communities to participate in local projects the last Saturday of each month but also to speak to a captive audience about the goals and requirements for this nation building project. The town halls following Umuganda community work, provided the space for each community to express their most urgent needs and discuss projects to be considered by the Umuganda leaders for the following months.[40] It mobilized the population to come together, it provided an avenue to make demands or proposals for what the community needed most first. Reimposing the practice of Umuganda did not meet much resistance from people because most projects were too large for any one family to undertake alone and all were to benefit from projects like building schools, hospitals, repairing roads, etc.

Uwimbabazi explained that in the precolonial period:

> patron-client ties were used to increase individuals' wealth and social standing, solidarity or communal work was more significant between occupational groups for mutual and communal benefit [. . .] the most inclusive and beneficial was community agricultural work, which was divided into two categories: one was known as *ubudehe* and the other as *umuganda*.[41]

Kigabo defines *ubudehe* as "the practice of communal digging of a field before the rains come and the planting season arrives" while Umuganda was usually centered on building houses in the community.[42] This important distinction is highlighted also by Uwimbabazi who compares the two practices and revealed that Ubudehe was only required of those who worked in the fields while Umuganda required everyone's participation and could benefit all people in the community.[43] This clarified why the Rwandan government chose the more inclusive practice of Umuganda. On the one hand, Umuganda was being invoked to get a head start on many streets, schools, and government building projects. On the other hand, Umuganda was required of all, not just those who worked in the field, and was intended to benefit all and increased trust in the government delivery of services in local areas.

So, in 2001, the government officially brought back Umuganda through the Ministry of Finance and Economic Planning (MINECOFIN). Umuganda was conceived as a multipronged strategy intended not only to reduce poverty, but also to help the government deliver services, give local populations an opportunity to participate in decision making, and opportunities to practice decentralization.[44] The practice of Umuganda had traditional roots in Rwandan society but had been manipulated over time by those in power to extract free labor from the community. In her analysis, Uwimbabazi explained that post-genocide, Umuganda became a powerful transformative tool.[45] The focus on Umuganda provided two essential ways of transforming identity. One by bringing the local communities together to work side by side on community projects (like construction or cleaning). Umuganda became an effective way to meet the objective of the Rwandan Decentralization Framework started in 2000 and revised in 2007 that stated it intended: "accountability and transparency [. . .] by making local leaders directly accountable to the communities they served."[46] Through community service, people internalized the added value of coming together as a community for progress that was visible and had a positive impact on their lives. Second, it gave a platform for local and national officials to share their vision with the people on a regular basis. Indeed, in Rwanda, Umuganda remained primarily orchestrated by the central government and its ministries, even when its purposes always included a more decentralized way of providing public service or opportunities for local community to share their input with the central government and an avenue to develop local leadership.[47] In 2008, Umuganda became institutionalized under the Ministry of Local Government, Good Governance, Community Development, and Social Affairs (MINALOC) with Law 53/2007.[48] The Rwandan government practiced Umuganda to save on labor for many projects essential to the continued growth and poverty eradication and to convey its messages of unity.[49]

Government documents such as the *Rwanda Decentralization Strategic Framework* lay out five objectives for Umuganda:

1. To invite the local population to participate and monitor decision making that considers local needs, priorities, capacities, and resources [. . .] in a decentralized fashion.

2. To strengthen accountability and transparency and to provide evidence and clear connections between the taxes people pay and the services the government provides.
3. To enable local leadership to develop organization structure and capacities that take into consideration the local environment and needs.
4. To facilitate sustainable economic planning and management capacity at the local levels.
5. To increase effectiveness and efficiency in the delivery of services.[50]

These objectives have been providing opportunities for local low-level officials and local community members to step up into leadership roles and participate in decision making processes that enhance their ability to respond to the needs of the local population while keeping in mind capacity and other crucial factors. Umuganda, in this sense, became a monthly governance workshop that helped officials and community members sharpen their collaboration, teamwork, public speaking, and other leadership skills.

Despite the Rwandan government's intention to use Umuganda to decentralize decision making processes and service delivery, Umuganda has remained mostly coordinated by the central government but has become a vehicle for social development and leadership training. In the conclusion of her extensive study of Umuganda, Uwimbabazi argued that the philosophy of Umuganda was based on the combination of good governance with social development to promote and achieve economic development.[51] Rwanda has been able to invest in its social capital while benefiting from using people's free labor. Through participation in Umuganda, people learn to follow guidelines for good governance and those who step up to participate in decision making and planning are helped to develop their own leadership skills further.[52]

Rwanda's use of Umuganda for nation building could not alone have brought the level of mobilization, healing, reconciliation, and development that Rwandans ushered for themselves. Transformation and reinforcement required more than a one Saturday a month program no matter how central, productive, and transformative Umuganda was. Two other important elements of transforming individual identity into the inclusive notion of Rwandan citizenship include justice on one end and mass media on the other. Justice and reconciliation came from another old communal practice: Gacaca or courts for collective justice that were brought back to address the massive backlog of genocide cases that had still not been brought to trial several years after the genocide took place.

GACACA: SEEKING JUSTICE FOR
UNITY AND RECONCILIATION

Gacaca courts provided a means for the government to continue building on the momentum it had gained by the mid-2000s. The central government brought back old traditional practices that were reintroduced with newer goals to promote unity and economic growth that could help promote reconciliation. Boudreaux and Ahlewalia point out that the institutionalization of local Gacaca courts was also intended to promote unity.[53] The Gacaca courts proceedings constructed a way to discuss the atrocities committed during the genocide, gave the community the ability to require some form of reparations rather than impose punishment, and tried over 150,000 perpetrators under their purview.[54] This form of local justice also brought controversies and opponents, in the same way they had opposed the unifying Rwandan citizenship identity transformation as well.

For Rwandans to be able to focus on their common Rwandan citizenship identity, they needed to overcome what had separated them and what had imposed so much trauma individually, had broken family ties, and had destroyed the fabric of tightknit communities during the 1994 Genocide Against Tutsi. Truth and reconciliation through transitional justice became another proactive way to support the reconstruction of identity.[55] When the government brought back the practice of Gacaca courts, its two-pronged intent included the need for justice and the compelling requirement for transforming identity. First, the government needed to deal with the very large number of genocidaires still in pre-trial detention several years after the genocide had ended. The government focused on restitutive and retributive forms of justice with emphasis on plea-bargaining and individual community service.[56] These elements provided the needed foundation to move beyond one's suffering and invited each Rwandan citizen to become a part of the solution through conflict resolution and development programs. In Kinyarwanda, the language shared by all Rwandans, *gacaca* means lawn or grass field, which was the traditional place where community members came together to resolve disputes between close relations or neighbors.[57] The government consulted civil society leaders, international non-governmental organizations (including Amnesty International), and major international donors which led to the decision to use Gacaca courts to handle the logjam of over 150,000 detainees in prisons intended to fit 15,000 prisoners only. Despite this inclusive decision-making process, Amnesty International became very critical of the way Gacaca courts conducted their affairs. The Rwandan Supreme Court argued in 2003 that considering the prohibition against indefinite detention next to the requirement for fair trials, in the case of Rwanda where the genocide had touched everyone's life presented a difficult conundrum especially since the country was still so underdeveloped.[58] The situation in the country was beyond dire; not only had all areas of the economy suffered major setbacks, so had all institutions including its judicial branch. Between 1996 and 2003 the 15 national specialized courts had only been able to render judgment on 9,700 cases; at that pace, Shabas estimated it would have taken another 80 years to bring all those accused of genocide to trial.[59] Others complained that the Gacaca process had excluded prosecuting any Tutsi alleged crimes during the period of the 1994 genocide.[60] These criticisms failed to take into account the fact that crimes committed to protect oneself from being killed and to stop the genocide could be addressed by regular Rwandan courts and represented a very small fraction in comparison. Furthermore, as Mamdani explained in his work *When Victims Become Killers,* published in 2001, establishing the Gacaca court to address the crimes of genocidaires also addressed Rwanda's dilemma in attempting to build democratic institutions by bringing together in the Rwandan political community the majority that bore the responsibility for the atrocities committed during the genocide who were working alongside the very small minority who remained fearful and lived in anguish each day.[61] Therefore, suggesting that the same process should have targeted both the crimes of acts of genocide and crimes against humanity of over 150,000 perpetrators versus the individual crimes of those who defended others and halted the genocide would not have provided the kind of retribution, reconciliation, and healing the Gacaca process intended. Kanyangara et al. explained that "Gacaca fosters an increase in social cohesion and a decrease in prejudicial attitudes."[62] They demonstrated that despite the egregious events discussed during the proceedings of the Gacaca courts, perceptions of positive climate did not deteriorate after the trials but did enhance social cohesion.[63] These findings were extremely important in the way they evidenced how this form of community justice provided a central element that supported the transformation of identity and the valuing of all Rwandans. Gibson's work on Apartheid in South Africa also suggested that the work of the Truth and Reconciliation Commission intended to build an inclusive national identity.[64] Transforming individual identity to prioritize belonging and inclusivity as Rwandan citizens was a tremendous undertaking but it needed one more way to reinforce these changes in one's daily lives by providing culturally relevant ways of teaching peace building and conflict resolution methods. This third element of this successful identity transformation project demonstrated the willingness from the government and the thirst from ordinary Rwandans to draw from culture and entertainment to find ways to resolve everyday issues. For this aspect, the Rwandan government turned to psychology experts and trauma specialists and the media. An unexpected group of academics, government officials, radio producers, and local actors created a novel program: *Musekeweya* that targeted ways of modeling forms of reconciliation, peace building, and local conflict resolutions.

MUSEKEWEYA: A RADIO PROGRAM FOR PEACEBUILDING AND CONFLICT RESOLUTION

One of the survivors of the Holocaust, Dr. Ervin Staub, a genocide scholar, psychologist, and author of the *Roots of Mass Violence,* dedicated his life to studying what brought people to becoming perpetrators or bystanders to the worst crimes against humanity.[65] In his quest to find answers he also devised methods that he tested to help different groups (especially children) around the world learn to become more altruistic and prevent future violence.[66]

Staub explained that there were several important elements that had to be integrated for prevention and that reconciliation provided an essential portion of early prevention.[67] He outlined that those principles of prevention and practice had to include:

> developing positive orientations to previously devalued groups, healing from past victimization and promoting altruism born of suffering; moderating respect for authority; creative constructive ideologies; promoting the understanding for the origins of violence, its impact, and avenues to prevention; promoting truth, justice, and a shared history; and raising inclusively caring morally courageous children.[68]

Drs. Staub and Pearlman (the trauma specialist) worked in Rwanda and ran several workshops and evaluated their impact. They then moved on to designing and implementing the most ambitious violence prevention and identity transforming nationwide project: *Musekeweya*.[69] Musekeweya, which means New Dawn in Kinyarwanda, started its broadcast in 2004 and has continued over the years.[70] *Musekeweya* used entertainment and culturally pertinent storylines to its nationwide audience to resolve inevitable conflicts and build peaceful institutions by playing out and peacefully resolving everyday challenges. *Musekeweya* integrated reconciliation as a step to prevent future violence in the region.[71] Staub stated that "listening to the radio drama also increased independence from authority" which represented an important indicator of future willingness to prevent violence against others.[72] Further workshops were implemented in Rwanda where small groups of local leaders after receiving training would evaluate whether policies that were introducing were more or less likely to increase violence.[73]

None of these identity transforming projects occurred in a vacuum. For example, Staub also examined how "a balance of different types of justice

[could] satisfy the need for justice without creating new hostility and violence."[74] After the first 8 years on the radio, the characters in *Musekeweya*
were not only able to resolve conflict but undertook Umuganda projects that
brought both separated communities together for the benefit of all in this
radio drama that mirrored much of the reality of everyday Rwandans. Finally,
while participating in the Gacaca process had tended to intensify the pain felt
by individual survivors, those surveyed explained that this had helped them
differentiate individuals from their previously assigned identity groups and
separate individual guilt from group responsibility.[75]

There are many other worthy elements one can study further in order to
better understand the interplay between all the facets of nation building and
reconciliation projects. In Rwanda, the integration of reconciliation with
nation rebuilding helps transform individual identity, fosters unity and inclusion in the way survivors, bystanders, and even perpetrators come together
and share a common Rwandan citizenship. The new Rwandan citizenship category was designed to be purposefully inclusive, forgiving, and a community
oriented for development identity.

CONCLUSION

This short chapter could not assess all the diverse elements that have contributed to the successful identity transformation undertaken by Rwandans and
their government for over two decades. I did not summarize in detail all criticisms against these programs for identity transformation.[76] One can question
whether this transformation of identity has taken root much more on the side
of the nation building and development processes rather than in the private
sphere of storytelling? Jessee and Watkins warned that "current scholars
[should] be well-read in Rwanda's contested past, including the precolonial
period, and particularly as written and debated in the pre-genocide period" to
examine the complexity of this subject.[77]

I highlighted that entire communities, including many diverse groups—
political leaders, clergy, the media and entertainment industry producers,
some academics, and ordinary citizens—partook and contributed some
important aspects to the process of successful identity transformation as
part of their nation building endeavor. The government created laws that set
hard parameters against genocide ideology, providing a proverbial stick to
avoid a return to previous exclusionary identity categories of Hutu, Tutsi,
and Twa. The government also provided very positive incentives. Umuganda
brought local communities together each month to participate in building and
improving one's community by serving their own most pressing needs for
schools, hospitals, roads, etc. Following the workshops and training programs

initiated by Staub and Pearlman and then sponsored by funding from the European Union, a radio program (then later TV broadcasts) sought to teach and reinforce the inclusionary identity of Rwandan citizenship to ordinary Rwandans to help them develop altruism towards other victims, bystanders, and even for perpetrators. While it is true that Rwandans comply with the required elements of this nation building process, it is their voluntary participation and support for all the other aspects of this nation building project that demonstrate the buy-in and individual mobilization and commitment to the transformation of their identity that they believe central to the continued development and peaceful future for their own country. Every day Rwandans benefit from organized and professional public services, from free education to free healthcare to new housing programs in collaboration with the World Bank to End Poverty for disabled Rwandan former combatants.[78]

Rwanda's progress on its nation building project slowly earned support at home and abroad, with many describing Rwanda as a 'Miracle' for its fast-paced development with subsequent years of 8% GDP growth.[79] However, as Drobac and Naughton explained in 2014, two decades after the genocide, "the word 'miracle' implied mystery, and there was no mystery there: the key was to link effective health care delivery systems to an equity agenda."[80] Unfortunately one could not isolate each factor to assess the extent to which each contributed to the outcomes in Rwanda. Drobac and Naughton list the many multipronged approaches that linked economic development programs with healthcare and equity to explain the ways in which Rwandans alongside their government met and exceeded expectations.[81] Identity transformation, good governance, community engagement—Umuganda, transitional justice—Gacaca, transparency, accountability, investing in education, Girinka (the one cow per poorest family development program), plus Vision 2020 Umurenge Program, that specifically aimed to eliminate extreme poverty by 2020 through the delivery of public works, employment, cash transfers to the poorest families, and conditional microloans, all reinforced the message of a unifying future. This vision for Rwanda called for equitable development, opportunities for employment, decentralizing the delivery of public services, and improving the overall standards of living for all and in particular for the poorest. The newest Vision 2050 subtitled: "The Rwanda We Want" was requested by the 13th National Umushyikirano Council in 2015.[82] In addition, Rwandans organized and took part each year, in Rwanda and abroad, major commemorative events: Kwibuka, Remember, Unite, Renew. These events that can take place over several days to several months were created to provide a narrative inclusive of all Rwandans and welcoming to non-Rwandans.[83] Local leaders in Rwanda, with the central government, and Rwandan Abroad Communities throughout the world, plan and implement these activities that provide the space to remember and witness individual experiences during the genocide, to share acts of forgiveness and attrition, and even help educate others about the 1994 Genocide Against Tutsi. Therefore, while there is an emphasis today on being all included as Rwandans, there is a concerted effort in not forgetting how exclusionary policies along with the mobilization and politicization of constructed ethnic categories led to the 1994 Genocide Against Tutsi and to the suffering it brought the entire nation.

Any top-down identity transformation process had to proceed cautiously. Early on, there were warnings of the dangers that simply removing the ethnic labels in Rwanda did not help address many of the issues of identity, reconciliation, and security.[84] It has become increasingly worrisome that elements of building a unified Rwandan citizenry and a nation building project through de-ethnicization were denounced by critics as tools of silencing political opposition or for curbing the freedom of the press.[85] However, it has also become clear that those who support and promote genocide ideology are denouncing specific aspects of government policies or decrying imposed unifying practices to challenge the progress made in unifying the country. Transforming identity required elements of changing the meaning, rewards, and motivations of identification of specific ethno-social groups in the Rwandan context. In the case of Rwanda, the government-imposed identity transformation accompanied many other essential elements to eradicate the extreme poverty in the country. Improving the lives of all Rwandan citizens (especially the lives of the poorest Rwandans), providing avenues for witnessing experiences of the genocide, and fostering justice through reconciliation with peace building and conflict resolution methods preempted and prevented violence, nurtured development, and maintained security in the country for close to three decades. These are quite extraordinary achievements considering that only two decades separated World War I and World War II which both included major genocides of Armenians and Jews respectively. In the Great Lakes of Africa, especially in the Eastern Democratic Republic of Congo, massive campaigns of human rights violations motivated by ethnic rationales of exclusions have continued since the 1990s. This meant that preventing a return to violence in Rwanda required major steps, even if a few were controversial ones. In the current political climate around the world, we see the acceleration of renewed exclusionary, divisive, and dehumanizing political rhetoric even by democratic governments often hindered in curtailing the dangerous politicization and mobilization of exclusionary ethnic or religious identities because of their allegiance to protecting free speech, potentially even above protecting life. Transforming Rwandan identity with inclusionary Rwandan citizenship and belonging to a national development project, supported and promoted economic growth, expanded literacy, increased investments in health and education, and helped Rwandans achieve living in a peaceful and safe society where all work to improve their country further.

NOTES

1. Catharine Newbury, "The Cohesion of Oppression: A Century of Clientship in Kinyaga, Rwanda" (PhD diss., University of Wisconsin, Madison, 1975); Catharine Newbury, *The Cohesion of Oppression: Clientship and Ethnicity in Rwanda 1860–1960* (New York: Columbia University Press, 1988).

2. Deborah Mayersen, "A Massive Rejection of the Tutsi as Fellow Nationals," in *On the Path to Genocide: Armenia and Rwanda Re-examined* (New York: Berghahn Books, 2014), 122–147.

3. Three major academic publications reviewed Newbury's book: Ronald Kassimir, "The Cohesion of Oppression: Clientship and Ethnicity in Rwanda, 1860–1960 (Book)," *American Journal of Sociology* 95, no. 4 (January 1990): 1063–65; Phyllis Martin, "The Cohesion of Oppression: Clientship and Ethnicity in Rwanda, 1860–1960," *American Historical Review*, October 1990, vol. 95, n. 4, 1264; and Aaron Segal, "A Look at Books," *Africa Today* 39, no. 3 (1992): 121. In addition, another review was published in *Foreign Affairs,* which has a large following by foreign policy practitioners of international relations ,in spring 1991: Gail M. Gerhart and Lucy Edwards Despard, "The Cohesion of Oppression: Clientship and Ethnicity in Rwanda, 1860–1960," *Foreign Affairs* 70, no. 2 (Spring 1991): 202.

4. Céline Jacquemin, "Human Rights Crises and International Response: Framing Rwanda and Kosovo" (PhD diss., University of California, Irvine, 2003).

5. UNHCR, "The Rwandan Genocide and Its Aftermath," in *The State of The World's Refugees 2000: Fifty Years of Humanitarian Action* (2000): 245–75.

6. Jacquemin, "Human Rights Crises."; Céline Jacquemin, "French Foreign Policy in Rwanda: Language, Personal Networks, & Changing Contexts," in *African Political Economy: The Way Forward for 21st Century Development*, eds. Toyin Falola and Jessica Archberger (Routledge, 2013), 322–340; Céline Jacquemin, "Hegemony and Counter-Hegemony: Colonial and Post-Colonial Roots of the Rwandan Genocide," in *The Roots of Ethnic Conflict in Africa: From Grievance to Violence,* ed. Wanjala S. Nasong'o (New York: Palgrave Macmilan, 2015), 93–123.

7. Jacquemin, "Hegemony," 93.

8. Africa for Results Initiative, "Africa's Emigration Crisis: Implications for Capacity Building" (2017), case 84, https://elibrary.acbfpact.org/acbf/collect/acbf/index/assoc/HASHdaad/beb28206/c62a3ebe/09.dir/AfCoPCaseStudy084.pdf.

9. Jacquemin, "Human Rights Crises," 186–202.

10. Ibid.

11. Ibid.; Jacquemin, "Hegemony." 93.

12. Andrea Purdekova, "'Even If I Am Not Here, There Are So Many Eyes': Surveillance and state Reach in Rwanda," *The Journal of Modern African Studies* 49, no. 3 (September 2011): 475–97.

13. Céline Jacquemin, "Rwandan Government & Diaspora: Harnessing the Power of Institutions Built for Unity & Democracy," in *Slavery, Migrations, and Transformations: Connecting Old and New Diasporas to the Homeland,* eds. Toyin Falola and Danielle Porter Sanchez (Amherst: Cambria Press Inc, 2015), 179–201.

14. Clare Akamanzi, Esteban Flores, and Richard Yarrow, "Rwanda's Push for Five-Star Development: An Interview with the CEO of the Rwandan Development Board on the Present and Future of Rwandan Economic Development," *Harvard International Review* 38, no. 4 (Fall 2017): 54–58.

15. Ibid.

16. "Rwanda: Justice After Genocide—20 Years On," Human Rights Watch, last modified March 28, 2014, https://www.hrw.org/news/2014/03/28/rwanda-justice -after-genocide-20-years.

17. Johan Pottier, "Land Reform for Peace? Rwanda's 2005 Land Law in Context," *Journal of Agrarian Change* 6, no. 4 (2006): 509–37.

18. Newbury, *Cohesion*; Jacquemin, "Human Rights Crises."; Jacquemin, "Rwandan Government."

19. "Rwanda Unveils New fFag and Anthem," *BBC News*, December 31, 2001, http://news.bbc.co.uk/2/hi/africa/1735405.stm.

20. Penine Uwimbabazi, "An Analysis of Umuganda: The Policy and Practice of Community Work in Rwanda" (PhD diss., University of KwaZulu-Natal, 2012), 64.

21. Audie Klotz and Cecelia Lynch, *Strategies for Research in Constructivist International Relations* (Armonk, New York: M. E. Sharpe, Inc., 2007).

22. Jacquemin, "Hegemony."

23. One should be careful not be swayed by an online network of genocide deniers who use the fact that a very small proportion of Hutu were killed during the 1994 Genocide Against Tutsi to deny the truth that this was a planned Genocide Against Tutsi. This version of suggesting the absurdity of a "double genocide" amounts to suggesting that since French Resistants targeted and killed Germans relentlessly, regardless of whether Nazis, SS, or Gestapo, there would have been a 'double' Holocaust. One cannot deny the intent of the ways the Holocaust was planned and carried out to target Jews during World War II. Therefore, one must acknowledge that in 1994 in Rwanda, there was a planned campaign of extermination that targeted Tutsi. The United Nations General Assembly "noted with concern any form of the denial of that genocide, [. . .] and designate[d] 7 April as the International Day of Reflection in the 1994 Genocide against the Tutsi in Rwanda"; A/72/L.31 12 December 2017.

24. Jacquemin, "Human Rights Crises," 95–101.

25. Ibid.; 95–101.

26. Jacquemin, "French Foreign Policy."

27. Bert Ingelaere, "Do We Understand Life After Genocide? Center and Periphery in the Construction of Knowledge in Postgenocide Rwanda," *African Studies Review* 53, no. 1 (April 2010): 41–59.

28. Catharine Newbury, "Ethnicity in Rwanda: The Case of Kinyaga: L'Ethnicite au Ruanda: Le Cas du Kinyaga," *Africa* 48, no. 1 (March 1978): 24–25.

29. Jacquemin, "Human Rights Crises"; Jacquemin, "Hegemony," 93.

30. Wanjala S. Nasong'o, *The Roots of Ethnic Conflict in Africa: from Grievance to Violence* (New York: Palgrave Macmillan, 2015); Jacquemin, "Hegemony," 93; Jacquemin, "Rwandan Government," 179–201.

31. Deborah Mayersen, "'Fraternity in Diversity' or 'Feudal Fanatics'? Representations of Ethnicity in Rwandan Presidential Rhetoric," *Patterns of Prejudice* 49, no. 3 (July 2015): 253–64.

32. In Kinyarwanda, the singular forms of these terms are Batutsi and Bahutu. Newbury, *Cohesion.*

33. Ibid.

34. Rene Lemarchand, *Rwanda and Burundi* (London: Pall Mall, 1970); Rene Lemarchand, *Ethnocide as Discourse and Practice* (Washington, D.C.: Woodrow Wilson Center Press, 1994).

35. André Guichaoua, *Rwanda 1994: les politiques du génocide à Butare* (Paris: Karthala, 2005); Filip Reyntjens, *Talking or Fighting? Political Evolution in Rwanda and Burundi, 1998–1999* (Uppsala: Nordiska Afrikainstitutet, 1999); Jacquemin, "French Foreign Policy," 322–340.

36. Purdekova, "Even if I am not here," 476, 478.

37. Ingelaere, "Do We Understand Life After Genocide," 44.

38. Amanda Breed, "Performing the Nation: Theatre in Post-Genocide Rwanda," *The Drama Review* 52, no. 1 (March 2008): 32–50.

39. Penine Uwimbabazi, "An Analysis of Umuganda: The Policy and Practice of Community Work in Rwanda" (PhD diss., University of KwaZulu-Natal, 2012), 53.

40. Ibid.

41. Ibid., 27.

42. Thomas Rusuhuzwa Kigabo, "Leadership, Policy-making, Quality of Economic Policies and Their Inclusiveness: The Case of Rwanda," *Commission on Growth and Development*, working paper no. 20 (2008): 12.

43. Uwimbabazi, "Umuganda," 28.

44. Ibid., 5–6, 53.

45. Ibid., 54.

46. Republic of Rwanda, *Rwanda Decentralisation Strategic Framework: Towards a Sector-Wide Approach for Decentralization Implementation* (Kigali: Ministry of Finance and Economic Planning, 2007), 7; Uwimbababzi, "Umuganda," 59.

47. Uwimbababzi, "Umuganda,"

48. Ibid., 53.

49. Penine Uwimbabazi and R. Lawrence, "Compelling Factors of Urbanization and Rural-urban Migration in Rwanda," *Rwanda Journal* 22 (2011): 19.

50. Republic of Rwanda, *Rwanda Decentralisation*, 7.

51. Uwimbababzi, "Umuganda," 53.

52. Ibid., 54.

53. Karol Bourdreaux and Ahluwalia Puja, "Cautiously Optimistic: Economic Liberalization and Reconciliation in Rwanda's Coffee Sector," *Denver Journal of International Law and Policy* 37, no. 2 (2009): 165–72.

54. Ariel Meyerstein, "Between Law and Culture: Rwanda's Gacaca and Postcolonial Legality," *Law & Social Inquiry* 32, no. 2 (June 2007): 468–70.

55. Kevin Avruch, "Truth and Reconciliation Commissions: Problems in Transitional Justice and the Reconstruction of Identity," *Transcultural Psychiatry* 47, no. 1 (January 2010): 33–49.

56. Meyerstein, "Between Law and Culture," 468.

57. Ibid.

58. Ibid., 469.

59. William A. Schabas, "Genocide Trials and Gacaca Courts," *Journal of International Criminal Justice* 3, no. 4 (September 2005): 888.

60. Allison Corey and Sandra F. Joireman, "Retributive Justice: The Gacaca Courts in Rwanda," *African Affairs* 103, no. 410 (January 2004): 73–89.

61. Mahmood Mamdani, *When Victims Become Killers: Colonialism, Nativism, and the Genocide in Rwanda* (Princeton: Princeton University Press, 2001), 46.

62. Patrick Kanyangara et al., "Collective Rituals, Emotional Climate and Intergroup Perception: Participation in 'Gacaca' Tribunals and Assimilation of the Rwandan Genocide," *Journal of Social Issues* 63, no. 2 (June 2007): 401.

63. Ibid., 399.

64. James L. Gibson, "Overcoming Apartheid: Can Truth Reconcile a Divided Nation?," *Politikon: South African Journal of Political Studies* 31, no. 2 (November 2004): 129–55.

65. Ervin Staub, *The Roots of Evil: The Origins of Genocide and Other Group Violence* (Cambridge: Cambridge University Press, 1989).

66. Ibid.; Ervin Staub, "Building a Peaceful Society: Origins, Prevention, and Reconciliation After Genocide and Other Group Violence," *American Psychologist* 68, no. 7 (October 2013): 576–89; Ervin Staub, "Promoting Healing and Reconciliation in Rwanda, and Generating Active Bystandership by Police to Stop Unnecessary Harm by Fellow Officers," *Perspectives on Psychological Science* 14, no. 1 (January 2019).

67. Staub, "Building a Peaceful Society," 576.

68. Ibid.

69. Staub and Pearlman, "Intergroup Prejudice," 588–93.

70. Staub, "Building a Peaceful Society," 589

71. Ibid., 583.

72. Ibid.

73. Staub et al., "Healing, Reconciliation, Forgiving, and the Prevention of Violence After Genocide or Mass Killing"; Staub, "Building a Peaceful Society."

74. Staub, "Building a Peaceful Society," 585.

75. Staub, "Promoting Healing," 60–64.

76. Yakaré-Oulé Jansen, "Denying Genocide or Denying Free Speech? A Case Study of the Application of Rwanda's Genocide Denial Laws," *Northwestern Journal of International Human Rights* 12 (2014): 191–213.

77. Erin Jessee and Sarah E. Watkins, "Good Kings, Bloody Tyrants, and Everything in Between: Representations of the Monarchy in Post-Genocide Rwanda," *History in Africa* 41 (June 2014): 35–62.

78. World Bank, Disabled Ex-combatants in Rwanda Regain Their Independence and Rebuild Their Lives, video in the series End Poverty, January, 24, 2019, accessed June 6, 2021, https://www.youtube.com/watch?v=yU1jywurfZE&t=14s

79. Saly Morgan, "Rwanda Today: A Complicated Miracle," *Ethos* 21, no. 4 (2013): 7–13; Remy K. Katshingu, *Du miracle rwandais au paradoxe congolais*

(RDC): de la pauvreté à l'émergence économique (Paris: L'Harmattan, 2015); Amy Sullivan, "Rwanda's 'Miracle' of Forgiveness," *USA Today*, February 15, 2010, https: //www.pressreader.com/usa/usa-today-us-edition/20100215/282729108048373.

80. Peter Drobac and Brienna Naughton, "Health Equity in Rwanda: The New Rwanda, Twenty Years Later," *Harvard International Review* 35, no. 4 (Spring 2014): 57.

81. Ibid., 61.

82. The Rwandan Constitution (Article 140) requires Umushyikirano to meet at least once per year to provide a forum where participants, the "President [. . .] and citizen representatives [. . .] debate issues relating to the state of the nation, the state of local government and national unity," 42.

83. Jacquemin, "Rwandan Government."

84. Lyndsay McLean Hilker, "Everyday ethnicities: identity and reconciliation among Rwandan youth," *Journal of Genocide Research* 11, no. 1 (March 2009): 96–97.

85. Laura Eramian, "Personhood, Violence, and the Moral Work of Memory in Contemporary Rwanda," *International Journal of Conflict and Violence* 8 (September 2014): 16–29; Kenneth W. Harrow, "'Un train peut en cacher un autre'1: Narrating the Rwandan Genocide and Hotel Rwanda," *Research in African Literatures* 36, no. 4 (2005): 223–32.

8

African Bureaucracies and the Implementation of Women Empowerment Programs

Abidemi Abiola Isola, Tolulope
Adeogun, and Victor Adesiyan

As African countries have taken the leadership in global rankings of women's parliamentary representation, many studies have focused on the factors and dynamics that have produced this result over the last twenty years.[1] Such explanations have included the role of post-conflict moments introduction of gender quotas, constitutional re-engineering women's activism, and different developmental approaches on women parity.[2] The twin puzzle has been, first, that women's political ascension as executives and heads of governments has not been commensurate with parliamentary progress on this score. Only a few African heads of state since the 2005–2006 election and inauguration of Ellen Johnson Sirleaf, (the First African woman democratically elected head of state), and her re-election in November 2011, have been elected females, indicating that there are continued and entrenched barriers to women's emergence in these positions. Second, the global leadership in the parliamentary representation of women has not trickled down to produce more gender-equitable societies, despite decades of global activism to achieve this aim. The barriers to achieving these ends are located in both institutional and societal factors. This chapter focuses on the national, institutional, and bureaucratic constraints and opportunities for achieving African women's empowerment towards greater gender equality in African states. It argues that bureaucratic impediments to African women's advancement spring from the colonial design of these institutions, leadership deficits, prebendal tendencies, lack of technical capacity, and lack of political will to implement women's empowerment programs, despite women's mobilization for political representation in Africa.

Women's empowerment is defined as improvement in the ability of women to access the essence of development, most importantly in health, education, earning opportunities, rights, and political participation.[3] According to Rowland, empowerment is bringing people who are outside decision-making spheres and giving access to intangible decision-making processes.[4] From a feminist perspective, empowerment is more than being involved in decision-making; it encompasses the process that led people to perceive themselves as able and entitled to occupy decision-making spaces.[5] Cornell Empowerment Group emphasized that empowerment is developing a sense of self, individual confidence, and capacity; the ability to negotiate and influence decisions made.[6] It also includes collectivity; i.e, individuals coming together to make a more extensive impact than each could have achieved alone. Political empowerment is "people's capacity to influence policy, make demands, and call to account the state institutions that impact upon their lives. This includes political representation and collective action."[7] Putting into consideration women's political representation, empowerment must also include women's access and mobilization within formal and informal political spaces. Mobilization is the process of bringing people in the society together to be involved in matters that bring changes to their existence. This could be either positive or negative. People in this context are women's groups, creating awareness and enlightenment on women's rights and influential policies that will help increase women's political representation.[8] The pressing need for women's rights led to the creation of the women's movement in Africa. Women's movements are pulling together, harnessing, and actualizing the potential in human resources to ensure development. Empowerment and many more are the main reasons for the creation of women's movements and their activities have been more of domestication, lobbying, advocacy, and media relations, but still constrained their impact on the political representation of women.[9]

Thus, women empowerment is the "process through which individuals attain the ability to make choices under the condition in which choices were previously denied."[10] In the context of this work, women's empowerment is creating an enabling environment where women can exercise control over desires, make decisions either individually or collectively, and be actively involved in the implementation of the decision process, resulting in social transformation.

Since the first United Nations Women's Conference and Decade of Women (1975–85), until the most recently concluded Sustainable Development Goals (SDGs) in 2015, many African nations have participated in the global efforts to enshrine women's rights in national policies and processes. African countries are signatories to the conventions and treaties, have dedicated ministries/departments/agencies for women's affairs, and many have national action plans for implementing women's programs; statistics on states that are signatories to the major women's rights conventions are 49; data of Ministry for women affairs in Africa, 24%; data on existence of national action plans for women, 34%. However, the indications are that these have not produced many results over the years, and various explanations have been proffered in the literature.[11] This chapter analyzes these arguments and evaluates them. The chapter addresses the following issues: historical overview of the development of African bureaucracies and their key features; key achievements of the women's agenda in post-independence African states; challenges of implementing women's empowerment programs; the mobilization around women's rights; and a conclusion including areas for further research.

The study employs both Maxine Molyneux's organizing theory and African feminist theory to justify the presence of institutional and societal factors in Africa that limit the efforts of women's organizations working towards the increase of representation of women in political participation and decision making both in substantive and descriptive ways, at both the national and international levels.

Maxine Molyneux conceptualized 'bottom-up development' as "greater attention to demand from the grassroots, more sensitive policy instruments, and changes like state–society relations."[12] This implies that women's involvement in the decision-making process using the bottom-up approach should be supported by the government via sensitive policy instrument which includes every aspect of customary laws that is put in place for the people at the grassroots level, making sure that these laws are not gendered biased. Furthermore, it is affirmed by Molyneux's theory, that institutional and societal barriers are the basis for discrimination against women which makes women's empowerment futile.

With regards to gender roles, African feminist theory explains the relationship between the affect, knowledge, and power, which has long been the concern of feminist theorists.[13] African feminism is a theoretical approach developed by Filimina Chioma Steady in 1981. It enlightens that the query of cultural, historical, political, and economic contexts influence the study of African women in management and leadership. The significance of this theory lies in understanding the impact of cultural and historical experiences on gender construction. The Eurocentric doctrine forced on African countries bastardized the paired role played by African men and women in discharging their duties.[14]

According to Bayu, the main principle of African feminism is the study of gender in Africa which must be based on the understanding of African sociocultural realities, feminist traditions, and philosophies rather than by the universalization of Western ideas that are contrary to gender relations in Africa and disempower women.[15]

THE CONCEPT OF BUREAUCRACY

Where there is the need for control and management of resources to ensure the accomplishment of aims and goals set by individuals working together cooperatively, written or unwritten rules and regulations are put in place for greater achievement. This is because it involves a large group of non-elected people who are involved in the running of government administration. Bureaucracy has to do with many complicated ways and manners of carrying out functions. It is usually marked by red-tape, hierarchy, rigidity, and proliferation. This was practiced in African countries like Nigeria, Ghana, South Africa, Rwanda, Liberia, Senegal, Mali, Morocco, Chad, Ivory Coast, Congo, etc., during the colonial era which placed women under subjugation socially, economically, educationally, and politically as policymakers and policy implementers were gender biased.

Bureaucratic practices narrow productive activity by focusing on those activities traditionally associated with men rather than women. It was the beginning of women's oppression, how this oppression has been sustained over time, consequent on the fact that it was characterized by the education of an "administrative elite" and the majority of women lacked privileged of formal education during the precolonial era, thus limiting women's opportunities within the colonial system. Women's activities were often assumed to be limited to domestic chores and the nursing of young children. However, African women were also responsible for harvesting many crops and growing of foods among many other roles they played that were essential to the communities in which they lived. African bureaucracy is a system that made use of both hierarchy and patriarchal systems to empower African men and place African women in subjugation positions, hence disempowering women with a lack of representative bureaucracy.[16] Bureaucracy, in the context of this chapter, helps us investigate where women are represented substantively or merely in numbers at all the levels of political decision making in administration.

HISTORICAL OVERVIEW OF THE DEVELOPMENT OF AFRICAN BUREAUCRACIES

African women in their traditional societies were empowered with all kinds of dignifying occupations. They dominated in matrilineal society. The Bantu ethnic group of Zaire, in Angola, and in the Great Lakes areas as well as the Shoma of Zimbabwe, the Ashanti of Ghana, and the Baddibunka of the North Bank of Gambia all accorded power to the matriarchs of their clans to a degree that their children were identified by their mother's name and owned by their mother's families. In some African countries, women did all jobs associated with men[17]—Women like warriors in Dahomey, the Maasai women who were house builders and also served as guards to defend such buildings. Yoruba women were resourceful traders in both short- and long-distance trades.[18] To mention just a few.

However, there are two opposing arguments in the literature about the link between women empowerment and matrilineality. First, women in the matrilineal group do not exercise more autonomy than those in the patrilineal group. The reason is that matrilines need to have connections to their male members who are decision-makers. Second, matrilineality does improve women's welfare and relative power through greater access to positions as village heads or clan leaders and direct or indirect access to land. Matrilineal descent systems exist globally but are less common than patrilineal descent. Based on ethnocultural groups in the world, 13% practice matrilineal descent, including 16% of all societies in Africa.[19] This descent appears in all regions of Africa; however, it is more concentrated in south-central surrounding the Zambezi River, and usually referred to as the 'matrilineal belt.'[20]

Women, from the creation of the world, have been resourceful and very impactful. In Yoruba cosmological myth, it is believed that Olodumare (Almighty God) sent seventeen primordial divinities to earth at the beginning of time, Osun was the only female among them. Osun was ignored by the sixteen male divinities from all decisions.[21] In reaction to this, Osun gathered all women together and formed the 'IyaMi' (i.e., My Mother) group, which disrupted the smooth running of the universe with their powers, and the earth became ungovernable for the sixteen other primordial divinities. 'Olodumare'(Omnipotent God) advised them to make peace with Osun so that all might be well again.[22] Women's involvement in the development of a community should not be brushed aside.

This traditional story is a social phenomenon involving supernatural beings referring to Almighty God, the gods, and the goddess in Yorubaland, who came together to make a decision that will benefit the whole earth. However, the only female (Osun) amidst was excluded from the decision-making process. This parallels the exclusion of women from decision making in the societies to which they belong. The exclusion of women from this public and private sphere by the sixteen primordial divinities led to a chaotic situation that made the earth ungovernable. But, when Osun, the only female primordial divinity, was included, smooth governance and development were achievable.[23]

In every political system, there is a need for the citizenry, that is men and women, to participate in governance and this can only be achieved through inclusive means of political participation. The inclusion of Osun in the decision-making process can be related to women's empowerment through the "IyaMi" group or My Mother's group. In the context of this work, this can be referred to as a women's movement that mobilized for women's rights.

In some African countries, despite the precolonial centralized and decentralized structure, women did all jobs associated with men including social security. Yoruba women were inclusive and resourceful leaders and traders. Oyěwùmí averred that as a result of non-gender categorization based on biological factors, women were made kings (*alaafin* i.e., owner of the place) and chiefs (*oloye* i.e., title holder) just like their male counterpart in the old Oyo Empire.[24] Besides, in the precolonial Igbo society, women participated in social, political, and religious systems to improve their lives enthusiastically and overtly. Women were described by Lord Fredrick Lugard as "ambitious, courageous, self-reliant, hardworking and independent." Igbo women claim full equality with their male counterparts and would seem to be the dominant partner.[25]

African women during the precolonial era were empowered to take part in the decision process. It was a period with no social categorization built on a gender system, Instead both sexes were involved in decision making. Instances of African societies where there was no socially gendered categorization includes Ancient Egypt, Ghana, and Liberia, among others.[26]

Akan and Asente oral tradition, according to Akyeampong and Fofack quipped that African women were empowered with a leadership position.[27] These include Queen Amina of Zaria, the Akan of Ghana, the So of Cameroon, among others. Rattray opined further that "in the matrilineal society in Ashanti with a paired male (chief) and female (queen mother) leadership, represented by stools as symbols of office."[28]

Women's prowess also allowed complacency as they helped men rule in some political areas. For instance, in Swazi kingdom, the mother of the king called Indlovukati helped her son rule, and under Bamileke of Cameroon power was shared equally between males and females. This can also be seen in the story of Yakoyo of Ashatiin in 1888. This example established the fact that women participated in politics which empowered them under both centralized and decentralized structures in the precolonial era.[29]

African women were landowners and farmers, which empowered them to carry out division of labor in both public and private spheres. African women were essential to the development of economic and social organization of production.[30] Documented fact proved that women's basic dominance in agricultural production was necessary even in a patriarchal society.[31] Women's prominence in agriculture in Africa did endow them with economic and political influence. Titles were based on economy and prosperity for both men and women. An instance is the 'Ekwe title in Nnobiq' (a title given to a woman) whose fortune looked prosperous. The involuntary title was open to all women, but for some men, it is reserved according to their lineage.[32] It is noteworthy that African communities, during the precolonial era, were agrarian. This empowered women since one of their main roles was farming. However, African gender inclusiveness and complementarity (socially, economically, and politically) during the precolonial period was destroyed all through the colonial era.

Colonialism brought educational, religious, economic, and political influences which redefined women's role and place within the society.[33] Alienation of women from land led to their loss of economic independence and intensified domestic patriarchy."[34] This could be referred to as the beginning of patriarchy and disempowerment. Adesokan reemphasized that the colonial economy was an export-oriented cash crop agriculture which seriously undermined the prestige of the traditional occupations of the African women.[35] Women began to experience oppression in its entirety. They were formally marginalized in the scheme of things and they seem to have lost any of the power they possessed during the precolonial era.[36] Pushed off the lands women previously cultivated, they lost access and control to all land, which made them economically dependent on men. Consequently, domestic patriarchy was reinforced by colonial social and economic institutions. Correspondingly, the introduction of wage labor had a negative impact as well.[37] Similarly, taxes introduced by the colonial economy led to male migration and labor taxes were then imposed on women as well. Finally, modernism, which Weberian bureaucracy preaches, led to the complete loss of access to land by women.[38]

The bureaucracy was introduced by Europeans as the practice that narrowed productive activity by focusing on those activities traditionally associated with men rather than women. It was the beginning of women's oppression and this oppression has been sustained over time. It was characterized by the education of an "administrative elite" and the majority of women lacked the privilege of formal education during the precolonial era, thus limiting their opportunity of working within the system during the colonial era.[39] Hence, their roles or activities were limited to domestic chores and the nursing of the young ones. The Eurocentric doctrine introduced to the African system paralleled women's prestige and dignity placing them in a subjugated position. According to Lugoes, gender is a social construct.[40] Thus, the gender roles of African women were no longer based on the African social construct definition of gender roles but rather on the European ones. African gender roles were no longer based on African culture but rather on the colonial masters' Western cultural principles.

According to Oyěwùmí, before the arrival of the colonial masters in Africa, same-sex relationships were recognized in many African societies.[41] Oyěwùmí is engaged in this deconstruction of categories. The woman category according to her would be a colonial invention.[42] Asserting that colonization in Africa, although violent, has a different impact on men and women, she explains this difference mainly by the fact that the colonizers were white men. The colonial state is, therefore, first, a patriarchal state. Despite the presence in the colonies of white women, although oppressed, enjoyed the privilege of the race. But, power and authority were exclusively concentrated in hands of white men.

The emergence of women as an identifiable category, defined by their anatomy and subordinated to men in all situations, resulted, in part, from the imposition of a patriarchal colonial state. For females, colonization was a twofold process of racial inferiorization and gender subordination.[43] The creation of "women" has a role in the colonial state. It is not surprising, therefore, that it was unthinkable for the colonial government to recognize female leaders among the colonized, such as among the Yoruba. The transformation of state power to male-gender power exclusively was accomplished by the exclusion of women from state structures. This was in sharp contrast to Yoruba state organization, in which power was not gender-determined.[44] However, it is important here to note that Oyěwùmí's work cannot be applied to the entire African continent, whose cultural realities are manifold. Even if we cannot extend Oyěwùmí's analysis to all African societies, it remains that colonization has influenced gender roles and identities on the continent. These dynamics of inequalities continue today and are characterized by the domination of patriarchy, the inequality between men and women.[45]

Despite all these challenges, women had made great attempts and are still forging ahead in making strides in different aspects of their society. African women keep struggling for their fair share of political influence, economic opportunities, and making an impact.

WOMEN'S AGENDA ACHIEVEMENT SINCE POST-INDEPENDENCE AND MOBILIZATION AROUND WOMEN'S RIGHTS

Despite the impediment created by colonial bureaucracies, there have been great achievements of women's agenda in Africa. Some of the key goals were achieved in both the public and private spheres. In the mid-20th century, building upon women's participation in anticolonial struggles across Africa, many political roles were taken on by African women in the post-independence period. In 1990, Tripp argued that for the first time in post-independence,

African women began to aspire to political leadership both at the national and local levels.[46] Women like Charity Ngilu and Wangari Maathai ran in the 1990 Kenyan presidential election. Rose Rugendo of Tanzania's party Chama Cha Mapinduzi sought her party's nomination in the 1995 presidential primaries and also Sarah Jibril in Nigeria in 1989. Although the bid for power did not reach fruition in that decade, these women set an important milestone in their respective countries.[47]

The first African women to emerge as leaders included Zauditu, Empress of Ethiopia (1917–1930); Dzeliwe Shongwe, Queen-regent of Swaziland (1982–1983); Ntombi Thwala, Queen-regent of Swaziland (1983–1986); and Elizabeth Domitien, Africa's first female prime minister in the Central African Republic (1975–1976).[48] Among these first few political leaders mentioned, only Elizabeth Domitien was appointed by the governing committee. The influence of the women's movement during this period was yet to be aggressive in mobilizing around women's rights as the main objective of the organization developmental activities. Their agendas did not yet involve lobbying for more gendered political representation.

When access to elected office in many countries in the early years after independence was barred by military and single-party rule, female and male combatants in southern African fought together for national liberation. Prior to the 1980s and 1990s, national gender machinery was established and fostered women's right through institutional infrastructure. Also, first lady-ism and national women's run by state, prompted state feminism in order to manipulate women's struggles for political gain. Furthermore, the severe impact of structural adjustment programs led to women's mobilization in the 1980s, locally organized programs, and focus on women's access to political office. Consequently, in the 1990s, new forms of mobilization emerged, providing women the opportunity to access political offices at the legislative, executive, and judiciary level in unprecedented numbers.[49]

Furthermore, an increase in political representation in the post-independence period in 1990 made possible the formation of new nonpartisan lobbying, civic education, and leadership training organizations as demonstrated by Orisadare.[50] This opening encouraged women to run for office and to the demise of mass organization tied to a single party. Examples include Umoja wa Wanawake wa Tanzania (UWT) that is linked to Chama cha Mapinduzi (CCM), the League of Malawi Women that is the women's wing of the Malawi Congress Party, and the Women's League of the United National Independence Party (UNIP) in Zambia.[51] The increase in women's political decision-making is progress measured in micro-steps, and representation is increasing, but at a stubbornly slow rate, to the exception of countries that introduced parity requirements in their constitutions such as Rwanda.[52]

Another achievement is the simultaneous emergence of independent women's associations which made it possible for the women's movement to select their leaders and agendas to ensure further mobilization. Countries like Uganda and South Africa that had the most independent women's movements seem to have gone the furthest in this regard. New nonpartisan organizations, also emerged to support women candidates and female political leadership.[53]

Lately, patriarchy failed as a society to incorporate women's issues into governance in Africa.[54] Many early feminist scholars discussed the existing women's movement as a major analytical focus.[55] While the women's movement was involved in educating voters, it was raising awareness about women's right issues, lobbying legislative bodies, and supporting the very few women daring to run for office.

Gouws, in Orisadare, quipped that women's organizations networking are across Africa on a unique scale, and creating welcoming laws and constitutions.[56] This indicates that women organizations no longer solely focus on development activities like income generation and welfare concerns but have evolved to become organizations lobbying for women in decision-making positions in politics, thereby politicizing previously assumed as nonpolitical agendas of women organizations.

Empowerment is essential for African women to thrive in their yearning to participate fully in the bright future of their continent. Thus, accelerating various empowerment programs in African states can bring the most significant changes and positive transformations. Several instruments have been adopted to put an end to women's marginalization and disempowerment.

Many international and national policies were put in place to ensure women's empowerment in various aspects within and outside her society. The African Union enshrined a legacy and protocol to the African Charter on Human and People's Rights of women. This is to ensure gender mainstreaming and nondiscrimination in some areas. This reflects and reinforces developments at the national level. The African Union also adopted from inception a 50 percent quota for women's representation. Angola, Mozambique, Namibia, Senegal, and South Africa have exceeded the 30 percent quota for their legislative representation.[57] Rwanda made great history when women exceeded 14 percent above the mandated 50% by law, in 2017. However, a slight reduction occurred in 2018. Women in Nigeria assumed nontraditional ministerial portfolios, in defense and finance. Liberia also had the first African female as head of state, Ellen Johnson Sirleaf. Besides, Ethiopia also took a great stride by electing a woman, Sahle-Work Zewde, as President in the year 2018. Nevertheless, this increase in women's representation has not catalyzed in favor of women in ensuring greater gender equality in Africa.

The colonial-era bureaucracy in Africa established patriarchal and racially stratified societies. At the Convention on the Elimination of all Forms of

Discrimination Against Women (CEDAW), new policies and guidelines were established to ensure African Women's Empowerment.[58] Only South Sudan and Somalia among African countries are yet to ratify CEDAW, adopted in 1979. Subsequently, in 1995, the Beijing Conference set ambitious targets to improve the lives of women worldwide, and African women had reason to expect changes in the area of gender equality.[59] However, the progress has been limited in Africa as a result of bureaucratic structures in place, hence the urgent need to overcome institutional obstacles.

As a result of pressure and mobilization by women, affirmative action policies were introduced in some African countries. This increased the number of women in decision-making positions to empower African women before the Beijing Conference.[60] For instance, Nigeria took certain steps towards mainstreaming gender issues. The Heads of State's wives embarked on programs to empower women. Better Life for Rural Women and family support programs, among others in Nairobi, Kenya, as well. Heads of State 'used' their wives to create awareness of women's issues. Although some of these empowerment programs had their critics, they provided some opportunities to empower women.[61]

In Rwanda, Zimbabwe, and Uganda, Ministries of Gender and Community Development were established (2003, 2011, and 1995, respectively) to foster gender equality and women's empowerment. Similarly, in Nigeria, Cameroon, Botswana, Ivory Coast, Malawi, Namibia, Gambia, and Egypt, the Ministry or Department of Women's Affairs were created for the same purpose.[62]

Following the adoption of the African Union Gender Policy, African leaders in 2009 launched the African Women Decade from 2010 to 2020 supported by the Fund for African Women to accelerate the implementation of all commitments on gender equality and women empowerment in African countries.[63] Many African countries are signatory to this continental framework.[64] However, most strategies and policies that yield general political mobilization are often not as effective to mobilize women in some African countries. It is a situation where implementation does not necessarily reach its intended goals. Despite the enormous achievements, there remain a plethora of issues hindering the empowerment of women in Africa.[65]

Policies and strategies are more theoretical than practical. Mobilization of women's political representation has not been as successful as it ought to be. Women's movements must find ways to translate mobilization into concrete improvements in levels of female leadership, addressing women's agendas, and providing more gender equal political representation. The reason for the lack of progress often comes back to the usurpation of gender activism, rendering the struggle for women's equality a mere technical exercise that seems best to be left to the government. The exploitation of customs, culture, and tradition to legitimize gender inequality remains a powerful force. There is the need, thus, to rethink the approach to women empowerment and gender equality, especially in the area of women's political participation.[66]

CHALLENGES OF IMPLEMENTING WOMEN'S EMPOWERMENT PROGRAMS

The implementation process involves different stages which include problem identification, proposal writing, appraisal, approval, implementation and monitoring, and finally, evaluation. More often than not, the implementation process of women's empowerment goes through all the early stages but stops at approval, while those that get all the way through to the implementation and monitoring stage do not reach the final stage of evaluation to learn from what has been achieved and generate new ideas.

Cultural barriers and poverty are bottlenecked to the implementation of women's empowerment. According to the 1995 United Nations Development Program, Human Development report, poverty has a woman's face. Out of 1.3 billion people in poverty, 70% are women (which means close to a billion of them are women and girls).[67] Women's inequality in the labor market, treatment under social welfare, their status and power in the family, can be linked to increase in poverty.

As long as women remain poor, they will continue to be oppressed and discriminated against in all spheres of life. This keeps women locked into a vicious cycle of dependency at all levels. When empowerment programs come to an end, because of poverty, women often have not been imbued with any skills to sustain themselves and fall back into a worse situation of poverty and dependency.[68] However, efforts are being made through women's movements by networking across the continent on an unprecedented scale, challenging laws and constitutions not propagating gender equality in the private and public sphere.[69] Enforcement of laws passed to give women a better life is slowly changing the shape of women's struggle region by region. However, several women's organizations and individuals are putting in more effort and working untiringly towards women's emancipation in Africa.

CONCLUSION INCLUDING AREAS FOR FURTHER RESEARCH

The study explores the beginning of African bureaucracy and the implementation of women's empowerment. This study's discussion started with what bureaucracy and African bureaucracy refer to, the precolonial era when women were empowered, and their role complemented their male counterpart. Male and female relations existed on an equal level where the construction of gender equity was socially assigned in many African cultures and societies. Until the emergence of the colonial master with the introduction of Eurocentric principles which constructed new gender roles, not based on African cultural norms but on Western cultural oppressive principles where all members deemed essential to the community were differentiated in levels of rights, power, and access to land. The colonial system elevated men in the position of authority over their wives, and subjugated both under colonial absolute power. This created an institutional barrier or a glass ceiling that has held back many African women from becoming empowered.

This study also shed light on the achievement of African women in the postcolonial era. In spite of barriers, achievements made were evident in the number of African women earning leadership roles in parliaments, ministries, in the economy, or in education realms. However, there were challenges as a cog in the wheel of the implementation of both national and international laws and treaties meant to empower women and encourage gender mainstreaming in Africa.

This paper recommends that the male power structure oppressing women should be destroyed in Africa's definition of gender roles. This can be achieved through indigenous teachings of African culture starting from home to school and through social gatherings where women leaders are present and mentor the next generations of girls and young women. Furthermore, teaching children the successful story of African women, hidden by Eurocentric doctrines, can help to further empower all members in African societies.

There is also the need for sensitivity in leadership selection of both men and women by citizens in African countries. Gender redistribution should also be considered to ensure redress is sought when imbalances were created by past discriminatory policies. And lastly, for the implementation of women's empowerment to be a reality, who gets what, when, and how should not be dictated only by men. Women should be involved in such edicts through mobilization and politicization for meaningful gender representation. Further studies should be carried out on the impact of African savings, credit culture, and women's empowerment.

NOTES

1. "Women in Politics: 2017," Inter-Parliamentary Union, accessed August 21, 2021, https://www.ipu.org/resources/publications/infographics/2017-03/women-in-politics-2017; "Women in parliament in 2018: The year in review," Inter-Parliamentary Union, accessed August 21, 2021, https://www.ipu.org/resources/publications/reports

/2019-03/women-in-parliament-in-2018-year-in-review; Pankaj Kumar, "Participation of Women in Politics: Worldwide experience," *Journal of Humanities and Social Science* 12, no. 6 (December 2017): 77–88.

2. For further reading on these topics, please see Tristan Anne Borer, "Gendered War and Gendered Peace: Truth Commissions and Postconflict Gender Violence: Lessons From South Africa," *Violence Against Women* 15, no. 10 (October 1, 2009): 1169–93; Aili Mari Tripp, *Women and Power in Postconflict Africa* (Cambridge: Cambridge University Press, 2015); Julie Ballington, *The Implementation of Quotas: African Experiences* (International Institute for Democracy and Electoral Assistance, IDEA, 2004); Nneamaka Mojekwu-Chikezie, *African Women Sentenced by Tradition* (Lagos, A.A. Nwokebi & Company, 2012); K.M. Omoragbon "Kicking Against the Pricks: 'The Nigerian Constitution as an Impediment to Women's Rights in Nigeria," in *The power of gender, the gender of power: women's labor, rights and responsibilities in Africa*, eds. Toyin Falola and Bridget Teboh (Trenton: Africa World Press, 2013): 703; S. Akinboye and D. Agbalajobi, "Gender –Based violence and the Quest for Sustainable Development," in *The Power of Gender, the Gender of Power: Women's Labor, Rights and Responsibilities in Africa*, eds. Toyin Falola and Bridget Teboh (Trenton: Africa World Press, 2013), 567; Myra Marx Ferree and Aili Mari Tripp, *Global Feminism: Transnational Women's Activism, Organizing, and Human Rights* (New York: NYU Press, 2006); Nwabufo Okeke Uzodike, "Women and Development in Africa: Competing Approaches and Contested Achievements," *Alternation* 20, no. 2 (January 2013), 27–51; Toyin Falola and Nana Akua Amponsah, *Women's Roles in Sub-Saharan Africa* (Santa Barbara: Greenwood, 2012).; and Toyin Falola and Nana Akua Amponsah *Women, Gender, and Sexualities in Africa* (Durham: Carolina Academic Press, 2013).

3. Esther Duflo, "Women's Empowerment and Economic Development," working paper, *National Bureau of Economic Research* (2011): https://www.nber.org/papers/w17702.

4. Jo Rowlands, "Empowerment Examined," in *Development and Social Diversity*, ed. Mary B. Anderson (Oxford: Oxfam: 1996), 3–4.

5. Ibid.; J. Rappaport, "In Praise of Paradox: A Social Policy of Empowerment over Prevention," *American Journal of Community Psychology* 9, no. 1 (1981): 1–25.

6. Rappaport, "Paradox," 1–25.

7. Rosalind Eyben, "Subversively Accommodating: Feminist Bureaucrats and Gender Mainstreaming," *IDS Bulletin* 41, no. 2 (2010): 54–61.

8. For more information, please see Claire Castillejo, *Women's Political Participation and Influence in Sierra Leone,* working paper no. 83 (Fride, Spain: Fundación Para Las Reflaciones Internacionales y el Diálogo Exterior, June 2009); and "South Africa," Country Data, International IDEA, accessed August 24, 2021, https://www.idea.int/data-tools/data/gender-quotas/country-view/310/35.

9. Monica Adele Orisadare, "An Assessment of the Role of Women Group in Women Political Participation, and Economic Development in Nigeria," *Front Sociol* 4, no. 52 (2019), doi: 10.3389/fsoc.2019.00052.

10. Naila Kabeer, "Gender Equality and Women's Empowerment: A Critical Analysis of the Third Millennium Development Goal 1," *Gender and Development* 13, no. 1 (2005): 13.

11. For further reading on these statistics, please see Aili Mari Tripp et al., *African Women's Movements: Transforming Political Landscapes* (Cambridge: Cambridge University Press, 2008); International Institute for Democracy and Electoral Assistance, *Women's Political Participation: Africa Barometer 2021* (International Institute for Democracy and Electoral Assistance: March 17, 2021), https://www.idea .int/publications/catalogue/womens-political-participation-africa-barometer-2021; Fredoline Anunobi, "Women and Development in Africa: From Marginalization to Gender Inequality," *African Social Science Review* 2, no. 2 (2002): 41–63; Toyin Falola, "Gender and Culture in Old and New Africa," in *The Toyin Falola Reader on African Culture, Nationalism, Development and Epistemology*, ed. Toyin Falola (Austin: Pan African University Press, 2018); Tolulope Adeogun and Abidemi Abiola Isola, "Democratic Governance and Women's Political Participation in Nigeria," in *Democratic Practice and Governance in Nigeria*, eds. Ebenezer Oluwole Oni et al. (New York: Routledge, 2021).

12. Maxine Molyneux "Gender and the Silences of Social Capital: Lessons from Latin America," *Development and Change* 33, no. 2 (2002): 183.

13. Annette Anigwe "Perceptions of Women in Political Leadership Positions in Nigeria," *Walden Dissertations and Doctoral Studies* 28 (2014), https://scholarworks .waldenu.edu/dissertations/28.

14. Pinkie Mekgwe, "Post Africa(n) Feminism?," *Third Text Third Text* 24, no. 2 (2010): 189–94.

15. Eyayu Kasseye Bayu, "A Comparative Analysis on the Perspectives of African Feminism Vs Western Feminism: Philosophical Debate with Their Criticism and its Implication for Women's Rights in Ethiopia Context," *International Journal of Sociology and Anthropology* 11, no. 4 (2019): 54–58.

16. Sebawit G. Bishu and Jean-Claude Garcia-Zamor, "Institutional Bureaucratic Representation in Gender Mainstreaming," *Global Journal of Interdisciplinary Social Sciences* 3, no. 3 (2014): 229–37.

17. Abidemi Abiola Isola and Bukola A. Alao, "African Women and Leadership Role," *Journal of Humanities and Social Science* 24, no. 9 (September 2019): 5–6.

18. Ibid., 5–6; Carol E. Morgan, "Women, Work and Consciousness in the Mid-nineteenth-century English Cotton Industry," *Social History* 17, no. 1 (January 1992): 23–41.

19. *Encyclopedia Britannica*, s.v. "Matrilineal Society," accessed December 3, 2021, https://www.britannica.com/topic/matrilineal-society.

20. Nava Ashraf et al., "Bride Price and Female Education," *Journal of Political Economy* 128, no. 2 (January 2020): 591–641.

21. Oyèrónké Oyěwùmí, *Gender Epistemologies in Africa: Gendering Traditions, Spaces, Social Institutions, and Identities* (New York: Palgrave Macmillan: 2011); Oyeronke Olajubu, "Seeing through a Woman's Eye: Yoruba Religious Tradition and Gender Relations," *Journal of Feminist Studies in Religion* 20, no. 1 (2004): 40–60; Pamela Machakanja. "Contested Spaces: Gender, Governance and Women's Political

Engagement in Postcolonial Africa," in *The Crises of Postcoloniality in Africa*, ed. Kenneth Omeje (Dakar: CODESRIA, 2015), 197–215.

22. Abidemi Abiola Isola and Bukola A. Alao, "African Women and Leadership Role," *Journal of Humanities and Social Science* 24, no. 9 (September 2019): 5–8.

23. Ibid.

24. O. Oyewumi, *Gender Epistemologies in Africa.*

25. Judith van Allen, "'Sitting on a Man': Colonialism and the Lost Political Institutions of Igbo Women," *Canadian Journal of African Studies/Revue Canadienne des Études Africaines* 6, no. 2 (1972): 165–81.

26. S. Franceschet and Jennifer M. Piscopo, "Gender Quotas and Women's Substantive Representation: Lessons from Argentina," *Politics & Gender* 4 (2008): 393–425.

27. Emmanuel Akyeampong and Hippolyte Fofack, *The Contribution of African Women to Economic Growth and Development: Historical Perspectives and Policy Implications—Part I: The Pre-Colonial and Colonial Periods,* SSRN Working Paper 6051 (Rochester, New York: Social Science Research Network, April 20, 2016), 111.

28. Ibid., 112–13; R.S. Rattray, 5.

29. Tarikhu Farrar, "The Queenmother, Matriarchy, and the Question of Female Political Authority in Precolonial West African Monarchy," *The Journal of Black Studies* 27, no. 5 (May 1997): 579–97.

30. Ibid., 581–82; Emmanuel Akyeampong and Hippolyte Fofack, The Contribution of African Women to Economic Growth and Development: Historical Perspectives and Policy Implications—Part I: The Pre-Colonial and Colonial Periods, SSRN Working Paper 6051, (Rochester, New York: Social Science Research Network, April 20, 2016), 111.

31. Lee Ndaba, "A Stolen Legacy: The Matrilineality of Pre-Colonial African Society," Medium, last modified November 14, 2018, https://medium.com/@MthiyaneShandu/a-stolen-legacy-the-matrilineality-of-pre-colonial-african-society-5307b8db3e5a.

32. Kirk Arden Hoppe, "IfiAmadiume. Male Daughters, Female Husbands: Gender and Sex in an African Society," *International Feminist Journal of Politics* 18, no. 3 (2016): 498–500.

33. Tristan Anne Borer, "Gendered War and Gendered Peace: Truth Commissions and Postconflict Gender Violence: Lessons from South Africa," *Violence Against Women* 15, no. 10 (October 2009): 1169–93.

34. Tolulope Adeogun and Abidemi Abiola Isola, "Evaluation of Women's Rights in the Perspective of Human Right Under Democratic Government in Nigeria. 1999–2009," *Babcock University Journal of Management and Social Sciences*, 8, nos. 1–2 (2011): 69.

35. Khadijah S. Adesokan, "Women Empowerment as a Catalyst for Sustainable Development in Nigeria: Adult Education as a Tool," *Journal of Education and Practice* 9, no. 11 (2018): 136–42.

36. Ibid.

37. Abidemi Abiola Isola and Bukola A. Alao, "African Women and Leadership Role," *Journal of Humanities and Social Science* 24, no. 9 (September 2019): 5–6.

38. Farrar, "The Queenmother Matriarchy," 582–83; Amy Mazur, Dorothy Mcbride, and Season Hoard, "Comparative Strength of Women's Movements over Time: Conceptual, Empirical, and Theoretical Innovations," *Politics, Groups, and Identities* 4, no. 4 (December 2015): 1–25.

39. Boris Bertolt, "Thinking Otherwise: Colonial/Modern Gender System in Africa," *Sociological Review* 22, no. 1 (September 2018): 3–17.

40. Lugoes cited in Obioma Nnaemeka, "Development, Cultural Forces, and Women's Achievements in Africa," *Law & Policy* 18, nos. 3–4 (July/October 1996): 251–80.

41. Oyèrónkẹ́ Oyěwùmí, *The Invention of Women: Making an African Sense of Western Gender Discourses* (Minneapolis: University of Minnesota Press, 1997), 22.

42. Bertolt, "Thinking Otherwise," 14.

43. Ibid.

44. Oyěwùmí, *The Invention of Women*, 124–25.

45. Bertolt, "Thinking Otherwise," 12–13.

46. Aili Mari Tripp, *Women in Power in Post Conflict Africa*, 33–54.

47. Ibid.

48. Ibid.

49. Aili Mari Tripp et al., "Preface," in *African Women's Movements: Transforming Political Landscapes*, eds. Aili Mari Tripp et al. (Cambridge: Cambridge University Press, 2008), xi–xvi.

50. Orisadare, "An Assessment of the Role of Women," 2.

51. Aili Mari Tripp, *Women in Power in Post Conflict Africa*, 33–54.

52. Yolanda Sadie, "Women, the Electoral System and Political Parties," in *Political Parties in South Africa: Do They Undermine or Underpin Democracy?* ed. Heather A. Thuynsma (Pretoria: Africa Institute of South Africa, 2017), 47–71.

53. Tripp et al., "Preface."

54. Pamela Machakanja, cited in Mechthild E. Nagel, "Patriarchal Ideologies and Women's Domestication," in *The End of Prisons: Reflections from the Decarceration Movement*, eds. Mechthild E. Nagel and Anthony J. Nocella II (Amsterdam: Rodopi, 2013), 147–67.

55. Drude Dahlerup, *The New Women's Movement: Feminism and Political Power in Europe and the USA* (London: Sage Publications, 1986); Orisadare, "An Assessment of the Role of Women"; Aili Mari Tripp, "New Trends in Women's Political Participation in Africa," (2001): 26–27.

56. Amanda Gouws, "Unpacking the Difference between Feminist and Women's movements in Africa," *The Conversation*, August 9, 2015, http://theconversation .com/unpacking-the-difference-between-feminist-and-womens-movements-in-africa -45258; Orisadare, "An Assessment of the Role of Women."

57. "Facts and figures: Women's Leadership and Political Participation," UN Women, last updated January 15, 2021, https://www.unwomen.org/en/what-we-do/ leadership-and-political-participation/facts-and-figures.

58. UN Human Rights Council, "Convention on the Elimination of All Forms of Discrimination against Women," December 18, 1979, https://www.ohchr.org/EN/ ProfessionalInterest/Pages/CEDAW.aspx.

59. United Nations Development Program, Human Development Report 1997: Human Development to Eradicate Poverty. http://www.hdr.undp.org/en/content/human-development-report-1997.

60. Ibid.

61. Mojekwu-Chikezie, *African Women Sentenced,* 22.

62. T. Jayeoba, "Evaluation of Socio-Political Rights of Women under Democratic Regimes in Nigeria (1960–2007)" (MSc Thesis, Obafemi Awolowo University, 2009).

63. African Union, "African Union Gender Policy," REV 2, February 10, 2009,

64. African Union, "African Union Gender Policy," REV 2, February 10, 2009, https://www.usip.org/sites/default/files/Gender/African_Union_Gender_Policy_2009 .pdf.

65. Meghan Corroon et al., "The Role of Gender Empowerment on Reproductive Health Outcomes in Urban Nigeria," *Maternal and Child Health Journal* 18, no. 1 (2014): 307–15.

66. Orisadare, "An Assessment of the Role of Women," 2–3.

67. United Nations Development Program, Human Development Report 1997: Human Development to Eradicate Poverty. http://www.hdr.undp.org/en/content/human-development-report-1997.

68. Patricia Made, "Defining an African Women's Agenda beyond Beijing," *African Journal of Political Science* 1, no. 1 (1996): 73–83.

69. Aili Mari Tripp, *Women in Power in Post Conflict Africa,* 33–54.

PART III

Internet and Social Media Foster Identity Change, Exploration, and Mobilization

9

Building Global Citizenship through the African Digital Public Humanities

The MaCleKi Collaborative

Meshack Owino and J. Mark Souther

After taking courses and engaging in various academic activities organized under the auspices of a grant-funded research project titled "Curating Kisumu: Adapting Mobile Humanities Interpretation in East Africa," a graduate student in the Department of History at Cleveland State University (hereinafter CSU), Cleveland, Ohio, and an undergraduate student in the Department of History and Archeology at Maseno University (hereinafter, MU), Kenya, started evincing sentiments that were eerily similar to one another as citizens whose aspirations and consciousness were becoming increasingly global. The CSU student, for example, shared in an email that he was going to serve in the Peace Corps in Tanzania, a choice he said was inspired by his work in the "Curating Kisumu" project. His counterpart at MU emailed to ask for advice on applying for scholarships to continue his studies in the United States.[1] The worldview, deportment, attitudes, and ambitions of these two students seemed to be changing, as, after finishing with the project, they started exploring opportunities for new experiences and ventures far away from their traditional local abodes. They started expressing interests in what was going on in other parts of the world, and what this meant for their future academic and professional careers as well as experiences as human beings. They started exploring opportunities for travel, study, work, and even residency in other parts of the world.

The interests that the two students exhibited in prospects and opportunities far away from their homes and in foreign lands after participating in the "Curating Kisumu" project lie at the center of the objective of this chapter. This chapter examines the attitudes, experiences, and worldviews of MU and CSU students and how they changed after the students interacted and learned with each other in the collaborative research project between their universities. It explores the transformation of the identity and worldview of the students who were involved in the project, and how the project helped in that transformation. Why and how did the MU and CSU students, after participating in the project, start expressing a desire to explore other parts of the world for academic and professional opportunities? Was this but a mere coincidence? Or did participation in the project actually play a role in expanding the students' mental horizons and worldviews? Did it shape how they saw themselves? Did it influence how they conceptualized their place in the world? What role did the project play in opening the minds of these two students to the possibility of other experiences in other parts of the world, and how they could avail themselves of those experiences?

Although the answers to these questions are not necessarily easy, fortunately students who participated in the research project produced a wealth of materials that can be mined for at least some glimpses of the answers to some of the questions. Apart from emails, students who participated in the project also filled out questionnaires that illuminate their experiences in the project. These data can help unravel the extent to which the research project helped to transform the students' views about themselves, their place in the world, their future, their identities, their aspirations; essentially, their worldview, their becoming global citizens.

An examination of the emails and questionnaires demonstrates that nearly all students who participated in the project loved working with what some of the students called "the outside world." The students asserted that they enjoyed "working with students from other cultures" or "people from other countries" during the project. Moreover, students from other parts of Kenya studying at MU also expressed appreciation that the project gave them an opportunity to visit new places in Kisumu, places that they had only heard about, but never visited or fully explored. The comments in the questionnaires demonstrate that the project had a major impact in changing students' attitudes, mindsets, worldviews, and orientations. It means that, after being involved in the research project, the students started seeing themselves in a different way. No longer merely disconnected individuals scattered in their isolated spaces, they were now learning to see themselves as part of something larger than their localities, their universities, or their countries. They started exhibiting bigger ambitions about their place in the world. They were now interested in experiencing other parts of the world. They were proud of working with students from other parts of the globe and were interested in the lives of those students. They became conscious of belonging to a global community, and they exhibited characteristics that are often associated with individuals that are often labeled as global citizens.

Global citizens are what we may literally call "globalized individuals," and globalized individuals are those who are curious about what goes on in other parts of the world beyond their immediate surroundings. They are aware of, and conversant with, issues, debates, and controversies around globalization, its impact on cultures, economies, communities, nations, and states, and the fear and anguish it provokes in the hearts and minds of certain individuals, and their culture and nations, but are nevertheless convinced that globalization is the natural, perhaps inevitable outcome of human progression and development.[2] They believe in the existence of a global community. They relish interdependence and communication with other individuals around the globe.[3] According to Gianluca Grimalda, Nancy Buchan, and Marilynn Brewer, a global citizen is an individual that is involved with and attached to other individuals in other parts of the world through global networks.[4] Kris Olds defines a global citizen as an international citizen with a firsthand experience of other cultures.[5] A global citizen is an individual who is interested in people and cultures in other parts of the world. He exhibits characteristics that are associated with self-awareness, and is interested in issues, events, and people around the world. He is conscious of the world and of his place in it. He understands that his community is not the only entity existing in the world, but, rather, is part of and connected to the rest of the wider world he lives in. In fact, the definition of a global citizen means that a global citizen is not just aware and conscious that he is part of a bigger world, lives in it, and operates in it, but also that what he does can affect others just as much as what others do affects him.

The emails and questionnaires from students who participated in the collaborative research project between their universities between 2015 and 2018 clearly show that the students developed or were in the process of developing interests in the world beyond their immediate, local surroundings after the project came to an end. The research project consisted of two successive phases, each of which was sponsored by the National Endowment for the Humanities (NEH). The first phase, titled "Curating Kisumu," ran from spring 2015 to fall 2016. After this phase ended, a similar, much bigger phase, titled "Curating East Africa: A Platform and Process for Location-based Storytelling in the Developing World," continued from fall 2017 to fall 2018. The two projects brought together students from MU and CSU in learning, studying, doing research, and writing essays on important topics in the history of the Kisumu region. After completing their work, the students posted essays on the topics they had researched on a website called MaCleKi (this name is an acronym based on the first two letters from the names of "Maseno," "Cleveland," and "Kisumu") specifically created to host work from the project.[6]

Between January 2015 and December 2018, more than 200 students from the two universities participated in the project. After participating in the project, these students expressed a deep desire to explore academic and professional opportunities where their research partners lived or came from. Nearly all the students who participated in the project also expressed an interest in the lives, affairs, experiences, and home areas of members of their groups after completing the work they did with each other in the project. The students in fact continued communicating with one another even after the project ended. Moreover, the students were not just interested in how each was doing, but also in visiting each other. They asserted that they learned a lot about each other's lives and would be grateful for an opportunity to visit the country of the students they worked with during the research project.

This chapter is therefore an examination of the transformation of the experiences, worldviews, and attitudes of students who participated in the research projects that their respective universities organized for them between 2015 and 2018. It examines how the research project transformed the attitude, experiences, and worldview of participating students, as well as how the project transformed the students from being merely focused on their individual, local interests into global citizens interested in what was going on around the globe.

THE RAISON D'ÊTRE OF THE TEACHING, LEARNING, AND RESEARCH COLLABORATION BETWEEN MASENO UNIVERSITY AND CLEVELAND STATE UNIVERSITY

The teaching, learning, and research collaboration between faculty and students in the Department of History at CSU, and Department of History and Archeology at MU started in spring 2015. The students and faculty who participated in the project from both universities were required to work with one another to identify research topics on important locations, sites, events, and people in the Kisumu region of Kenya and write essays on those subjects while taking concurrent courses offered by the two universities. After writing the essays, the students were expected to post them on the MaCleKi website (www.macleki.org). The students were expected to use the website not only to help in disseminating historical knowledge about Kisumu, but also to engage their audience in discussing their stories, and, where needed, provide updates to the stories. This was live history. The project began with Kisumu, but there were plans to extend the same strategy of collaboration in teaching, learning, research, and dissemination of historical knowledge to other parts of Kenya, East Africa, Africa, and ultimately, perhaps, to other parts of the developing world.

This collaborative research project was inspired by innovative but cheap technological programs that were emerging in Africa following the digital revolution that was taking the continent by storm during the 1990s and 2000s. Such programs depended on the maximization of the utility of the mobile handsets that were helping people from all walks of life on the African continent to break social, economic, political, and technological barriers that had long hampered Africans' access to much-needed services. With tech-savvy entrepreneurs and creative innovators harnessing the potentialities opened up by the handset, by far the most easily and cheaply available device, communication became easier; problems became easier to identify and resolve; more opportunities opened up more easily. The emergence of the M-Pesa financial transaction program, for example, was based on the innovative idea of using the mobile phone handset to transfer and exchange money between people more easily and conveniently, helping people to bypass bureaucratic red tape, technological obstacles, infrastructural problems, and geographical barriers that had impeded financial transactions in the African continent for a very long time. The Ushahidi program was also based on the use of mobile handsets to seek or provide help during crises, thus enabling people to communicate with one another and overcome problems during natural disasters and catastrophes as happened during the disastrous earthquake that hit Haiti in 2010, and the devastating double tragedy of an earthquake and a tsunami that hit Japan in 2011. There were also similar innovative programs enabling people, communities, and cities to overcome challenges and solve problems. One such program was created to help farmers learn from one another about the best farm practices, how weather and other environmental problems could affect their crops and animals, the best prices for their farm products, and the best markets to visit if they were interested in selling their farm products for higher returns. Such programs were helping farmers to exchange information and maximize on economic opportunities in ways that were not possible in the past. These were highly innovative programs and they were all based on the utilization of the cellphone handset because it was the cheapest, and most easily accessible means for people to communicate and share ideas on the African continent.

Following on these innovative programs utilizing the mobile handset to spur social, economic, technological, and political development of the African continent, the faculty and students at MU and CSU decided to develop a research project to explore the possibility of deploying the mobile handset in the classroom to facilitate teaching, learning, dissemination of information, and exchange of knowledge between faculty and students from different parts of the world. It was interested in how to exploit the mobile handset to promote teaching, learning, research together between faculty and students who did not have access to the same amount or type of resources, for example, between students and faculty in the classroom in an industrialized, Western country, and those in a developing country, between say, students in a classroom in a university in the United States of America, and students in a university in Kenya. Could such a program be developed? How could it work? What were the challenges and pitfalls, and the opportunities and possibilities?

Apart from the need to explore the possibility of faculty and students from different parts of the world exchanging knowledge in a digital classroom, the project was also set up to help salvage, document, and share knowledge of important historical sites, places, locations, events, and people around the world. With the expansion of the modern economy, many important historical sites, locations, places, events, and people especially in the developing world are in jeopardy and disappearing. Important historical sites are being torn down to make way for new roads, new buildings, and other new projects. Prominent individuals that have contributed to the history of places are dying with their knowledge disappearing because they have not had the opportunity to write down or record their memories for posterity. It is therefore critically important to identify these individuals, places, sites, events, and locations; write about their history; store, preserve, and curate it; and then disseminate it to the rest of the world. In short, the research project was motivated by the need to salvage and share the history of such places before it was too late. Kisumu was just the beginning of such efforts.

Another reason behind the project was to examine the possibility and practicality of collecting, collating, storing, and preserving raw historical data such as oral interviews, photographs, questionnaires, and students' notes already collected during research for future generations of readers and scholars to consult and learn from. There was an interest in exploring the possibility of saving the collected raw primary research materials digitally for future generations. Students involved in the project were required to interview members of the local community during their research, and to engage them in debating their research findings online. This meant that the research project was also creating room for community members to be involved in telling their own stories, and engaging students and scholars in validating their findings with comments and suggestions on the stories even after the students had published their stories. Thus, in this way, the project facilitated linkages between students and faculty in the university and members of communities where the universities were located. The project was exploring the possibility of bridging gaps and dissolving barriers between the university and the community. It was trying to bring the university down from the vaunted ivory tower and into the community where the university scholars would engage the public in identifying and discussing issues of broad societal importance. Moreover, by facilitating such connections between the university and the community, the students and faculty were literally giving knowledge back to the community. The project was therefore interested in exploring innovative ways through which the university and the community could work together as equals, sharing knowledge as equals, identifying problems and challenges and proposing solutions together, again as equals, as opposed to the usual method where the university considers itself the sinecure of knowledge with a mission of letting knowledge trickle from it from the top down to communities at the bottom, where the elite think and behave as if they are better than members of the community. In short, this project embodied the ethos and methods of public history.[7]

Another factor behind the creation of the project was the need to examine how to inculcate certain skills that are critical to the welfare, well-being, and success of students in the modern world. Such skills are difficult for certain students to acquire in a regular classroom because the students have been born, brought up, and educated in schools in regions suffering from scarcity of resources or lack of opportunities. The project was interested in imbuing such students with digital skills necessary to survive and thrive in the fast technologically evolving world. While other students have had access to opportunities to acquire and hone such skills, there are students especially in the developing world who can benefit from access and opportunities to develop such skills. Those skills include collaboration, group work, social interaction, leadership, critical thinking, analysis, oral communication, writing, adaptability, and, most importantly for this essay, global awareness. The project was initiated with the aim of imbuing students with skills they would need to successfully function in the modern society after graduation. Students participating in the project were expected to acquire such skills through identifying topics for their research, collecting and analyzing data, and synthesizing and writing stories on their topics. By involving students in conducting research on their topics, the project was also going to help students gain fieldwork experience that they would otherwise not be able to acquire in a typical classroom environment.

After writing their stories, the students were expected to have their work published on the MaCleKi research website that, as we have already seen, was created specifically for that purpose. The publication of such research work marked the first time that many of the students had their work published. Moreover, this would be the first time their work would be available for the rest of the world to see. This was a terrifying yet fulfilling moment for many of the students. The students participating in the project would become empowered, seeing their work published where readers could make comments and suggestions. The students would become inspired and motivated by achieving such milestones even before graduating from school, and they would aspire for more in their future academic and professional careers. Apart from providing students with skills that would put them in good stead in life after graduation, the project also provided them an opportunity to be active in the learning process. By participating in identifying their research topics, collecting and analyzing data, writing, and publishing their research findings, the students would be actively engaged in learning in a way that they would not in a typical classroom.

Another project objective was an examination of how to make the modern student aware of and engaged with global issues while they are still young and still in school since the world is becoming more and more connected today than ever before. The project provided an important avenue for facilitating contacts and collaboration between students from different parts of the world, and making them aware of issues and events affecting the students with whom they were collaborating. Thus, in this particular instance, students at MU and CSU were brought together to learn in the courses they had registered for at both the institutions while at the same time working together on their research topics. The project therefore expected the students from the two universities to work together and collaborate with one another. They worked together in identifying topics for their research, apportioning duties and responsibilities on the research among themselves, collecting data, analyzing and synthesizing data, writing about the topics they had selected, and then posting their essays on MaCleKi. The way the project assignments were organized therefore required students to collaborate closely with one another. There was simply no other alternative for them to succeed in the course without learning how to work together. Such students were expected to eventually learn about and acquire skills of teamwork, leadership, collaboration, and to be aware of the geographical, cultural, familial, financial, health, educational, and political environment in which their research partners lived and worked. It was expected that these students would become aware and appreciative of the social, cultural, economic, and political circumstances of their research partners, and eventually would have more context for evaluating their own. In short, they would become aware of how the other side of the world lived, and how it compared to how they themselves lived.

THE ARCHITECTURE OF COLLABORATIVE RESEARCH AND WRITING OF STORIES ABOUT KISUMU, KENYA

The collaboration between MU and CSU started with the faculty from the two universities identifying and developing a joint course for their students, creating a syllabus for the course, and identifying and describing activities and assignments for students participating in the project. The first cohort of students started participating in the project during the spring 2015 semester. Many other students have been involved in collaborative courses between the two universities from spring 2015, when the collaboration began, to fall 2018, when the second phase of the project ended. The students were organized into groups based on the topics they had selected for their research. The students were then required to reach out to their group members via text, WhatsApp, Skype, Facebook, or email, introduce themselves, share contact information, pictures of themselves, and any other information they deemed important for becoming acquainted.

During this phase, the group members discussed the parameters of activities of their groups; distributing tasks and responsibilities; and reminding themselves of deadlines and due dates. Most of the students at CSU allocated themselves the task of identifying, reading, and collecting materials from secondary sources because they happened to be in an institution with access of the most up-to-date secondary materials (books, articles, etc.), while students at MU usually took the responsibility of collecting primary materials such as pictures/photographs, and oral interviews. The students at CSU were mostly involved in doing research at local libraries, but students at MU were more involved in doing fieldwork. After allocating themselves the tasks required to finish their research, the students moved on to the actual process of collecting and analyzing data and writing their essays. For example, they wrote abstracts, and identified and collected pictures/photographs, and other materials for their essays. The students engaged in these activities while working closely with their professors at CSU and MU. There were grades for these regular consultations. Once the students had finished their research and written their essays, they received comments from their professors, revised the essays accordingly, and, once the essays were deemed ready, uploaded them on the website. These essays were accompanied with photographs, and, where necessary, other audio-visual materials, and maps directing the reader to the locations, places, events, sites, and people that the students' essays were based on. The names of the students involved in writing the essays were included on the essays on the project website. Receiving full credit for the essays they wrote and published on the website was a powerful motivator because most students were eager to be recognized as authors.

Since the project started in 2015, the CSU and MU students have collaboratively written and published many essays on critical aspects of the history of Kisumu that were under threat of disappearing and knowledge about them being lost forever. But, this was not easy. The first semester, when the project began, was particularly challenging. Since the universities operate under different academic programs and sometimes courses are placed on the calendar well in advance (in the case of CSU, two years in advance), there was no uniform course that students at CSU and MU could take together. The students at CSU had already enrolled for a course on South Africa, while students at Maseno were enrolled for a course on modern Africa. This problem forced students who enrolled for the project to conduct research comparing certain aspects of the history of Kisumu and South Africa. Thus, due to programmatic challenges, the first students' essays under the project were comparative rather than singularly focused on Kisumu. These were 10 essays in total that dealt with Kisumu and South Africa. They included the following essays: "The Mega City Mall in Kisumu: Mega City's Role in the Importation of Goods and Services into Kisumu from South Africa"; "The Mamboleo Murram Extraction Site: Miners' Experience in Murram Mining in Kisumu and Gold Mining in South Africa"; "The East African Community and the South African Development Community: A Comparison of Regional Bodies in Terms of Their Origin, Functions, and Impact"; and "Miracle Healers in Kisumu: Comparing Father Juma Pesa of Kisumu, and Pastor Lesego Daniel of South Africa." The other essays were "The Kisumu Port: The Challenges and Promise of a Port City on Lake Victoria"; "From Single-faith-based Religious to Multi-faith-based, Integrated Education: A History of Religious and Secular Schools in Kisumu"; "Political Protests, Resistance, and Unrest in Kisumu: An Examination of Protests in Kondele and Nyalenda during the 2007–08 Post-Election Violence in Kenya"; "Kisumu Girls High School: From a Mixed Boys-Girls School to a Single Girls-Only High School"; "The Kenya-Uganda Railway: How the Railroad Shaped the Development of Kenya"; and "Land Alienation and Its Impact in Kisumu: Miwani Sugar Company and the Creation of Kabonyo Settlement Scheme."

Using experience gained from the first semester, the subsequent semesters were more organized, structured, and efficient. Students' work was more focused. The students were able to conduct research and produce many essays focusing on important places, sites, locations, people, and events in the history of Kisumu. During the fall 2015 semester, the students at MU and CSU collaborated in writing essays on the following topics: "The Bombay of East Africa: Asian and African Relations in Kisumu"; "Jaramogi Oginga Odinga and the Rise of Opposition Politics in Kisumu"; "Kibuye Market, Kisumu"; "The Livestock Trade"; "Oginga Odinga Hut at Maseno National School"; "History of Maseno National School"; "Archdeacon Owens Monument in

Kisumu"; "Kisumu War Cemetery"; "The Ramogi Press"; "Ambrose Ofafa Memorial Hall"; "Jaramogi Oginga Odinga Referral Hospital ('Russia'— Nyanza Provincial Hospital)"; and "The Jua Kali, and Other Informal Business Sectors in Kisumu."

During the fall 2016 semester, the students conducted research and wrote essays on the "The Old Nyanza Provincial Headquarter"; "People's Parliament"; "The Origin and Impact of Maseno National School"; "History of Maseno University"; "Maseno Mission Hospital"; "The Origin of Maseno Town"; "The Anglican Church in Maseno"; "Chief Nindo and the Colonial Administration of Kenya"; and "Living with the Hyacinth Weed in Lake Victoria."

The research project did not run during the spring 2017 semester due to lack of funds, but a semester later, we received our second grant from the NEH and resumed work. The students who participated in the subsequent project collaborated in writing essays on the following topics: "Chief Ogola Ayieke"; "Nyalenda Peri-Urban Neighborhood"; "Manyatta Peri-Urban Neighborhood"; "Fishing at Usoma Beach"; "Kisumu Boys High School"; and "Bishop Ogonyo Ngede and Power of Jesus Around the World Church."

During the spring 2018 semester, there was a faculty strike at MU that prevented collaborative content development between MU and CSU. Consequently, the CSU students partnered with the Kisumu Museum, and this partnership enabled the CSU students to write essays on the following topics: "Fishing at Dunga Beach, Kisumu, Focusing on Traditional Fishing Methods"; "A General History of Kit Mikayi"; "Kit Mikayi in the History of Migration, Dispersal, and Settlement among the Seme People"; "Traditional Homesteads among the Luo"; "Traditional Food such as Vegetables, Meat, and Fish among the Luo"; "Traditional Elders' and Leaders' Meetings"; "Funerals, Burials, and Memorialization of the Dead among the Luo"; "Kit Mikayi Between Tradition and Modernity: Is Tourism Perverting Local Cultural Beliefs and Practices?"; and "The Place and Status of the Mikayi Woman in the Luo Community."

During the fall 2018 semester, a new cohort of students at MU and CSU working together wrote essays on the following 12 topics: "Kisumu Social Hall: A Brief Glimpse at its History, Role, and Impact on Social, Economic, and Political Development of Kisumu"; "Makasembo Road, Kisumu, Kenya: A Rambunctious, Boisterous, and Busy Thoroughfare Full of Modern City Conveniences"; "The Equator Bottlers Co. of Kisumu: Exploring the History of the Complex Relationship between the Company, and the Local People"; "Kisumu Museum: The Cultural Significance of the Kisumu Museum"; "Kisumu Cotton Mills (KICOMI): The Rise and Fall of an Important Industry in Kisumu"; "Kisumu Municipal Hall: Its History and Role in the Social, Economic, and Political Development of Kisumu"; "Sunset Hotel: Kisumu's

First Post-Independence Luxury Hostelry"; "Odera Street, Kisumu, Kenya: A Historical Look at the Bazaar around Odera Street"; and "St. Stephen's Cathedral, Kisumu, Kenya."

Thus, by the end of fall 2018, the MU and CSU students had researched and written 54 essays dealing with critical aspects of the history of Kisumu, ranging from the coming of colonialism to Kisumu, infrastructural development, Western schools and the introduction of Western education in the region, land problems and the emergence of slums, racism, religion, leaderships, soil erosion, and environmental degradation, livestock keeping and fishing, entertainment, wars, and opposition politics. These students wrote their essays without ever meeting with each other in person. They did all this work in the virtual classroom, without meeting in a common physical space. They collaborated closely with one another, apportioned each other tasks and responsibilities, and communicated by phone, email, and social media sites such as Facebook. They did it all digitally. The work they did required discipline, trust, interdependence, confidence in each other, cooperation, and leadership. In the process, they also learned about one another. They came to learn that they were not just students working with each other to acquire good grades and pass the courses they were taking together, but also that they were real people with varying degrees of problems, challenges, opportunities, and prospects.

THE TRANSFORMATION OF THE ATTITUDES, WORLDVIEWS, AND EXPERIENCES OF STUDENT PARTICIPANTS

In the course of collaborating, the students communicated regularly and developed close bonds with one another. They exchanged cellphone numbers, email addresses, and even photographs of each other to facilitate communication and collaboration. They talked to each other by phone and got to learn about each other. They learned about how their research partners lived. They learned how to pronounce each other's names, what kinds of food they ate in their homes, and how they spent their free time. They learned about life in their respective countries. They learned about each other's educational programs, economic systems, and political institutions. They learned about issues that they could not have easily heard about, let alone learned about in the typical classroom. There were many students during this project who, for example, learned, for the first time, that their countries were not just separated from each other by vast distances, but also by huge time differences. They learned that MU students were ahead of CSU in terms of time by eight hours during the winter period, and by seven hours during the spring and summer seasons. There were many students who learned, again, for the first time, about each other's geographical environment—the temperature, the snow, the different climate zones they lived in. The students also learned about each other's occupations, family lives, health issues, financial opportunities, and challenges. Some students learned that some of them had cars, and that others did not. The students started appreciating each other's culture and ways of life. The students started developing a new sense of friendship and camaraderie with each other even though they were separated by time and space. The students started developing a new sense of themselves. Working with students from other parts of the world enabled them to start seeing themselves as part of something bigger, beyond their local communities. They realized that, although they lived apart from their research partners, they were connected to them in ways they had never envisaged. They developed a new consciousness.

A few examples should illustrate the heightened global consciousness gained from this transnational collaboration. A 19-year-old student from Murang'a studying at MU commented in his questionnaire that the project "enables me to get more information about places I only heard of." The student also added that he enjoyed participating in the project because it helped him to "know more about places from other countries."[8] Another student, 20 years old, from Embu, wrote that what he enjoyed the most about the project was the opportunity to "interact with different people."[9] Another student who chose to be anonymous while filling the questionnaires remarked that he liked the project because "it is an exposing exercise. It made me mingle and relate with people I never thought I would meet." The same student also observed that "information gathered is shared with people within and without the continent."[10] A 22-year-old MU student liked the project because it provided him with an opportunity for "gathering information and socializing with other MaCleKi students." He went on to suggest that the project should not simply end with students participating in the project. It should lead to a "student exchange programme [*sic*]."[11] His sentiments were shared by another student who liked the project because it also provided him with an opportunity for "gathering information and socializing with other MaCleKi students."[12] The students increasingly became aware that the project gave them "exposure to the outside world . . . I got to meet great people in relation to my research."[13] Another student observed that "I have liked the research in finding new ideas and share of information with my Cleveland partners."[14] A 21-year-old student liked the project because it provided him with an opportunity for "social interactions" and observed that the "project is so informative and educative hence helps me gather a lot of field experience." The student also noted that during the project, there was "close interaction with sharing knowledge and ideas with other partners."[15] Another student observed that the project enabled him to "interact with people." The student observed that he liked the project because you "get to interact with people from other countries for example our partners from Cleveland University [*sic*]."[16]

In fact, the students were not just appreciative of working with students from Cleveland or another country, they were also grateful for the project providing them with an opportunity to learn about Kisumu. Kenya is a big country, the size of Texas. Students at MU come from many different parts of Kenya. Many of these students travel only between their homes and MU. They had never even had the opportunity to travel around Kisumu, the biggest city near their university. Many of these students were quite grateful for participating in the project because it provided them with an opportunity to also know about their own city. One 22-year-old student at MU, for example, observed that the project helped him to understand "my environment and . . . understood humans as a resource for production."[17] A 19-year-old student from Kiambu, near Nairobi, commented that the project helped "non residents in Kisumu to know more about Kisumu City."[18] Another 22-year-old student said that he enjoyed "travelling and knowing more places within Kisumu Town."[19] One of his classmates observed that his friends liked the project and have "browsed the MaCleKi and fight [seems he meant 'find'] the story of Kisumu very interesting."[20] In fact, some of these students, inspired by the research they were doing on Kisumu, wished that the project could be extended to "feature other areas other than Kisumu."[21]

There were students who saw a lot of potential in the project exposing them to bigger and better opportunities in the future. A 21-year-old student from Nairobi remarked that one of his relatives told him that participating in "MaCleKi . . . will help me big time in my career."[22] The idea that the project might provide better opportunities in the future was echoed by another student who observed that his friends told him "to be very serious with it [the project] because better opportunities may come out of it."[23] Echoing this interest in opportunities for traveling, another student observed that he "heard that someone can be taken for a trip to Cleveland."[24] The students who participated in the project wanted to continue interacting with one another even after the project came to an end. They did not want their relationship and partnership with other students to end. One student observed that "communication between students of both universities should be increased through social media such as WhatsApp and etc."[25] Echoing these sentiments, a student who participated in the project wished that there was a forum for "discussion," among, presumably, the students who had participated with each other in the project.[26] One student noted that, even if they could not visit each other, the "relationship between the MaCleKi students, for example, the Cleveland Students and those of Maseno students should be improved through various social media such as WhatsApp, Facebook, Email, Twitter among others."[27]

Still another student observed that the website "should be added to social media pages so as to help the researchers to connect with each other."[28] The foregoing comments demonstrate an evolving awareness among the students. The students were appreciative of the opportunity to learn about themselves, their city, their partners, and the world as a whole. They were learning of their connectedness to the outside world, the people living in it, and the opportunities available in it.

The students' comments and sentiments about the research projects were effervescent even among collaborators, stakeholders, and partners that helped run the project from Kisumu. Among some of these collaborators, stakeholders, and partners were staff at the Kisumu Museum in Kenya. Their comments and views leave no doubt that the project provided an important link between Kisumu City and the larger world. One member of the Kisumu Museum staff observed that the project is "very positive to bring this history of the Luo people to entire world."[29] Another museum staff member observed that the people say that the project is good because it "will enable tourists and Kisumu residents learn more about the town."[30] A third Kisumu Museum staff member observed that the project has "put Kisumu Museum in the world map as one of the tourist attractions within Kisumu."[31] A fourth museum staffer also observed that the project "gives our culture exposure to the world, enabling other communities understand us better and what we stand for."[32]

Similar views and sentiments about the project facilitating global connections were expressed by the ordinary members of the public who were given an opportunity to view the stories on the MaCleKi website. These are public members living and working in Kisumu. After going through the website, members of the public were given an opportunity to fill out questionnaires and make comments about the research project. The comments and views left by the public on the questionnaires also demonstrate an awareness that the project was facilitating global contacts between Kisumu and the outside world. One Kisumu woman, for example, was impressed by the research project because of the potential for "proper relay of the authentic culture of the Luo for the consumption of both local and international tourists."[33] Another member of the public was asked to review the MaCleKi website and make comments about the research project. He subsequently observed that the project "acts as a better marketing tool for Kisumu County. . . ."[34] A man from Siaya observed that the project can "help connect society with attractions."[35] A man from Homa Bay observed that the project could "help the current generation understand their past."[36] These sentiments were shared by an anonymous observer who wrote, "I think it is a good project since the young generation who have been in position to get this information from their grandparents and parents can get it from here."[37]

An analysis of the emails and questionnaires written or filled by students, ordinary members of the public, and research partners clearly indicates an evolving consciousness and awareness about the world. The students, in particular, increasingly became conscious of their connections and relationships with one another, or of the potential for the development of such connections and relationships. The students in fact wanted to continue their communications even after the completion of their research projects. Their comments show an appreciation of the new relationships they were developing with each other, and that they wanted these to continue after the project came to an end, even if only through social media such as Facebook or WhatsApp. It is no wonder, therefore, that after taking the course the two students mentioned at the outset of this chapter were curious about opportunities existing in the home areas of their research partners. After participating in the project, the MU student expressed a desire to continue with his studies abroad, and, more instructively, at CSU, where some of his research partners studied. Similarly, his CSU counterpart, after finishing his studies, decided to travel, work, and live in Africa. He explored the easiest and fastest opportunity for him to do that, and subsequently settled on the Peace Corps, which, coincidentally, if not ironically, decided to post him to Tanzania, a country, which, again interestingly, is adjacent to Kenya and not far from the research partners he had worked with while studying at CSU. The desire by such students as these to expand their social, academic, and professional relationships and experiences after finishing with the research project strongly suggests that the project played an important role in the transformation of their experiences, attitudes, worldviews, and interests, as well as those of the other students who participated in it. Their ambitions and aspirations are examples of the evolution of the consciousness of the students into global citizens. But, such students were not alone. Their fellow students harbored similar ambitions and aspirations. They had become, or were in the process of becoming, global citizens.

CONCLUSION

This chapter was interested in the extent to which the "Curating Kisumu" and "Curating East Africa" research project imbued the MU and CSU students with a new sense of consciousness as members and citizens of the global community. Since the commencement of the project between CSU and MU students, more than 200 students between those two universities have worked together on learning and doing research on various aspects of the history of the Kisumu region, and Kenya as a whole. After taking part in this project, the students filled questionnaires documenting their experiences, expectations, and hopes.

An analysis of the students' questionnaires demonstrates that the project catapulted the students beyond their comfort zones and made them increasingly conscious of their place as citizens of the world. The students became proud of working with students from other parts of the globe. Their consciousness as members of the global community increased. This consciousness as global citizens is what might be called globalization. An overwhelming majority of the students indicated that they enjoyed interacting and working with students living in another part of the world while participating in the project. The students expressed a keen interest in the lives, affairs, and experiences of members of their groups after finishing with the research project.

NOTES

1. CSU graduate student (anonymous), email to Dr. Meshack Owino, July 10, 2017; MU undergraduate student (anonymous), email to Dr. Mark Souther, December 9, 2015.

2. There are many debates on globalization, its nature, and impact on individuals, cultures, countries, nations, and continents. See, for example, Joseph Stiglitz, *Globalization and Its Discontents* (New York: W. W. Norton & Company, 2003); Dani Rodrik, *The Globalization Paradox: Democracy and the Future of the World Economy* (New York: W.W. Norton, 2011); Melinda Mills, "Globalization and Inequality," *European Sociological Review* 25, no. 1 (2009): 1–8; Adam McKeown, "Periodizing Globalization," *History Workshop Journal* 63 (Spring, 2007): 218–30; Gary Teeple, "What Is Globalization?" in *Globalization and Its Discontents*, eds. S. McBride and J. Wiseman (New York: St. Martin's Press, 2000); Pippa Norris, "Global Governance and Cosmopolitan Citizens," in *Governance in a Globalizing World*, eds. J.S. Nye, Jr. and J.D. Donahue (Washington, DC.: Brookings Institution Press, 2000); Richard A. Falk, *Predatory Globalization: A Critique* (Cambridge: Polity Press, 1999); Arie M. Kacowicz, "Regionalization, Globalization, and Nationalism: Convergent, Divergent or Overlapping?," *Alternatives* 24, no. 4 (1999): 527–55; Stephen Gill, "Globalization, Market Civilization and Disciplinary Neo-Liberalism," *Millennium: Journal of International Studies* 24, no. 3 (1995): 399–423; Andrew Hurrell and Ngaire Woods, "Globalization and Inequality," *Millennium: Journal of International Studies* 24, no. 3 (1995): 447–70; Eleonore Kofman and Gillian Youngs, "Introduction: Globalization—The Second Wave," in Eleonore Kofman and Gillian Youngs, eds., *Globalization: Theory and Practice* (London: Pinter, 1996), 1–8; Jan Aart Scholte, "Beyond the Buzzwords: Toward a Critical Theory of Globalization," in Eleonore Kofman and Gillian Youngs, eds., *Globalization: Theory and Practice* (London: Pinter, 1996), 43–57. As far as globalization and Africa is concerned, see, for example, Usman A. Tar, et al., eds., *Globalization in Africa: Perspectives on Development, Security, and the Environment* (London: Lexington Books, 2016), especially Lucky Imade, "How Globalization Underdeveloped Africa," in Usman A. Tar, et al., eds., *Globalization in Africa: Perspectives on Development, Security, and*

the Environment (London: Lexington Books, 2016), 47–78; George Klay Kieh, *Africa and the New Globalization* (Aldershot: Ashgate Publishing, Ltd., 2008); Jake Bright and Aubrey Hruby, *The Next Africa: An Emerging Continent Becomes a Global Powerhouse* (New York: St. Martin's Press, 2015); J. Shola Omotola, "Political Globalization and Citizenship: New Sources of Security Threats in Africa," *Journal of African Law* 52, no. 2 (2008): 268–83; Rok Ajulu, "Thabo Mbeki's African Renaissance in a Globalizing World Economy: The Struggle for the Soul of the Continent," *Review of African Political Economy* 87 (2001): 27–42; Nana K. Poku, "Poverty, AIDS and the Politics of Response in Africa," *International Relations* 15, no. 3 (2000): 390–452; Giles Mohan, "Globalization and Governance: The Paradoxes of Adjustment in Sub-Saharan Africa," in Eleonore Kofman and Gillian Youngs, eds., *Globalization: Theory and Practice* (London: Pinter, 1996), 289–303. Sometimes the sentiments against globalization in the African continent are expressed in the form of critiques against the IMF, the World Bank, the United States, and the Chinese in Africa. For more information on transformation, see, for example, David Held, Anthony McGrew, David Goldblatt, and Jonathan Perraton, *Global Transformation: Politics, Economics, and Culture* (Palo Alto, CA: Stanford University Press, 2000); Kenichi Ohmae, *The End of the Nation-State: The Rise of Regional Economies* (New York: Free Press, 1995); Francis Fukayama, *The End of History and the Last Man* (New York: Free Press, 1992).

3. Paul Tarc, "The Uses of Globalization in the Shifting Landscape of Educational Studies," *Canadian Journal of Education* 35, no. 3 (2012): 4–29.

4. Gianluca Grimalda, Nancy Buchan, and Marilynn Brewer, "Social Identity Mediates the Positive Effect of Globalization on Individual Cooperation: Results from International Experiments," in *PLOSONE*, December 14, 2018, https://journals .plos.org/plosone/article?id=10.1371/journal.pone.0206819.

5. Kris Olds, "Global Citizenship—What Are We Talking About and Why Does It Matter?" in *Inside Higher Education*, March 11, 2012, https://www.insidehighered .com/blogs/globalhighered/global-citizenship-%E2%80%93-what-are-we-talking -about-and-why-does-it-matter.

6. MaCleKi homepage, https://macleki.org.

7. Cherstin M. Lyon, Elizabeth M. Nix, and Rebecca K. Shrum, eds., *Introduction to Public History: Interpreting the Past, Engaging Audiences* (Lanham, MD: Rowman & Littlefield, 2017), 1–19.

8. An anonymous, 19-year-old MU student from Muranga.

9. An anonymous, 20-year-old MU student from Embu.

10. An anonymous, 23-year-old MU student from Bomet.

11. An anonymous, 22-year-old MU student from Nandi.

12. An anonymous, 23-year-old MU student from Bomet.

13. An anonymous, 21-year-old MU student from Nairobi.

14. An anonymous, 20-year-old MU student from Mumias.

15. An anonymous, 21-year-old MU student from Siaya.

16. An anonymous, 18-year-old MU student from Bondo.

17. An anonymous, 22-year-old MU student from Kisumu.

18. An anonymous, 19-year-old MU student from Kiambu.

19. An anonymous, 22-year-old MU student from Kavatanzoli.

20. An anonymous, 20-year-old MU student from Kakamega.

21. An anonymous, 22-year-old MU student from Taita.

22. An anonymous, 21-year-old MU student from Nairobi.

23. An anonymous, 21-year-old MU student from Siaya.

24. An anonymous, 20-year-old MU student from Mombasa.

25. An anonymous, 20-year-old MU student from Nairobi.

26. An anonymous, 22-year-old MU student from Kisumu.

27. An anonymous 20-year-old MU student from Luanda.

28. An anonymous, 20-year-old MU student from Nairobi. In fact, the project team regularly shares excerpted material from MaCleKi on social media, including Facebook.

29. An anonymous Kisumu Museum staff member from Siaya.

30. An anonymous Kisumu Museum staff member from Kisumu.

31. An anonymous Kisumu Museum staff member from Migori.

32. An anonymous Kisumu Museum staff member from Kisumu.

33. An anonymous woman from Kisumu.

34. An anonymous man from an unknown location in the Nyanza region of Kenya.

35. An anonymous man from Siaya.

36. An anonymous man from Homa Bay.

37. An anonymous observer from Ang'urai.

10

Mobilizing Student Interest in African Identity

An Academic Project for the Real World

Bradford Whitener

This chapter reports on an educational experiment that showcases the mobilization effect that opportunities for online publications gave university students. A small number of students chose themes that connected to African history. These students' projects illustrate the impact of technology, particularly that of Internet publications, on how technology mobilized students to research and write about cases of identity politicization in Africa.

In the summer of 2016, I began to put the pieces together for a new approach to my teaching that has since evolved into something far beyond what I could have anticipated. The "problem" that I sought to solve with this new approach is one familiar to all teachers of college students, namely the lack of student motivation to master the research and writing skills they will need for their chosen professional career paths. But what happens when our best efforts to motivate our students fail to gain their "buy-in"? For me, what happened was the expenditure of a tremendous amount of energy, on my part and on that of my students, to produce research papers that largely reflected a casual approach to the "assignment," resulting in inadequately researched papers and half-hearted efforts to write and revise their work. There was a safe assumption that my eyes would be the only ones ever to read these papers. And, under those circumstances, their efforts would rise only as far as their concern for my feedback was valued. They viewed the task as a "mere assignment," one of many such assignments that they, as students, had to perform for their professors in various classes. If they regarded themselves as an A student, they typically raised their efforts to that A level; and if they saw themselves as a C student, they made sure to put just enough into their assignment to achieve what they expected of themselves.

As I grappled with this dynamic over the course of the better part of a decade of teaching at the university, I came to realize that, to a certain extent, there was no problem here. What I was observing was simply the functioning of a normal distribution of the "Bell Curve." The upper 20% of grade maximizers gave me the satisfaction that there was little slippage between the energy expended and the desired outcome. But what about the other 80% of my students who were not maximizers, who were merely approaching the assignment as so much paper to push, mechanically going through the motions of "doing the assignment," without much concern over the actual research and writing skills that I was hoping to cultivate in them? Could I find a way to improve on this "20 percent–80 percent" split, even to the point of flipping it to 80/20, where 80% of my students would find complete success in the skills I wished to develop in them?

During that summer of 2016, I began to redesign my courses to address the issue of motivation and mobilization or "buy-in." It started with the simple question: "What if it wasn't just my eyes seeing their work?" What if the whole world could read their work? Would that change the way they would view this research "assignment" in my class? My bet was that it would provide the needed mobilization effect. And without any experience with blogging or with website creation, I became a quick study in setting up a WordPress website that would become the vehicle for sharing the research and writing of my students in that Fall semester. I believed that if students could see themselves as participants in something beyond themselves, as members of a real-world publishing organization doing something that the real world valued and could benefit from, I might be able to flip that 20/80 success rate to 80/20 and get students to see themselves as real researchers and professional authors doing something real, rather than as mere students doing mundane assignments in a required class for a grade. Thus was born the StMU History Media organization, with StMUHistoryMedia.org as its public face, with the banner tagline "Featuring the Historical Research, Writing, and Media of students at St. Mary's University."[1]

On the first day of the semester, I introduced students to the *StMU History Media* project by telling them that they were not only students who had signed up for my class, but that they had been "hired" by the *StMU History Media* organization, with the job title of "Writer" as their position in the organization. The role of Writer gave them the opportunity to research and write a Descriptive article for the organization's website.[2] They would receive their "paycheck" for their published article, and that first success would entitle them to apply for a promotion in the organization, namely to "Senior Writer."[3] As a Senior Writer, they then had the opportunity to write not only Descriptive articles, but two types of Explanatory articles as well, giving them opportunities to develop deeper research skills, stronger analytical skills, and more advanced writing skills.[4] From the first day of class, I reassured all students that they would not be doing any of these things by themselves. As members of the organization, we were all collaborating in this project. I informed them that I would not publish anything with their name on it that would make them look bad. Their articles would make them look anywhere from good to great. And their contributions to the website will help the organization look good, and it would make the university look good.

The *StMU History Media* organization collaborates with several university services to assist our "Writers" and "Senior Writers." Members are encouraged to seek out professors, or "consulting experts," on campus who have special expertise in the areas of their topics. Members are encouraged to make appointments with our research librarians for assistance in finding high-quality sources for their research projects, as well as to deepen their own research skills by sitting down with librarians who tutor them in navigating research databases and search portals. Members are encouraged to make appointments with our Learning Assistance Center's writing tutors, who help them with all stages of their research and writing.[5] Members are also encouraged to make appointments with our Career Services Center staff for assistance in developing a professional résumé and letter of application for their promotion to Senior Writer.

As the Fall semester of 2016 got underway, the organization came to life. Research projects were launched, raw articles were submitted to the editorial workflow of our *WordPress* software, and I began to interact with my students in a completely new way, thanks largely to the functionality of that software. What had been final drafts of students' work in prior semesters now became starting points for a back-and-forth editorial revision process. For the first time in my teaching career, I was taking some eighty students through a one-on-one revision process that is usually reserved for graduate-level engagements. At first, I did not comprehend just how transformative that editorial process was. I now see that it is the most important aspect of the entire project. For students willing to see the process as truly collaborative, the editorial process can completely transform their attitudes toward research and writing, not just in my classes, but in their majors and in their other classes as well. Their buy-in deepens as they see themselves contributing something substantial to the project, and they are mobilized by the collective momentum of the class to celebrate each member's fresh publication. The magic moment for them comes when I send them an email congratulating them on having just published their article. It looks good! The world—their family and friends—the public can now read a polished piece of writing that has their name as author. They feel a sense of immense pride at having accomplished something that they never dreamed they could do. And that was the goal I had for them, to help them develop the skills as well as the confidence to do something real for the real world. Students gravitated towards diverse themes that related to their identity whether it was themes connected to their majors, to their ethnicity, to their immigration status, or to their cultural heritage. In the first few semesters, the number of articles relating to African and African-American identities remained relatively small, but once students started writing more pieces about social justice and human rights, the number of articles linked to African history and identity more than doubled. Student articles examined elements of identity politicization, of transformation, and mobilization. Some articles looked at their roots in the African diaspora in the United States. For example, one examined how W.E.B. Du Bois and Booker T. Washington's very different backgrounds impacted their fight for human rights so differently.[6]

One of these articles, published originally on the StMU Research Scholars website as "Institutional Change and Identity: Unexpected Impact from the Arab Spring," by its author, Auroara Nikkels, was selected to be revised and expanded for inclusion in this volume as a chapter that details the way the Internet transformed mobilization in the North African countries of Tunisia and Libya during the Arab Spring.[7] The project of publishing student research online provided an important instrument for mobilizing students' interest often based on elements that related to their own identity. For many, the elements of their identity connected with their own roots in various immigration stories from Latin America or from the African continent.[8] Over time, it became apparent that each semester a small group of students gravitated towards issues that connect to identity politicization and mobilization, and for some, this was localized on the African continent or in the African-American diaspora.

As our website's homepage started accumulating published articles, I encouraged students to read the articles on our site and post comments to them. I found that this served multiple purposes. It helped students who were fearful of the process to see that others *just like them* were finding success at writing. It also helped students see more clearly what kind of research topics they too could take up. The commenting assignment aided in establishing a positive feedback loop to student "buy-in." And once that buy-in began to kick in, they were unstoppable. They wanted their high school history teachers to know about our website. And in keeping with the "real-world organization" theme, we started our first organization-wide "committee," which was a voluntary meeting of students who wanted to do some form of outreach to the community. We called it the Outreach Committee.

As more articles were published, I pitched the idea of having a committee that would evaluate the published articles and select twenty of the best articles to be elevated to a "Showcase Edition," which would be a "best-of-the-best" collection of articles to be included in a virtual magazine. This committee would be our organization's "quality control" committee. We then needed a committee that would create the magazine for the Showcase Editions. Students with a background in magazine layout and experience with software like Adobe *InDesign* then formed the Publication Committee.

At the outset of the 2016 Fall semester, I announced that we would not be taking a final exam in my classes. Instead, as an organization committed to producing a real-world product, we would have an Award Ceremony to celebrate the hard work they had done that semester. Our "quality control" committee would be responsible for establishing the categories that we would have for awards, and they would then nominate the five or six best articles in each of those categories.[9] Toward the end of the semester, all members of the organization would vote on articles that were nominated. Then, the Award Ceremony would take place during their normally scheduled final exam time. Envelopes were prepared. Slideshows for each award category were displayed to honor those nominated. Students, serving as presenters, opened the envelopes and announced the winning articles. Trophies, medals, and certificates were presented to the runners-up and winners. Photos were taken. And that's how the first semester of the project came to an end.

Even in that first semester, I had the vision of an Award Ceremony that more nearly approximated the "Academy Awards" versions of such ceremonies. Instead of four small and separate ceremonies at four different final exam times, we needed one large evening gathering in a real banquet room. It needed to be semiformal attire to raise the dignity of the occasion, and it needed to be run completely by the students. In the third semester of the project, we formed our Award Ceremony committee, and our humble beginnings took main stage. We knew we had a fantastic show to offer. University dignitaries were invited and students who were nominated for an award could invite guests. Those who were nominated for an award and those who were involved in our five committees were invited to be presenters of awards. The Award Ceremony committee selected a Master of Ceremonies, invited a key-note speaker to address the assembly, and solicited funding for banquet food, room decorations, and trophies and medals. The 3rd Semi-Annual StMU History Media Award Ceremony was a major success. One of the reasons this celebration succeeded came from the many ways in which it transformed the identity of the students selected to be Masters of Ceremony and from the ways they wrote scripts for the celebration that connected to all the students who had been involved for the semester. The MCs, for example, took on leadership roles completely unexpected for first- or second-year university students and they explained that their identity transformed from an individual student working for personal grades to that of a leader and motivator for their team whose responsibility was to help others shine. All of them saw a higher purpose in the creation and celebration of a community of student researchers and writers above and beyond themselves. The students who served as Masters of Ceremony also wrote their own scripts for the event. Maria Mancha, who had just published days before "The Love Story of the Lovings" recounting how racial injustice in marriage was finally redressed by the 1967 Supreme Court decision, illustrated the centrality of themes of social justice, respect, and identity in community in her own speech.[10] While the concepts of Ubuntu philosophy were not necessarily discussed in these terms with the students, Dr. Celine Jacquemin, the faculty in charge of the Award Ceremony from Spring 2018 to Spring 2020, teaches all major courses on African Politics and African Security, and specializes in team building following these important principles.

Maria Mancha understood her role as Master of Ceremony was not to make herself shine, but instead she had a very clear commitment to the project and to her peers, no matter how successful they had been or no matter how much they struggled. She wrote in her script for the Spring 2018 ceremony: "The purpose of this ceremony is to make sure that each student is recognized. From the late nights writing alone in our rooms, to [. . . the] late nights editing peer articles, we all gave it our best. As authors in training, we first learned by reading published articles, and writing constructive comments to cheer each other on."[11] She as the MC felt a responsibility to represent all members of the projects. She mentioned several times the importance of her peers who were still struggling to complete their own articles and she cheered them on to complete their articles before the end of the semester. She felt the celebration should intentionally value all members, not just those nominated or winning. As the faculty who prepared video clips of the nominated articles, I too echoed the importance of valuing all of the students' contributions and I prepared slide shows of all published articles that were not nominated to display the excellent work of all students.

In learning from previously published articles, new students are given the opportunity to learn from their peers. They get to build strong ties to the project and to students, some they know and some who might have already graduated and moved on. In Fall 2018, Sarah Nguyen explained the community's results from the project:

> This semester with 7 classes and over 150 students, 3 faculty, several librarians, technology support, and embedded tutors, we embarked on a different educational journey, one that called us to take part in high impact activities. A journey that, regardless of our majors or initial interest, emboldened us to explore our world to conduct historical research and publish our first articles, for so many of us in our first year and first semester at the St. Mary's University.[12]

Students invest so much into the project and become champions and advocates with their peers and with the guests on the day of the ceremony. Michael Mengler declared during his opening speech for the Fall 2019 ceremony:

> On the most fundamental level, this project celebrates multidisciplinary study as a means to explore not just our own areas of interest, but those of our peers and faculty mentors. This fostering of integrated liberal arts education is made manifest in many ways—but perhaps no more readily than in the exposure to the new ideas, insight, and passions of our peers and mentors; this support and encouragement throughout our struggles and successes . . . these highs and lows that we've all experienced one way or another . . . the persistence along this path of academic growth, and the cultivation of curiosity . . . this is surely the essence of the community we at St. Mary's value, together.[13]

So many of these values center around the importance of community and of the contributions and roles of each of the members of the project, past, present, and future. These connections to central themes of Ubuntu philosophy and to students' African roots and other personal heritage and passions have become more evident over time. Certainly, being at a Hispanic-serving institution, we expected that their Hispanic, Latinx, and Chicano roots would come through, yet seeing how many ways students were delving into African and African-American historic and identity themes has become additionally rewarding. For most students, the links came from their aspiring to shedding light on issues of social justice required to foster supportive symbiotic communities that strive to serve the common good.

The set of interrelated concepts in Ubuntu philosophy, as illustrated in the chapter by Asike and Onwuluorah, that include the spirit of reciprocity, collaboration, inclusiveness, and even nationalism, were emerging in very unexpected ways from a group of students not familiar with Ubuntu philosophy but who understood that for their community of scholars to thrive, further collaboration and support needed to be provided to each.[14] As Lutz explains in his 2009 article "African Ubuntu Philosophy and Global Management," building a community in our globalizing world based on principles for the common good can anchor members in earlier traditions rooted in African Ubuntu philosophy. The students who had active roles in this new real publishing organization gravitated towards principles of belonging to a community more important than each individually. Lutz wrote:

> Ubuntu philosophy One of the most striking features of the cultures of sub-Saharan Africa is their non-individualistic character: "Although African cultures display awesome diversity, they also show remarkable similarities. Community is the cornerstone in African thought and life" (Mbigi, 2005a, p. 75). An African is not a rugged individual, but a person living within a

community. In the words of Mbiti (1969, pp. 108, 109), "I am, because we are;
and since we are, therefore I am." Or, as Turaki (2006, p. 36) puts it: "People
are not individuals, living in a state of independence, but part of a community,
living in relationships and interdependence."[15]

And that success in building a community of student scholars immediately
led to new levels of collaboration, with the joining of a second professor to
the project, who believed in the project and in the benefits it offered to all of
our students. We discovered that the project was malleable enough to accommodate the different curricular demands of the disciplines of history and
political science. It was also scalable enough to include larger numbers of students participating in the project. And having two or more professors participating in the project meant that it was no longer limited to my own vision for
what was possible for the project; other professors joining the project brought
their own successes in teaching and their own visions of possibilities for the
project that I would not have thought of. With each semester, we continue to
add additional faculty to the project. As of the Fall semester of 2021, we had
ten faculty members from six different disciplines in the project. This was far
beyond what I had believed possible for this little pedagogical experiment.
Indeed, as our community of student scholars and diverse faculty continued
growing, we felt compelled to better reflect our more diverse identities and
interests and decided to rename the project *StMU Research Scholars* to
respond to our community's needs as it expanded.

In her 2016 article on "The Ubuntu Paradigm in Curriculum Work,
Language of Instruction and Assessment," Brock-Utne makes the point that:
"In the African tradition knowledge is experientially and socially based
rather than propositionally derived."[16] She goes on to quote Roger Averstrop:
"There could hardly be a greater contrast than between Descartes' contextless
mentalist individualism in Cogito ergo sum (I think therefore I am) and the
African contextually pregnant, social constructivist relationalism of umuntu
umuntu bahuntu (I am because you are)."[17] In her earlier work, Brock-Utne
with co-author Azaveli Lwaitama in 2010 urged researchers to study "indigenous systems of thoughts" that drew upon Ujamaa and Ubuntu that define
sharing, togetherness, and familyhood in the extended versions.[18]

While Brock-Utne targets language instruction as one of the tools to foster
Ubuntu principles in knowledge formation, the StMU Research Scholars
project has been able to reach some of these goals through this publication
collaborative project.

But what have the results been? Has it made a difference? Has it bent the
Bell Curve? Below is a graph that best illustrates how successful I was at
solving the problem I identified, namely, how to motivate students to achieve
an A-level of skill development in research and writing. At the beginning of

the project, in Fall 2016, I estimated that my students were only about 20% successful at achieving that A level, but that was just an estimate. My goal was to flip that 20% success rate to 80%. After analyzing the data, I discovered that before implementing the *StMU History Media* project, only 15% of my students were scoring 90% or higher on their research projects. Once I started the *StMU History Media* project, the percent of students who have been successful at having at least one published article per semester is 71%. That means that 71% of my students are achieving the equivalent of 90% or higher on their research projects. I think I have made a substantial dint into the normal distribution of the Bell Curve.[19]

But these quantitative numbers are only the beginning measurement of the project's success. Students have been encouraged to take up topics that are truly meaningful to them in some way. Since these articles will make up a substantial part of their online profiles, their choice of topics can be crucial in opening doors to future opportunities, both in their academic careers and in their professional careers beyond graduation. By encouraging students to take up topics of interest to them, I have found that many students use this opportunity to explore aspects of their own identity. For many of my African and African-American students, that has meant taking up topics that explore the African and African-American identities and experiences. As of September 2021, there were 124 articles on the *StMU Research Scholars* website that were tagged "African Diaspora Studies," which was 12% of the total. Of those articles, 43 were about Africa, and 81 were about the African Diaspora (mostly in the United States). Twenty-three of those articles were written by student authors of African descent, either as international students from Africa, or as African-American students. Two of my students used the opportunity to explore aspects of the Rwandan Genocide.[20] One student researched the origins of the Barbados Slave Codes.[21] Another student explored aspects of Rosa Parks's life *after* her famed Montgomery bus protest.[22] A number of

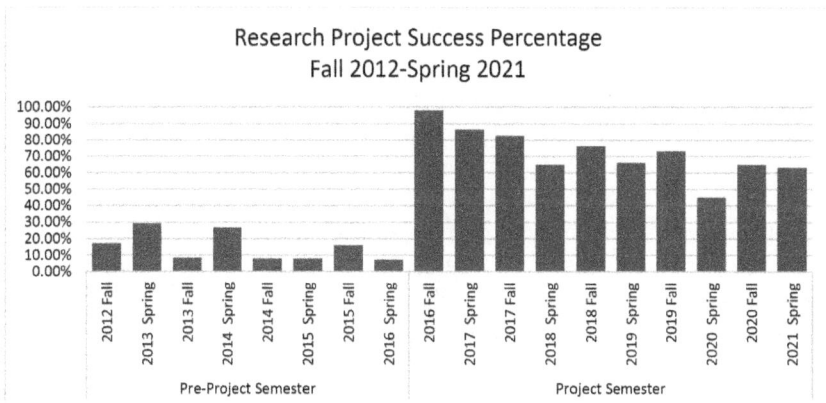

Research Project Success Percentage
Fall 2012-Spring 2021

students took the opportunity to explore aspects of African-American culture that were meaningful to them in some way. One student, who was raised in Detroit, researched the origins of Motown music.[23] Another student examined a cultural first for African Americans in film by looking at the career of Dorothy Dandridge.[24] And another student brought to life an incredible sports event involving basketball star Kobe Bryant.[25] And one of my students explored the life of the Egyptian film-star Abdul Halim Hafez.[26] St. Mary's University is a Hispanic-serving institution with over 70% Hispanic students. Seeing such large numbers of articles with connections to African and African-American themes and heritage was somewhat surprising at first. However, as communities of color with long experiences of oppression in the United States, discovering the yearning students had to use this community of research and writing to share some of their most meaningful needs for community improvement through stories seeking social justice made perfect sense.

The theme of African and African-American identity has not been limited to my African and African-American students. We have over 100 articles on the theme published by students who are not of African descent, but who have found the theme meaningful because of their shared oppression. There were 68 articles tagged as "African Diaspora Studies" written by students of Hispanic descent. Here are the titles of some of these articles:

- "The Lynching Era: The Tragic Hanging of Laura and L. D. Nelson"[27]
- "The Rage of Nina Simone: 'Mississippi Goddam'"[28]
- "The Power of a Ball: How Soccer Star Didier Drogba Ended the Côte D'Ivoire Civil War"[29]
- "The Young and Courageous: Ruby Bridges"[30]
- "Forty Years of 'Bad Blood': The Tuskegee Syphilis Study"[31]
- "'Cause Freedom Ain't Free: Freedom Summer Movement in 1964 Mississippi"[32]
- "Black Codes, Jim Crow, and Social Control in the South"[33]
- "He Would Have Killed Me: The Story of Jennifer Teege, Granddaughter of Nazi Commandant Amon Goeth"[34]
- "The Immortal Woman: Henrietta Lacks"[35]
- "The Love Story of the Lovings"[36]

Students are finding success in an area of academics that they have always feared or avoided in the past. That success is translated into confidence in their research and writing abilities that carries over into other areas of their academic pursuits. An assignment that used to benefit only the top 20% of my students is now benefiting the majority. It is possible that as many as 80% of my students now find the research and writing assignment of this project to be very meaningful and beneficial to them in ways that the traditional research paper assignment did not. It has also benefited me as well. The *StMU History Media* project that I created is now a collaborative project with numerous colleagues from disciplines across the university joining the project. We are implementing interdisciplinarity, collaboration, and high-impact learning on a scale that is truly transformative, with implications that go far beyond our classrooms. But one of the greatest rewards of the project for me has been seeing the pride that students express when they realize that a great little thing exists on the Internet that has their name attached to it.

What has been my biggest take-away from this experiment? It would have to be my own discovery of the power of *collaboration*. It started with my desire to create an environment that brought my students and myself out of the classroom and into a place where we all were mobilized to do something real together, to contribute our own energies to something bigger than ourselves. That transformed my relationship with my students into being a *collaborator with them* instead of an *instructor for them*. We were working on many themes that connected our identities together and finding a lot of interest in the area of African identities and African history. We were helping each other, cheering each other on, applauding each other's successes, and supporting each other as needed. We, as members of an organization, naturally reached out to other collaborators of the university, drawing them in to our organization as ancillary collaborators, from librarians and tutors to support staff and professors from across the university, and even beyond the university. It was this environment of collaboration that generated a tremendous mobilization effect, which could be seen in almost every aspect of the project and especially in how it built an interdisciplinary community of students, staff, and faculty. Students were motivated to assist others, often just because they could, regardless of whether it would contribute to their grade. Many students who were no longer taking classes in the project still volunteered to serve as editors or committee members, and in two cases, volunteers served as MCs for our award ceremonies. Professors were likewise mobilized to offer their expertise to other professors, especially to those who were new to the project, in sharing experiences and learning-curve shortcuts, or just in how to engage in the most meaningful and efficient ways to offer feedback on their writing to large numbers of students. We started calling ourselves a "team," and we had a mission: to model collaboration to our students and to our support staff and colleagues. And, at this point, in late 2021, the collaboration loop just keeps getting larger, and the energy and mobilization keep getting stronger.

The project has become recognized by the university community for its dynamism and for its collaboration. I am blessed and honored to be in such company. And it all started with a problem that needed to be solved: how to motivate students to do meaningful research and writing. The solution created highlighted that in our community of learners, writers, and researchers, students' interests either overlapped or connected to many major themes including African and African-American identity and to elements of Ubuntu philosophy.

NOTES

1. Five years into the project, it has grown to include ten professors from various disciplines across the university. We collectively decided to rebrand the project to be reflective of academic excellence from all disciplines of the university, thereby losing the strong focus that the original project had on the discipline of History. The new project is called "StMU Research Scholars" and the new URL for the project is www .stmuscholars.org.

2. "Descriptive article" became the first genre of writing that we established for the website. Using Jack Hart's book *Storycraft: The Complete Guide to Writing Narrative Nonfiction* (Chicago: The University of Chicago Press, 2012), I introduced my students to the genre of storytelling and encouraged them to pick topics of interest that could be emplotted into a narrative arc story structure.

3. In the first two years of the project, students were expected to publish three articles. Each publication would allow them to advance in the organization, from their initial position of Writer to that of Senior Writer, and finally to Editor. Each promotion would entitle them to tackle more challenging research and writing projects called "Explanatory articles," and those more challenging projects would earn them more in salary, or grade points.

4. The "Academic Explanatory article" is actually the standard thesis-driven research paper that most college disciplines routinely assign to students to help them learn how to address a question or problem of scholarship, develop deep research skills in finding out how other scholars have approached that question or problem, develop analytical skills in articulating the arguments of other scholars and their use of evidence, synthesize all of that material to articulate their own answer to that question or problem (their thesis), and design their own arguments to defend their thesis. The "Journalistic Explanatory article," which Jack Hart presents in Chapter 12 of his book *Storycraft*, follows a microlevel process of some sort, and in the journey of that process there will be moments for digressions where the author feels that further explanation is required in order for the reader to understand that part of the process.

5. After the first two years of the project, virtually all the tutors assigned to serving the students in the project were themselves veterans of the project who had won awards for their own published articles.

6. Alexandria Garcia, "The Cry of the American Negro: Northern vs. Southern Demands for Human Rights," *StMU Research Scholars*, November 5, 2020, https:

//stmuscholars.org/the-cry-of-the-american-negro-the-demand-for-human-rights-by
-the-north-and-the-south/.

7. See Auroara-Juhl Nikkels, "Institutional Change & Identity: Unexpected Impact of the Arab," *StMU Research Scholars*, April 7, 2019, https://stmuscholars.org/institutional-change-identity-impact-of-the-arab-spring/, revised as Chapter 11 in this volume.

8. See Genesis Vera, "CARELESS: Excluding DACA Recipients from the Covid-19 CARES Act," *StMU Research Scholars*, November 30, 2020, https://stmuscholars.org/careless-excluding-daca-recipients-from-the-covid-19-cares-act/; Rodriguez Manuel, "In the Shadows: Undocumented Life and Human Rights Abuses in the U.S.," *StMU Research Scholars*, November 30, 2020, https://stmuscholars.org/in-the-shadows-living-undocumented-and-enduring-human-rights-abuses-in-the-u-s; Perez Angela, "Colonias in the Rio Grande Valley: La Monjita En La Bicicleta," *StMU Research Scholars*, November 1, 2020, https://stmuscholars.org/colonias-in-the-rio-grande-valley-la-monjita-en-la-bicicleta/; see also Vanessa Tombo, "The Art of Forgiveness: How Immaculée Ilibagiza Survived the Painful Losses from the Rwandan Genocide," *StMU Research Scholars*, March 21, 2018, https://stmuscholars.org/the-art-of-forgiveness-the-story-of-immaculee-ilibagiza/.

9. We ended up calling this committee the Nominating Committee.

10. Maria Mancha, "The Love Story of the Lovings," *StMU Research Scholars*, April 29, 2018, https://stmuscholars.org/the-love-story-of-the-lovings/.

11. Maria Mancha, *Master of Ceremony: StMU History Media Award Ceremony Script*, Spring 2018, St. Mary's University.

12. Sarah Nguyen, "Master of Ceremony Speech," 5th Semi-Annual StMU History Media Award Ceremony, St. Mary's University, San Antonio, November 28, 2018. This text was provided to the editor as a draft prior to the official ceremony.

13. Michael Mengler, "Master of Ceremony Speech," 7th Semi-Annual StMU History Media Award Ceremony, St. Mary's University, San Antonio, December 4, 2019. This text was provided to the editor as a draft prior to the official ceremony.

14. *Editor's note*: For further reading on this topic, please see Chapter 2 of this volume.

15. This quote is presented in its entirety from David W. Lutz, "African Ubuntu Philosophy and Global Management," *Journal of Business Ethics* 84, no. 53 (February 2009): 314. The citations that are included in the blocked quote are maintained from the original source.

16. Birgit Brock-Utne, "The Ubuntu Paradigm in Curriculum Work, Language of Instruction and Assessment," *International Review of Education* 62, no. 1 (February 2016): 30.

17. Roger Avenstrup, quoted in Brock-Utne, "The Ubuntu Paradigm," 30.

18. Birgit Brock-Utne and Azaveli Lwaitama, "The Prospects for and Possible Implications of Teaching African Philosophy in Kiswahili in East Africa: A Tanzanian Perspective," in *Educational Challenges in Multilingual Societies. Loitasa Phase Two Research,* eds. Zubeida Desai, Martha Qorro, and Birgit Brock-Utne (Cape Town: African Minds, 2010), 333–49.

19. In order to have a meaningful comparison of results, I've had to compare two things that are not qualitatively the same. The results of the Pre-Project semesters are measuring the percentage of students who scored 90% or better on their research papers. It represents the right-hand side of the standard distribution of grades. But it also represents the percentage of students who maximally benefited from the assignment, acquiring and displaying their ability to engage in meaningful research and writing at a high academic level. This is something we want for all of our students, not just the 15% who do so with a standard research paper assignment. The results of the Project semesters after Spring 2016 represent those students who succeeded in getting at least one article published. Getting published requires a different mindset from simply turning in an assignment as done. Getting published requires collaboration with others; it requires a demonstration of deep and meaningful research; and it requires the engagement in a writing process that demands a professional level of writing, requiring as many revisions as it takes to reach the level of excellence required for being published. The graph shows a very high percentage in Fall 2016 and a somewhat downward slope from the beginning of the project. This slope is due to my own learning curve about what constitutes excellence. Over the span of ten semesters, I've encouraged fewer and longer articles over shorter and more numerous ones. I started the project requiring three articles for an A in the class. Over time, I've reduced that number to one article. The average word-length of articles has gone from 815 words to 2500 words. And the last three semesters also represent the onset of the COVID-19 pandemic, affecting especially the Spring semester of 2020.

20. See Troy Leonard, "Rwanda's Genocide of 1994," *StMU Research Scholars*, October 20, 2017, https://stmuscholars.org/rwandas-genocide-of-1994/, and Vanessa Tombo, "The Art of Forgiveness: How Immaculée Ilibagiza Survived the Painful Losses from the Rwandan Genocide," *StMU Research Scholars*, March 21, 2018, https://stmuscholars.org/the-art-of-forgiveness-the-story-of-immaculee-ilibagiza/.

21. See Maalik Stansbury, "Barbados Slave Codes," *StMU Research Scholars*, October 19, 2016, https://stmuscholars.org/barbados-slave-codes/.

22. See Erik Shannon, "From Montgomery to Detroit: Rosa Parks," *StMU Research Scholars*, October 31, 2017, https://stmuscholars.org/from-montgomery-to-dertoit-rosa-parks/.

23. See Soteria Banks, "Berry Gordy: The Man Who Broke Barriers in the Music Industry," *StMU Research Scholars*, November 3, 2017, https://stmuscholars.org/berry-gordy/.

24. See Aaiyanna Johnson, "How Many of You Will Remember Me, Dorothy Dandridge?," *StMU Research Scholars*, October 13, 2017, https://stmuscholars.org/how-many-of-you-will-remember-me-dorothy-dandridge/.

25. See Lamont Traylor, "'Mama There Goes That Man': The Story of Kobe Bryant's Miraculous 81 Point Game," *StMU Research Scholars*, November 15, 2018, https://stmuscholars.org/mama-there-goes-that-man-the-story-of-kobe-bryants-miraculous-81-point-game/.

26. See Faten Al Shaibi, "'My Father Is up the Tree': Abdul Halim Hafez and Egyptian Cinema," *StMU Research Scholars*, October 7, 2018, https://stmuscholars.org/my-father-is-up-the-tree/.

27. Gabriela Serrato, "The Lynching Era: The Tragic Hanging of Laura and L. D. Nelson," *StMU Research Scholars*, February 14, 2017, https://stmuscholars.org/the -lynching-era-the-tragic-hanging-of-laura-and-l-d-nelson/.

28. Amanda Figueroa, "The Rage of Nina Simone: 'Mississippi Goddam,'" *StMU Research Scholars*, October 18, 2017, https://stmuscholars.org/the-rage-of-nina -simone/.

29. Josemaria Soriano, "The Power of a Ball: How Soccer Star Didier Drogba Ended the Côte d'Ivoire Civil War," *StMU Research Scholars*, October 24, 2017, https://stmuscholars.org/the-power-of-a-ball-how-soccer-star-didier-drogba-ended -the-cote-divoire-civil-war/.

30. Gabriela Serrato, "The Young and Courageous: Ruby Bridges," *StMU Research Scholars*, October 15, 2017, https://stmuscholars.org/the-young-and-courageous-ruby -bridges/.

31. Amanda Figueroa, "Forty Years of 'Bad Blood': The Tuskegee Syphilis Study," *StMU Research Scholars*, September 19, 2017, https://stmuscholars.org/bad-blood -the-tuskegee-syphilis-study/.

32. Cameron Adelman, "'Cause Freedom Ain't Free: Freedom Summer Movement in 1964 Mississippi," *StMU Research Scholars*, April 16, 2017, https://stmuscholars .org/cause-freedom-aint-free-freedom-summer-movement-in-1964-mississippi/.

33. Roberto Tijerina, "Black Codes, Jim Crow, and Social Control in the South," *StMU Research Scholars*, March 22, 2017, https://stmuscholars.org/the-south-and -vigilante-justice/.

34. Maria Esquivel, "He Would Have Killed Me: The Story of Jennifer Teege, Granddaughter of Nazi Commandant Amon Goeth," *StMU Research Scholars*, April 21, 2018, https://stmuscholars.org/he-would-have-killed-me-the-story-of-jennifer -teege-granddaughter-of-nazi-commandant-amon-goeth/.

35. Belia Camarena, "The Immortal Woman: Henrietta Lacks," *StMU Research Scholars*, April 16, 2018, https://stmuscholars.org/the-immortal-woman-henrietta -lacks/.

36. Maria Manch, "The Love Story of the Lovings." *StMU Research Scholars*, April 29, 2018, https://stmuscholars.org/the-love-story-of-the-lovings.

11

Institutional Change and Identity

Impact of the Arab Spring and Mobilization in North Africa

Auroara Nikkels

December of 2010 saw what would become a massive wave of demand for change throughout the Middle Eastern and North African (MENA) areas. Governments were toppled, militaries took over, and civil wars broke out.[1] The three countries in this chapter, Morocco, Libya, and Tunisia, are members of the 22-country Arab League and three of the five states in the Maghreb. The Maghreb region of five countries was organized to help integrate economic and political characteristics of the five countries.[2] The population in Morocco was estimated at 34 million in July 2018, with approximately 40% of the population who is Berber.[3] In Libya, the population is around 6 million, which was last estimated in July 2018, with Berbers and Arabs making up 97% and the other 3% including Greeks, Maltese, Italians, Egyptians, Pakistanis, Turks, Indians, and Tunisians 96.6% are Muslims and 2.7% Christians.[4] In Tunisia, the estimated population as of July 2018 is around 11 million, which consists of 98% Arab, 1% European, 1% Jewish, under 1% Berber and a few other very small groups. Morocco and Tunisia have a similar religious makeup, which is 99% of the population being Muslim and the other 1% Christian, Jewish, Shia Muslim, and Baha'i.[5]

This chapter examines these three countries for their uniqueness. During the Arab Spring, Morocco was one of the only North African countries to not have a regime change, Libya was the first country to experience NATO interference, and Tunisia marked the beginning of the Arab Spring when Mohamed Bouazizi set himself on fire to protest the government and the lack of economic opportunity that he felt he had in December of 2010.[6]

Since the overthrow of former president Ben Ali, Tunisia has had multiple elections, including one in 2019, that have been more successful than some of the other countries, yet alarming events have taken place since July 25, 2021.[7] The difference in outcomes for Tunisia during the Arab Spring versus Morocco and Libya was explained by the fact that Tunisia is one of the most educated countries of those that saw their populations mobilizing for change during the Arab Spring. According to the Human Development Report, in 2011, 34% of the population, both male and female, 25 years of age and up, had some secondary education in Tunisia; 21.9% in Morocco; and in Libya 58% of the population.[8] Education in Libya is high due partly to the fact that education was free and compulsory for the first nine years in 2011.[9] The Arab Spring outcome in Libya has continued to bring increasing challenges unlike with Tunisia and Morocco because Libya has since dissolved into what many consider a "failed state." After the 2011 uprising and overthrow of the authoritarian regime, the country held democratic elections in 2011 and 2014, but after the 2014 elections, the country dissolved into a civil war and worked with the United Nations to bring peace back to the country. Morocco had a different experience within the context of the Arab Spring, with the creation of the main protest group in 2011 which was referred to as the *February 20th Movement* that demanded the transition from an executive monarchy to a parliamentary monarchy.[10] Furthering the differences, in Libya and Tunisia, people called for a regime change. However, the people of Morocco did not ask for their King to step down, only for there to be reforms, which King Muhamad partly agreed to follow as with the 2011 constitutional reform.[11]

This chapter will start with an examination of how governments have changed and how effective the demands for change have been and how these changes have connected to the identities of the people in these North African countries. Questions include how did the governments adapt or resist against demands for change, how has the Arab Spring of 2011 affected Berber people, and how are identities transformed through conflict? These questions help assess the extent to which the differences between these three states saw populations mobilize for different demands during the Arab Spring and which led them on diverging paths since.

GOVERNMENTAL RESPONSES TO DEMANDS FOR CHANGE

The death of Mohamed Bouazizi in Tunisia sparked a revolution that spread throughout the MENA countries. On December 17, 2010, Mohamed Bouazizi was selling fruit from his cart when a policewoman stopped him and confiscated his cart and products, despite the Office for Employment and

Independent Work not requiring a permit to sell fruit from a cart. While the events of what happened in this altercation are contested, it is believed that the policewoman either slapped Bouazizi or threw his cart across the street. Hours later, Bouazizi, in front of the governor's office, shouted "How do you expect me to make a living?" and then set himself on fire.[12] Bouazizi's act of self-immolation burned away the fear others felt of government repression and violence and sparked outrage that mobilized mass protests for better economic and employment opportunities. Aside from thousands of protesters, lawyers took to the streets and the Chairman of the National Bar Association declared that lawyers were on strike after the torture of lawyers at protests.[13] Approximately three weeks after protests began, President Zine el Abidine Ben Ali was overthrown and fled to Saudi Arabia, where there is no extradition agreement with Tunisia, and where he died at the age of 83 having been sentenced by a Tunisian court but never serving any of his sentence. After Ben Ali fled, Ghanouchi took place as Prime Minister, but resigned in February 2011 due to continued protests over the involvement of any members of Ben Ali's Constitutional Democratic Rally (RDC) in the new government. The National Constituent Assembly (NCA) took the Prime Minister's place as the new government and declared that political parties were no longer outlawed and that elections were to take place, proposed to happen in July 2011 but postponed to October to allow for more time to properly set up elections.[14] Ennahdha, the Islamist party, won 89 seats and the rest went to the Congress for the Republic (CPR) and Ettakatol parties. These first elections set the country up to be run by a Parliament in which the Prime Minister, in this case political party Ennahda's Hamadi Jebali, was the most powerful. The President's position was won by the political party CPR, who elected Moncef Marzouki, and Ettakatol's Mustapha Ben Jaafar led the assembly.[15] On February 6, 2013, the first political assassination since the elections took place and a member of the Patriots Party, Chokri Belaid, was murdered.[16] It is suspected that the political party Ennahda had ordered the assassination, but the head of the party denied this. In response to the assassinations, Prime Minister Jebali proposed a council run by technocrats, but it failed, and Prime Minister Jebali resigned.[17]

In 2014, the National Constitution Committee released a new constitution that was approved with 200 to 12 votes.[18] This new constitution included many changes and added 71 articles. Because the youth in Tunisia were such a large part of the protests, the voting age was decreased from 22 to 18 years of age.[19] Furthermore, the 2014 constitution determined that "Education shall be mandatory up to the age of sixteen years."[20]

Also in 2014, the second set of elections was held, with almost a complete power change. The political party Nidaa Tounes won 85 seats and the leader of the party, Beji Caid Essebsi, was elected President while Ennahda won

69 seats. President Essebsi took office, though many worried whether this is a return to the earlier regime, as President Essebsi previously worked as Tunisia's Foreign Minister in the 1980s, and then as Parliament's Speaker in the early 1990s. Presidential elections were scheduled to be held in 2019.[21] Kais Saied was elected President in October 2019.[22] Just a few weeks earlier, youths were taking their protests into the streets to denounce the presidential power grab after Saied dismissed his prime minister, suspended Parliament, and granted himself judicial powers.[23]

While the two paths that Libya and Tunisia took were very different, they are similar in that eventually both authoritarian governments were overthrown and new ones were established via elections. This is where their similarities end, however. Libya had only ever had one king, King Idris, in 1951 when Libya gained its independence from Italy. Gadhafi, a military officer, overthrew King Idris in 1969, abolished the constitution, and ran the country with his "Green Book" which was his philosophy on laws that should be followed. In the "Green Book," Gadhafi specifically mentions constitutions: "Constitutions cannot be considered the law of society."[24] A constitution is fundamentally a (man-made) positive law and lacks the natural source from which it must derive its justification." Furthermore, he discusses his view on political parties which is that they are created "to rule over non-members of the party" to gain more power.

February 15, 2011, started the past decade of political struggle when protesters demanded more freedoms and better economic opportunities. Ten days after protests started, the National Transitional Council (NTC), a group of "high profile individuals," met in the city of Bayda.[25] They established that Mustafa Abdual Jalil, former Justice Minister, would be chair. On March 5, 2011, the NTC announced that it was the "sole representative of all Libya."[26]

On February 26, 2011, the United Nations Security Council (UNSC) passed Resolution 1970, which placed arms embargoes, travel bans, and froze the assets of individuals mentioned in an annex in an effort to stop the conflict and violence on civilians.[27] The next resolution came on March 17 and established a no-fly zone, strengthened the arms embargo, allowed for measures to protect citizens, and established a panel of experts to report to the council and offer advice on the situation.[28] Following this resolution, the North Atlantic Treaty Organization (NATO) allies began to intervene to protect citizens; this operation was called Operation Unified Protector (OUP). OUP had three main goals while in Libya: enforce the arms embargo, enforce the no-fly zone, and "conducting air and naval strikes against military forces involved in attacks or threatening to attack Libyan civilians and civilian populated areas."[29] In September 2011, the UNSC passed Resolution 2009, which changed terms of the arms embargo, unfroze some Libyan assets, and established the United Nations Support Mission in Libya (UNSMIL).[30] From then until October 31, 2011, NATO conducted air strikes on Libyan military bases and delivered humanitarian support to civilians.

In October of 2011, after approximately eight months of the intervention through air strikes from NATO, and 10,000 deaths, Gadhafi was overthrown by the NTC, who then established the Constitutional Drafting Assembly (CDA).[31] Initially, the CDA was going to be comprised of members that the NTC chose, but after protests where the population mobilized once again, the NTC amended the law so that members would be selected by voters. Changes provided for the three regions, Fezzan, Cyrenaica, and Tripolitania, to be represented as well.[32] The Constitutional Drafting Assembly published a constitutional draft based off the 1951 constitution, though there were amendments made, such as Article 30 which set parameters and responsibilities for the National Transitional Council (NTC). The NTC led for an interim period during which some smaller-scale protests continued. On January 4, 2012, the ban on political parties was lifted and in July of 2012, the General National Congress (GNC) held elections, where 62% of the Libyan population showed up to vote.[33] The GNC was dominated by the National Forces Alliance (NFA) who won the largest share of the plurality of the seats with 39%. The Muslim Brotherhood's Justice and Construction Party (PCJ) won 17% and the rest of the seats were won by smaller parties and independents.[34]

Differing from Tunisia, the Libyan elections were not peaceful, as multiple voting booths across the state had to be shut down from protesters and violence. Voters and candidates were under threat for the 2014 election because of differences in ideologies of how the government should be run. In 2014, these differences came to a head briefly after the elections and another round in the civil war broke out. A key event that spurred more turmoil was the 2012 attack in Bengasi, where four American officials were killed, including J. Christopher Stevens, the U.S. Ambassador. This attack was orchestrated by a number of terrorists' groups.[35] Furthermore, the security sector in Libya was spread between multiple armed groups, some of which got their arms from across the border. Two main armed groups that grew in power were the Libyan Shield Force (LSF) and the Supreme Security Committee (SSC), which are led respectively by the chief of staff and the Interior Ministry, but both groups function more or less autonomously, with political gains in mind.[36] The SSC was formed as a policing unit while the LSF was a reserve army.[37] In May 2013, these two groups pushed for the passage of the political isolation law in which officials from the Gadhafi era would be unable to run for any future government positions, though this was repealed in 2015. Part of the reason so many armed groups other than the military were able to rise up is because Gadhafi severely limited the military's function, cutting funding, support, training, and equipment which had severely handicapped the ability of the military to secure the entire country.[38]

While the SSC and LSF were pushing for the Political Isolation Law, the General National Congress split into two groups: one for forbidding former Gadhafi officials to hold future offices, while the others were against this law. The National Force Alliance had a less stringent view, while the Justice and Construction Party had hard lines. Despite this split, elections to form the House of Representatives (HOR) went ahead with candidates running as independents. However, coalitions formed, linked to the National Forces Alliance, who established the House of Representatives. This political divide allowed General Haftar to launch Operation Dignity against the Islamists while the Islamists launched the Libya Dawn in response.[39]

When the 'Libya Dawn' and 'Operation Dignity' clashed at Tripoli International Airport, the Libya Dawn beat General Haftar and took control of Tripoli.[40] The elected House of Representatives, Prime Minister Abdullah al-Thinni, and his cabinet fled to Tobruk, where they were internationally recognized by the European Union, United States, Egypt, and the United Arab Emirates. In Tripoli, the Libya Dawn enacted their own government under a new GNC.[41]

However, in December 2015, the United Nations was able to broker a peace deal, the Libyan Political Agreement (LPA), between both rival governments that led to the creation of the Government of National Accord run by a nine-person Presidency Council.[42] The Presidency Council was allowed two years of executive authority or until a constitution was drafted, which happened in 2016.[43] The HOR would remain the only legislative authority in Libya, while the GNC would form a State Council to advise the newly formed Government of National Accord (GNA). The Presidency Council had the power to appoint the head of the military, who was General Haftar, but the HOR opposed this option because they feared it would limit their power. However, the HOR had yet to ratify this new government due to the delayed voting because of the failure to produce the required number of members to convene a session until late August 2016. Even once the HOR convened, the GNA was rejected because of the magnitude of the involvement that the Libya Dawn group would have. Further crippling the GNA, a group led by the former prime minister of the Libya Dawn took control of the State Council and reclaimed executive authority from the GNA.[44]

As previously mentioned, in Morocco, protesters did not demand that King Muhamad step down.[45] This is because of the idea of the "Holy Trinity" which consists of the "God, King, and Country." The King is seen as a direct descendant from the Prophet of Islam. It is suspected that King Muhamad VI addressed previous grievances from the population preempting protests and demands that might have asked for his removal during the Arab Spring. King Muhamad VI started making changes to the constitution and laws years before when the population mobilized to voice grievances. For example, in

2003, he passed a law—*Mudawwana*—which made it illegal for women to be abused by a male and for divorce to be unilateral. A few years prior, the Equity and Reconciliation Commission opened case files filled with stories of torture from the King Hassan II reign. When protests started in Spring 2011, King Mohamed VI responded to the February 20 Movement, and proposed a constitution referendum to be held in July 2011.[46]

Demands from the people included recognition of central elements of their identity as fighting for the rightful place of the Berber language, and also mobilized for broader political and economic access requesting equal rights and more employment opportunities, which were primarily demanded by youth.[47] The discussion of whether to remain an Islamic state also arose during the protests. The constitution included an increase in articles, from 108 to 180. As per the people's demands, the King redistributed his power to the Prime Minister in several ways. In November 2011, the first elections were held and Abdelilah Benkirane, leader of the Islamist Justice and Development Party (PJD), won majority. This is one of the first times that an Islamist party had control. The JPD won 107 seats, which was 61 more than the 2007 elections. There was also a new quota created that designated 60 seats for women and 30 seats for men under 30. Prime Minister Benkirane can now appoint government ministers and has to ability to dissolve the Parliament, which was previously a power of the King only. Although the Prime Minister gained more powers, the King still has the sole ability to call on the cabinet to convene and retained veto powers. Despite these constitutional changes and slight change in allocations of power, the King bypassed the former prime minister Benkirane to approve the arrest of 130 allegedly corrupt customs officers in the Tangier Port.[48] Benkirane argued that the power to give orders to other ministers was not within the King's rights and rests with the current prime minister.[49]

In 2016, a protest movement mobilized in response to a death, in a similar way to how protest had started in December 2010 in Tunisia. Mouhcine Fikri was crushed to death in a garbage truck when he was attempting to retrieve the swordfish he caught that police had confiscated, asserting it was the wrong time of year to catch swordfish. It was speculated that the officers ordered the garbage truck to start compacting the trash, which resulted in Fikri's death as he dove in after the fish to retrieve it. This happened in Al Hoceima, a primarily Berber-speaking town. From Fikri's death, Nasser Zefzaf formed the Hirak Protest Movement. The Hirak Movement has been more liberal in terms of welcoming women's involvement, with the second in command a mother of four named Nawale Ben Aissa.[50]

IMPACT OF ARAB SPRING ON BERBERS
AND THEIR FIGHT TO PROTECT THEIR
IDENTITY AND POLITICAL RIGHTS

Berbers—*Imazighen* ("free people")—are a primary focus because they are indigenous people of North Africa who have lived throughout the region for over 3,000 years, well before the Arab invasions of the 7th century.[51] For most of recent history, the case of the Berbers is much like the case of every minority: minimal rights. King Hassan II, King Muhamad's father, made a step recognizing Berber as something that should be taught in schools, though that has not happened.[52] However, after the 2011 uprisings, Berber was recognized as an official language in Article 5, which states "Likewise, Tamazight [which is the Berber word that designates Berber languages] constitutes an official language of the State, being common patrimony of all Moroccans without exception." Furthermore, the preamble of the constitution was amended to include "Its unity, is forged by the convergence of its Arab-Islamist, Berber and Saharan-Hassanic components, nourished and enriched by its African, Andalusian, Hebraic and Mediterranean influences."[53]

Only 1–2% of the population of Tunisia claims to be purely Berber. Success for the Berber people in Tunisia includes the creation of the Tunisian Association for Amazigh Culture in July of 2011, the appointment of a Tunisian Amazigh to the federal Council, and the inclusion of some Berber films at a film festival in Nebeul.[54] Since they are such a small minority, there is no mention of Berbers in the Tunisian constitution.

In Libya, the Berber population makes up about 8–9% of the population.[55] When the GNC held elections in 2012, the Imazighen (plural of Amazigh) boycotted the elections on the basis that there was not enough representation of minorities in the council. To combat this issue, the GNC allotted six seats for women and two seats for minority ethnic group representation: Tuareg and Tebu.[56] While the Tuareg and Tebu took their two seats, Imazighen continued to boycott through the 2014 elections.[57] In Article 1 of the 2011 constitution, the government of Libya recognizes that "Arabic shall be the official language, while the linguistic and cultural rights of the Amazigh, the Tebus, the Tuareg and the other components of the Libyan society shall be guaranteed."[58] However, this was changed with the 2016 constitution which fails to mention any minorities by name but does say that languages spoken by any other Libyan people are also national languages. Again, the text of the constitution was changed in the 2017 constitution to include further protection beyond recognition of the diversity of the identity elements for the minority ethnic groups in Libya: "The languages spoken by the Libyans or part of them, including Arabic, Amazigh, Tuareg, or Tebu are considered a cultural and linguistic heritage . . . The state shall guarantee taking the necessary measures to protect them, preserve their originality and develop their teaching to and usage by those who speak them."[59]

In 2014, the first Libyan Berber, Nouri Abusahmain, was elected to Libya's National General Congress, which was the government that overthrew the House of Representatives. Abusahmain called on the LSF to defend the government that took control in Tripoli.[60] This has led to much controversy regarding his position and beliefs.[61] He has been sanctioned by the European Union, along with two others, for his actions regarding the attempted peace deal. Further adding to the controversy, in 2016, he rejected the LPA in a discussion with the United Nations.[62]

IMPACT OF ARAB SPRING ON IDENTITY TRANSFORMATION

Identities transform when faced with hard decisions and hard situations. First and foremost, the biggest factor that affects individual lives and identity: death. While death can no longer affect the person who died, their death forever alters the lives of every individual in these countries. People lost wives, mothers, sisters, husbands, fathers, brothers, and children. From what is considered the first death of the Arab Spring, Mohamed Bouazizi, to the death of Gadhafi, to the people whose names we will never know. This can be highlighted in a first-person account of a young woman in Tunisia. This woman was Ahlem Yazidi, who lost her cousin in a protest outside her home. She had been in the capital just days before preparing to join the protests. Turned away by an undercover policeman, she eventually returned close to her hometown, where she met with her cousin, Wael. A few days later, he participated in what was supposed to be a peaceful protest and instead sat "lying motionless on the ground with a bullet in his chest" after police opened fire.[63] She then speaks about how her cousin's death was a great sadness to her, but despite that she was "proud of him and his courage."[64] She says that people accused them of losing their identity, but she believes that they lived up to being what a Tunisian meant: "heroic people, willing to sacrifice everything for the pursuit of freedom and dignity."[65]

A young man named Abdulmonem Allieby from Libya spoke about his feelings for the protests and how he responded to them, saying,

> Imagine a person oppressed, beaten, and humiliated for decades and when he finally speaks, he still is strangled. While slowly awaiting death, the oppressor is momentarily disoriented and releases his grip. Knowing that this is absolutely your last and only chance at survival, what would you do? In my case, I fought.[66]

Many others expressed similar feelings. They found themselves in the Arab Spring and realized what they were on this earth for: to fight for change and equality.

Social media, thanks to the growth of access and reach in the MENA countries, is another factor within the context of the Arab Spring that opened new avenues for validating and showcasing identity and to mobilize large groups of people who gathered in protest. The platforms that exist allow people to express how they feel and who they are, providing a voice to those with diverse identities. Social media allows for change to occur through education of the events that are happening. News of events were shared, protests were organized, and people found their voice, sharing their opinions and stories. Social media had a major impact on the women's movement in these three countries. Platforms such as Twitter, Facebook, Instagram, etc., allowed women to post their faces along with their messages, "unfazed by the possibility of getting arrested," allowing them to decide how to define themselves and be seen.[67] Sexual assault typically results in the shame and humiliation of the victim by the family; thus, those assaulted rarely speak out against crimes committed against them. However, with social media, there has been a movement of women who have been sexually assaulted and record their story to publish on social media platforms, refusing to be shamed into silence.[68]

In Morocco, the 20 February Movement was comprised of mainly youth seeking better employment opportunities but also labor unions, Berbers, women, and some political parties. The 20 February Movement used social media to inform their community and the world of their mission and demands, as well as livestream protests. Videos were recorded and uploaded of protesters that were beaten by police and forced into what the government hoped would be silence.[69] The King in Morocco has the primary power of the media and can appoint the heads of public radio and television stations. After the 2011 elections and Prime Minister Benkiran's election, speeches addressed to the public were spread much faster because of how quickly they were shared over social media. Recognizing the importance of social media, the Ministry of Communication held a public hearing with over 500 representatives invited from over 250 e-news outlets.[70] Further exacerbating the media problems was the fact that many journalists were shut out, their stories buried, when they touched on certain subjects like criticizing the King, government, or Islam. Many journalists were also arrested. Another setback was that many businesses were tied to the crown and were paid to only show certain advertisements.[71]

In Tunisia, social media played a critical role. From the very beginning, videos were uploaded to Twitter, YouTube, and Facebook.[72] When Mohamed Bouazizi set himself on fire, the video was posted immediately to Twitter and people responded by organizing protests, demanding that President Ben Ali step down and that there be democratic elections and better economic opportunity, specifically for the youth. Through the sharing of videos, news channels like Al-Jazeera were able to spread the news of what was happening on the ground in real time. Although Al-Jazeera was banned in Tunisia, it is a satellite station and it is estimated that about half of the population with access to television connects to international satellite networks like Al-Jazeera.[73] Much like in Morocco, the press and news channels are controlled by the government and only show content approved by the government.[74]

Social media was not as widely used in Libya as it was in Tunisia, but it still allowed people to view news articles from Al-Jazeera and other news sources. In 1996 in Libya, 1,200 political prisoners were killed in Abu Salim prison and every year since, mothers and families march to remember them. On February 15, 2011, families of the Abu Salim victims marched in Benghazi, with many other protesters who joined in. During the protests, lawyer Fathi Terbal, who represented the families of the victims, was arrested. Two days later, the Day of Rage was announced on Facebook in response.[75]

Aside from those residing within the countries, social media provided a window for those outside these countries, specifically students studying abroad. A Fulbright student was studying in Pennsylvania when protests broke out in Tunisia. In January of 2011, the student stated that he "was connected to [his] computer twenty-four hours a day" to stay connected to his friends and family in Tunisia, as well as staying up to date on events happening.[76] He used Facebook to share news articles, some of which he was able to confirm as true because of the ability that social media gave him to contact those in Tunisia and confirm whether news articles were accurately reporting the events. He believed that "the revolution was all about media."[77] On multiple occasions, his activity on social media gave him the ability and access to be a keynote speaker at his university and other places to share his knowledge and opinions of the events. However, he does not believe that all social media was positive, because it allowed people to express their views and opinions more easily. While this was a positive thing, it caused conflict between people. He provides the example of his brother and his best friend who fought over their beliefs of the government because of such high tensions. Comments can be made when emotions are running high that are less than peaceful and exacerbate conflict.[78]

Outside of social media, identity was targeted and transformed through the experiences of the Tebu and Tuareg people, specifically in Libya.[79] Prior to the Arab Spring, Gadhafi stripped the Tebu of their citizenship by declaring that all those with IDs issued in Aouzou, a region that the Tebu were previously forced to relocate to, would be considered foreigners in the 1996 Decree. This made it incredibly difficult to acquire official papers. Because of this institutional barrier, many were unable to receive proper health care and education, which led to a very high illiteracy rate and rapid spread of illnesses. Therefore, the majority of the Tebu were mobilized and sided with protesters against the Gadhafi regime, demanding citizenship and other basic human rights in the 2011 protests. Their vocal protests in 2011 forced the government to nullify the 1996 Decree, though it has been harder to overcome in smaller villages where the Tebu population is small. When the House of Representatives fled to Tobruk in the 2014 civil war, Tebu people again sided with them. The villages that the Tebu lived in were controlled by them and therefore gave them a more serious role in politics and their own economy.[80]

The Tuareg people have a slightly different story, as they primarily sided with Gadhafi and then supported the government based in Tripoli.[81] In the 1970s, Gadhafi recruited Tuareg fighters to join the military, making promises of equality. In 2004, he created a section of the military called the Maghawir Brigade, made entirely of Tuareg people. Because of their association with Gadhafi, the villages where Tuareg people live were impoverished and disenfranchised. However, inside of the Tuareg community, there is conflict over whether it is the right decision to back the government in Tripoli as opposed to the one in Tobruk. Many Tuareg argue that the Tripoli government will continue to oppress them. Those that were in the Maghawir Brigade defected and went on to form the Ténéré Brigade in 2011. Further, the relations between the Tuareg born in Libya versus those born in the surrounding states fuel the conflict because of economic and political differences.[82]

CONCLUSION

In the words of Ahlem Yazidi, "[Tunisia] demonstrated to the whole world that the greatness of a nation resides not just in economic, political or demographic power, but also in its strong will."[83] The revolts of the 2011 Arab Spring in Tunisia, Morocco, and Libya have forever altered the countries' and the regions' history and brought a higher level of recognition for ethnic groups previously subsumed, fostered by the ubiquity of social media and its power. People will not rest until they see a government in charge that accomplishes the changes that they want and need to have equality. The Arab Spring set in motion many different kinds of transformation and mobilization that continue to impact current events in these three countries. The developments in Tunisia have become extremely alarming as it was the country that seemed to take the most hopeful of steps and even changed its constitution to foster more democratic developments and to strengthen its democratic institutions. North African countries have continued to see significant mobilization of their citizens to challenge the status quo in Algeria with growing Friday protests of the Hirak Movement and to renewed protests in Tunisia revolting against the authoritarian turns taken by the current president.[84]

NOTES

1. An earlier version of this article appeared on the website for the *StMU History Media Project*: Auroara Nikkels, "Institutional Change & Identity: Unexpected Impact of the Arab Spring," *STMU Research Scholars* (blog), April 7, 2019.

2. Robert W. McKeon Jr., "The Arab Maghreb Union: Possibilities of Maghrebine Political and Economic Unity, and Enhanced Trade in the World Community," *Penn State International Law Review* 10, no. 2 (1992): 263–302.

3. Bruce Maddy-Weitzman, "A Turning Point? The Arab Spring and the Amazigh Movement," *Ethnic and Racial Studies* 38, no. 14 (2015): 2499–2515.

4. *Encyclopedia Britannica*, s.v. "Libya—People," accessed December 1, 2021, https://www.britannica.com/place/Libya/People.

5. Ibid.; *Encyclopedia Britannica*, s.v. "Morocco, " accessed December 1, 2021, https://www.britannica.com/place/Morocco.

6. Thessa Lageman, "Remembering Mohamed Bouazizi: The Man Who Sparked the Arab Spring," *Al Jazeera*, December 17, 2020, https://www.aljazeera.com/features/2020/12/17/remembering-mohamed-bouazizi-his-death-triggered-the-arab.

7. "Kais Saied Freezes All Parliamentary Activities, Lifts Immunity of All MPs and Dismisses PM," *Agency Tunis Afrique Press*, July 26, 2021, http://search.ebscohost.com.blume.stmarytx.edu:2048/login.aspx?direct=true&db=n5h&AN=f73b76ce8949fe29bf2a537cfa420e8f0012&site=ehost-live&scope=site.

8. United Nations Development Programme, "Population with at Least Some Secondary Education, Female (% Ages 25 and Older)," Human Development Reports, 2020, http://hdr.undp.org/en/indicators/23906.

9. Delinda C. Hanley, "Libya Invests in Its People's Education," *Washington Report on Middle East Affairs—WRMEA*, March 20, 2001, https://www.wrmea.org/001-march/libya-looking-toward-a-post-lockerbie-future-libya-invests-in-its-people-s-education.html.

10. Ahmed Zakarya Mitiche, "Morocco's February 20 Movement: Demands Still Alive, " *Al Jazeera*, February 22, 2017, https://www.aljazeera.com/features/2017/2/22/moroccos-february-20-movement-demands-still-alive

11. Marina Ottaway, "The New Moroccan Constitution: Real Change or More of the Same?," Carnegie Endowment for International Peace, June 20, 2011, https://carnegieendowment.org/2011/06/20/new-moroccan-constitution-real-change-or-more-of-same-pub-44731.

12. Joseph Pugliese, "Permanent Revolution: Mohamed Bouazizi's Incendiary Ethics of Revolt," *Law, Culture and the Humanities* 10, no. 3 (2014): 408–20.

13. Imad El-Anis and Ashraf Hamed, "From Spring to Summer? Revolutionary Change in Tunisia, Egypt and Libya—CIAO," *Bilgi* 27, no. 2 (2013): 75–102.

14. News Wires, "Vote Delayed until October, Tunisia's Interim PM says," *France 24*, June 8, 2011, https://www.france24.com/en/20110608-elections-postponed-until-october-tunisia-interim-prime-minister-sebsi-essebsi.

15. Ibid.

16. Andrej Zwitter, "Constitutional Reform and Emergency Powers in Egypt and Tunisia," *Middle East Law and Governance* 7, no. 2 (August 31, 2015): 257–84.

17. "Tunisia Prime Minister Hamadi Jebali Resigns," *BBC News*, February 19, 2013, https://www.bbc.com/news/world-africa-21508498.

18. Md. Muddassir Quamar, "Tunisia: Presidential and Parliamentary Elections, 2014," *Contemporary Review of the Middle East* 2, no. 3 (September 1, 2015): 269–88.

19. Tunisian Constitution, Article 54, 2014.

20. Tunisian Constitution, Article 39, 2014.

21. Quamar, "Tunisia," 269–88; "Kais Saied Freezes All Parliamentary Activities, Lifts Immunity of All MPs and Dismisses PM," *Agency Tunis Afrique Press*, July 26, 2021, https://allafrica.com/stories/202107260461.html.

22. BBC News, "Tunisia Election: Kais Saied to Become President," *BBC News*, October 14, 2019, https://www.bbc.com/news/world-africa-50032460.

23. *Al Jazeera*, "In Pictures: Tunisians Rally to Denounce Saied's Power Grab," *Al Jazeera* November 14, 2021, https://www.aljazeera.com/gallery/2021/11/14/tunisia-96.

24. Muammar al-Gaddafi, *The Green Book* (CreateSpace Independent Publishing Platform, 2016), 27.

25. "National Transitional Council—Libya," NTC Libya, 2011, http://ntclibya.org/.

26. Ibid.

27. United Nations Security Council resolution 1970, S/RES/1970 (February 26, 2011), available from https://www.nato.int/nato_static_fl2014/assets/pdf/pdf_2011_02/20110927_110226-UNSCR-1970.pdf.

28. United Nations Security Council resolution 1973, S/RES/1973 (March 17, 2011), available from https://www.nato.int/nato_static/assets/pdf/pdf_2011_03/20110927_110311-UNSCR-1973.pdf.

29. NATO, "NATO and Libya (Archived)," NATO, November 9, 2015, http://www.nato.int/cps/en/natohq/topics_71652.htm.

30. United Nations Security Council resolution 2009 S/RES/2009 (September 16, 2011), available from: https://www.nato.int/nato_static_fl2014/assets/pdf/pdf_2011_09/20110927_110916-UNSCR-2009.pdf.

31. El-Anis and Hamed, "Spring," 75–102

32. Darin E.W. Johnson, "Conflict Constitution-Making in Libya and Yemen," *University of Pennsylvania Journal of International Law* 39, no. 2 (2017): 293.

33. El-Anis and Hamed, "Spring," 75–102.

34. Lisa Watanabe, "Libya's Future: Uncertain, Despite a Political Agreement," *Middle East Policy* 23, no. 4 (2016): 114–22.

35. Daniel L. Byman, "Terrorism in North Africa: Before and After Benghazi," *Brookings*, July 10, 2013, https://www.brookings.edu/testimonies/terrorism-in-north-africa-before-and-after-benghazi/.

36. Frederic Wehrey and Peter Cole, "Building Libya's Security Sector," *Carnegie Endowment for International Peace*, August 6, 2013.

37. Watanabe, "Libya's Future," 114–22.

38. Frederic Wehrey and Peter Cole, "Building Libya's Security Sector," *Carnegie Endowment for International Peace*, August 6, 2013.

39. Watanabe, "Libya's Future," 114–22.

40. Daveed Gartenstein-Ross and Nathaniel Barr, "Dignity and Dawn: Libya's Escalating Civil War," *Terrorism and Counter-Terrorism Studies* (2015): 1–58.

41. Johnson, "Conflict," 293.

42. Watanabe, "Libya's Future," 114–22.

43. Johnson, "Conflict," 293.

44. Watanabe, "Libya's Future," 114–22.

45. Larbi Sadiki and Youcef Bouandel, "The Post Arab Spring Reform: The Maghreb at a Cross Roads," *Digest of Middle East Studies* 25, no. 1 (2016): 109–31.

46. Ibid.

47. Ibid.

48. Ibid.

49. Maati Monjib, "All the King's Islamists," Carnegie Endowment for International Peace, September 12, 2012, https://carnegieendowment.org/sada/49433.

50. Marvine Howe, "Year-Old Hirak Protest Movement Galvanizes Northern Morocco's Neglected Rif Region," *Washington Report on Middle East Affairs—WRMEA*, October 2017, https://www.wrmea.org/017-october/year-old-hirak-protest-movement-galvanizes-northern-moroccos-neglected-rif-region.html.

51. Jane E. Goodman, *Berber Culture on the World Stage: From Village to Video* (Bloomington: Indiana University Press, 2005), 31; Bruce Maddy-Weitzman, *The Berber Identity Movement and the Challenge to North African States* (Austin: University of Texas Press, 2011), 196–97.

52. Sarah R. Fischer, "Amazigh Legitimacy through Language in Morocco," *Human Rights & Human Welfare*, 32–45, https://www.academia.edu/7660870/Amazigh_Legitimacy_through_Language_in_Morocco.

53. Morocco Constitution, Preamble, 2011, https://www.constituteproject.org/constitution/Morocco_2011.pdf.

54. Bruce Maddy-Weitzman, "A Turning Point? The Arab Spring and the Amazigh Movement," *Ethnic and Racial Studies* 38, no. 14 (2015): 2499–2515.

55. Ibid.

56. Agnese Boffano, "Libya's Stateless Ethnic Minorities and an Upcoming Election," *Al Jazeera*, June 28, 2021, https://www.aljazeera.com/news/2021/6/28/libyas-stateless-ethnic-minorities-and-an-upcoming-election

57. Darin E.W. Johnson, "Conflict Constitution-Making in Libya and Yemen," *University of Pennsylvania Journal of International Law* 39, no. 2 (2017): 293.

58. Libyan Constitution, 2011.

59. Libyan Constitution, 2016.

60. Candice Moore, "Four Years After the Fall of Gaddafi," ACCORD, April 11, 2015, https://www.accord.org.za/conflict-trends/four-years-fall-gaddafi/

61. Bruce Maddy-Weitzman, "A Turning Point? The Arab Spring and the Amazigh Movement," *Ethnic and Racial Studies* 38, no. 14 (2015): 2499–2515.

62. Tarek Megerisi, "Plot Twist: How Europe Should Deal with Libya's New Government—European Council on Foreign Relations," European Council on Foreign Relations, February 12, 2021, https://ecfr.eu/article/plot-twist-how-europe-should -deal-with-libyas-new-government/.

63. Ahlem Yazidi, "The Death of My Cousin and the Birth of a New Tunisia," in *Voices of the Arab Spring: Personal Stories from the Arab Revolutions*, ed. Asaad Alsaleh (New York: Columbia University Press, 2015), 29.

64. Ibid.

65. Ibid, 25.

66. Abdulmonem Allieby, "The Dark Night on the Tripoli Front," in *Voices of the Arab Spring: Personal Stories from the Arab Revolutions*, ed. Asaad Alsaleh (New York: Columbia University Press, 2015), 128.

67. Fereshteh Nouraie-Simone, *On Shifting Ground: Muslim Women in the Global Era* (New York: The Feminist Press at CUNY, 2014), 51–54.

68. Ibid.

69. Ibid.

70. Bouziane Zaid, "Internet and Democracy in Morocco: A Force for Change and an Instrument for Repression," *Global Media and Communication* 12, no. 1 (2016): 49–66.

71. Jackie Spinner, "How Morocco Has Weakened Its Press, Pushing Readers to Social Media for News," *Pulitzer Center*, January 2, 2018, https://pulitzercenter.org /stories/how-morocco-has-weakened-its-press-pushing-readers-social-media-news.

72. Noureddine Miladi, "Tunisia: A Media Led Revolution?," *Al Jazeera*, January 17, 2011, https://www.aljazeera.com/opinions/2011/1/17/tunisia-a-media-led -revolution.

73. Al Jazeera, "Al Jazeera Condemns Raid on Its Office by Tunisian Forces," *Al Jazeera*, July 26, 2021, https://www.aljazeera.com/news/2021/7/26/al-jazeera -condemns-bureau-raid-by-tunisian-security-forces.

74. Miladi, "Tunisia: A Media Led Revolution?"

75. Ali Abdullatif Ahmida, "Libya, Social Origins of Dictatorship, and the Challenge for Democracy," *The Journal of the Middle East and Africa* 3, no. 1 (2012): 70–81.

76. Noureddine Cherif, "Revolution from the Outside," in *Voices of the Arab Spring: Personal Stories from the Arab Revolutions*, ed. Asaad Alsaleh (New York: Columbia University Press, 2015), 34.

77. Ibid, 36.

78. Ibid.

79. Laura van Waas, "The Stateless Tebu of Libya?" (Tilburg Law School Research Paper, Social Science Research Network, 2013).

80. Ibid.

81. Rebecca Murray, "Southern Libya Destabilized," *Small Arms Survey*, April 2017.

82. Ibid.

83. Yazidi, "The Death of My Cousin," 25.

84. Arab Center for Research & Policy Studies, *Algeria 2019: From the Hirak Movement to Elections* (Arab Center for Research & Policy Studies, 2020), 1–42.

12

Tracking Political and Religious Mobilization Against Queer Men in Senegal

Grayson Michael Posey

It is regrettable that in 2022 we continue reading about the atrocities committed against gay and gender nonconforming individuals all over the world. From so-called "honor killings" in Iran to unidentified assailants on killing sprees in Guatemala, human rights violations against people who do not fit into the well-defined mold of heterosexual binary genders are on the rise.[1] While the topic of political and ideological mobilization against queer people could be written about any corner of the African continent—because there is unfortunately no shortage of incidents—some of the most recent and most concerning cases involve Senegal because of the intersection of previously established discriminatory laws and their stringent recent application by the state.

In June 2021, at least four men were assaulted and over 150 were threatened on the suspicion of homosexuality.[2] That, in and of itself, is a strange sentence to write, but in Senegal to be accused of homosexuality amounts to guilt. There are no appeals in the court of public opinion where Senegalese homosexuality is concerned. Senegal presents a unique case study in that collective affirmation elicits collective retaliation despite Senegalese people's historically tolerant attitudes towards homosexuality and gender nonconforming men. Article 319.3 of Senegal's Criminal Code first introduced in 1965 imposes a maximum of five years imprisonment and up to $3,000 for homosexual acts, stating:

Sans préjudice des peines plus graves prévues par les alinéas qui précédent ou par les articles 320 et 321 du présent Code, sera puni d'un emprisonnement

*d'un à cinq ans et d'une amende de 100.000 à 1.500.000 francs, quiconque
aura commis un acte impudique ou contre nature avec un individu de son sexe.*

[Without prejudice to the more serious penalties provided for by the preceding
paragraphs or by articles 320 and 321 of this Code, will be punished by imprisonment from one to five years and a fine of 100,000 to 1,500,000 francs, who-
ever has committed an indecent or unnatural act with an individual of his sex.]

It should also be noted that, while theoretically this law can apply to both
cisgendered (a person whose sense of identity and gender are consistent with
their biological sex) men and women equally, the purpose of this examination
deals primarily with the study of how queer and gender nonconforming men
have been affected by political and religious mobilization against them.[3] This
is not to imply the importance of one over the other, nor that queer or gender
nonconforming women are in any way less targeted by either Senegalese
Criminal Code 319.3 or the calls for harsher punishments for Senegalese
homosexuals. However, the issue that began this exploration into identity
and mobilization was one that specifically targeted Senegalese men, and as
such, this study will be in reference to them. However, each of the issues that
are discussed herein affect queer men and women equally and should in no
way be read as either exclusionary or dismissive of the plight of Senegalese
lesbians or gender nonconforming women.[4]

   While this work aims to emphasize the importance of studying gender
nonconformity and sexual fluidity within an otherwise binary society, it
requires that we accept the very existence of a dichotomous system which
can be both frustrating and limiting. In this sense we are continuing the
exploration of constructivist scholars such as Wanjala Nasong'o through a
rainbow-tinted lens.[5] While it is true that most studies on political African
identity do not include explorations of African queerness, it is nevertheless
an important field of international political investigation. In many ways,
queer identity mirrors constructivist interpretations of ethnic identity in that
queer groups are not naturally occurring phenomena, but rather, they are
products of human actions. This should not be read as an indication that
homosexuality as a characteristic is any more a personal choice than being
left-handed. Instead, it should be understood that queer communities are
established when self-identifying queer individuals seek others with whom
they share a common identity for a sense of community and belonging.
Benedict Anderson's exploration of imagined communities gives insight
into ethnic social constructions, and Nasong'o discusses complex theories
of cultural objectification—both of which provide valuable insight into the
formation and preservation of fringe communities, even against the threat of
political mobilization.[6] It is my hope that this study further establishes the

importance of understanding queer identities in the realm of international relations. As it stands, few scholars embark on this line of political thought, yet it is within these discussions that we discover the tangential existence of theoretical imagined communities with the volatile realities of mobilization against queer identities.

What is interesting to note within the Senegalese Criminal Code is the explicit mention of *acts committed*, not merely the *existence of*, and yet, these recent attacks are not the result of men being found *en flagrante delicto*, rather these resulted from guilt by association, guilt by appearance, and ultimately guilt by assumption. This poses significant security questions for Senegalese citizens whose identities do not conform to the societal (Islamic) heterosexual cisgendered norms, queer travelers and tourists from other more tolerant home countries, and for health and medical aid workers looking to stop the spread of HIV/AIDS in the region.

For the context of this examination of identity politics and mobilization, some definitions provide required specificity. LGBTQAI+ refers to the population of self-identifying lesbian, gay, bisexual, transgender, queer, asexual, and intersex individuals. The "+" refers to the other unmentioned, though still relevant sexual and gender minorities including but not limited to pansexual, gender nonconforming (GNC), and two-spirit identities. "Queer" is an umbrella term that encompasses all of these sexual and gender minorities; therefore, its use will be most frequent as we progress.[7] Sex refers to the biological classification of humans into two groups based on reproductive capability, whereas gender refers to the social and cultural construct of masculine and feminine. Traditionally, biological men are expected to present masculine whereas biological women are expected to present feminine. The term "gender nonconforming" will refer to persons not adhering to social or cultural expectations of a person's assigned biological sex. In the case of Senegal, this can include clothing, makeup, jewelry, and mannerisms.

How did we get here? How did the focus on this specific group become such a mobilizing target for a population that was largely indifferent to sexual and gender nonconformity? What role does social media and technology play in targeting sexual and gender minority groups? To be sure, homosexuality was never a protected status, nor was it looked upon favorably by either secular or religious leaders. And yet, Senegal was widely considered a haven for gay and gender nonconforming men in the African Francophonie, and Criminal Code 319.3 was sparsely and unevenly enforced until very recently.[8] What catalyst element(s) mobilized so many against an already vulnerable population? To better understand recent shifts in attitudes and behaviors towards gay and gender nonconforming men in Senegal, we must address historical precedents and the recent rise in Islamic extremism in the Sahel region.[9] This will give way to further understanding how political mobilization against queer people should be seen as a dire security issue for the African continent as a whole.

QUEERING UP THE PAST: SENEGALESE
QUEER CULTURE THEN AND NOW

It goes without saying that despite contemporary African leaders claiming homosexuality is a product of Western imperialism, homosexuality, though perhaps not so explicitly defined, was not alien to the people of Senegal prior to and during French colonialism.[10] A great deal of anthropological work has been done on alternative sexualities and gender roles in Africa, and certainly the 1998 groundbreaking work *Boy Wives and Female Husbands* by Murray and Roscoe is quickly becoming required reading in the field of African queer theory.[11] That said, the contexts by which we analyze historical trends on queer Africa do little to ameliorate the attitudes and behaviors of modern societies. It is not enough to know that same-sex activity existed and was tolerated in precolonial times. We must understand why and how, decades after independence, these attitudes and behaviors have shifted negatively even further. For without this knowledge our exploration of the security concerns for queer Senegalese would remain woefully incomplete.

While the particulars of linguistic equivalence are beyond the scope of this work, it should be noted that misinterpretation, and by extension, misrepresentation of Senegalese-Wolof, plays a large part in how queer culture has (d)evolved for much of Senegal. The word *goordjiggen* in Senegalese-Wolof loosely refers to a gender nonconforming man.[12] Wolof does not have an explicit word for "homosexual," "queer," or "transgendered," nor was *goordjiggen* synonymous with these terms prior to 2008, owing to the colonial and postcolonial African notions of modest ambiguity when it came to matters of sex and sexuality.[13] This is an important distinction as we explore political mobilization against Senegalese queer groups, because prior to 2008 *goordjiggen* were largely tolerated and even celebrated among many social circles. Senegalese writer Ken Bugul often depicted *goordjiggen* in her works, and even referred to these gender nonconforming men as "part of our daily lives."[14] The *goordjiggen*, according to Bugul, were often sought after and became socialites in their own rights in the 1950s and 60s. They were not only tolerated but welcomed by Senegalese social elites. Even religious leaders accepted, though they did not fully understand, the *goordjiggen*. Muslim clerics would often tolerate gender nonconformity if the offender made note that he was intent on renouncing it later in life to be in line with Islamic teachings.[15]

It was not until 2008 that *goordjiggen* took on a decidedly negative connotation after the unlicensed publication of gay wedding photos of two
Senegalese men taken in 2006. The wedding photos, first published in the
Senegalese local magazine *Icône*, led to the arrest of several men on the suspicion of homosexual activity which was quickly reported on by the BBC.[16]
Human Rights Watch reported in *Fear for Life* in 2010 that after *Icône*'s initial publication, other media outlets republished the images leading to "massive public outcry" and "sensationalist media coverage."[17]

The rapid dissemination of information through media made the collective condemnation of queer citizens, either self-identified or assumed,
swift and unrelenting. Pape Mbaye, the alleged organizer of the wedding
who self-identifies as gay, is currently a Senegalese refugee living in New
York—though his journey to safety in the United States involved a harrow-
ing trip through the Gambia and Ghana, where he says he was "hunted" for
his sexuality.[18] The publication of these photos led to a definitive correlation
of *goordjiggen* with "gay," and it ushered in heightened antagonism of gay
and gender nonconforming people.[19] While Coly does not specifically cite the
mistranslation by Mansour Dieng, the editor ultimately responsible for the
publication of the photos, *Le Nouvel Afrik* does: "In Senegal, 'goordjiguènes'
[homosexual, in Wolof] are kinds of matchmakers, they accompany singers
and put them in contact with politicians. To be homosexual in Senegal is to
rise socially, to be part of the world of the rich."[20] This equivocation was the
moment that served as a catalyst not only for gay men to become the target
of collective retaliation, but for those associated with the perceived promotion of homosexuality and queer identities in Senegal to be targeted as well.
According to Dieng, he published these photos to contest an earlier article
denying the existence of gay men in Senegal.[21]

Along with Dieng, five wedding guests that appeared in the photos were
arrested as well. While it may be correctly inferred that the grooms in the
photo were self-identifying gay men (or, at the very least, self-identifying
men-who-marry-men), the wedding guests in the photos give no indication
that they were anything other than supportive family or friends. Perhaps it
was the nature of the article itself that began the targeted mobilization against
gay and gender nonconforming men. This article showed that queer identities
were visible and undeniable even within conservative Senegalese borders,
and as a result, the grooms, the guests, the publisher, and the organizer were
all equally perceived as guilty by public denouncement. The psychoanalysis
of collective homophobic thought should be examined further to better understand the security risk of collective thought as a danger to queer people and
to those identified by others as queer.

Whether or not the misrepresentation of *goordjiggen* as strictly synonymous with "homosexual" was a product of Dieng's journalistic oversight of

Wolof linguistic particularities, or of willful comparison is not essential. The fact remains that this is the moment when the presumption of homosexuality, not only the act itself, was seen as worthy of public outcry. The widespread circulation of these photos called for citizens to alert the authorities to the rise of homosexuality among young people and to march against "the depravity of morals and the liberation of homosexuals" in a rally that was held in Dakar days after the photos were published.[22]

This misidentification, in and of itself, was a sort of societal appropriation of a word—a word that up to this point had not carried with it the negative or perverse connotations associated with "gay" or "homosexual" in either English or French. By unilaterally linking gay men with *goordjiggen*, Dieng, in many ways, created the 'Senegalese homosexual.'[23] Before, the word never existed, and so it was not questioned. But identifying the *others* of a society is far easier when there is a label attached.

Despite these rather glaring truths, Senegal maintains that it does not criminalize homosexuality as an identity—instead it criminalizes the actions of homosexuals. Foreign Affairs Minister Madické Niang said to the 2009 UN Human Rights committee that:

> [Senegalese] people are not prosecuted for their sexual orientation. Sexual orientation in Senegal is a private matter. For many years now we have seen homosexuality in our country and that has never led to situations where homosexuals are harassed, persecuted or prosecuted . . . No one was shocked when the president authorized a man to adopt the woman's name. But when homosexuality becomes blatantly public, it leads to embarrassing situations.[24]

President Macky Sall doubled down on this affirmation in 2013 when speaking with U.S. President Obama, saying that homosexuals were not persecuted unless they engaged in acts that violated the law.[25] This echoes the point above that Senegalese Criminal Code 319.3 does not criminalize *identities*, only *actions*.

Semantics aside, we know this is not the case. The same-sex wedding photos sparked a change in Senegalese discourse—both politically and socially—and an already vulnerable population was targeted by increasing calls for harsher punishment, ostracization, and death by Islamic vigilantes.[26] To be sure, the men mentioned at the beginning of this report were the victims of the devolution of language *and* the power of mobilization through media. While beating the men, the attackers yelled "*goordjiggen*."[27] And yet, the assailants were not charged with any crime. By President Sall's own admission gay men (or *goordjiggen*—the distinction is moot at this point) are not targeted unless they are caught engaging in homosexual acts. And so, we must ask—what alleged homosexual acts was this teacher engaging in, in broad daylight and in public on June 6, 2021? Why was the collective affirmation of this man's guilt readily accepted by the crowd in spite of government officials' assurance that homosexuals are not harassed?

As we progress, we will begin to see how political mobilization against anyone who can be identified externally as queer was not produced solely by increasing fundamentalist rhetoric (both Christian and Islamic), but also directly resulted from scapegoating by politicians motivated by public opinion and appeals to their collective outrage.

MOBILIZATION AND IDENTITY

Demonization of queer and gender nonconforming individuals throughout the African continent provides scholars with a host of material in which to analyze mobilization and public opinion against sexual and gender minorities.[28] While the specific reasons behind each country and culture's disapprobation for homosexuality may be different, the result is often the same: religious leaders and government officials calling for an 'extermination' (and this word is chosen specifically) of gay men.[29] In the case of Senegalese officials, the rallying cry against gay and gender nonconforming men has increased since 2008. Since the collective outcry against the wedding photos began, political officials began capitalizing on the public trend of vilifying their own citizens for political clout.

The concept of political homophobia first introduced by Weiss and Bosia "refers to purposeful [strategies], especially as practiced by state actors; as embedded in the scapegoating of an 'other' that drives processes of state building and retrenchment; as the product of transnational influence-peddling and alliances; and as integrated into questions of collective identity and the complicated legacies of colonialisms."[30] Bertolt and Masse expand on the exploration of political homophobia with respect to Senegalese politics, and rightfully conclude that political and religious authorities politicize and weaponize homophobia as a strategy to strengthen their positions of power by framing homosexuality as a "crisis," with dangerous effects.[31] What the exact "crisis" is, though, remains conveniently vague from the perspective of a politician looking for a scapegoat. The concepts of political homophobia and political mobilization against queer and gender nonconforming citizens are intrinsically linked in that both concepts build on one another. While the state is a product of socially constructed homophobic laws, it is the political leaders who utilize the state as a weapon against minority populations. For President Sall in 2013, refusal to grant protections to queer Senegalese citizens meant earning political clout by standing up to U.S. President Obama. "He's courageous to have spoken like that, in front of the greatest power on earth. Even if they turn off the spigots, we won't give in."[32] This dog whistle tactic signaled to religious and politically conservative groups within Senegal that President Sall was strong, fearless, and morally homologous with their values. In short, President Sall earned political points from constituents for his refusal to give in, while simultaneously risking almost no political backlash.

In 2015, denying legalization of same-sex relations was a means to ward off Western influence on a broader scale beyond simply saying "no." For President Sall, in this instance, maintaining the status quo against gay and gender nonconforming men meant reaffirming the cultural identity of the Senegalese.[33] And just as recently as 2020, Canadian Prime Minister Justin Trudeau's calls for human rights in Senegal were summarily dismissed by President Sall, saying "It's our way of living and being. It has nothing to do with homophobia."[34]

In all these instances, political support was gained by the castigation of queer Senegalese citizens. Notably, this denouncement-support-denouncement routine functions cyclically. The public denounces wedding photos in 2008 which thereby causes those in power to take positions that affirm the public's negative and discriminatory opinions. This then leads to greater support of the politicians by the populace, causing them to double down on their denouncement of queer people, thus further mobilizing the masses against this minority. What was once only discussed in hushed tones in a language that did not have a word for it, took suddenly and violently center stage in the political realm in Senegal by way of social media and traditional media sensationalism.

To emphasize this, we must understand that not only everyday people became targets of homophobic vitriol, but political opponents and open-minded supporters were affected as well. Djamil Bangoura, head of the Senegalese LGBTQAI+ support group *Association Prudence*, told Reuters that during elections, candidates will often refer to their opponents as gay, to emphasize their undesirability. Candidates will also attack queer rights to show religious voters that they are in line with their communities.[35] Beyond this, association with or support of queer Senegalese is used as continued elements of politicization for the purpose of mobilizing votes.[36]

Despite the Senegalese government's refusal to acknowledge that their actions led to increased attacks and harassment of queer citizens, these instances demonstrate that political mobilization against queer citizens directly influenced the attacks that took place in June 2021. And while it is true that the organizers of these rallies in Dakar have called for *harsher* punishments for homosexual actions and identities whether real or assumed, the government's failure to provide even basic protections for its citizens emboldened rallygoers and antigay communities.

The use of technology and dissemination of information through media is growing among religious and politically active citizens. These rallies are largely organized through Facebook. Annd Samm Jikko Yi, a civil society collective, organized the June 2021 rally in Dakar which called for harsher punishments and criminalization of homosexual identities.[37] The group's Facebook page, their main communication channel it seems, also calls for movements against women's rights, opposition to the COVID-19 vaccine, and regularly posts graphic depictions of mutilated bodies and Islamic prayers.[38]

Attendees of the rallies, including Ousmane Kouta, a representative of a student religious group, told Africa News that "[Senegal] is homophobic and will remain so forever."[39] The ardent support of antiqueer sensibilities and movements by Islamic groups, such as Annd Samm Jikko Yi, requires us to ask why Muslims, who were primarily perceived as tolerant in general, have become fundamentally immovable on the question of human rights protections for their fellow citizens. Amidst so many other pressing economic issues in the country, why is the mobilization against this one specific identity so successful in politicizing and mobilizing the communities?

To explore this question further, we must examine how the demonization of queer people in Senegal does not emanate from a single unilateral voice. There are multiple actors and motivations behind the security issues we see in this region and a major player is the impending threat of radical Islamic fundamentalists.

The influence of Islamic teachings in Senegal goes back centuries, of course, but it is only recently, relatively speaking, that religious fundamentalism has raised serious security concerns in the region. Senegal, a decidedly Muslim society with 95.9% of the population, adheres to the Sunni Islamic faith tradition.[40] While Senegal is known to tolerate religious differences, that tolerance does not extend to queer and gender nonconforming Senegalese citizens.[41]

In recent years in the Sahel, there have been rising incidents of violence carried out by al-Qaeda, ISIS, and Boko Haram.[42] According to President Sall, "excessive forms of Islam" are condemned within Senegalese borders, yet this has not stopped radical Islamic ideologies from creeping into Senegalese society.[43] The 2021 Counter Extremism Project reports no less than 23 "major" incidents of Islamic extremist and terrorist attacks within Senegal, and The International Centre for Counter-Terrorism report shows one in ten Senegalese citizens have a favorable opinion of al-Qaeda and ISIS.[44] In spite of what Senegalese leaders say to the public, it is clear that religious extremism is a growing concern for the security of the region.

While motivations and end goals for each of these Islamic extremist groups are beyond the scope of this study, what can be noted is that each of these groups stem from Salafism, a puritanical and literal interpretation of the Koran which calls for harsh punishments for offenses.[45] In each of these interpretations of Islam, homosexuality—again, either actions or identities—is an offense punishable by death. Human Rights Watch reports in *Fear for Life* that Islamic imams were calling for the execution of homosexual men after the release of the 2008 wedding photographs.[46] And while it is true that the rallies in Dakar in 2021 did not call for the public stoning of *goordjiggen*, they did call for an expanded interpretation of Criminal Code 319.3. This shows that the ideological influence of fundamentalist Islamic groups has begun seeping into Senegalese society since 2008, despite President Sall asserting that Senegal is a tolerant and accepting country. Religious mobilization against gay and gender nonconforming men in Senegal remains a threat to citizens further condoned by the government.

Islamic fundamentalist ideologies are not the only religious threats to gay and gender nonconforming men within Senegal, or throughout the African continent. Uganda's infamous "Kill the Gays" bill was ultimately influenced and supported by U.S. evangelical Christians.[47] Even the religious minority, it seems, is staunch in its opposition to the human rights of the queer population of Senegal.

The combined efforts of politicians and religious groups make for a strong and terrifying adversary for queer people of Senegal. The mobilization of both camps, political and religious, against a common enemy indicates a growing and unyielding security threat for gay and gender nonconforming men in the region.

Recent attacks were the result of a collective affirmation. The men attacked in June 2021 have so far not self-identified as homosexuals, nor was this an isolated incident. In 2009, two Senegalese teenagers were tried and convicted for suspected homosexual activity and not for actually engaging in homosexual sex.[48] And yet, these attacks and arrests are the result of collectively affirming the sexual orientation of several men based on either their association or their clothing rather than on actions.[49] It is unnerving to think that mere *appearance* can incite violence and arrests—not for the attackers, but of the victims. What does this mean for other areas of security? How does guilt-by-assumption affect other, more volatile areas of public concern? As we continue, we will see exactly how the growing insecurity for the rights of identity further impact Senegalese society at large.

FURTHER IMPLICATIONS FOR
HEALTH AND SURVIVAL

Despite Senegal's relative success at managing the HIV/AIDS epidemic, the assumption of guilt looms large overhead. Senegal is heralded as a leader in West Africa in the fight against the spread of HIV/AIDS, yet stigmas for people living with the disease remain high.[50] David Ansari and Allyn Gaestel encourage organizations to sensitize religious and government officials to the realities of HIV/AIDS prevention by promoting the use of condoms.[51]

This, however, is far easier said than done.

In 2015, seven men were convicted of homosexual activity after police discovered condoms and lubricant in a house where they were arrested.[52] This delivered a serious blow to health organizations hoping to further contain the spread of HIV/AIDS in Senegal. Once again, we see that the men were not caught in the act, as it were. Rather, it was the possession of socially taboo contraceptives that led a panel of judges to issue a six-month prison sentence in less than a minute.

Djamil Bangoura, President of *Association Prudence* who was quoted previously in this study, told Reuters that this trial meant gay men (or, rather, any man that might be perceived as gay) were "prevented" from carrying condoms.[53]

The implications were clear. If men were accused of illegal homosexual activity on the basis of owning or carrying condoms, it is safer legally, though not medically, not to have any at all. As the risk of infection becomes preferable to the risk of conviction, numbers of infections will likely rise over time. Officials might be attempting to quell the act of homosexuality, but they are endangering the health of the population at large. A man is not required to self-identify as homosexual to engage in homosexual activity—and men in heterosexual marriages can at times seek the sexual companionship of other men.[54] By equating the tools of safer sexual activities with homosexuality, Senegalese officials threaten the health and physical safety of all citizens—homosexual or otherwise.

UNAIDS reports that 27.6% of the 52,500 men who have sex with men are currently HIV positive. This rate is staggeringly high, considering that the report estimates only 39,000 people in Senegal—both heterosexual and homosexual—are currently living with HIV. Even among the 22,000 estimated sex workers in Senegal, only 4.8% are HIV positive. While UNAIDS does not provide data on demographics and rate of new infections of men who have sex with men, it does provide us with a "condom use" statistic. According to UNAIDS, in 2020, 75.8% of men who have sex with men used condoms to protect against viral transmission. By using the carrying and owning of this means of protection to convict of homosexuality, the Senegalese government risks exacerbating the HIV/AIDS infection rates within an already at-risk population.[55]

Though the act of owning contraceptives is not necessarily illegal, the guilt-by-assumption displayed in 2015 should serve as a chilling reminder that collective retaliation against gay and gender nonconforming men in Senegal has and will continue to be a security concern for public health as time goes on. Though international rights organizations have spoken out against cases such as these, we are left with the question of what can be done to better ensure security for men in Senegal who are gay or gender nonconforming.[56] What can foster dignity and respect for this incredibly vulnerable group in an oppressive society?

DANGERS OF POLITICIZATION AND MOBILIZATION FOR THE EXCLUSION OF MINORITY GROUPS

Societies are fragile ecosystems. As in nature, societies are made of many parts hanging in the balance, each carefully constructed over centuries of cultural evolution. To suggest rapid and sudden changes to a society, even if intended altruistically, is not advisable. Despite calls for a more tolerant and accepting Senegalese populace, expeditious decriminalization of homosexual activity might not bring lasting security to this minority of the region—not with the multipronged fight against queer acceptance from multiple camps.

Still, simply acknowledging that these problems exist does little to ameliorate current political and religious mobilization against queer and gender nonconforming citizens in Senegal. In this instance, silence is compliance.

The use of social media and technology to accelerate public opinion against minority groups has grown in the last decade. From the international dissemination of gay wedding photos in 2008 to the June 2021 rallies in Dakar calling for harsher punishments for homosexual identities *and* actions, scholars are provided with ample source material for future study. That said, the dangers of mobilization against queer identities in Senegal are not concepts that can be addressed in theoretical terms. For queer Senegalese citizens such as Pape Mbaye, Mansour Dieng, and Djamil Bangoura, political mobilization through media has increasingly become a source of fear and insecurity.

The following section provides strategies for further security against political and religious mobilization for queer people in Senegal. They are presented in order of most pressing, to long-term strategies. The most pressing security issues involve those who are most affected by the mobilization now: citizens incarcerated, in hospital, and without food, water, shelter, and medical security. Secondary, tertiary, and long-term strategies can be implemented incrementally—though the exact increments need not be determined at this stage. Consider Senegalese protections for queer people to be analogous to a marathon, not a sprint.

Queer identity may present a challenge in Senegal; however, rights of identity is a growing area of concern for other areas of the African continent. Consensual same-sex activity is only legal in 22 out of 54 countries.[57] Therefore, it may not be pertinent to examine too closely the methods and actions taken by other African governments where decriminalization is concerned. We cannot expect the legislative reform that came to Angola in February 2021, nor the High Court's decision in Botswana to have the same effect in Senegal.[58] Different countries require different approaches. On this point, President Sall and I are in agreement.

Senegalese organizations such as *Association Prudence* are giving voices to the voiceless within Senegal. These important organizations remain small, poorly funded, and have few allies.[59] The *Association Prudence*'s website, *Senegal Tomorrow*, is not even connected to a domain—and therefore is not published on the Internet. If they were to partner with larger, more easily recognizable names in the queer rights agencies of the world (Amnesty International, Human Rights Watch), further assistance might reach citizens who are ostracized and cannot obtain financial, medical, or legal support anywhere currently. By solving for the immediate problem of security for those most in danger (the incarcerated, the hospitalized, etc.), it would decrease the number living in constant fear.

Groundwork is important, and can alleviate some of the immediate negative impact brought on by political and religious mobilization against queer individuals, but without eventual governmental declarations of committed support, these organizations may be playing a losing game. Fighting for and ultimately securing human rights for these groups will require time.

The most pressing issue facing queer security in Senegal is the mobilization of Islamic extremism in the Sahel. It is important to directly implicate fundamentalist Islamic groups in this assessment of religious mobilization, because even though there are Christians denouncing homosexuality and requesting the removal of all protection for queer citizens, the potential political power of a group of this size makes Muslims a priority. That is, it is easier to radicalize a moderate Muslim to ISIS, al-Qaeda, or Boko Haram than it is to convert one of the few Christians in the country *and then* radicalize them. Therefore, the primary focus from a governmental level must be on slowing the spread of radical Islam. This serves two purposes: 1) the stalling of radical Islamic groups will slow the spread of radical ideologies, thus bringing some semblance of security to queer people in the region; and 2) it will provide political and personal security for all citizens regardless of sexual orientation. The exact methods of this strategy are beyond the scope of this study, though multinational militaristic options would seem to be the most effective. This is one area where diplomacy, sadly, has failed.

The second strategy for the protection of queer citizens' human rights against the politicization of identity and religious mobilization must be slow governmental protection. While this is secondary on our list of strategies, we must understand that these changes cannot be full sweeping and rapid to avoid the risk of a snap-back effect. Pulling too hard and too fast in one direction can have deleterious effects that cause more suffering than originally expected in the aftermath of newly imposed measures. It needs to be something palatable that can be relatively easily accepted by the broad population—something like employment protections, or hate crime legislation can be important places to start. Again, this is a two-pronged solution. While neither of these issues would sufficiently ensure full governmental protection, it would, 1) ease Senegalese society into an understanding that protections for queer citizens do not in any great way affect them or their livelihoods; and 2) offer better security for queer citizens in their own self-sufficiency without the need for international aid organizations suggested previously. By providing employment discrimination protection, queer people are better financially secure to deal with the realities of living in a homophobic society—thus slowing weaning them from the necessity of the financial support of the international organizations suggested for immediate action.

It should be noted here that for the Senegalese government to even consider a proposal such as this, there must be pressure from the outside. We know that Senegal is unwilling to listen to either the United States or Canada on matters of queer security, and they summarily rejected the UN Resolution on Human Rights, Sexual Orientation and Gender Identity, but we do not yet know how they would respond to pressure from within the African Union.[60] While I am not advocating for Angola to offer an Angolan solution to a Senegalese problem, the fact that the suggestion is coming from an equal—and not a world superpower—might be easier to consider. Theoretically speaking, when coming from a stronger, wealthier, more influential, and better equipped player on an international stage, a request does not feel like a request, but rather an implied order. This is perhaps why President Sall refused to acquiesce to President Obama or Prime Minister Trudeau's suggestion of queer protection. His stance was praised highly among his constituents. If the request were to come from Angola, Botswana, South Africa, or Cape Verde, perhaps the necessity to dig their heels in might be avoided.

It may be argued that it is better to remove Senegalese Criminal Code 319.3 before addressing employment or hate crime legislation; however, I disagree. If we accept that under Senegalese Criminal Code 319.3 identities are not the immediate subject of criminalization and that it is only queer actions that are subject to criminal offenses, removing 319.3 does little for the pressing security concerns of gay and gender nonconforming men that are simply walking down a street, as these men in June 2021 were. By making hate crime legislation a priority over decriminalization of queer actions, it better protects queer citizens from further political and religious mobilization in the immediate threat of violence against minority identities from fellow citizens. Protecting human rights of all Senegalese people can be framed in much less controversial terms than attacking the existing law directly. This should not be read as an exoneration of Senegalese Criminal Code 319.3; quite the opposite. Rather, it should be read as the best means to ensure future political and physical security for queer and gender nonconforming citizens from collective retaliation by citizens, and from state-sponsored apathy of human rights abuses.

Addressing this issue is difficult when we consider that Senegalese officials have little to gain, domestically speaking, by extending protections to queer Senegalese citizens. Yet, these protections, along with multinational militaristic operations against radical Islamic groups in the Sahel, could propel Senegal as a leading advocate in West Africa in the fight against human rights abuses. While Senegal has made little effort in gaining international support on this front in recent years, added pressure from other African leaders could tip the scales for the betterment of human rights in West Africa. The Human Rights Campaign hypothesizes that other countries in the Southern African region could be influenced by the recent decriminalization of same-sex activities in Botswana, just as Botswana was likely influenced by decriminalization in South Africa, Mozambique, and Angola.[61] Influence and pressure from within the African continent could potentially do more for human rights in Senegal than orders from the United States or Canada ever could.

The final long-term suggestion that I can offer is the education and acclimation of queer people by the youth of Senegal. Senegal is a very young country, with 60% of the population being under 25.[62] While high fertility and population growth is an increasingly important security concern on the African continent, it also provides an opportunity for a generation to be exposed to, and learn from, minority groups in different ways. Television, music, literature, even popular video games with queer characters, can be ways to connect with Senegalese youth that better explain the plight of all minority groups. In this way, social media—which has until this point been used primarily in Senegal as a means to target and abuse minority groups— can be used once again as a way to protect and uplift minority groups that are the target of negative political and religious mobilization. This is not an overnight fix for Senegal's problems. President Sall is right: these things take time.[63] Culture does not necessarily improve because of a governmental decree. This solution, combined with the other strategies provided, can help to alleviate the political suffering experienced by queer Senegalese citizens.

This will not solve every problem. But it would move Senegal forward in acknowledging the rights of all, including gay or gender nonconforming citizens and their quest for security.

NOTES

1. Jo Yurcaba, "Gay Iranian Man Dead in Alleged 'Honor Killing,' Rights Group Says." *NBC News*, May 11, 2021, https://www.nbcnews.com/feature/nbc-out/gay-iranian-man-dead-alleged-honor-killing-rights-group-says-n1266995; "Guatemala: 3 Killings of LGBT People in a Week," Human Rights Watch, June 22, 2021; and Enrique Anarte, "Hate Crimes against LGBT+ People in Germany Rise 36% in 2020," *Reuters*, May 4, 2021. See also Madeleine Roberts, "HRC Releases Report on Violence Against Trans, GNC People," Human Rights Campaign, November 19, 2020, https://www.hrc.org/press-releases/marking-the-deadliest-year-on-record-hrc-releases-report-on-violence-against-transgender-and-gender-non-conforming-people

2. Corentin Bainier, "Terror Sweeps Senegal's Gay Community After a Series of Assaults," *The Observers*, June 15, 2021, https://observers.france24.com/en/africa/20210615-senegal-gay-community-homophobia-assaults.

3. B. Aultman, "Cisgender," *TSQ: Transgender Studies Quarterly* 1, no. 1–2, 61–62.

4. For further readings on Senegalese lesbianism, please see Loes Oudenhuijsen, "Quietly Queer(ing): The Normative Value of Sutura and Its Potential for Young Women in Urban Senegal," *Africa* 91, no. 3 (April 26, 2021): 434–52.

5. Wanjala S. Nasong'o, "From Grievance to Ethnic Mobilization," in *The Roots of Ethnic Conflict in Africa*, ed. Wanjala S. Nasong'o (New York: Palgrave Macmillan, 2015), 1–9.

6. Benedict Anderson, *Imagined Communities: Reflections on the Origin and Spread of Nationalism* (London: Verso, 2016).

7. "Glossary of Terms," Human Rights Campaign, accessed July 28, 2021, https://www.hrc.org/resources/glossary-of-terms.

8. Ayo Coly, "The Invention of the Homosexual," in *Gender and Sexuality in Senegalese Societies: Critical Perspectives and Methods*, eds. Babacar Mbaye and Besi Brillian Muhonja (Lanham, MD: Lexington Books, 2019), 27–51.

9. The Sahel region is comprised of Senegal, the Gambia, Mauritania, Mali, Guinea, Burkina Faso, Nigeria, Niger, Chad, and Cameroon.

10. See Rose Troup Buchanan, "Robert Mugabe Tells UN General Assembly 'We Are Not Gays!,'" *The Independent*, September 29, 2015, https://www.independent.co.uk/news/people/robert-mugabe-tells-un-general-assembly-we-are-not-gays-a6671316.html; contested with Babacar M'Baye, "The Origins of Senegalese Homophobia: Discourses on Homosexuals and Transgender People in Colonial and Postcolonial Senegal," *African Studies Review* 56, no. 2 (2013): 109–28.

11. Stephen O. Murray and Will Roscoe, *Boy-Wives and Female Husbands. Studies in African Homosexualities* (New York: Palgrave Macmillan, 1998).

12. Coly, "Invention of the Homosexual," 33.

13. Ibid., 33–34.

14. Arona Basse, "Homosexualité et Médias," *Seneplus,* April 5, 2014, https://www.seneplus.com/article/homosexualit%C3%A9-et-m%C3%A9dias. For further reading on *goordjiggen*, see Babacar Mbaye, "Representations of the Gor Djiguene [Man Woman] in Senegalese Culture, Films, and Literature," in *Gender and Sexuality in Senegalese Societies: Critical Perspectives and Methods*, eds. Babacar Mbaye and Besi Brillian Muhonja (Lanham, MD: Lexington Books, 2019), 77–106.

15. Cheikh Ibrahima Niang et al., "'It's Raining Stones': Stigma, Violence and HIV Vulnerability among Men Who Have Sex with Men in Dakar, Senegal," *Culture, Health & Sexuality*, no. 6 (2003): 499–512.

16. "Senegalese Homosexuals Flee," *afrol News,* February 25, 2008, http://www.afrol.com/articles/28112; "Arrests for Senegal 'Gay Wedding,'" *BBC News*, February 4, 2008, http://news.bbc.co.uk/2/hi/africa/7226346.stm.

17. Dipika Nath, "Fear for Life," Human Rights Watch, November 30, 2010, https://www.hrw.org/report/2010/11/30/fear-life/violence-against-gay-men-and-men-perceived-gay-senegal.

18. Kirk Semple and Lydia Polgreen, "Persecuted in Africa, Finding Refuge in New York," *New York Times*, October 5, 2008, https://www.nytimes.com/2008/10/06/nyregion/06pape.html.

19. Coly, "Invention of the Homosexual," 34.

20. This is a direct quote from Stéphanie Plasse, "Sénégal: Les Homosexuels Traqués," *Afrik.com*, February 5, 2008, https://www.afrik.com/senegal-les-homosexuels-traques. The mistranslation in the brackets is provided by the original author and is included to show how the misrepresentation of *goordjiggen* entered into Senegalese discourse.

21. "Arrests for Senegal 'Gay Wedding,'" *BBC News*, February 4, 2008.

22. Jean Christophe Servant, "Homosexuels: Cibles Émouvantes, Boucs Émissaires," Le Monde Diplomatique, October 21, 2009, https://blog.mondediplo.net//2009-10-21-Homosexuels-cibles-emouvantes-boucs-emissaires; Habibou Bangré, "L'homophobie Se Radicalise Au Sénégal," *Afrik.com*, February 21, 2008, https://www.afrik.com/l-homophobie-se-radicalise-au-senegal.

23. Coly, "Invention of the Homosexual," 34–36.

24. United Nations Human Rights Council, "Human Rights Council—Universal Periodic Review," February 6, 2009, https://www.ohchr.org/EN/HRBodies/UPR/Pages/Highlights6February2009pm.aspx.

25. "Senegalese President Defends Anti-Gay Law," *CBS News*, June 28, 2013, https://www.cbsnews.com/news/senegalese-president-defends-anti-gay-law/.

26. Habibou Bangré, "L'homophobie Se Radicalise Au Sénégal," *Afrik.com*, February 21, 2008, https://www.afrik.com/l-homophobie-se-radicalise-au-senegal

27. Bainier, "Terror."

28. Boniface Dulani et al., "Good Neighbours? Africans Express High Levels of Tolerance for Many, but Not for All," Afrobarometer, March 1, 2016, https://afrobarometer.org/sites/default/files/publications/Dispatches/ab_r6_dispatchno74_tolerance_in_africa_eng1.pdf; Lucas Ramon Mendos et al., "State Sponsored Homophobia: Global Legislation Overview Update," IGLA World, December 2020,

https://ilga.org/downloads/ILGA_World_State_Sponsored_Homophobia_report
_global_legislation_overview_update_December_2020.pdf.

29. Ishaan Tharoor, "Gambia's President Threatens to Slit the Throats of Gay Men,"
Washington Post, May 2, 2019, https://www.washingtonpost.com/news/worldviews/
wp/2015/05/12/gambias-president-threatens-to-slit-the-throats-of-gay-men/.

30. Meredith L. Weiss and Michael J. Bosia, *Global Homophobia: States, Movements, and the Politics of Oppression.* (Urbana: University of Illinois Press, 2013).

31. Boris Bertolt and Lea E.J.S. Masse, "Mapping Political Homophobia in Senegal," *African Studies Quarterly* 18, no. 4 (October 2019): 21–39.

32. Adam Nossiter, "Senegal Cheers Its President for Standing Up to Obama on
Same-Sex Marriage," *New York Times*, June 28, 2013. https://www.nytimes.com
/2013/06/29/world/africa/senegal-cheers-its-president-for-standing-up-to-obama-on
-same-sex-marriage.html

33. Bertolt and Masse, "Mapping Political Homophobia," 25–26.

34. Babacar Dione, "Canadian PM Trudeau Raises Gay Rights with Senegal Leader," *ABC News.* February 12, 2020. https://abcnews.go.com/International/
wireStory/canadian-pm-trudeau-raises-gay-rights-senegal-leader-68941144.

35. Nellie Peyton, "'Fighting for Survival,' Senegal's Gay Community Is on
Its Own." *Reuters.* September 27, 2018. https://www.reuters.com/article/senegal
-lgbt-rights/feature-fighting-for-survival-senegals-gay-community-is-on-its-own
-idUSL8N1W454T.

36. Bertolt and Masse, "Mapping Political Homophobia," 32.

37. Senegalese Rally against LGBTQ Rights," *Africanews*, May 24, 2021. https://
www.africanews.com/2021/05/24/senegalese-rally-against-lgbtq-rights//.

38. Annd Samm Jiko Yi. *Facebook*. 2021. https://www.facebook.com/Annd-Samm
-Jikko-Yi-246734129175772/?ref=page_internal

39. "Senegalese Rally against LGBTQ Rights," *Africanews*, May 24, 2021. https://
www.africanews.com/2021/05/24/senegalese-rally-against-lgbtq-rights//.

40. "Senegal," *The World Factbook,* Washington, DC: Central Intelligence Agency,
continually updated, https://www.cia.gov/the-world-factbook/countries/senegal/.

41. Peyton, "Fighting for Survival."

42. Stephanie Höppner, "Terrorism Poses Growing Threat in Africa's Sahel, Germany Warns: DW: 27.12.2019." *DW.COM*, December 27, 2019. https://www.dw.com
/en/terrorism-poses-growing-threat-in-africas-sahel-germany-warns/a-5181326.

43. "Senegal's President Sall Condemns 'Excessive Form of Islam,'" *BBC News*,
November 10, 2015. https://www.bbc.com/news/world-africa-34774985.

44. Alex P. Schmid, "Public Opinion Survey Data to Measure Sympathy and Sup-
port for Islamic Terrorism," International Centre for Counter-Terrorism, The Hague,
February 2017, https://icct.nl/app/uploads/2017/02/ICCT-Schmid-Muslim-Opinion
-Polls-Jan2017-1.pdf.

45. John Campbell, "ISIS, Al Qaeda, and Boko Haram: Faces of Terrorism," Council on Foreign Relations, November 23, 2015, https://www.cfr.org/blog/isis-al-qaeda
-and-boko-haram-faces-terrorism.

46. Nath, "Fear for Life."

47. Tim Walker, "How Uganda Was Seduced by Anti-Gay Conservative Evangelicals," *The Independent,* March 14, 2014, https://www.independent.co.uk/news/world/africa/how-uganda-was-seduced-anti-gay-conservative-evangelicals-9193593.html.

48. "Senegalese Court to Try Teenagers for Homosexuality." Voice of America, November 2, 2009. https://www.voanews.com/archive/senegalese-court-try-teenagers-homosexuality.

49. Bainer, "Terror."

50. "Senegal," *UNAIDS,* Accessed July 15, 2021, https://www.unaids.org/en/keywords/senegal-0.

51. David A. Ansari and Allyn Gaestel, "Senegalese Religious Leaders' Perceptions of HIV/AIDS and Implications for Challenging Stigma and Discrimination," *Culture, Health & Sexuality* 12, no. 6 (2010): 633–48, https://doi.org/10.1080/13691051003736253.

52. Makini Brice, "Jailing of Gay Men in Senegal Poses Setback to HIV Fight in Africa," *Reuters,* August 26, 2015, https://www.reuters.com/article/us-africa-aids/jailing-of-gay-men-in-senegal-poses-setback-to-hiv-fight-in-africa-idUSKCN0QV1OZ20150826; Nath, "Fear for Life."

53. Brice, "Jailing."

54. Joseph Larmarange, Annabel Desgrées du LoÛ, Catherine Enel, and Abdoulaye Wade, "Homosexuality and Bisexuality in Senegal: A Multiform Reality," *Population (English edition)* 64, no. 4 (2009): 635–66, https://doi.org/10.3917/pope.904.0635.

55. "Country factsheets Senegal 2020," UNAIDS, accessed July 29, 2021, https://www.unaids.org/en/regionscountries/countries/senegal This UNAIDS statistics do not distinguish between genders of sex workers.

56. Brice, "Jailing."

57. Lucas Ramon Mendos et al., "State Sponsored Homophobia: Global Legislation Overview Update," IGLA World, December 2020.

58. Graeme Reid, "Angola Decriminalizes Same-Sex Conduct," Human Rights Watch, January 23, 2019, https://www.hrw.org/news/2019/01/23/angola-decriminalizes-same-sex-conduct;

Max Bearak, "Botswana Legalizes Gay Sex, Striking down Colonial-Era Laws," *Washington Post,* June 11, 2019, https://www.washingtonpost.com/world/africa/botswana-legalizes-homosexuality-striking-down-colonial-era-laws/2019/06/11/7b3f9376-8c0f-11e9-b08e-cfd89bd36d4e_story.html.

59. Peyton, "Fighting for Survival."

60. Nossiter, "Senegal Cheers Its President"; Dione, "Canadian PM Trudeau"; United Nations, General Assembly, *Human Rights, Sexual Orientation, and Gender Identity,* A/HRC/17/L.9/Rev.1 (June 15, 2021) available from https://documents-dds-ny.un.org/doc/UNDOC/LTD/G11/141/94/PDF/G1114194.pdf?OpenElement

61. Milagros Chirinos, "Botswana High Court Overturns Colonial-Era Law Criminalizing Same-Sex Relations," Human Rights Campaign, June 11, 2019, https://www.hrc.org/press-releases/breaking-botswana-high-court-overturns-colonial-era-law-criminalizing-same

62. "Senegal," *The World Factbook.*

63. Dione, "Canadian PM Trudeau."

Bibliography

"£2m. Ghana Treasury Bill Issue." *Financial Times*, February 6, 1960, 7.

Abdul, Mariam Marwa, Olayinka Adeleke, Olajumoke Adeyeye, Adenike Babalola, Emilia Eyo, Maryam Tauhida Ibrahim, Monica Voke, and Martha Onose. "Analysis of the History, Organisations and Challenges of Feminism in Nigeria." Nigerian Group, October 2011. http://www.nawey.net/wp-content/uploads/downloads/2012/05/Feminism-in-Nigeria.pdf.

Abdullahi, Suleiman, Victor E, and Binta M. "The Menace of Cattle Rustling and Banditry in North-West Nigeria: A Case Study of Katsina State." *Journal of Research & Method in Education* 7, no. 6 (2017): 40–47.

Abdullahi, U.S., H.N. Daneyel, and Y.H. Aliyara. "Grazing Reserves and Pastoralism in Nigeria: A Review." *Vom Journal of Veterinary Science* 10 (2015): 137–42.

ActionAid International. "Publications." Accessed August 9, 2021. https://actionaid.org/publications.

Adamu, Fatima L. "Women's Struggle and the Politics of Difference in Nigeria," 2006, 11.

———. "Women's Struggle and the Politics of Difference in Nigeria." *Gender...Pol itik...Online*, 2006.

Adedeji, Femi, and Tayo Omosilade. "'I Say No': The Rebuff of Anti-Democratic Forces in Orlando Owo's Music." *Nsukka Journal of Musical Arts Research* 1 (2012): 67–80.

Adeleke, Tunde. "Africa and Afrocentric Historicism: A Critique." *Advances in Historical Studies* 04, no. 15 (2015): 200–215. https://doi.org/10.4236/ahs.2015.43016.

Adelman, Cameron. "'Cause Freedom Ain't Free: Freedom Summer Movement in 1964 Mississippi." *StMU Research Scholars*, April 16, 2017. https://stmuscholars.org/cause-freedom-aint-free-freedom-summer-movement-in-1964-mississippi/.

Adeogun, Tolulope, and Abidemi Abiola Isola. "Evaluation of Women's Rights in the Perspective of Human Right Under Democratic Government in Nigeria. 1999-2009." *Babcock University Journal of Management and Social Sciences* 8, no. 1–2 (2011).

Adesokan, Khadijah S. "Women Empowerment as a Catalyst for Sustainable Development in Nigeria: Adult Education as a Tool." *Journal of Education and Practice* 9, no. 11 (2018): 136–42.

Adeyemi, O. Oluwatobi. "The Politics of States and Local Governments Creation in Nigeria: An Appraisal." *European Journal of Sustainable Development* 2, no. 3 (October 1, 2013): 155–74. https://doi.org/10.14207/ejsd.2013.v2n3p155.

Afigbo, A. E. *The Poverty of African Historiography*. Lagos: Afrografika, 1977.

Africa for Results Initiative. "Africa's Emigration Crisis: Implications for Capacity Building." Case Study. African Community of Practice on Management for Development Results at the African Capacity Building Foundation. Accessed September 2, 2021. https://elibrary.acbfpact.org/acbf/collect/acbf/index/assoc/HASHdaad/beb28206/c62a3ebe/09.dir/AfCoPCaseStudy084.pdf.

African Union. "African Union Gender Policy." African Union, February 10, 2009. https://www.usip.org/sites/default/files/Gender/African_Union_Gender_Policy_2009.pdf.

———. "Decisions, Declarations, and Resolution." Presented at the Assembly of the Union. Twenty-Fifth Ordinary Session, Johannesburg, South Africa, June 14, 2015. https://au.int/sites/default/files/documents/36086-doc-assembly_decisions_on_the_cfta_e.pdf.

AfricaNews. "Senegalese Rally against LGBTQ Rights." *Africanews*, May 24, 2021. https://www.africanews.com/2021/05/24/senegalese-rally-against-lgbtq-rights/.

Afrol News. "Senegalese Homosexuals Flee." *Afrol News*, February 25, 2008. http://www.afrol.com/articles/28112.

Agbiboa, Daniel Egiegba, and Andrew Emmanuel Okem. "Unholy Trinity: Assessing the Impact of Ethnicity and Religion on National Identity in Nigeria." *Peace Research* 43, no. 2 (2011): 98–125.

Agency Tunis Afrique Press. "Kais Saied Freezes All Parliamentary Activities, Lifts Immunity of All MPs and Dismisses PM." *Agency Tunis Afrique Press*, July 26, 2021. https://allafrica.com/stories/202107260461.html.

Agu, Dan C.C. "Traditional African Music: Contributions to Contemporary Music Creation and Performance Techniques." In *Humanities and All of Us*, edited by E. Oguegbu, 80–86. Ontisha: Watch Word Publications, 1990.

Agunbiade, Tayo. "Hajiya Gambo Sawaba: 'The Most Jailed Nigerian Female Politician.'" *Al Jazeera*, February 15, 2021. https://www.aljazeera.com/features/2021/2/15/hajiya-gambo-sawaba-the-most-jailed-nigerian-female-politician.

———. "Remembering Funmilayo Ransome-Kuti: Nigeria's 'Lioness of Lisabi.'" *Al Jazeera*, October 1, 2020. https://www.aljazeera.com/features/2020/10/1/the-lioness-of-lisabi-who-ended-unfair-taxes-for-nigerian-women.

———. "Remembering Margaret Ekpo and the Enugu Strike Massacre." *Al Jazeera*, December 12, 2020. https://www.aljazeera.com/features/2020/12/12/remembering-margaret-ekpo-and-enugu-strike-massacre.

Ahktar, Marium. "Role of Identity Crisis and Relative Deprivation as Catalysts of Political Violence and Terrorism: Case Study of Kurd Fighters in Turkey."

RAIS Journal for Social Sciences 2, no. 1 (2018): 49–66. https://doi.org/10.5281/zenodo.1196532.

Ahmida, Ali Abdullatif. "Libya, Social Origins of Dictatorship, and the Challenge for Democracy." *The Journal of the Middle East and Africa* 3, no. 1 (2012): 70–81. https://doi.org/10.1080/21520844.2012.666646.

Ajulu, Rok. "Thabo Mbeki's African Renaissance in a Globalising World Economy: The Struggle for the Soul of the Continent." *Review of African Political Economy* 28, no. 87 (2001): 27–42.

Akamanzi, Clare, Esteban Flores, and Richard Yarrow. "Rwanda's Push For Five-Star Development: An Interview with the CEO of the Rwandan Development Board on the Present and Future of Rwandan Economic Development." *Harvard International Review* 38, no. 4 (Fall 2017): 54–58.

Ake, C. "What Is the Problem of Ethnicity in Africa?" *Transformations* 22 (1993). https://www.semanticscholar.org/paper/WHAT-IS-THE-PROBLEM-OF-ETHNICITY-IN-AFRICA1-Ake/45f01f5c8414f97b6a2a0c339428d775a68fb94f.

Akerjiir, Anastasia Sandra. "Increasing Farmer-Herder Conflict in Nigeria: An Assessment of the Clashes Between The Fulani Herdsmen and Indigenous Farmers in Ukpabi-Nimbo Community Enugu State." M.Sc Diss, Wageningen University, 2018. https://edepot.wur.nl/460818.

Akinyemi, Bolaji. "The New Country We Need." *Vanguard News*, December 20, 2015. https://www.vanguardngr.com/2015/12/the-new-country-we-need-by-prof-bolaji-akinyemi/.

Akinyetun, Tope Shola. "Staff to Gun: Fulani Herdsmen in Nigeria." *Asian Journal of Multidisciplinary Studies* 4, no. 8 (July 15, 2016): 38–44.

Akov, Emmanuel. "The Resource-Conflict Debate Revisited: Untangling the Case of Farmer–Herdsman Clashes in the North Central Region of Nigeria." *African Security Review* 26, no. 3 (July 3, 2017): 288–307. https://doi.org/10.1080/10246029.2017.1294088.

Akyeampong, Emmanuel, and Hippolyte Fofack. "The Contribution of African Women to Economic Growth and Development: Historical Perspectives and Policy Implications—Part I: The Pre-Colonial and Colonial Periods." Working Paper. Rochester, NY: Social Science Research Network, April 20, 2016. https://papers.ssrn.com/abstract=2045947.

Al Jazeera. "Al Jazeera Condemns Raid on Its Office by Tunisian Forces." *Al Jazeera*. July 26, 2021. https://www.aljazeera.com/news/2021/7/26/al-jazeera-condemns-bureau-raid-by-tunisian-security-forces.

———. "In Pictures: Tunisians Rally to Denounce Saied's Power Grab." *Al Jazeera*, November 14, 2021. https://www.aljazeera.com/gallery/2021/11/14/tunisia-96.

Allen, Judith van. "'Sitting on a Man': Colonialism and the Lost Political Institutions of Igbo Women." *Canadian Journal of African Studies/Revue Canadienne Des Études Africaines* 6, no. 2 (1972): 165–81. https://doi.org/10.2307/484197.

Allieby, Abdulmonem. "The Dark Night on the Tripoli Front." In *Voices of the Arab Spring: Personal Stories from the Arab Revolutions*, edited by Asaad Alsaleh, 126–28. New York: Columbia University Press, 2015.

Alsaleh, Asaad. *Voices of the Arab Spring: Personal Stories from the Arab Revolutions*. New York: Columbia University Press, 2015.

AlSayyad, Nezar, and Muna Guvenc. "Virtual Uprisings: On the Interaction of New Social Media, Traditional Media Coverage and Urban Space during the 'Arab Spring.'" *Urban Studies* 52, no. 11 (August 1, 2015): 2018–34. https://doi.org/10.1177/0042098013505881.

Alubo, Ogoh. "Citizenship and Identity Politics." In *Conference Proceeding on Citizenship and Identity Politics in Nigeria*, 1–18. Monograph Series 5. Lagos, Nigeria: CLEEN Foundation, 2009.

Aluko, Olajide. *Ghana and Nigeria, 1957-70: A Study in Inter-African Discord*. London: Rex Collins, 1976.

Aly, Bamidele. "Monetary Creations in Nigeria: From the Nigerian Sterling to the Naira (1967-1974)," 2017.

———. "The Status of the West African Sterling in Southern Nigeria in 1916." In *There Came a Time: Essays on the Great War in Africa—Edited Collection*, edited by Anne Samson, Ana Paula Pires, and Dan Gilfoyle, 327–41. Rickmansworth: The Great War in Africa Association/TSL Publications, 2018.

Amarquaye Laryea, A.D., and Bernardin Senadza. "Trade and Exchange Rate Policies since Independence and Prospects for the Future." In *The Economy of Ghana Sixty Years after Independence*, edited by Ernest Aryeetey and Ravi Kanbur, 103–16. Oxford: Oxford University Press, 2017. https://doi.org/10.1093/acprof:oso/9780198753438.001.0001.

Amnesty International. "Harvest of Death: Three Years of Bloody Clashes between Farmers and Herders in Nigeria." Abuja: Amnesty International Ltd, December 17, 2018. https://www.amnesty.org/en/documents/afr44/9503/2018/en/.

Anarte, Enrique. "Hate Crimes against LGBT+ People in Germany Rise 36% in 2020." *Reuters*, May 4, 2021, sec. Big Story 10. https://www.reuters.com/article/us-germany-lgbt-crime-idUSKBN2CL1TN.

Anderson, Benedict. *Imagined Communities: Reflections on the Origin and Spread of Nationalism*. London: Versp, 1983.

———. *Imagined Communities: Reflections on the Origin and Spread of Nationalism*. Revised edition. London New York: Verso, 2016.

Anderson, Lisa. "Demystifying the Arab Spring: Parsing the Differences Between Tunisia, Egypt, and Libya." *Foreign Affairs* 90, no. 3 (2021): 2–7.

Anigwe, Annette. "Perceptions of Women in Political Leadership Positions in Nigeria." *Walden Dissertations and Doctoral Studies*, January 1, 2014. https://scholarworks.waldenu.edu/dissertations/28.

An-Na'im, Abdullahi Ahmed. *Islam and the Secular State: Negotiating the Future of Shari`a*. Cambridge, Mass.: Harvard University Press, 2010.

"Annd Samm Jikko Yi." Facebook. Accessed July 20, 2021. https://www.facebook.com/pages/category/Art/Annd-Samm-Jikko-Yi-246734129175772/.

Anonymous. "Student Emails with Feedback on the Impact of Participating in the MaCleKi Project." Meshack Owino and J. M. Souther eds., 2015–2021.

———. "Questionnaires for MaCleKi Project" Meshack Owino and J. M. Souther eds., 2015–2021.

Ansari, David A., and Gaestel Allyn. "Senegalese Religious Leaders' Perceptions of HIV/AIDS and Implications for Challenging Stigma and Discrimination." *Culture, Health & Sexuality* 12, no. 6 (August 1, 2010): 633–48. https://doi.org/10.1080/13691051003736253.

Apter, David E., and Carl Gustav Rosberg, eds. *Political Development and the New Realism in Sub-Saharan Africa*. Charlottesville: University Press of Virginia, 1994.

Arab Center for Research & Policy Studies. "Algeria 2019: From the Hirak Movement to Elections." Arab Center for Research & Policy Studies, 2020. https://www-jstor-org.blume.stmarytx.edu/stable/pdf/resrep24409.pdf?ab_segments=0%2Fbasic_search_gsv2%2Fcontrol&refreqid=fastly-default%3A7323222282fb0293c97c31c6913c3e5e.

Arndt, Jochen S. "Engineered 'Zuluness': Language, Education, and Ethnic Identity in South Africa, 1835–1990." *The Journal of the Middle East and Africa* 10, no. 3 (July 3, 2019): 211–35. https://doi.org/10.1080/21520844.2019.1652049.

Aryeetey, Ernest, and Ama Pokuaa Fenny. "Economic Growth in Ghana: Trands and Structure, 1960-2014." In *The Economy of Ghana Sixty Years after Independence*, edited by Ernest Aryeetey and Ravi Kanbur, 45–65. Oxford: Oxford University Press, 2017. https://doi.org/10.1093/acprof:oso/9780198753438.001.0001.

Aryeetey, Ernest, and Ravi Kanbur, eds. *The Economy of Ghana Sixty Years after Independence*. Oxford: Oxford University Press, 2017. https://doi.org/10.1093/acprof:oso/9780198753438.001.0001.

Ashraf, Nava, Natalie Bau, Nathan Nunn, and Alessandra Voena. "Bride Price and Female Education." *Journal of Political Economy* 128, no. 2 (January 9, 2020): 51.

Asiegbu, Martin F. "Contemporary African Philosophy: Emergent Issues and Challenges." *OGIRISI: A New Journal of African Studies* 12 (August 2, 2016): 1–24. https://doi.org/10.4314/og.v12i0.1.

Asike, Jude C. "The Interplay between Philosophy and Religion: The Perspectives of the Igbos, South-East, Nigeria." *Journal of Religion and Culture* 16, no. 2 (2016): 177–80.

———. "The Philosophical Concept of 'Ubuntu' as Dialogic Ethic and the Transformation of Political Community in Africa." *OGIRISI: A New Journal of African Studies* 12, no. 1 (2016): 1–16. https://doi.org/10.4314/og.v12is1.1.

Asike, Jude C, and Ogugua Patricia Anwuluorah. "Ubuntu Dialogic Ethics: Towards a Liberal Theory of Virtue for Development of Common Good." *Oracle of Wisdom Journal of Philosophy and Public Affairs* 2, no. 2 (2018): 1–7.

Associated Press. "Senegalese President Defends Anti-Gay Law." *CBS NEWS*, June 28, 2013. https://www.cbsnews.com/news/senegalese-president-defends-anti-gay-law/.

Atkinson, Ronald R. "The (Re)Construction of Ethnicity in Africa: Extending the Chronology, Conceptualization and Discourse." In *Ethnicity and Nationalism in Africa: Constructivist Reflections and Contemporary Politics*, edited by P. Yeros, 15–44. London: Palgrave Macmillan UK, 1999. https://doi.org/10.1007/978-1-349-27155-9.

Attah, Noah Echa. "Contesting Exclusion in a Multi-Ethnic State: Rethinking Ethnic Nationalism in Nigeria." *Social Identities* 19, no. 5 (September 1, 2013): 607–20. https://doi.org/10.1080/13504630.2013.835515.

Aultman, B. "Cisgender." *TSQ: Transgender Studies Quarterly* 1, no. 1–2 (January 1, 2014): 19–21. https://doi.org/10.1215/23289252-2399470.

Avenstrup, Roger. "Introduction to the Proceedings of the Sub-Regional Curriculum Conference: Shaping Africa's Future Through Innovative Curricula." In *Shaping Africa's Future Through Innovative Curricula*, edited by Roger Avenstrup, 1–6. Windhoek: Gamsberg Macmillan, 1997.

———, ed. *Shaping Africa's Future Through Innovative Curricula*. Windhoek: Gamsberg Macmillan, 1997.

Avruch, Kevin. "Truth and Reconciliation Commissions: Problems in Transitional Justice and the Reconstruction of Identity." *Transcultural Psychiatry* 47, no. 1 (January 2010): 33–49. https://doi.org/10.1177/1363461510362043.

Azam, Jean-Paul. "The Redistributive State and Conflicts in Africa." *Journal of Peace Research* 38, no. 4 (2001): 429–44.

Azide, J. "Culture and National Identity." In *Basic Foundations in Arts and Social Sciences*, edited by M.E. Onuora and C.O.N. Oguji, 491–98. Enugu: Frefabag, 2006.

Baaz, Maria Eriksson, and Maria Stern. "Why Do Soldiers Rape? Masculinity, Violence, and Sexuality in the Armed Forces in the Congo (DRC)." *International Studies Quarterly* 53, no. 2 (June 2009): 495–518. https://doi.org/10.1111/j.1468-2478.2009.00543.x.

Babalola, Dele. "Nigeria: Federalism Works." *IPI Global Observatory* (blog), August 25, 2014. https://theglobalobservatory.org/2014/08/nigeria-federalism-works/.

Badger, JS. "The Central Bank." *Financial Times*, October 30, 1962, IV.

Bagai, Huma. "The Role of Ethnicity in the Conflict Spectrum of South Asia." *Pakistan Horizon* 57, no. 4 (October 2004): 57–68.

Bailey, Robert W. *Gay Politics, Urban Politics: Identity and Economics in the Urban Setting*. Power, Conflict, and Democracy. New York: Columbia University Press, 1999.

Bainier, Corentin. "Terror Sweeps Senegal's Gay Community after a Series of Assaults." *The Observers–France 24*, June 15, 2021, sec. africa. https://observers.france24.com/en/africa/20210615-senegal-gay-community-homophobia-assaults.

Bakunin, Michail Aleksandrovič. *Marxism, Freedom and the State*. Translated by K. J Kenafick. London: Freedom Press, 1950.

Baldwin, Kate, and John D. Huber. "Economic versus Cultural Differences: Forms of Ethnic Diversity and Public Goods Provision." *American Political Science Review* 104, no. 4 (November 2010): 644–62. https://doi.org/10.1017/S0003055410000419.

Bangré, Habibou. "L'homophobie se radicalise au Sénégal." *Afrik.com*, February 21, 2008. https://www.afrik.com/l-homophobie-se-radicalise-au-senegal.

"Bank of British West Africa." *Financial Times*, May 22, 1957, 7.

"Bank of West Africa." *Financial Times*, May 21, 1958, 13.

"Bank of West Africa Limited." *Financial Times*, June 3, 1959, 7.

"Bank of West Africa Limited." *Financial Times*, May 25, 1960, 6.

Barber, James. "South Africa: The Search for Identity." *International Affairs* 70, no. 1 (January 1994): 67. https://doi.org/10.2307/2620716.

Baregu, Mewiga. "Congo in the Great Lakes Conflict." In *Security Dynamics in Africa's Great Lakes Region*, edited by Gilbert M. Khadiagala, First Edition., 59–79. Boulder, Colorado: Lynne Rienner Pub, 2006.

Barnhart, Jaclyn. "Umuganda: The Ultimate Nation-Building Project?" *Pursuit—The Journal of Undergraduate Research at the University of Tennessee* 2, no. 1 (2011).

Barth, Fredrik, ed. *Ethnic Groups and Boundaries: The Social Organization of Culture Difference*. Long Grove: Waveland Press, 1998.

Bartrop, Paul. "The Relationship between War and Genocide in the Twentieth Century: A Consideration." *Journal of Genocide Research* 4, no. 4 (December 2002): 519–32. https://doi.org/10.1080/146235022000000445.

Basse, Arona. "Homosexualité et Médias." *SenePlus*, April 5, 2014, sec. Société. https://www.seneplus.com/article/homosexualit%C3%A9-et-m%C3%A9dias.

Basu, Saroj Kumar. *Central Banking in the Emerging Countries: A Study of African Experiments*. New York: Asia Pub. House, 1967.

Bateye, O. O. *Defining African Traditional Musical Traits: Resource Material for African Art Music Composition*. Nigerian Music Review, 2007.

Bauer, Gretchen, Akosua Darkwah, and Donna Patterson. "Women and Post-Independence African Politics." In *Oxford Research Encyclopedia of African History*, by Gretchen Bauer, Akosua Darkwah, and Donna Patterson. Oxford University Press, 2017. https://doi.org/10.1093/acrefore/9780190277734.013.202.

BBC News. "Arrests for Senegal 'Gay Wedding.'" *BBC News*, February 4, 2008. http://news.bbc.co.uk/2/hi/africa/7226346.stm.

———. "Nigerian Senator 'Busts Open' $37,500 Expenses Payments." *BBC News*, March 12, 2018, sec. Africa. https://www.bbc.com/news/world-africa-43377690.

———. "Rwanda Unveils New Flag and Anthem." *BBC News*, December 31, 2001. http://news.bbc.co.uk/2/hi/africa/1735405.stm.

———. "Senegal's President Sall Condemns 'Excessive Form of Islam.'" *BBC News*, November 10, 2015, sec. Africa. https://www.bbc.com/news/world-africa-34774985.

———. "Tunisia Election: Kais Saied to Become President." *BBC News*, October 14, 2019, sec. Africa. https://www.bbc.com/news/world-africa-50032460.

———. "Tunisia Prime Minister Hamadi Jebali Resigns." *BBC News*, February 19, 2013, sec. Africa. https://www.bbc.com/news/world-africa-21508498.

Bearak, Max. "Botswana Legalizes Gay Sex, Striking down Colonial-Era Laws." *Washington Post*, June 11, 2019. https://www.washingtonpost.com/world/africa/botswana-legalizes-homosexuality-striking-down-colonial-era-laws/2019/06/11/7b3f9376-8c0f-11e9-b08e-cfd89bd36d4e_story.html.

Behalal, Zobel, Nelson Alusala, Ledio Cakaj, Virginie Monchy, Bart Vanthomme, and David Zounmenou. "Final Report of the Group of Experts on the Democratic Republic of the Congo." United Nations Security Council, June 4, 2018. https://www.undocs.org/pdf?symbol=en/S/2018/531.

Bell, Wendell, and Walter E. Freeman. *Ethnicity & Nation Building: Comparative, International, and Historical Perspectives*. Beverly Hills, Calif.: SAGE Publications, Inc, 1974.

Bell, Wendell, Walter E. Freeman, and René Lemarchand, eds. "Status Differences and Ethnic Conflict: Rwanda and Burundi." In *Ethnicity & Nation Building: Comparative, International, and Historical Perspectives*. Beverly Hills, Calif.: SAGE Publications, Inc, 1974.

Bennett, David. *Multicultural States: Rethinking Difference and Identity*. London; New York: Routledge, 1998.

Bennett, W. Lance. "The UnCivic Culture: Communication, Identity, and the Rise of Lifestyle Politics." *PS: Political Science and Politics* 31, no. 4 (1998): 741–61. https://doi.org/10.2307/420711.

Berman, Bruce, Dickson Eyoh, and Will Kymlicka, eds. *Ethnicity & Democracy in Africa*. Oxford: J. Currey; Athens : Ohio University Press, 2004.

Bernstein, Mary. "Identity Politics." *Annual Review of Sociology* 31 (2005): 47–74.

Bertelsmann, Stiftung. "BTI 2018 Country Report—Libya." Gütersloh: Bertelsmann Stiftung, 2018.

Bertolt, Boris. "Thinking Otherwise: Colonial/Modern Gender System in Africa." *Sociological Review* 22, no. 1 (September 9, 2018): 3–17.

Bertolt, Boris, and Lea E.J.S. Masse. "Mapping Political Homophobia in Senegal." *African Studies Quarterly* 18, no. 4 (2019): 21–39.

Bishu, Sebawit G., and Jean-Claude Garcia-Zamor. "Institutional Bureacratic Representation in Gender Mainstreaming." *Global Journal of Interdisciplinary Social Sciences* 3, no. 3 (2014): 229–37.

Bisina, Joel. "Reducing Small Arms, Increasing Safety and Security and Minimizing Conflicts in the Niger Delta Region." Benin City, Nigeria: African Strategic and Peace Research Group, 2003.

Blacking, John. *How Musical Is Man?* London: Faber & Faber, 1976.

Blumin, Stuart Mack. *The Emergence of the Middle Class: Social Experience in the American City, 1760–1900*. 1st edition. Cambridge, England; New York: Cambridge University Press, 1989.

Boafo-Arthur, K. "Neo-Liberalism, Human Security, and Pan-Africanist Ideals: Synergies and Contradictions." *African Journal of International Affairs* 5, no. 1–2 (July 29, 2010). https://doi.org/10.4314/ajia.v5i1-2.57193.

Boffano, Agnese. "Libya's Stateless Ethnic Minorities and an Upcoming Election." *Al Jazeera*, June 28, 2021. https://www.aljazeera.com/news/2021/6/28/libyas-stateless-ethnic-minorities-and-an-upcoming-election.

Bourdreaux, Karol, and Ahluwalia Puja. "Cautiously Optimistic: Economic Liberalization and Reconciliation in Rwanda's Coffee Sector." *Denver Journal of International Law and Policy* 37, no. 2 (2009): 147–99.

Breed, Ananda. "Performing the Nation: Theatre in Post-Genocide Rwanda." *The Drama Review* 52, no. 1 (March 2008): 32–50. https://doi.org/10.1162/dram.2008.52.1.32.

Breusers, Mark, Suzanne Nederlof, and Teunis van Rheenen. "Conflict or Symbiosis? Disentangling Farmer-Herdsman Relations: The Mossi and Fulbe of the Central Plateau, Burkina Faso." *The Journal of Modern African Studies* 36, no. 3 (1998): 357–80.

Brice, Makini. "Jailing of Gay Men in Senegal Poses Setback to HIV Fight in Africa." *Reuters*, August 26, 2015, sec. Healthcare & Pharma. https://www.reuters.com/article/us-africa-aids-idUSKCN0QV1OZ20150826.

Bright, Jake, and Aubrey Hruby. *The Next Africa: An Emerging Continent Becomes a Global Powerhouse*. New York: St. Martin's Press, 2015.

Brock-Utne, Birgit. "The Ubuntu Paradigm in Curriculum Work, Language of Instruction and Assessment." *International Review of Education* 62, no. 1 (February 2016): 29–44. https://doi.org/10.1007/s11159-016-9540-2.

Brock-Utne, Birgit, and Azaveli Lwaitama. "The Prospects for and Possible Implications of Teaching African Philosophy in Kiswahili in East Africa: A Tanzanian Perspective." In *Educational Challenges in Multilingual Societies. Loitasa Phase Two Research*, edited by Zubeida Desai, Martha Qorro, and Birgit Brock-Utne, 333–49. Cape Town: African Minds, 2010.

Brooks, Aaron. "Only Africa Can Put a Stop to Drain Brain." *East Africa Monitor* (blog), April 28, 2017. https://eastafricamonitor.com/only-africa-can-put-a-stop-to-drain-brain/.

Buchanan, Rouse Troup. "Robert Mugabe Tells UN General Assembly: 'We Are Not Gays!'" *The Independent*, September 29, 2015, sec. News. https://www.independent.co.uk/news/people/robert-mugabe-tells-un-general-assembly-we-are-not-gays-a6671316.html.

Bukari, Kaderi Noagah, Papa Sow, and Jürgen Scheffran. "Cooperation and Co-Existence Between Farmers and Herders in the Midst of Violent Farmer-Herder Conflicts in Ghana." *African Studies Review* 61, no. 2 (July 2018): 78–102. https://doi.org/10.1017/asr.2017.124.

Burgess, Thomas. "Introduction to Youth and Citizenship in East Africa." *Africa Today* 51, no. 3 (2005): vii–xxiv.

Buzan, Barry, Ole Wæver, and Jaap De Wilde. *Security: A New Framework for Analysis*. UK ed. Boulder, Colo.: Lynne Rienner Publishers, 1997.

Byman, Daniel L. "Terrorism in North Africa: Before and After Benghazi." *Brookings*, July 10, 2013. https://www.brookings.edu/testimonies/terrorism-in-north-africa-before-and-after-benghazi/.

Cain, P. J., and A. G. Hopkins. *British Imperialism: Crisis and Deconstruction, 1914-90*. London; New York: Longman, 1993.

———. *British Imperialism: Innovation and Expansion 1688-1914*. London; New York: Addison-Wesley Longman Ltd, 1993.

Calhoun, Craig. "The Problem of Identity in Collective Action." In *Macro-Micro Linkages in Sociology*, edited by Joan Huber, 51–75. Newbury Park, CA: SAGE Publications, 1991.

Camarena, Belia. "The Immortal Woman: Henrietta Lacks." *StMU Research Scholars*, April 16, 2018. https://stmuscholars.org/the-immortal-woman-henrietta-lacks/.

Campbell, John. "ISIS, Al Qaeda, and Boko Haram: Faces of Terrorism." *Council on Foreign Relations* (blog), November 23, 2015. https://www.cfr.org/blog/isis-al-qaeda-and-boko-haram-faces-terrorism.

Caselli, Francesco, and Wilbur John Coleman. "On the Theory of Ethnic Conflict." *Journal of the European Economic Association* 11 (January 2013): 161–92.

Castells, Manuel. *The Power of Identity*. 2nd ed., with s New Preface. *The Information Age: Economy, Society, and Culture*. Malden, MA: Wiley-Blackwell, 2010.

Castillejo, Claire. "Women's Political Participation and Influence in Sierra Leone." Working Paper. Fride, Spain: Fundación Para Las Reflaciones Internacionales y el Diálogo Exterior, June 2009.

"Central Bank for Ghana." *Financial Times*, February 20, 1957, 9.

"Central Bank for Ghana." *Economist*, February 23, 1957, 670.

"Central Banks for New Dominions." *Economist*, August 11, 1956, 507+.

Central Intelligence Agency. "CIA World Factbook: Nigeria." Official Government site. The World Factbook, February 4, 2022. https://www.cia.gov/the-world-factbook/countries/nigeria/#government.

———. "Senegal—The World Factbook." Washington, D.C., Continually updated. https://www.cia.gov/the-world-factbook/countries/senegal/.

Cerulo, Karen A. "Identity Construction: New Issues, New Directions." *Annual Review of Sociology* 23, no. 1 (August 1997): 385–409. https://doi.org/10.1146/annurev.soc.23.1.385.

Chabal, Patrick. *Africa: The Politics of Suffering and Smiling*. 1st edition. New York and London: New Zed, 2009.

Chabal, Patrick, and Jean-Pascal Daloz. *Africa Works: Disorder as Political Instrument*. African Issues. Oxford: James Currey, 1999.

Charbonnier, Nathanaël. "'Au Sénégal, les homosexuels sont considérés comme des animaux', témoigne un défenseur des droits LGBT." *Franceinfo*, May 23, 2021. https://www.francetvinfo.fr/monde/afrique/senegal/au-senegal-les-homosexuels-sont-consideres-comme-des-animaux-temoigne-un-defenseur-des-droits-lgbt_4634005.html.

Chazan, Naomi, Robert A. Mortimer, John Ravenhill, and Donald S. Rothchild. *Politics and Society in Contemporary Africa*. Boulder, Colorado: Lynne Rienner Publishers, 1992.

Cheikh, Ibrahima Niang, Placide Tapsoba, Ellen Weiss, Moustapha Diagne, Youssoupha Niang, Amadou Mody Moreau, Dominique Gomis, Abdoulaye Sidbé Wade, Karim Seck, and Chris Castle. "'It's Raining Stones': Stigma, Violence and HIV Vulnerability among Men Who Have Sex with Men in Dakar, Senegal." *Culture, Health & Sexuality* 5, no. 6 (2003): 499–512.

Cherif, Noureddine. "Revolution from the Outside." In *Voices of the Arab Spring: Personal Stories from the Arab Revolutions*, edited by Asaad Alsaleh, 34–37. New York: Columbia University Press, 2015.

Chiegboka, A.B.C., T.C. Utoh-Ezeajgh, and G.I. Udechukwu, eds. *The Humanities and Globalization in the Third Millennium*. Nimo: Rex Charles and Patrick, 2010.

Chirico, JoAnn. *Globalization: Prospects and Problems*. Thousand Oaks: SAGE Publications, 2014.

———. "Setting the Stage." In *Globalization: Prospects and Problems*, 60–84. Thousand Oaks: Sage Publications, 2014.

Chirinos, Milagros. "Botswana High Court Overturns Colonial-Era Law Criminalizing Same-Sex Relations." Human Rights

Campaign, June 11, 2019. https://www.hrc.org/press-releases/breaking-botswana-high-court-overturns-colonial-era-law-criminalizing-same.

Chukwuma, Kodili Henry. "Constructing the Herder–Farmer Conflict as (in)Security in Nigeria." *African Security* 13, no. 1 (January 2, 2020): 54–76. https://doi.org/10.1080/19392206.2020.1732703.

Clarke, Killian, and Korhan Kocak. "Launching Revolution: Social Media and the Egyptian Uprising's First Movers." *British Journal of Political Science* 50, no. 3 (July 2020): 1025–45. https://doi.org/10.1017/S0007123418000194.

Cohen, Ronald, and John Middleton, eds. *From Tribe to Nation in Africa: Studies in Incorporation Processes*. English Language edition. Scranton: Chandler Pub. Co, 1970.

Coly, Ayo. "The Invention of the Homosexual." In *Gender and Sexuality in Senegalese Societies: Critical Perspectives and Methods*, edited by Babacar Mbaye and Besi Brillian Muhonja, 27–51. Critical African Studies in Gender and Sexuality. Lanham, Maryland: Lexington Books, 2019.

"Commodity Market Reports and Prices." *Financial Times*, July 11, 1967, 2.

"Commonwealth Central Banks." *Financial Times*, August 29, 1957, 3.

Constitution of the Federal Republic of Nigeria, § 66, 131, 106, 131 and 177 (1999).

Corey, Allison, and Sandra F. Joireman. "Retributive Justice: The Gacaca Courts in Rwanda." *African Affairs* 103, no. 410 (January 2004): 73–89. https://doi.org/10.1093/afraf/adh007.

Corroon, Meghan, Ilene S. Speizer, Jean-Christophe Fotso, Akinsewa Akiode, Abdulmumin Saad, Lisa Calhoun, and Laili Irani. "The Role of Gender Empowerment on Reproductive Health Outcomes in Urban Nigeria." *Maternal and Child Health Journal* 18, no. 1 (January 2014): 307–15. https://doi.org/10.1007/s10995-013-1266-1.

Council on Foreign Relations. "Violence in the Democratic Republic of Congo." Global Conflict Tracker. Accessed March 3, 2019. https://cfr.org/global-conflict-tracker/conflict/violence-democratic-republic-congo.

Cramp, Andy, and Catherine Lamond. "Engagement and Kindness in Digitally Mediated Learning with Teachers." *Teaching in Higher Education* 21, no. 2 (January 2016): 1–12.

Cronin, Bruce. *Community Under Anarchy: Transnational Identity and the Evolution of Cooperation*. New York: Columbia University Press, 1999.

Cundy, Jaime Booth. "Music and the Millennium Development Goals." Canadian Artists for African Aid, 2019. https://www.psychologytoday.com/files/attachments/45883/music-and-the-millennium-development-goals.pdf.

Dahlerup, Drude, ed. *The New Women's Movement: Feminism and Political Power in Europe and the USA*. Sage Modern Politics Series, v. 12. London: Sage Publications, 1986.

Danfulani, Umar Habila Dadem. "Factors Contributing to the Survival of the Bori Cult in Northern Nigeria." *Numen* 46, no. 4 (1999): 412–47.

Davidheiser, Mark, and Aniuska Luna. "From Complementarity to Conflict: A Historical Analysis of Farmer- Fulbe Relations in West Africa." *African Journal* on *Conflict Resolution* 8, no. 1 (July 1, 2008): 77–104. https://doi.org/10.4314/ajcr.v8i1.39421.

Davies, Carole Boyce. "Gender/Class Intersections and African Women's Rights." *Meridians* 13, no. 1 (2015): 1–25. https://doi.org/10.2979/meridians.13.1.1.

Dawson, Kara, and Nancy Fichtman Dana. "When Curriculum-Based, Technology-Enhanced Field Experiences and Teacher Inquiry Coalesce: An Opportunity for Conceptual Change?" *British Journal of Educational Technology* 38, no. 4 (July 2007): 656–67.

British Museum. "De La Rue." Accessed December 8, 2021. https://www.britishmuseum.org/collection/term/BIOG147804.

Deleon, Richard, and Katherine Naff. "Identity Politics and Local Political Culture: The Politics of Gender, Race, Class, and Religion in Comparative Perspective." Philadelphia, 2003.

Derrida, J. *Margins of Philosophy*. Translated by A. Bass. Brighton: Harvester Press, 1982.

Desai, Zubeida, Martha Qorro, and Birgit Brock-Utne, eds. *Educational Challenges in Multilingual Societies. Loitasa Phase Two Research*. Cape Town: African Minds, 2010.

Desan, Christine. *Making Money: Coin, Currency, and the Coming of Capitalism*. Oxford: Oxford University Press, 2014.

Devy, G. N., Geoffrey V. Davis, and K.K. Chakravarty, eds. *Performing Identities: Celebrating Indigeneity in the Arts*. New Delhi: Routledge, Taylor and Francis Group, 2015.

Dickson, E. Ekpe, Eja Eni, and John Egbe Inyang. "Women, Gender Equality in Nigeria: A Critical Analysis of Socio-Economic and Political (Gender Issues)." *Journal Research in Peace, Gender and Development (JRPGD)* 4, no. 1 (2014): 11–20.

Dione, Babacar. "Canadian PM Trudeau Raises Gay Rights with Senegal Leader." *ABC News*, February 12, 2020. https://abcnews.go.com/International/wireStory/canadian-pm-trudeau-raises-gay-rights-senegal-leader-68941144.

Dlamini, Simangele, Solomon G. Tesfamichael, and Tholang Mokhele. "A Review of Place Identity Studies in Post-Apartheid South Africa." *South African Journal of Psychology* 51, no. 1 (March 2021): 121–33. https://doi.org/10.1177/0081246320954040.

Doornbos, Martin, and Wim van Binsbergen. *Researching Power and Identity in African State Formation: Comparative Perspectives*. Pretoria: Unisa Press, 2017.

Doughty, Kristin. "Law and the Architecture of Social Repair: Gacaca Days in Post-Genocide Rwanda: Law and the Architecture of Social Repair." *Journal of the Royal Anthropological Institute* 21, no. 2 (June 2015): 419–37. https://doi.org/10.1111/1467-9655.12213.

Drobac, Peter, and Brienna Naughton. "Health Equity in Rwanda: The New Rwanda, Twenty Years Later." *Harvard International Review* 35, no. 4 (Spring 2014): 57–61.

Dukor, Maduabuchi. *African Freedom: The Freedom of Philosophy*. Saarbrücken: LAP LAMBERT Academic Publishing, 2010.

————. *African Philosophy in the Global Village Theistic Panpsychic Rationality, Axiology and Science.* Saarbrücken: LAP LAMBERT Academic Publishing, 2010. https://nbn-resolving.org/urn:nbn:de:101:1-2015011414602.

Dulani, Boniface, Gift Sambo, and Kim Yi Donne. "Good Neighbours? Africans Express High Levels of Tolerance for Many, but Not for All | Afrobarometer." Afrobarometer, March 1, 2016. https://afrobarometer.org/publications/tolerance-in-africa.

Dzurgba, Akpenpuun. *Principles of Ethics.* Ibadan: Agape Publications, 2000.

Edwards, John. "Record Turnover as Cocoa Slumps." *Financial Times,* July 11, 1967, 2.

Egbuta, Ugwumba. "Understanding the Herder-Farmer Conflict in Nigeria." *Conflict Trends* 3 (2018): 40–48.

Eichstaedt, Peter. *Consuming the Congo: War and Conflict Minerals in the World's Deadliest Place.* Reprint edition. Chicago, Ill: Lawrence Hill Books, 2016.

Eifert, Benn, Edward Miguel, and Daniel N. Posner. "Political Competition and Ethnic Identification in Africa." *American Journal of Political Science* 54, no. 2 (2010): 494–510.

Ekeh, Peter P. "Colonialism and the Two Publics in Africa: A Theoretical Statement." *Comparative Studies in Society and History* 17, no. 1 (1975): 91–112.

Ekundare, R. Olufemi. *An Economic History of Nigeria, 1860-1960.* London: Methuen & Co. Ltd, 1973.

Ekweariri, C.S., and N. Mbara. "Ethnic Sentimentality and the Search for Social Stability in Nigeria. A Reading of Kinsley Agubom's 'The Bitter Truth.'" In *The Humanities and National Identity,* edited by P.A. Uchechukwu, E.U. Ibekwe, N.M. Obi, and C. Okoye, 62–66. Awka: Fab Anieh, 2013.

El-Anis, Imad, and Ashraf Hamed. "From Spring to Summer? Revolutionary Change in Tunisia, Egypt and Libya—CIAO." *Bilgi* 27, no. 2 (2013): 75–102.

Encyclopedia Britannica. "Libya—People." In *Encyclopedia Britannica.* Accessed December 1, 2021. https://www.britannica.com/place/Libya/People.

Enloe, Cynthia H. *Ethnic Conflict and Political Development.* Lanham [Md.: University Press of America, 1986.

Eramian, Laura. "Personhood, Violence, and the Moral Work of Memory in Contemporary Rwanda." *International Journal of Conflict and Violence* 8 (September 1, 2014): 16–29.

Ernest, John. *Liberation Historiography: African American Writers and the Challenge of History, 1794-1861.* Chapel Hill: University of North Carolina Press, 2004.

Esimone, C. C., and E.C. Umezinwa. "Music: An Instrument of Identity and Social Security." In *The Humanities and National Identity,* edited by P.A. Uchechukwu, E.U. Ibekwe, N.M. Obi, and C. Okoye, 34–37. Awka: Fab Anieh, 2013.

Esquivel, Maria. "He Would Have Killed Me: The Story of Jennifer Teege, Granddaughter of Nazi Commandant Amon Goeth." *StMU Research Scholars,* April 21, 2018. https://stmuscholars.org/he-would-have-killed-me-the-story-of-jennifer-teege-granddaughter-of-nazi-commandant-amon-goeth/.

"Etymology Meaning of Virtue." Google Search. Accessed November 11, 2016. https://www.google.com/search?q=etymology%20meaning%20of%20virtue.

Eyben, Rosalind. "Subversively Accommodating: Feminist Bureaucrats and Gender Mainstreaming." *IDS Bulletin* 41, no. 2 (2010): 54–61. https://doi.org/10.1111/j.1759-5436.2010.00123.x.

Eyo, Ekpo. *Nigeria and the Evolution of Money.* Lagos: Central Bank of Nigeria in association with the Department of Antiquities, 1979.

Fabusoro, E., and C.I. Sodiya. "Institutions for Collective Action among Settled Fulani Agro-Pastoralists in Southwest Nigeria." *The Journal of Agricultural Education and Extension* 17, no. 1 (February 1, 2011): 53–68. https://doi.org/10.1080/1389224X.2011.536349.

Fagothey, Austin. *Right and Reason: Ethics in Theory and Practice.* St. Louis: Mosby, 1981.

Falk, Richard A. *Predatory Globalization: A Critique.* Reprint. Cambridge, UK: Polity Press, 1999.

Falola, Toyin. "Ethnic Nationalism." In *The Power of African Cultures*, 128–65. Rochester, NY: University of Rochester Press, 2003. https://www-jstor-org.blume.stmarytx.edu/stable/pdf/10.7722/j.ctt1bh2m2w.9.pdf?ab_segments=0%2Fbasic_search_gsv2%2Fcontrol&refreqid=fastly-default%3A3fe4f6b1e16e7f1e0e17e737c4ff1327.

———. *The Power of African Cultures.* Rochester, NY: University of Rochester Press, 2003.

Falola, Toyin. *The Toyin Falola Reader on African Culture, Nationalism, Development and Epistemologies.* Austin: Pan-African Univeristy Press, 2018.

Falola, Toyin, and Augustine Agwuele. *Africans and the Politics of Popular Culture, Augustine.* Rochester Studies in African History and the Diaspora, Variation: Rochester Studies in African History and the Diaspora. Rochester, NY: University of Rochester Press, 2009.

Falola, Toyin, and Nana Akua Amponsah. *Women, Gender, and Sexualities in Africa.* Durham, N.C: Carolina Academic Press, 2013.

Falola, Toyin, and Ann Genova *Orisa: Yoruba Gods and Spiritual Identity in Africa and the Diaspora.* Trenton, N.J.; London: Africa World; Turnaround [distributor], 2006.

Falola, Toyin, and Matthew M. Heaton. *A History of Nigeria.* Cambridge, UK; New York: Cambridge University Press, 2008.

———. *A History of Nigeria.* Illustrated edition. Cambridge, UK; New York: Cambridge University Press, 2008.

Falola, Toyin, and Martin S. Shanguhyia. *The Palgrave Handbook of African Colonial and Postcolonial History.* New York, NY: Palgrave Macmillan, 2018.

Falola, Toyin, and Aribidesi Usman, eds. *Movements, Borders, and Identities in Africa.* Rochester, NY: University of Rochester Press, 2009.

Farrar, Tarikhu. "The Queenmother, Matriarchy, and the Question of Female Political Authority in Precolonial West African Monarchy." *Journal of Black Studies* 27, no. 5 (May 1997): 579–97. https://doi.org/10.1177/002193479702700501.

Fearon, James D., and David D. Laitin. "Explaining Interethnic Cooperation." *The American Political Science Review* 90, no. 4 (1996): 715–35. https://doi.org/10.2307/2945838.

Feavearyear, Albert E. *The Pound Sterling: A History of English Money.* London: Oxford University Press, 1931.

"February 12, 1957: Nkrumah and Busia Agree on a Draft Constitution for Independence." Edward A. Ulzen Memorial Foundation. Accessed January 19, 2022. https://www.eaumf.org/ejm-blog/2018/2/12/february-12-1957-nkrumah-and-busia-agree-on-a-draft-constitution-for-independence.

"Federal Ministry of Women Affairs and Social Development." In *Wikipedia*, September 17, 2021. https://en.wikipedia.org/w/index.php?title=Federal_Ministry_of_Women_Affairs_and_Social_Development&oldid=1044879918.

Federal Republic of Nigeria. Constitution of the Federal Republic of Nigeria (n.d.). https://wipolex.wipo.int/en/text/179202.

———. "Federal Ministry of Women Affairs." Official Government site. Nigerian Information Portal, February 12, 2022. https://nigeria.gov.ng/executive/federal-ministry-of-women-affairs/.

———. "Federal Ministry of Women Affairs: Who We Are." Official Government site. Federal Ministry of Women Affairs, 2016. https://www.womenaffairs.gov.ng/index.php/about-us/about-us.

———. "National Assembly." Members of the House of Representatives. https://nass.gov.ng/mps/members. Accessed on October 27, 2021.

———. "National Assembly." Federal Republic of Nigeria, Senators. https://nass.gov.ng/mps/senators. Accessed on October 27, 2021.

Figueroa, Amanda. "Forty Years of 'Bad Blood': The Tuskegee Syphilis Study." *StMU Research Scholars*, September 19, 2017. https://stmuscholars.org/bad-blood-the-tuskegee-syphilis-study/.

———. "The Rage of Nina Simone: 'Mississippi Goddam.'" *StMU Research Scholars*, October 18, 2017. https://stmuscholars.org/the-rage-of-nina-simone/.

Fischer, Sarah R. "Amazigh Legitimacy through Language in Morocco." *Human Rights & Human Welfare*, n.d., 32–45.

Fonkoué, Ramon A. *Nation without Narration: History, Memory and Identity in Postcolonial Cameroon.* Cambria African Studies Series; Variation: Cambria African Studies Series. Amherst, New York: Cambria Press, 2019.

Foucault, Michel. "Nietzsche, Genealogy, History." In *The Foucault Reader*, edited by P. Rabinow. New York: Pantheon, 1984.

Fowler, Ian. "Voicing Identity." In *Encounter, Transformation and Identity: Peoples of the Western Cameroon Borderlands, 1891-2000/Fanso, Verkijika G.*, edited by Ian Fowler and Verkijika G. Fanso, 2–15. New York: Berghahn Books, 2009.

Fowler, Ian Njeuma, and Verkijika G. Fanso, eds. *Encounter, Transformation and Identity: Peoples of the Western Cameroon Borderlands, 1891-2000/Fanso, Verkijika G.* Cameroon Studies; v. 8; Variation: Cameroon Studies ;; v. 8. New York: Berghahn Books, 2009.

France 24. "Uganda's Brutal Lord's Resistance Army, Past and Present." *France 24*, June 5, 2021. https://www.france24.com/en/live-news/20210506-uganda-s-brutal-lord-s-resistance-army-past-and-present.

Franceschet, S., and Jennifer M. Piscopo. "Gender Quotas and Women's Substantive Representation: Lessons from Argentina." *Politics & Gender* 4 (2008): 393–425. https://doi.org/10.1017/S1743923X08000342.

Francis, David J. "Peace and Conflict Studies: An African Overview of Basic Concepts." In *Introduction to Peace and Conflict Studies in West Africa: A Reader*, edited by Shedrack Gaya Best. Ibadan, Nigeria: Spectrum Books, 2006.

Franck, Raphaël, and Ilia Rainer. "Does the Leader's Ethnicity Matter? Ethnic Favoritism, Education, and Health in Sub-Saharan Africa." *American Political Science Review* 106, no. 2 (May 2012): 294–325. https://doi.org/10.1017/S0003055412000172.

Fukuyama, Francis. "Identity, Immigration, and Liberal Democracy." *Journal of Democracy* 17, no. 2 (2006): 5–20. https://doi.org/10.1353/jod.2006.0028.

———. *The End of History and the Last Man*. 1st Free Press trade pbk. ed. New York: Free Press, 1992.

Fullinwider, Robert K., ed. *Civil Society, Democracy, and Civic Renewal*. Lanham, MD: Rowman & Littlefield Publishers, 1999.

Gaddafi, Muammar al-. *The Green Book*. CreateSpace Independent Publishing Platform, 2016.

Gartenstein-Ross, Daveed, and Nathaniel Barr. "Dignity and Dawn: Libya's Escalating Civil War." *Terrorism and Counter-Terrorism Studies*, 2015, 1–58. https://doi.org/10.19165/2015.1.01.

Gauba, O.P. *An Introduction to Political Theory*. Fourth Edition. New Delhi: Macmillan India Limited, 2003.

Gavin, Michelle. "The Conflict in Ethiopia's Tigray Region: What to Know." Council on Foreign Relations, February 10, 2021. https://www.jstor.org.blume.stmarytx.edu:2048/stable/resrep31163.

Gaya Best, Shedrack, ed. *Introduction to Peace and Conflict Studies in West Africa: A Reader*. Ibadan, Nigeria: Spectrum Books, 2006.

Geertz, Clifford, ed. *Old Societies and New States*. New York: Free Press, 1963.

———, ed. *Old Societies and New States: The Quest for Modernity in Asia and Africa*. Committee for the Comparative Study of New Nations. New York: Free Press, 1967.

———. "The Integrative Revolution: Primordial Sentiments and Civil Politics in the New States." In *Old Societies and New States*, edited by Clifford Geertz, 105–57. New York: Free Press, 1963.

Gerhart, Gail M., and Lucy Edwards Despard. "The Cohesion of Oppression: Clientship and Ethnicity in Rwanda, 1860-1960." *Foreign Affairs* 70, no. 2 (Spring 1991): 202–202. https://doi.org/10.2307/20044810.

"Ghana Bank Note Circulation." *Financial Times*, July 23, 1958, 5.

"Ghana Bank Report." *Financial Times*, August 28, 1958, 5.

"Ghana Cocoa Financing." *Financial Times*, October 16, 1961, [1].

Ghana Independence Act (1957). https://www.cvce.eu/content/publication/2015/10/14/631f7166-5664-41f3-a5d1-7cc9d2387f58/publishable_en.pdf.

"The Ghana Independence Bill." House of Commons, November 28, 1956. British Library Social Science Room.

"Ghana Independence Bill. Order for Second Reading." Official Report of Fifth Series Parliamentary Debates—Commons 1956-1957, December 10—December 21. British Library Social Science Room.

"Ghana Issues 5% Stock." *Financial Times*, May 30, 1961, 11.

"Ghana Remains Undecided." *Financial Times*, November 21, 1967, 29.

Gibson, James L. "Overcoming Apartheid: Can Truth Reconcile a Divided Nation?" *Politikon: South African Journal of Political Studies* 31, no. 2 (November 2004): 129–55. https://doi.org/10.1080/0258934042000280698.

Giddens, Anthony. *Modernity and Self-Identity: Self and Society in the Late Modern Age*. 1st edition. Stanford, Calif.: Stanford University Press, 1991.

Gill, Stephen. "Globalisation, Market Civilisation, and Disciplinary Neoliberalism." *Millennium: Journal of International Studies* 24, no. 3 (December 1, 1995): 399–423. https://doi.org/10.1177/03058298950240030801.

Glantz, Michael H., ed. *Drought and Hunger in Africa: Denying Famine a Future*. Cambridge: Cambridge University Press, 1987.

Glazer, Nathan, Daniel Patrick Moynihan, and Corinne Saposs Schelling, eds. *Ethnicity: Theory and Experience*. Harvard University Press, 1975.

"Gold Coast Currency." *Financial Times*, September 20, 1955, 9.

Goodman, Jane E. *Berber Culture on the World Stage: From Village to Video*. Bloomington: Indiana University Press, 2005.

Gordon, David. "Identity, Religion, and Politics in South Africa's Remote and Recent Past." *The Journal of African History* 53, no. 1 (2012): 118–20. https://doi.org/10.1017/S0021853712000114.

Gouws, Amanda. "Unpacking the Difference between Feminist and Women's Movements in Africa." The Conversation, August 9, 2015. http://theconversation.com/unpacking-the-difference-between-feminist-and-womens-movements-in-africa-45258.

Graff, Peter van der, Lynne F. Forrest, Jean Adams, Janet Shucksmith, and Martin White. "How Do Public Health Professionals View and Engage with Research? A Qualitative Interview Study and Stakeholder Workshop Engaging Public Health Professionals and Researchers." *BMC Public Health* 17 (November 22, 2017): 1–10.

Green, Elliott. "The Politics of Ethnic Identity in Sub-Saharan Africa." *Comparative Political Studies* 54, no. 7 (June 2021): 1197–1226. https://doi.org/10.1177/0010414020970223.

Green, James W. *Cultural Awareness in the Human Services: A Multi-Ethnic Approach*. Boston: Allyn & Bacon, 1999.

Greenland, Jeremy. "Ethnic Discrimination in Rwanda and Burundi." In *Case Studies on Human Rights and Fundamental Freedoms: A World Survey: 2*, edited by Ruut Veenhoven, Vol. 4. The Hague: Springer, 1975.

Grimalda, Gianluca, Nancy Buchan, and Marilynn Brewer. "Social Identity Mediates the Positive Effect of Globalization on Individual Cooperation: Results from

International Experiments." *PLOS ONE* 13, no. 12 (December 14, 2018): e0206819. https://doi.org/10.1371/journal.pone.0206819.

Guichaoua, André, ed. *Les Crises Politiques Au Burundi et Au Rwanda, 1993-1994: Analyses, Faits et Documents.* 2nd ed. Villeneuve d'Ascq : Paris: Université des sciences et technologies de Lille, Faculté des sciences économiques et sociales; Diffusion Karthala, 1995.

———. *Rwanda 1994: Les Politiques Du Génocide à Butare.* Hommes et Sociétés. Paris: Karthala, 2005.

Gurr, Ted Robert, and Barbara Harff. *Ethnic Conflict in World Politics.* Boulder, Colo.: Westview Press, 1994.

Gurr, Ted Robert, Woodrow Wilson School of Public and International Affairs, and Center of International Studies. *Why Men Rebel.* Princeton, New Jersey: Published for the Center of International Studies, Princeton University [by] Princeton University Press, 1970.

Habyarimana, James, Macartan Humphreys, Daniel N. Posner, and Jeremy M. Weinstein. "Why Does Ethnic Diversity Undermine Public Goods Provision?" *American Political Science Review* 101, no. 4 (November 2007): 709–25. https://doi.org/10.1017/S0003055407070499.

Habyarimana, James P., Macartan Humphreys, Daniel N. Posner, and Jeremy Weinstein. *Coethnicity: Diversity and the Dilemmas of Collective Action.* Russell Sage Foundation Series on Trust; Variation: Russell Sage Foundation Series on Trust. New York: Russell Sage Foundation, 2009.

Hall, Stephen G. *A Faithful Account of the Race: African American Historical Writing in Nineteenth-Century America.* The John Hope Franklin Series in African American History and Culture. Chapel Hill: University of North Carolina Press, 2009.

Hallen, Barry. *A Short History of African Philosophy.* Bloomington: Indiana University Press, 2002. https://muse.jhu.edu/book/13116.

Hanley, Delinda C. "Libya Invests in Its People's Education." *Washington Report on Middle East Affairs—WRMEA*, March 20, 2001. https://www.wrmea.org/001-march/libya-looking-toward-a-post-lockerbie-future-libya-invests-in-its-people-s-education.html.

Harbeson, John W., and Donald Rothchild. *Africa In World Politics: The African State System In Flux.* 1st edition. Boulder, Colo.: Westview Press, 2000.

Harff, Barbara, and Ted Robert Gurr. *Ethnic Conflict in World Politics.* Oxfordshire: Routledge, 2019. https://nls.ldls.org.uk/welcome.html?ark:/81055/vdc_100061914567.0x000001.

Harris, Eddy L. *Native Stranger: Black American's Journey into the Heart of Africa.* New York: Simon & Schuster, 1992.

Harrow, Kenneth W. "'Un Train Peut En Cacher Un Autre'1: Narrating the Rwandan Genocide and Hotel Rwanda." *Research in African Literatures* 36, no. 4 (2005): 223–32.

Held, David, Anthony G. McGrew, David Goldblatt, and Jonathan Perraton, eds. *Global Transformations: Politics, Economics and Culture.* Palo Alto, CA: Stanford Univ. Press, 2000.

Helleiner, Eric. *The Making of National Money: Territorial Currencies in Historical Perspective*. 1st edition. Ithaca: Cornell University Press, 2002.

Heywood, Andrew. *Political Ideologies: An Introduction*. 3rd ed. New York: Palgrave Macmillan, 2003.

Higazi, Adam. "Farmer-Pastoralist Conflicts on the Jos Plateau, Central Nigeria: Security Responses of Local Vigilantes and the Nigerian State." *Conflict, Security & Development* 16, no. 4 (July 3, 2016): 365–85. https://doi.org/10.1080/146788 02.2016.1200314.

Hilker, Lyndsay McLean. "Everyday Ethnicities: Identity and Reconciliation among Rwandan Youth." *Journal of Genocide Research* 11, no. 1 (March 2009): 81–100. https://doi.org/10.1080/14623520802703640.

Hintjens, H. M. "When Identity Becomes a Knife: Reflecting on the Genocide in Rwanda." *Ethnicities* 1, no. 1 (March 1, 2001): 25–55. https://doi.org/10.1177/146879680100100109.

Hoppe, Kirk Arden. "Ifi Amadiume. Male Daughters, Female Husbands: Gender and Sex in an African Society." *International Feminist Journal of Politics* 18, no. 3 (2016): 498–500.

Höppner, Stephanie. "Terrorism Poses Growing Threat in Africa's Sahel, Germany Warns | DW | 27.12.2019." *DW.COM*, December 12, 2019. https://www.dw.com/en/terrorism-poses-growing-threat-in-africas-sahel-germany-warns/a-51813261.

Hornby, Albert Sydney. *Oxford Advanced Learner's Dictionary*. Edited by Joanna Turnbull, Diana Lea, Dilys Parkinson, and Patrick Phillips. 8th edition. Oxford: Oxford University Press, 2010.

Hornby, Albert Sydney, and Michael Ashby. *Oxford Advanced Learner's Dictionary of Current English*. Edited by Sally Wehmeier. Oxford: Oxford University Press, 2000.

Horowitz, Donald L. *Ethnic Groups in Conflict*. Berkeley: University of California Press, 1985.

Horowitz, Michael M., and Peter D. Little. "African Pastoralism and Poverty: Some Implications for Drought and Famine." In *Drought and Hunger in Africa: Denying Famine a Future*, edited by Michael H. Glantz, 59–82. Cambridge: Cambridge University Press, 1987.

Hountondji, Paulin J. *African Philosophy: Myth and Reality*. 2nd ed. African Systems of Thought. Bloomington, Ind.: Indiana University Press, 1996.

House of Representatives. The Growing Crisis In Africa's Sahel Region, Pub. L. No. Serial No. 113-72, § Subcommittee on Africa, Global Health, Global Human Rights, an International Organizations (2013). https://www.govinfo.gov/content/pkg/CHRG-113hhrg81167/html/CHRG-113hhrg81167.htm.

"House of Representatives (Nigeria)." In *Wikipedia*, November 22, 2021. https://en.wikipedia.org/w/index.php?title=House_of_Representatives_(Nigeria)&oldid=1056495534.

Howe, Marvine. "Year-Old Hirak Protest Movement Galvanizes Northern Morocco's Neglected Rif Region." *Washington Report on Middle East Affairs—WRMEA*, October 2017. https://www.wrmea.org/017-october/year-old-hirak-protest-movement-galvanizes-northern-moroccos-neglected-rif-region.html.

Huber, Joan, ed. *Macro-Micro Linkages in Sociology.* Newbury Park, CA: SAGE Publications, 1991.

Human Rights Campaign. "Glossary of Terms." Human Rights Campaign. Accessed July 28, 2021. https://www.hrc.org/resources/glossary-of-terms.

Human Rights Council. "Human Rights, Sexual Orientation, and Gender Identity." United Nations General Assembly, June 15, 2011.

Human Rights Watch. "Guatemala: 3 Killings of LGBT People in a Week." Human Rights Watch, June 22, 2021. https://www.hrw.org/news/2021/06/22/guatemala-3-killings-lgbt-people-week.

———. "Rwanda: Justice After Genocide—20 Years On." Human Rights Watch, March 28, 2014. https://www.hrw.org/news/2014/03/28/rwanda-justice-after-genocide-20-years.

———. "Senegal: Quash Conviction of 7 for 'Acts Against Nature.'" Human Rights Watch, August 28, 2015. https://www.hrw.org/news/2015/08/28/senegal-quash-conviction-7-acts-against-nature.

Hurrell, Andrew, and Ngaire Woods. "Globalisation and Inequality." *Millennium: Journal of International Studies* 24, no. 3 (December 1, 1995): 447–70. https://doi.org/10.1177/03058298950240031001.

Hussain, Muzammil M. "Digital Infrastructure Politics and Internet Freedom Stakeholders after the Arab Spring," 2021, 21.

Hussain, Muzammil M., and Philip N. Howard. "What Best Explains Successful Protest Cascades? ICTs and the Fuzzy Causes of the Arab Spring." *International Studies Review* 15, no. 1 (March 2013): 48–66. https://doi.org/10.1111/misr.12020.

Huyse, Lucien, and Mark Salter, eds. *Traditional Justice and Reconciliation after Violent Conflict: Learning from African Experiences.* Stockholm: International Idea, 2008.

Ighobor, Kingsley. "New AU Chair DRC's President Felix Tshisekedi Sets Ambitious Agenda for 2021." Africa Renewal, February 9, 2021. https://www.un.org/africarenewal/magazine/february-2021/new-au-chair-drc-president-felix-tshisekedi-sets-ambitious-agenda-2021.

Ijere, Thomas Chukwuma. "Political Parties, Identities and Violent Conflict in Nigeria." *International Journal of African and Asian Studies* 13 (2015): 110–18.

Ikwuemesi, C. Krydz, ed. *Astride Memory and Desire Peoples, Cultures, and Development in Nigeria.* Eugu, Nigeria: ABIC Books, 2012.

Imade, Lucky. "How Globalization Underdeveloped Africa." In *Globalization in Africa: Perspectives on Development, Security, and the Environment*, edited by Usman A. Tar, Etham B. Mijah, and Moses E. U. Tedheke, 47–78. London: Lexington Books, 2016.

"The Implications of Exchange Control." *Financial Times*, July 7, 1961, 5.

Ingawa, S. A., G. Tarawali, and R. von Kaufmann. "Grazing Reserves in Nigeria: Problems, Prospects and Policy Implication." Network Paper. Addis Ababa: International Livestock Centre for Africa, 1989. https://agris.fao.org/agris-search/search.do?recordID=QT2016105834.

Ingelaere, Bert. "Do We Understand Life After Genocide? Center and Periphery in the Construction of Knowledge in Postgenocide Rwanda." *African Studies Review* 53, no. 1 (April 2010): 41–59. https://doi.org/10.1353/arw.0.0307.

International Center for Transitional Justice. "Significance of the Bemba Case at the ICC." International Center for Transitional Justice, January 1, 2009.

International Crisis Group. "Herders against Farmers: Nigeria's Expanding Deadly Conflict." Brussels, Belgium: International Crisis Group, September 19, 2017. https://www.crisisgroup.org/africa/west-africa/nigeria/252-herders-against-farmers-nigerias-expanding-deadly-conflict.

International Institute for Democracy and Electoral Assistance. *Women's Political Participation: Africa Barometer 2021*. International Institute for Democracy and Electoral Assistance, 2021. https://doi.org/10.31752/idea.2021.21.

International Institute for Democracy and Electoral Assistance (International IDEA). "South Africa." International Institute for Democracy and Electoral Assistance (International IDEA). Accessed August 24, 2021. https://www.idea.int/data-tools/data/gender-quotas/country-view/310/35.

Inter-Parliamentary Union. "Women in Parliament in 2018: The Year in Review." Inter-Parliamentary Union. Accessed September 4, 2021. https://www.ipu.org/resources/publications/reports/2019-03/women-in-parliament-in-2018-year-in-review.

———. "Women in Politics: 2017." Inter-Parliamentary Union. Accessed September 4, 2021. https://www.ipu.org/resources/publications/infographics/2017-03/women-in-politics-2017.

Iroegbu, Pantaleon. *Metaphysics, the Kpịm of Philosophy*. Owerri, Nigeria: International Universities Press, 1995.

Isaacs, Harold. "Basic Group Identity: The Idols of the Tribe." In *Ethnicity: Theory and Experience*, edited by Nathan Glazer, Daniel Patrick Moynihan, and Corinne Saposs Schelling, 29–52. Cambridge: Harvard University Press, 1975.

Isajiw, Wsvvolod W. "Definition and Dimensions of Ethnicity: A Theoretical Framework." Ontario, 1992. https://tspace.library.utoronto.ca/bitstream/1807/68/2/Def_DimofEthnicity.pdfLeo.

Isin, Engin F., and Bryan S. Turner, eds. *Handbook of Citizenship Studies*. 1st edition. London; Thousand Oaks, Calif.: SAGE Publications Ltd, 2003.

Isola, Abidemi Abiola, and Bukola A. Alao. "African Women and Leadership Role." *Journal of Humanities and Social Science* 24, no. 9 (September 2019): 5–8.

Jackson, Joseph. "Roots of Revolution: The African National Congress and Gay Liberation in South Africa." *SSRN Electronic Journal* 44, no. 2 (2019): 613–70. https://doi.org/10.2139/ssrn.3619433.

Jacquemin, Céline A.. "French Foreign Policy in Rwanda: Language, Personal Networks, & Changing Contexts." In *African Political Economy: The Way Forward for 21st Century Development*, edited by Toyin Falola and Jessica Achberger, 322–40. Routledge African Studies. Routledge, 2013.

———. "Hegemony and Counterhegemony. The Roots of Rwandan Genocide." In *The Roots of Ethnic Conflict in Africa: From Grievance to Violence*, edited by Wanjala S. Nasong'o, 93–123. New York: Palgrave Macmillan, 2015.

———. "Rwandan Government & Diaspora: Harnessing the Power of Institutions Built for Unity & Democracy." In *Slavery, Migrations, and Transformations: Connecting Old and New Diasporas to the Homeland*, edited by Toyin Falola and Danielle Porter Sanchez, 179–201. Amherst: Cambria Press Inc., 2015.

———. "Human Rights Crises and International Response: Framing Rwanda and Kosovo." Ph.D., Political Science, University of California, Irvine, 2003.

Jakande, L. K., ed. *West Africa Annual, 1964-1965*. Lagos: John West Publications Ltd., 1964.

Jansen, Yakaré-Oulé. "Denying Genocide or Denying Free Speech? A Case Study of the Application of Rwanda's Genocide Denial Laws." *Northwestern Journal of International Human Rights* 12, no. 2 (2014): 191–213.

Jayeoba, T. "Evaluation of Socio-Political Rights of Women under Democratic Regimes in Nigeria (1960–2007)." MSc Thesis, Obafemi Awolowo University, 2009.

Jessee, Erin, and Sarah E. Watkins. "Good Kings, Bloody Tyrants, and Everything in Between: Representations of the Monarchy in Post-Genocide Rwanda." *History in Africa* 41 (June 2014): 35–62. https://doi.org/10.1017/hia.2014.7.

Jili, Philani. "African Identity and an African Renaissance." Master's thesis, University of Natal, 2000.

Johnson, Darin E.W. "Conflict Constitution-Making in Libya and Yemen." *University of Pennsylvania Journal of International Law* 39, no. 2 (2017): 293.

Jucker-Fleetwood, Erin E. *Money and Finance in Africa*. New York: Frederick A. Praeger Publishers, 1964.

Kabengele Mpinga, Emmanuel, Mapendo Koya, Jennifer Hasselgard-Rowe, Emilien Jeannot, Sylvie B. Rehani, and Philippe Chastonay. "Rape in Armed Conflicts in the Democratic Republic of Congo: A Systematic Review of the Scientific Literature." *Trauma, Violence, & Abuse* 18, no. 5 (December 2017): 581–92. https://doi.org/10.1177/1524838016650184.

Kacowicz, Arie M. "Regionalization, Globalization, and Nationalism: Convergent, Divergent, or Overlapping?" *Alternatives* 24, no. 4 (1999): 527–55.

Kadankavil, Thomas. *Ethical World: A Study on the Ethical Thought in the East and the West*. Bangalore: Dharmaram Publications, 1995.

Kalemba, Joshua. "'Being Called Sisters': Masculinities and Black Male Nurses in South Africa." *Gender, Work & Organization* 27, no. 4 (July 2020): 647–63. https://doi.org/10.1111/gwao.12423.

Kanyangara, Patrick, Bernard Rimé, Pierre Philippot, and Vincent Yzerbyt. "Collective Rituals, Emotional Climate and Intergroup Perception: Participation in 'Gacaca' Tribunals and Assimilation of the Rwandan Genocide." *Journal of Social Issues* 63, no. 2 (June 2007): 387–403. https://doi.org/10.1111/j.1540-4560.2007.00515.x.

Kasfir, Nelson. "Reviewed Work(s): Institutions and Ethnic Politics in Africa by Daniel N. Posner." *Political Science Quarterly* 121, no. 2 (Summer 2006): 330–32.

Kassimir, Ronald. "The Cohesion of Oppression: Clientship and Ethnicity in Rwanda, 1860-1960 (Book)." *American Journal of Sociology* 95, no. 4 (January 1990): 1063–65. https://doi.org/10.1086/229393.

Katshingu, Remy K. *Du Miracle Rwandais Au Paradoxe Congolais (RDC): De La Pauvreté à l'émergence Économique*. Paris: L'Harmattan, 2015.

Keller, Edmond J., and Ruth Iyob, eds. *Religious Ideas and Institutions: Transitions to Democracy in Africa*. Pretoria: Unisa Press, 2012.

Kelly, Jocelyn. "Rape in War: Motives of Militia in DRC." Special Report. Washington, D.C.: United States Institute of Peace, June 2010. https://www.usip.org/sites/default/files/SR243Kelly.pdf.

Khadiagala, Gilbert M., ed. *Security Dynamics in Africa's Great Lakes Region*. First Edition. Boulder, Colo.: Lynne Rienner Pub., 2006.

Kieh, George Klay. *Africa and the New Globalization*. Aldershot: Ashgate Publishing, Ltd., 2008.

Kigabo, Thomas Rusuhuzwa. "Leadership, Policy Making, Quality of Economic Policies, and Their Inclusiveness: The Case of Rwanda." Working Paper. Washington, DC: World Bank, 2008. https://openknowledge.worldbank.org/handle/10986/28051.

Kimonyo, Jean Paul. *Rwanda, Un Génocide Populaire*. Hommes et Sociétés. Paris: Karthala, 2008.

Kinzer, Stephen, Miguel Pimentel, and Carol Kim. "Reconciliation and Development in Kagame's Rwanda." *The Brown Journal of World Affairs* 20, no. 2 (2014): 93–101.

Kirshner, Jonathan. *Currency and Coercion : The Political Economy of International Monetary Powers*. Princeton: Princeton Univ. Press, 1995.

Klandermans, P. G. "Identity Politics and Politicized Identities: Identity Processes and the Dynamics of Protest." *Political Psychology* 35, no. 1 (2014): 1–22.

Klosowicz, Robert. "Identity, Ethnic Conflict, and Communal Conflict in Sub-Saharan Africa." *Politeja* 17, no. 5 (2020): 171–90.

Klotz, Audie, and Cecelia Lynch. "Identities." In *Strategies for Research in Constructivist International Relations*, 65–85. International Relations in a Constructed World. Armonk, New York: M.E. Sharpe, Inc., 2007.

———. *Strategies for Research in Constructivist International Relations*. International Relations in a Constructed World. Armonk, New York: M.E. Sharpe, Inc., 2007.

Kofman, Eleonore, and Gillian Youngs, eds. *Globalization: Theory and Practice*. London: Pinter, 1996.

———. "Introduction: Globalization—The Second Wave." In *Globalization: Theory and Practice*, edited by Eleonore Kofman and Gillian Youngs, 1–8. London: Pinter, 1996.

Kohl, Ines. "Libya's 'Major Minorities'. Berber, Tuareg and Tebu: Multiple Narratives of Citizenship, Language and Border Control." *Middle East Critique* 23, no. 4 (October 2, 2014): 423–38. https://doi.org/10.1080/19436149.2014.970384.

Krasner, Stephen D. *Power, the State, and Sovereignty: Essays on International Relations*. London: Routledge, 2009.

Kubalkova, Vendulka, Nicholas Onuf, and Paul Kowert. *International Relations in a Constructed World*. 1st edition. Armonk, N.Y.: Routledge, 1998.

Kukah, M. H. *Religion, Politics and Power in Northern Nigeria*. Ibadan, Nigeria: Spectrum Books, 1993.

Kumar, Pankaj. "Participation of Women in Politics: Worldwide Experience." *Journal of Humanities and Social Science* 22 (December 19, 2017): 77–88. https://doi.org/10.9790/0837-2212067788.

Kuper, Leo, and Michael G. Smith, eds. *Pluralism in Africa*. Berkeley: Univ. of California Press, 1969.

Kwaja, Chris M. A., and Bukola I Ademola-Adelehin. "Responses to Conflicts Between Farmers and Herders in Middle-Belt, Nigeria: Mapping Past Efforts and Opportunities for Violence Prevention." Washington, D.C.: Search for Common Ground, January 2018.

———. "The Implications of the Open Grazing Prohibition and Ranches Establishment Law on Farmer-Herder Relations in the Middle Belt of Nigeria." Washington, D.C.: Search for Common Ground, December 2017.

Kymlicka, Will, and Wayne Norman. "Return of the Citizen: A Survey of Recent Work on Citizenship Theory." *Ethics* 104, no. 2 (1994): 352–81.

Laclau, Ernesto, and Chantal Mouffe. *Hegemony and Socialist Strategy: Towards a Radical Democratic Politics*. 2nd ed. London; New York: Verso, 2001.

Laessing, Ulf, and Ahmed Aboulenein. "Iraq Power Vacuum Deepens after PM-Designate Quits." *Reuters*, March 2, 2020, sec. Healthcare. https://www.reuters.com/article/iraq-protests-idUSL8N2AV265.

Lageman, Thessa. "Remembering Mohamed Bouazizi: The Man Who Sparked the Arab Spring." *Al Jazeera*, December 17, 2020. https://www.aljazeera.com/features/2020/12/17/remembering-mohamed-bouazizi-his-death-triggered-the-arab.

Laïdi, Zaki. *A World without Meaning: The Crisis of Meaning in International Politics*. London; New York: Routledge, 1998.

Lame, Danielle de. *A Hill Among a Thousand: Transformations and Ruptures in Rural Rwanda*. Madison, WI: University of Wisconsin Press, 2005.

Larmarange, Joseph, Annabel Desgrées Du LoÛ, Catherine Enel, and Abdoulaye Wade. "Homosexuality and Bisexuality in Senegal: A Multiform Reality." *Population* 64, no. 4 (September 2009): 635–66. https://doi.org/10.3917/pope.904.0635.

Laswell, Harold. *Politics: Who Gets What, When, and How*. New York: World Publishing Company, 1930.

Leatherman, Janie. "Sexual Violence and Armed Conflict: Complex Dynamics of Re-Victimization." *International Journal of Peace Studies* 12, no. 1 (2007): 53–71.

Lemarchand, René. "Disconnecting the Threads: Rwanda and the Holocaust Reconsidered." *Journal of Genocide Research* 4, no. 4 (2002): 499–518.

———. *Ethnocide as Discourse and Practice*. Woodrow Wilson Center Series. Washington, D.C.: Woodrow Wilson Center Press; Cambridge University Press, 1994.

———. *Rwanda and Burundi*. Pall Mall Library of African Affairs. London: Pall Mall, 1970.

———. "The Crisis in the Great Lakes." In *Africa in World Politics: The African State System in Flux*, edited by John W. Harbeson and Donald Rothchild, 1st edition., 338. Boulder, Colo.: Westview Press, 2000.

Lenz, Renate. "Michiel Heyns's Lost Ground: The White Man's Sense of Identity and Place in a Decolonised Africa and a Democratic South Africa." *Literator* 38, no. 1 (March 27, 2017): 1–10. https://doi.org/10.4102/lit.v38i1.1329.

Lesley, Elena. "Death on Display: Bones and Bodies in Cambodia and Rwanda." In *Necropolitics: Mass Graves and Exhumations in the Age of Human Rights*, edited by Francisco Ferrándiz and Antonius C. G. M. Robben, 213–39. Philidelphia: University of Pennsylvania Press, 2015.

Levinson, David. *Ethnic Relations: A Cross-Cultural Encyclopedia*. 1st edition. Santa Barbara: ABC-CLIO, 1995.

Lewis, Peter, and Michael Bratton. "Attitudes toward Democracy and Markets in Nigeria: Report of a National Opinion Survey, January-February 2000." Washington, DC: International Foundation for Election Systems, 2000.

Libya Constitution (2011). https://www.constituteproject.org/constitution/Libya_2011.pdf.

"Local Government Areas of Nigeria." In *Wikipedia*, November 30, 2021. https://en.wikipedia.org/w/index.php?title=Local_government_areas_of_Nigeria&oldid=1057983074.

Lomasky, Loren E. "Towards a Liberal Theory of Vice (and Virtue)." In *Civil Society, Democracy, and Civic Renewal*, edited by Robert K. Fullinwider. Lanham, MD: Rowman & Littlefield Publishers, 1999.

Longman, Timothy. "Genocide and Socio-Political Change: Massacres in Two Rwandan Villages." *Journal of Public Opinion* 13, no. 2 (1995): 18–21.

Love, Heather. "Queer." *TSQ: Transgender Studies Quarterly* 1, no. 1–2 (January 1, 2014): 172–76. https://doi.org/10.1215/23289252-2399470.

Loyle, Cyanne E., and Christian Davenport. "Some Left to Tell the Tale: Finding Perpetrators and Understanding Violence in Rwanda." *Journal of Peace Research* 57, no. 4 (July 2020): 507–20. https://doi.org/10.1177/0022343319885173.

Lundgren, Berit, and Eileen Scheckle. "Hope and Future: Youth Identity Shaping in Post-Apartheid South Africa." *International Journal of Adolescence and Youth* 24, no. 1 (January 2, 2019): 51–61. https://doi.org/10.1080/02673843.2018.1463853.

Lundy, Brandon D., and Solomon Negash, eds. *Teaching Africa: A Guide for the 21st-Century Classroom*. Bloomington: Indiana University Press, 2013.

Lutz, David W. "African Ubuntu Philosophy and Global Management." *Journal of Business Ethics* 84, no. S3 (February 2009): 313–28. https://doi.org/10.1007/s10551-009-0204-z.

Lyon, Cherstin M., Elizabeth M. Nix, and Rebecca K. Shrum, eds. "Introducing Public History." In *Introduction to Public History: Interpreting the Past, Engaging Audiences*, 1–19. American Association for State and Local History Book Series. Lanham, MD: Rowman & Littlefield, 2017.

———, eds. *Introduction to Public History: Interpreting the Past, Engaging Audiences*. American Association for State and Local History Book Series. Lanham, MD: Rowman & Littlefield, 2017.

Lyotard, Jean-François. *The Postmodern Condition: A Report on Knowledge*. Translated by Geoffrey Bennington and Brian Massumi. Manchester: Manchester University Press, 1984.

Mace, Ruth, David M. Anderson, Thomas Bierschenk, Lee Cronk, Ilse Köhler-Rollefson, William Lancaster, Fidelity Lancaster, Peter D. Little, Elizabeth Ann Morris, and Jacqueline Rossignol. "Transitions Between Cultivation and Pastoralism in Sub-Saharan Africa." *Current Anthropology* 34, no. 4 (1993): 363–82.

Machakanja, Pamela. "Contested Spaces: Gender, Governance and Women's Political Engagement in Postcolonial Africa." In *The Crises of Postcoloniality in Africa*, edited by Kenneth Omeje, 197–215. Dakar: CODESRIA, 2015. https://doi.org/10.2307/j.ctvh8r3k3.

MaCleKi. "MaCleKi." Accessed July 20, 2021. https://macleki.org/.

"MaCleKi: Engaging the African Public in Their History, One Story at a Time." *Items* (blog). Accessed February 9, 2022. https://items.ssrc.org/parameters/macleki-engaging-the-african-public-in-their-history-one-story-at-a-time/.

Maddy-Weitzman, Bruce. "A Turning Point? The Arab Spring and the Amazigh Movement." *Ethnic and Racial Studies* 38, no. 14 (November 14, 2015): 2499–2515. https://doi.org/10.1080/01419870.2015.1061139.

———. *The Berber Identity Movement and the Challenge to North African States*. Austin: University of Texas Press, 2011. https://utpress.utexas.edu/books/madber.

Made, Patricia. "Defining an African Women's Agenda beyond Beijing." *African Journal of Political Science* 1, no. 1 (1996): 73–83.

Maedl, Anna. "Rape as Weapon of War in the Eastern DRC? The Victims' Perspective." *Human Rights Quarterly* 33, no. 1 (2011): 128–47.

Maha, M. "Italo Festival of the Igala as Panacea for Fostering National Identity." In *The Humanities and National Identity*, edited by P.A. Uchechukwu, E.U. Ibekwe, N.M. Obi, and C. Okoye, 81–88. Awka: Fab Anieh, 2013.

Maiangwa, Benjamin. "'Conflicting Indigeneity' and Farmer–Herder Conflicts in Postcolonial Africa." *Peace Review* 29, no. 3 (July 3, 2017): 282–88. https://doi.org/10.1080/10402659.2017.1344527.

Malkki, Liisa H. *Purity and Exile: Violence, Memory, and National Cosmology among Hutu Refugees in Tanzania*. Chicago: University of Chicago Press, 1995.

———. "Speechless Emissaries: Refugees, Humanitarianism, and Dehistoricization." *Cultural Anthropology* 11, no. 3 (1996): 377–404.

Mamdani, Mahmood. "Beyond Settler and Native as Political Identities: Overcoming the Political Legacy of Colonialism." *Comparative Studies in Society and History* 43, no. 4 (2001): 651–64.

———. "Making Sense of Political Violence in Postcolonial Africa." *Identity, Culture and Politics* 32, no. 2 (2002): 1–24. https://doi.org/10.1142/9789812795496_0005.

———. *When Victims Become Killers: Colonialism, Nativism, and the Genocide in Rwanda*. Princeton, N.J.: Princeton Univ. Press, 2001.

Mancha, Maria. "The Love Story of the Lovings." *StMU Research Scholars*, April 29, 2018. https://stmuscholars.org/the-love-story-of-the-lovings/.

———. *Master of Ceremony: StMU History Media Award Ceremony Script*, Spring 2018, St. Mary's University.

Mann, F. A. *Legal Aspect of Money*. 3rd edition. Oxford: Oxford University Press, 1971.

Maquet, Jacques. "Societal and Cultural Incorporation in Rwanda." In *From Tribe to Nation in Africa: Studies in Incorporation Processes,* edited by Ronald Cohen and John Middleton, English Language edition. Scranton: Chandler Pub. Co, 1970.

———. *A Study of Political Relations in a Central African Kingdom.* London: Oxford University Press, 1961.

Martin, Phyllis M. "The Cohesion of Oppression: Clientship and Ethnicity in Rwanda, 1860-1960." *American Historical Review* 95, no. 4 (October 1990): 1264–1264. https://doi.org/10.2307/2163650.

Masson, Paul R., and Catherine Pattillo. *The Monetary Geography of Africa.* Washington, D.C.: Brookings Institution Press, 2005.

Mathieson, Susan, and David Attwell. "Between Ethnicity and Nationhood: Shaka Day and the Struggle over Zuluness in Post-Apartheid South Africa." In *Multicultural States: Rethinking Difference and Identity,* edited by David Bennett. London; New York: Routledge, 1998.

Mayersen, Deborah. "A Massive Rejection of the Tutsi as Fellow Nationals." In *On the Path to Genocide: Armenia and Rwanda Re-Examined,* 122–47. New York: Berghahn Books, 2014.

———. "'Driven by Ethnic Exclusivism': On the Timing of Genocide." In *On the Path to Genocide: Armenia and Rwanda Re-Examined.* New York: Berghahn Books, 2014.

———. "'Fraternity in Diversity' or 'Feudal Fanatics'? Representations of Ethnicity in Rwandan Presidential Rhetoric." *Patterns of Prejudice* 49, no. 3 (July 2015): 249–70.

———. *On the Path to Genocide: Armenia and Rwanda Re-Examined.* New York: Berghahn Books, 2014.

Mazrui, Ali. "Violent Contiguity and the Politics of Retribalization in Africa." *Journal of International Affairs* 23, no. 1 (1969): 89–105.

Mazur, Amy, Dorothy Mcbride, and Season Hoard. "Comparative Strength of Women's Movements over Time: Conceptual, Empirical, and Theoretical Innovations." *Politics, Groups, and Identities* 4, no. 4 (December 7, 2015): 1–25. https://doi.org/10.1080/21565503.2015.1102153.

M'Baye, Babacar. "Representations of the Gor Djiguene [Man Woman] in Senegalese Culture, Films, and Literature." In *Gender and Sexuality in Senegalese Societies: Critical Perspectives and Methods,* edited by Babacar Mbaye and Besi Brillian Muhonja, 77–106. Critical African Studies in Gender and Sexuality. Lanham, Maryland: Lexington Books, 2019.

———. "The Origins of Senegalese Homophobia: Discourses on Homosexuals and Transgender People in Colonial and Postcolonial Senegal." *African Studies Review* 56, no. 2 (2013): 109–28.

Mbaye, Babacar, and Besi Brillian Muhonja, eds. *Gender and Sexuality in Senegalese Societies: Critical Perspectives and Methods.* Critical African Studies in Gender and Sexuality. Lanham, Maryland: Lexington Books, 2019.

McBride, Stephen, and John Richard Wiseman, eds. *Globalization and Its Discontents.* Houndmills, Basingstoke, Hampshire; New York: Macmillan Press; St. Martin's Press, 2000.

McKeon, Robert W., Jr. "The Arab Maghreb Union: Possibilities of Maghrebine Political and Economic Unity, and Enhanced Trade in the World Community." *Penn State International Law Review* 10, no. 2 (1992): 263–302.

McKeown, Adam, Marx, Engels, Robert Park, M. F. Millikan, W. W. Rostow, and Manuel Castells. "Periodizing Globalization." *History Workshop Journal*, no. 63 (2007): 218–30.

Meester, Jos, and Nancy Ezzeddine. "A Transition at Work? The Ethnicization of Ethiopia's Informal Sector." The Hague: Clingendael, February 23, 2021.

Megerisi, Tarek. "Plot Twist: How Europe Should Deal with Libya's New Government—European Council on Foreign Relations." *European Council on Foreign Relations* (blog), February 12, 2021. https://ecfr.eu/article/plot-twist-how-europe-should-deal-with-libyas-new-government/.

Meier, August, and Elliott M. Rudwick. *Black History and the Historical Profession, 1915-1980*. Blacks in the New World. Urbana: University of Illinois Press, 1986.

Melucci, Alberto. *Nomads of the Present: Social Movements and Individual Needs in Contemporary Society*. Philadelphia: Temple Univ Pr, 1989.

Mendos, Lucas Ramon, Kellyn Botha, Rafael Carrano Lelis, Enrique López de la Peña, Ilia Savelev, and Daron Tan. "State-Sponsored Homophobia Report—2020 Global Legislation Overview Update." Geneva: ILGA World, December 14, 2020. https://ilga.org/state-sponsored-homophobia-report-2020-global-legislation-overview.

Mengler, Michael. "Master of Ceremony Speech." Speech presented at the 7th Semi-Annual StMU History Media Award Ceremony, St. Mary's University, December 4, 2019.

Mercy Corps. "The Economic Costs of Conflict in Nigeria." Mercy Corps, June 11, 2015. https://www.mercycorps.org/research-resources/economic-costs-conflict-nigeria.

Meyerstein, Ariel. "Between Law and Culture: Rwanda's Gacaca and Postcolonial Legality: Between Law and Culture." *Law & Social Inquiry* 32, no. 2 (June 7, 2007): 467–508. https://doi.org/10.1111/j.1747-4469.2007.00066.x.

Miladi, Noureddine. "Tunisia: A Media Led Revolution?" *Al Jazeera*, January 17, 2011. https://www.aljazeera.com/opinions/2011/1/17/tunisia-a-media-led-revolution.

Miller, Susan Gilson, Nevill Barbour, L. Carl Brown, Will D. Swearingen, and Abdallah Laroui. "Morocco." In *Encyclopedia Britannica*, n.d. https://www.britannica.com/place/Morocco.

Mills, Ivy. "Sutura: Gendered Honor, Social Death, and the Politics of Exposure in Senegalese Literature and Popular Culture." Dissertation, UC Berkeley, 2011. https://escholarship.org/uc/item/7x37t9qs.

Mills, Melinda. "Globalization and Inequality." *European Sociological Review* 25, no. 1 (2009): 1–8.

Ministry of Local Government, Good Governance, Community Development, and Social Affairs. "Rwanda Decentralization Strategic Framework." Kigali: Ministry of Local Government, Good Governance, Community Development, and Social Affairs, August 2007. https://www.minaloc.gov.rw/fileadmin/user_upload/Minaloc/Sector_docs/Rwanda_Decentralisation_Strategic_Framework_10_August_2007.pdf.

Mohan, Giles. "Globalization and Governance: The Paradoxes of Adjustment in Sub-Saharan Africa." In *Globalization: Theory and Practice*, edited by Eleonore Kofman and Gillian Youngs, 289–303. London: Pinter, 1996.

Monjib, Maati. "All the King's Islamists." Carnegie Endowment for International Peace, September 20, 2012. https://carnegieendowment.org/sada/49433.

Monroe, Kristen Renwick. *Ethics in an Age of Terror and Genocide: Identity and Moral Choice*. Princeton: Princeton University Press, 2012.

———. "The Holocaust and Genocide." In *Ethics in an Age of Terror and Genocide: Identity and Moral Choice*, 9–31, 2012.

Montague, Dena, and Frida Berrigan. "The Business of War in the Democratic Republic of Congo." Third World Traveler, 2001. https://thirdworldtraveler.com/Africa/Business_War_Congo.html.

Montalvo, José G., and Marta Reynal-Querol. "Ethnic Polarization, Potential Conflict, and Civil Wars." *American Economic Review* 95, no. 3 (June 2005): 796–816. https://doi.org/10.1257/0002828054201468.

MONUSCO. "The Foreign Armed Groups." MONUSCO, February 22, 2016. https://monusco.unmissions.org/en/foreign-armed-groups.

Moore, Candice. "Four Years After the Fall of Gaddafi." ACCORD, April 11, 2015. https://www.accord.org.za/conflict-trends/four-years-fall-gaddafi/.

Morgan, Carol E. "Women, Work and Consciousness in the Mid-Nineteenth-Century English Cotton Industry." *Social History* 17, no. 1 (January 1992): 23–41.

Morgan, Saly. "Rwanda Today: A Complicated Miracle." *Ethos* 21, no. 4 (2013): 7–13.

Moritz, Mark. "Changing Contexts and Dynamics of Farmer-Herder Conflicts across West Africa." *Canadian Journal of African Studies* 40, no. 1 (2006): 1–40.

Morocco Constitution (2011). https://www.constituteproject.org/constitution/Morocco_2011.pdf.

Moss, Sigrun Marie. "Identity Hierarchy Within the Sudanese Superordinate Identity: Political Leadership Promoting and Demoting Subordinate Groups: Identity Hierarchy Within a Superordinate Identity." *Political Psychology* 38, no. 6 (December 2017): 925–42. https://doi.org/10.1111/pops.12378.

Mueller, John. "The Banality of 'Ethnic War.'" *International Security* 25, no. 1 (2000): 42–70.

Murray, Rebecca. "Southern Lybia Destabalized." *Small Arms Survey*, April 2017, 20.

Murray, Stephen O., and Will Roscoe. *Boy-Wives and Female Husbands. Studies in African Homosexualities*. New York: Palgrave Macmillan, 1998. http://www.arcados.ch/wp-content/uploads/2012/06/MURRAY-ROSCOE-BOY-WIVES-FEMALE-HUSBANDS-98.pdf.

Muthien, Yvonne, and Meshack Khosa. "Constructing a Regional Political Identity in South Africa." *Social Identities* 4, no. 3 (October 1998): 457. https://doi.org/10.1080/13504639851726.

Nagel, Mechthild E. "Patriarchal Ideologies and Women's Domestication." In *The End of Prisons: Reflections from the Decarceration Movement*, edited by Mechthild E. Nagel and Anthony J. Noella II. Amsterdam: Rodopi, 2013.

Nagel, Mechthild E., and Anthony J. Noella II, eds. *The End of Prisons: Reflections from the Decarceration Movement*. Amsterdam: Rodopi, 2013.

Nahimana, Marie-Rosette, Candide Tran Ngoc, Olushayo Olu, Jose Nyamusore, Ayodeji Isiaka, Vedaste Ndahindwa, Lakruwan Dassanayake, and André Rusanganwa. "Knowledge, Attitude and Practice of Hygiene and Sanitation in a Burundian Refugee Camp: Implications for Control of a Salmonella Typhi Outbreak." *Pan African Medical Journal* 28 (September 2017): 1–8.

Narayan, Anjana. "Matrilineal Society." In *Encyclopedia Britannica*. Accessed December 3, 2021. https://www.britannica.com/topic/matrilineal-society.

Nasong'o, Wanjala S. "Deep-Seated Historical and Socioeconomic Grievances: The North-South Conflict in Sudan." In *The Roots of Ethnic Conflict in Africa: From Grievance to Violence*, 21–36. New York: Palgrave Macmillan, 2015. http://site.ebrary.com/id/11118000.

———. "Explaining Ethnic Conflicts: Theoretical and Conceptual Perspectives." In *The Roots of Ethnic Conflict in Africa: From Grievance to Violence*, 11–20. New York: Palgrave Macmillan, 2015. http://site.ebrary.com/id/11118000.

———. *The Roots of Ethnic Conflict in Africa: From Grievance to Violence*. New York: Palgrave Macmillan, 2015. http://site.ebrary.com/id/11118000.

———. "From Grievance to Ethnic Mobilization." In *The Roots of Ethnic Conflict in Africa: From Grievance to Violence*, edited by Wanjala S. Nasong'o, 1–9. Houndmills, Basingstoke, Hampshire; New York: Palgrave Macmillan, 2015.

Nath, Dipika. "Fear for Life." Human Rights Watch, November 30, 2010. https://www.hrw.org/report/2010/11/30/fear-life/violence-against-gay-men-and-men-perceived-gay-senegal.

"National Assembly | Federal Republic of Nigeria." Accessed February 12, 2022. https://nass.gov.ng/mps/members.

NATO. "NATO and Libya (Archived)." NATO, November 9, 2015. http://www.nato.int/cps/en/natohq/topics_71652.htm.

———. "NATO and Libya (Archived)." NATO. Accessed November 30, 2021. http://www.nato.int/cps/en/natohq/topics_71652.htm.

Ndaba, Lee. "A Stolen Legacy: The Matrilineality of Pre-Colonial African Society." *Medium* (blog), November 14, 2018. https://medium.com/@MthiyaneShandu/a-stolen-legacy-the-matrilineality-of-pre-colonial-african-society-5307b8db3e5a.

Ndubisi, Frank Okenna. "The Philosophical Paradigm of African Identity and Development." *Open Journal of Philosophy* 3, no. 1 (February 25, 2013): 222–30. https://doi.org/10.4236/ojpp.2013.31A037.

"New Bank for Ghana." *Financial Times*, June 17, 1957, 7.

Newbury, Catharine. "Colonialism, Ethnicity, and Rural Political Protest: Rwanda and Zanzibar in Comparative Perspective." *Comparative Politics* 15, no. 3 (April 1983): 253. https://doi.org/10.2307/421681.

———. "Ethnicity in Rwanda: The Case of Kinyaga: L'Ethnicite Au Ruanda: Le Cas Du Kinyaga." *Africa* 48, no. 1 (March 1978): 17–29. https://doi.org/10.2307/1158708.

———. "The Cohesion of Oppression: A Century of Clientship in Kinyaga, Rwanda." PhD diss, University of Wisconsin Madison, 1975. http://gateway.

proquest.com/openurl?url_ver=Z39.88-2004&rft_val_fmt=info:ofi/fmt:kev:mtx:dissertation&res_dat=xri:pqdiss&rft_dat=xri:pqdiss:7602500.

———. *The Cohesion of Oppression: Clientship and Ethnicity in Rwanda 1860-1960*. New York: Columbia University Press, 1988.

Newbury, David. "Minding the Gap. Re-Imagining Rwanda: Conflict, Survival and Disinformation in the Late Twentieth Century." By Johan Pottier. Cambridge: Cambridge University Press, 2002. *The Journal of African History* 45, no. 1 (2004): 171–73.

Newman, Saul. *Power and Politics in Poststructuralist Thought: New Theories of the Political*. Routledge Innovations in Political Theory 17. London: Routledge, 2005.

News Wires. "Vote Delayed until October, Tunisia's Interim PM Says." *France 24*, June 8, 2011, sec. Africa. https://www.france24.com/en/20110608-elections-postponed-until-october-tunisia-interim-prime-minister-sebsi-essebsi.

Nguyen, Sarah. "Master of Ceremony Speech." Speech presented at the 5th Semi-Annual StMU History Media Award Ceremony, St. Mary's University, November 28, 2018.

"Nigerian Bank Note Order." *Financial Times*, May 16, 1958, 1.

Nigerian Independence Act (1960). https://www.legislation.gov.uk/ukpga/1960/55/pdfs/ukpga_19600055_en.pdf.

"Nigerian Note Circulation." *Financial Times*, August 9, 1961, 6.

"Nigerian Pound Still Strong." *Financial Times*, September 14, 1967.

"Nigerian Senators of the 9th National Assembly." In *Wikipedia*, November 18, 2021. https://en.wikipedia.org/w/index.php?title=Nigerian_Senators_of_the_9th_National_Assembly&oldid=1055944035.

Nikkels, Auroara. "Institutional Change & Identity: Unexpected Impact of the Arab Spring." *STMU Research Scholars* previously known as *StMU History Media* (blog), April 7, 2019. https://stmuscholars.org/institutional-change-identity-impact-of-the-arab-spring/ .

———. "Sticks & Stones May Break My Bones, But My Words Will Build an Army Against Apartheid." *STMU Research Scholars* (blog), April 7, 2019. https://stmuscholars.org/sticks-and-stones-may-break-my-bones-but-words-will-build-an-army-apartheid.

Njogu, Kimani, Kabiri Ngeta, and Mary Wanjau, eds. *Ethnic Diversity in Eastern Africa: Opportunities and Challenges*. Nairobi: Twaweza Communications, 2010.

Nkrumah, Kwame. *Neo-Colonialism: The Last Stage of Imperialism*. London: Nelson & Sons, 1965. marxist.org.

Nkwi, Paul Nchoji, ed. *The Anthropology of Africa: Challenges for the 21st Century*. Bamenda, Cameroon: Langaa RPCIG, 2015. https://doi.org/10.2307/j.ctvh9vxg1.

Nnaemeka, Obioma. "Development, Cultural Forces, and Women's Achievements in Africa." *Law & Policy* 18, no. 3–4 (October 1996): 251–80.

Nnoli, Okwudiba. *Ethnic Politics in Nigeria*. Enugu, Nigeria: Fourth Dimension Publishers, 1978.

Norris, Pippa. "Global Governance and Cosmopolitan Citizens." In *Governance in a Globalizing World*, edited by Joseph S. Nye and John D. Donahue, 155–77. Cambridge, Mass.; Washington, D.C.: Visions of Governance for the 21st Century; Brookings Institution Press, 2000. http://site.ebrary.com/id/10026257.

Nossiter, Adam. "Senegal Cheers Its President for Standing Up to Obama on Same-Sex Marriage." *The New York Times*, June 28, 2013, sec. World. https://www.nytimes.com/2013/06/29/world/africa/senegal-cheers-its-president-for-standing-up-to-obama-on-same-sex-marriage.html.

Nouraie-Simone, Fereshteh, ed. *On Shifting Ground: Muslim Women in the Global Era*. Revised edition. New York: The Feminist Press at CUNY, 2014.

NTC Libya. "NTC Libya | National Transitional Council—Libya," 2011. http://ntclibya.org/.

Ntung, Alex. "Dynamics of Local Conflict in the Democratic Republic of Congo: Challenges Ahead for President Felix Tshisekedi Tshilombo." *The Fletcher Forum of World Affairs* 43, no. 2 (2019): 131–50.

Nussbaum, Arthur. *Money in the Law*. Chicago: Foundation Press, 1939. http://books.google.com/books?id=nnw_AAAAIAAJ.

Nwosu, Onyebuchi, Obinna Ibezim, and Ngozi G. Ugochukwu. "Didactic and Pedagogical Dimensions of Igbo Oral Children's Songs." *Journal of Language and Cultural Education* 9, no. 2 (September 1, 2021): 84–98. https://doi.org/10.2478/jolace-2021-0014.

Nyankanzi, Edward L. *Genocide: Rwanda and Burundi*. Rochester, VT: Schenkman Books, 1998.

———. *The Rwanda Crisis: History of a Genocide*. Rochester, VT: Schenkman Books, 1995.

Nye, Joseph S., and John D. Donahue, eds. *Governance in a Globalizing World*. Cambridge, Mass.; Washington, D.C.: Visions of Governance for the 21st Century; Brookings Institution Press, 2000. http://site.ebrary.com/id/10026257.

Nyerere, Julius K. *Ujamaa. English Ujamaa-Essays on Socialism*. Dar-es-Salaam: Oxford University Press, 1968.

Nyiayaana, Kialee. "Voting Without Choosing? Ethnic Voting Behaviour and Voting Patterns in Nigeria's 2015 Presidential Election and Implications for Institutionalisation of Social Conflicts," *NOKOKO, Institute of African Studies*, vol. 7. Carleton University, Ottawa: Canada. 2019. 79 –112.

Nzewi, Meki. *Learning the Musical Arts in Contemporary Africa: Derived from Indigenous Knowledge Systems*. 1st ed. Ciimda Series. Pretoria: Centre for Indigenous Instrumental African Music and Dance (Ciimda), 2005.

———. *Musical Practice and Creativity: An African Traditional Perspective*. Bayreuth, Germany: IWALEWA-Haus, Univ. of Bayreuth, 1991.

Nzomiwu, John Paul C. *The Concept of Justice among the Traditional Igbo: An Ethical Inquiry*. Awka: Fides Publications, 1999.

Obiefuna, B.A.C., and S.C. Izuegbu. "The Igbo Value of Justice: A Tool for Good Governance in Nigeria." In *Humanities and African Values*, edited by E.C. Umezinwa, K.L. Nwadialor, and I.L. Umeanolue, 141–53. Awka: Fab Anieh, 2016.

Odetola, Theophilus Olatunde. *Military Politics in Nigeria: Economic Development and Political Stability*. New Brunswick, N.J: Transaction Books, 1978.

Odette, Yaya Fonye. "Africa and Its Philosophical Thought," 2021, 29.

Odoemene, Akachi. "Whither Peacebuilding Initiatives? The Escalation of Herder-Farmer Conflicts in Nigeria." *Kujenga Amani* (blog), April 7, 2017.

https://kujenga-amani.ssrc.org/2017/04/07/whither-peacebuilding-initiatives-the-escalation-of-herder-farmer-conflicts-in-nigeria/.

Oguegbu, E. *Humanities and All of Us*. Ontisha: Watch Word Publications, 1990.

Oguejiofor, I.O., ed. *The Hermeneutics of Culture Religion and Society*. Onitsha: Wisdom Technologies Entertainment, 2015.

Ogunrinade, D.O.A. "Music Education as a Pillar to Sustainable Development in Nigeria." *Journal of Economics and Sustainable Development* 6, no. 3 (2015). https://www.iiste.org/Journals/index.php/JEDS/article/viewFile/19919/20425.

Ohmae, Kenichi. *The End of the Nation State: The Rise of Regional Economies*. New York: Free Press, 1995.

Okafor, Richard. *Music in Nigeria Society*. Enugu: New Generation Books, 2005.

Okafor, Richard, and Lawrence Emeke. *Nigerian Peoples and Culture*. 5th edition. Enugu: New Generation Ventures LTD, 2013.

Okeke, T.J. "Cultural Diplomacy and Ethnic Tension in a Multi-Religious Society: An Example of Nigeria." In *The Humanities and Globalization in the Third Millennium*, edited by A.B.C. Chiegboka, T.C. Utoh-Ezeajgh, and G.I. Udechukwu, 248–54. Nimo: Rex Charles and Patrick, 2010.

Okeke Uzodike, Nwabufo, and Hakeem Onapajo. "Women and Development in Africa: Competing Approaches and Contested Achievements." *Alternation* 20, no. 2 (January 1, 2013): 27–51.

Okeke–Ihejirika, Philomina E., and Susan Franceschet. "Democratization and State Feminism: Gender Politics in Africa and Latin America." *Development and Change* 33, no. 3 (2002): 439–66. https://doi.org/10.1111/1467-7660.00262.

Okere, T. "Addressing Multi-Cultural and Human Rights Issues in the Formation of Priests and Religious in Africa." In *The Hermeneutics of Culture Religion and Society*, edited by I.O. Oguejiofor, 75–83. Onitsha: Wisdom Technologies Entertainment, 2015.

Okoli, Al Chukwuma, and Cornelius O. Ogayi. "Herdsmen Militancy and Humanitarian Crisis in Nigeria: A Theoretical Briefing." *African Security Review* 27, no. 2 (April 3, 2018): 129–43. https://doi.org/10.1080/10246029.2018.1499545.

Okpu, Ugbana. *Ethnic Minority Problems in Nigerian Politics, 1960-1965*. Stockholm: Univ., 1977.

Olajubu, Oyeronke. "Seeing through a Woman's Eye: Yoruba Religious Tradition and Gender Relations." *Journal of Feminist Studies in Religion* 20, no. 1 (2004): 41–60.

Olaniyan, Azeez, and Aliyu Yahaya. "Cows, Bandits, and Violent Conflicts: Understanding Cattle Rustling in Northern Nigeria." *Africa Spectrum* 51, no. 3 (2016): 93–105.

Olanrewaju, Surajujul. "Pursuing Its Self-Serving Agenda, National Assembly Kills 'Not Too Young to Run' Bill." *Sahara Reporters*, July 16, 2017. http://saharareporters.com/2017/07/16/pursuing-its-self-serving-agenda-national-assembly-kills-not-too-young-run-bill.

Olds, Kris. "Global Citizenship—What Are We Talking About and Why Does It Matter? | Inside Higher Ed." Inside Higher Education, March 11, 2012. https://www.insidehighered.com/blogs/globalhighered/global-citizenship-%E2%80%93-what-are-we-talking-about-and-why-does-it-matter.

O'Loughlin, Ed. "Identities of Zaire's Rebels Hint at Rwanda Link." *Christian Science Monitor* 89, no. 3 (November 27, 1996): 6.

Omeihe, Emeka. "Cattle Colonisation!" *The Nation*, January 22, 2018. https://thenationonlineng.net/cattle-colonisation/.

Omeje, Kenneth, ed. *The Crises of Postcoloniality in Africa*. Dakar: CODESRIA, 2015. https://doi.org/10.2307/j.ctvh8r3k3.

Omonubi-McDonnell, Morolake. *Gender Inequality in Nigeria*. Ibadan, Nigeria: Spectrum Books, 2003.

Omotola, J. Shola. "Political Globalization and Citizenship: New Sources of Security Threats in Africa." *Journal of African Law* 52, no. 2 (2008): 268–83.

Oni, Ebenezer, and Samuel Okunade. "The Context of Xenophobia in Africa: Nigeria and South Africa in Comparison." In *The Political Economy of Xenophobia in Africa*, edited by Adeoye O. Akinola, 37–51, 2018. https://doi.org/10.1007/978-3-319-64897-2_4.

Onoh, J. K. *Money and Banking in Africa*. London; New York: Longman, 1982.

Onuigbo, Richard Amaechi, and Eme Okechukwu. "State Governors and Revenue Allocation Formula in Nigeria: A Case of the Fourth Republic." *International Journal of Accounting Research* 2, no. 7 (2015): 14–36.

Onuora, M.E., and C.O.N. Oguji, eds. *Basic Foundations in Arts and Social Sciences*. Enugu: Frefabag, 2006.

Onwudiwe, Ebere, and Rotimi T. Suberu, eds. *Nigerian Federalism in Crisis: Critical Perspectives and Political Options*. Ibadan: John Archers, 2005.

Onwuegbuna, Ikenna Emmanuel. "Music as an Embodiment of Culture and Philosophy: A Survey of Nigerian Folk Songs." In *Astride Memory and Desire Peoples, Cultures, and Development in Nigeria*, edited by C. Krydz Ikwuemesi, 291–309. Eugu, Nigeria: ABIC Books, 2012.

Onyeji, Christian. "Towards Nigerian Social and Cultural Integrity: The Contributions of the Nigerian Indigenous Musicians (with Particular Reference to Abigbo Music of Mbaise)." *Nsukka Journal of Musical Arts Research* 1 (2012): 48–66.

Onyima, Blessing Nonye, and Victor Chidubem Iwuoha. "New Dimensions to Pastoralists–Farmers Conflicts and Sustainable Agricultural Development in Agadama and Uwheru Communities, Niger Delta." *African Security* 8, no. 3 (2015): 166–84.

Oommen, T. K. *Citizenship, Nationality, and Ethnicity: Reconciling Competing Identities*. Cambridge, UK; Oxford, UK; Cambridge, MA, USA: Polity Press; Blackwell Publishers, 1997.

Orisadare, Monica Adele. "An Assessment of the Role of Women Group in Women Political Participation, and Economic Development in Nigeria." *Frontiers in Sociology* 4 (2019). https://www.frontiersin.org/article/10.3389/fsoc.2019.00052.

Ortega y Gasset, José, and Howard Lee Nostrand. *Mission of the University*. New York: The Norton Library, 1966.

Osaghae, Eghosa E. "Ethnicity and Contested Citizenship in Africa." In *Citizenship, Belonging, and Political Community in Africa*, edited by Emma Hunter, 256–81. Cambridge Centre of African Studies. Athens: Ohio University Press, 2016.

———. "Foreword: Nigerian Federalism—A Project in Crisis." In *Nigerian Federalism in Crisis: Critical Perspectives and Political Options*, edited by Ebere Onwudiwe and Rotimi T. Suberu, i–vii. Ibadan: John Archers, 2005.

———. "Structural Adjustment and Ethnicity in Nigeria." Uppsala: Nordiska Afrikaninstitutet, 1995. https://www.jstor.org/stable/3601872?origin=crossref.

Osaghae, Eghosa E., and Rotimi T. Suberu. "A History of Identities, Violence, and Stability in Nigeria." Working Paper. University of Oxford: Centre for Research on Inequality, Human Security and Ethnicity, 2005.

Osei, Robert Darko, and Henry Telli. "Sixty Years of Fiscal Policy in Ghana: Outcomes and Lessons." In *The Economy of Ghana Sixty Years after Independence*, edited by Ernest Aryeetey and Ravi Kanbur, 66–87. Oxford: Oxford University Press, 2017. https://doi.org/10.1093/acprof:oso/9780198753438.001.0001.

Osiander, Andreas. "Sovereignty, International Relations, and the Westphalian Myth." *International Organization* 55, no. 2 (2001): 251–87. https://doi.org/10.1162/00208180151140577.

Oswin, Natalie. "Researching 'Gay Cape Town', Finding Value Added Queerness." *Social & Cultural Geoography* 6, no. 4 (August 2005): 567–87.

Ota, Ejitu N., Chinyere Ecoma, and Chiemela Godwin Wambu. "Creation of States in Nigeria, 1967-1996: Deconstructing the History and Politics." *American Research Journal of Humanities and Social Sciences* 6, no. 1 (April 2020): 1–8.

Otite, Onigu. *Ethnic Pluralism and Ethnicity in Nigeria: With Comparative Materials.* Ibadan, Nigeria: Shaneson, 1990.

———. *Ethnic Pluralism Ethnicity and Ethnic Conflict in Nigeria.* Ibadan: Shaneson, 2000.

Ottaway, Marina. "The New Moroccan Constitution: Real Change or More of the Same?" Carnegie Endowment for International Peace, June 20, 2011. https://carnegieendowment.org/2011/06/20/new-moroccan-constitution-real-change-or-more-of-same-pub-44731.

Oudenhuijsen, Loes. "Quietly Queer(Ing): The Normative Value of Sutura and Its Potential for Young Women in Urban Senegal." *Africa* 91, no. 3 (April 26, 2021): 434–52. https://doi.org/10.1017/S0001972021000243.

"Our History." De La Rue. Accessed December 8, 2021. https://www.delarue.com/about-us/our-history-orig.

Oviawe, Joan Osa. "Introduction: How to Rediscover the Ubuntu Paradigm in Education." *International Review of Education* 62, no. 1 (2016): 1–10.

Owino, Meshack, and J. M. Souther. "MaCleKi: Engaging the African Public in Their History, One Story at a Time" Blog. *Items: Insight from the Social Sciences.* Accessed February 9, 2022. https://items.ssrc.org/parameters/macleki-engaging-the-african-public-in-their-history-one-story-at-a-time.

Oyěwùmí, Oyèrónkẹ́. *The Invention of Women: Making an African Sense of Western Gender Discourses.* Minneapolis: University of Minnesota Press, 1997.

Oyoybaire, S. Egite. "On the Concept of Ethnicity and African Politics." *Présence Africaine*, no. 92 (1974): 178–89.

Palmberg, Mai. *Playing with Identities in Contemporary Music in Africa/Kirkegaard, Annemette.* Uppsala: Nordiska Afrikainstitutet in cooperation with the Sibelius Museum/Dept. of Musicology, Åbo Akademi University, Finland, 2002.

Paluck, Elizabeth Levy, and Donald P. Green. "Deference, Dissent, and Dispute Resolution: An Experimental Intervention Using Mass Media to Change Norms and Behavior in Rwanda." *American Political Science Review* 103, no. 4 (November 2009): 622–44. https://doi.org/10.1017/S0003055409990128.

Percival, Val, and Thomas Homer-Dixon. "Environmental Scarcity and Violent Conflict: The Case of South Africa." *Journal of Peace Research* 35, no. 3 (1998): 279–98.

Pérez, Efrén O. "Ricochet: How Elite Discourse Politicizes Racial and Ethnic Identities." *Political Behavior* 37, no. 1 (March 2015): 155–80.

Peyton, Nellie. "FEATURE—'Fighting for Survival', Senegal's Gay Community Is on Its Own." *Reuters*, September 27, 2018, sec. LGBT. https://www.reuters.com/article/senegal-lgbt-rights-idUSL8N1W454T.

Phillips, R. "Keywords." *TSQ: Transgender Studies Quarterly* 1, no. 1–2 (January 1, 2014): 19–21. https://doi.org/10.1215/23289252-2399470.

Pinxteren, Bert van. "African Identities: A New Perspective." African Studies Centre, Leiden University, 2018.

Pithouse, Richard Michael. "Forging New Political Identities in the Shanty Towns of Durban, South Africa." *Historical Materialism* 26, no. 2 (June 2018): 178–97. https://doi.org/10.1163/1569206x-00001644.

Plasse, Stéphanie. "Sénégal: les homosexuels traqués." *Afrik.com*, February 5, 2008. https://www.afrik.com/senegal-les-homosexuels-traques.

Plessis, Anton Du. "Exploring the Concept of Identity in World Politics." In *Politics of Identity and Exclusion in Africa: From Violent Confrontation to Peaceful Cooperation*, 13–25. Pretoria: University of Pretoria, 2001.

Pojman, Louis P. *Philosophy: The Pursuit of Wisdom.* Canada: Wadsworth, 2001.

Poku, Nana K. "Poverty, AIDS and the Politics of Response in Africa." *International Relations* 15, no. 3 (December 1, 2000): 390–452. https://doi.org/10.1177/004711 7800015003005.

Posner, Daniel N. *Institutions and Ethnic Politics in Africa.* Political Economy of Institutions and Decisions; Variation: Political Economy of Institutions and Decisions. Cambridge; New York: Cambridge University Press, 2005.

———. "Regime Change and Ethnic Cleavages in Africa." *Comparative Political Studies* 40, no. 11 (November 2007): 1302–27. https://doi.org/10.1177/0010414006291832.

———. "The Political Salience of Cultural Difference: Why Chewas and Tumbukas Are Allies in Zambia and Adversaries in Malawi." *The American Political Science Review* 98, no. 4 (2004): 529–45.

Post, Ken, and Michael Vickers. *Structure and Conflict in Nigeria, 1960-1965.* London: Heinemann, 1973.

Pottier, Johan. "Land Reform for Peace? Rwanda's 2005 Land Law in Context." *Journal of Agrarian Change* 6, no. 4 (2006): 509–37.

————. *Re-Imagining Rwanda: Conflict, Survival and Disinformation in the Late Twentieth Century.* African Studies Series 102. Cambridge [U.K.]; New York: Cambridge University Press, 2002.

"The Proposed Constitution of Ghana," February 1957. British Library Social Science Room.

Prunier, Gérard. *The Rwanda Crisis: History of a Genocide.* New York: Columbia University Press, 1995.

Pugliese, Joseph. "Permanent Revolution: Mohamed Bouazizi's Incendiary Ethics of Revolt." *Law, Culture and the Humanities* 10, no. 3 (2014): 408–20. https://doi.org/10.1177/1743872112448339.

Purdeková, Andrea. "'Even If I Am Not Here, There Are so Many Eyes': Surveillance and State Reach in Rwanda." *The Journal of Modern African Studies* 49, no. 3 (September 2011): 475–97. https://doi.org/10.1017/S0022278X11000292.

Putnam, Robert D. "Bowling Alone: America's Declining Social Capital." *Journal of Democracy* 6, no. 1 (1995): 65–78. https://doi.org/10.1353/jod.1995.0002.

Quamar, Md. Muddassir. "Tunisia: Presidential and Parliamentary Elections, 2014." *Contemporary Review of the Middle East* 2, no. 3 (September 1, 2015): 269–88. https://doi.org/10.1177/2347798915603277.

"Queen's Speech Debate on Address," November 6—November 23. British Library Social Science Room.

Rabinow, P., ed. *The Foucault Reader.* New York: Pantheon, 1984.

Raleigh, Clionadh, Braden Fuller, Danyal Kamal, Katerina Bozhinova, Sandra Pellegrini, Franklin Holcomb, Bhavani Castro, et al. "Ethiopia: At Risk of Multiplying Conflicts Stretching the Capacity of the State." Ten Conflicts to Worry About in 2021. Armed Conflict Location & Event Data Project, 2021. https://www.jstor.org.blume.stmarytx.edu:2048/stable/resrep28646.4.

Randall, Amy E. *Genocide and Gender in the Twentieth Century: A Comparative Survey.* London; New York: Bloomsbury Academic, 2015.

Refugees, United Nations High Commissioner for. "The State of the World's Refugees 2000: Fifty Years of Humanitarian Action—Chapter 10: The Rwandan Genocide and Its Aftermath." UNHCR. Accessed September 18, 2021. https://www.unhcr.org/publications/sowr/3ebf9bb60/state-worlds-refugees-2000-fifty-years-humanitarian-action-chapter-10-rwandan.html.

Reid, Graeme. "Angola Decriminalizes Same-Sex Conduct." Human Rights Watch, January 23, 2019. https://www.hrw.org/news/2019/01/23/angola-decriminalizes-same-sex-conduct.

Republic of Rwanda. "Constitution Republic of Rwanda," with Amendments through 2015 2013. https://www.constituteproject.org/constitution/Rwanda_2015.pdf?lang=en.

————. "Rwanda Decentralisation Strategic Framework: Towards a Sector-Wide Approach for Decentralization Implementation." Kigali: Ministry of Finance and Economic Planning, 2007. www.minecofin.gov.rw.

Reyntjens, Filip. *Again the Crossroads: Rwanda and Burundi, 2000-2001.* Translated by K. Couper. Current African Issues, 24 0280-2171. Uppsala: Nordiska Afrikainstitutet, 2001.

―――. *L'Afrique Des Grands Lacs En Crise: Rwanda, Burundi, 1988-1994*. Les Afriques. Paris: Karthala, 1994.

―――. "Rwanda: Genocide and Beyond." *Journal of Refugee Studies* 9, no. 3 (1996).

―――. "Rwanda, Ten Years On: From Genocide to Dictatorship." *African Affairs* 103, no. 411 (2004): 177–210.

―――. *Small States in an Unstable Region--Rwanda and Burundi, 1999-2000*. Current African Issues, no. 23. Uppsala: Nordiska Afrikainstitutet, 2000.

―――. *Talking or Fighting? Political Evolution in Rwanda and Burundi, 1998-1999*. Vol. 21. Current African Issues. Uppsala: Nordiska Afrikainstitutet, 1999.

Riedl, RB. "Transforming Politics, Dynamic Religion: Religion's Political Impact in Contemporary Africa." *African Conflict and Peacebuilding Review* 2, no. 2 (2012): 29–50. https://doi.org/10.2979/africonfpeacrevi.2.2.29.

Rimé, Bernard, Patrick Kanyangara, Vincent Yzerbyt, and Dario Paez. "The Impact of Gacaca Tribunals in Rwanda: Psychosocial Effects of Participation in a Truth and Reconciliation Process after a Genocide." *European Journal of Social Psychology* 41, no. 6 (October 2011): 695–706. https://doi.org/10.1002/ejsp.822.

Roberts, Madeleine. "HRC Releases Report on Violence Against Trans, GNC People." Human Rights Campaign, November 19, 2020. https://www.hrc.org/press-releases/marking-the-deadliest-year-on-record-hrc-releases-report-on-violence-against-transgender-and-gender-non-conforming-people.

Rodrik, Dani. *The Globalization Paradox: Democracy and the Future of the World Economy*. First published as a Norton paperback. New York, London: W.W. Norton & Company, 2011.

Rotberg, Robert I. "Overcoming Difficult Challenges: Bolstering Good Governance." *The ANNALS of the American Academy of Political and Social Science* 652, no. 1 (March 2014): 8–19. https://doi.org/10.1177/0002716213513542.

Rotberg, Robert I., and Ali Mazrui. *Protest and Power in Black Africa*. New York: Oxford University Press, 1970.

Ryan, Sarah. "The Dilemmas of Post-Identity Organizing: Unmaking Feminist Ties in Southern Rwanda." *Women & Language* 34, no. 2 (2011): 61–78.

Sadie, Yolanda. "Women, the Electoral System and Political Parties." In *Political Parties in South Africa*, edited by Heather A. Thuynsma, 47–71. Do They Undermine or Underpin Democracy? Africa Institute of South Africa, 2017. https://www.jstor.org.blume.stmarytx.edu:2048/stable/j.ctvh8r24c.11.

Sadiki, Larbi, and Youcef Bouandel. "The Post Arab Spring Reform: The Maghreb at a Crossroads." *Digest of Middle East Studies* 25, no. 1 (2016): 109–31. https://doi.org/10.1111/dome.12079.

Saleh, Heba. "Libya's Political Vacuum Opens Way for Isis, UN Envoy Warns." *Financial Times*, September 6, 2018. https://www.ft.com/content/8176b6fe-b1ed-11e8-8d14-6f049d06439c.

Sambanis, Nicholas. "Do Ethnic and Nonethnic Civil Wars Have the Same Causes? A Theoretical and Empirical Inquiry." *Journal of Conflict Resolution* 45, no. 3 (2001): 259–82.

Sambanis, Nicholas, and Moses Shayo. "Social Identification and Ethnic Conflict." *The American Political Science Review* 107, no. 2 (2013): 294–325.

Samson, Anne, Ana Paula Pires, and Dan Gilfoyle, eds. *There Came a Time: Essays on the Great War in Africa—Edited Collection*. Rickmansworth: The Great War in Africa Association/TSL Publications, 2018.

Sassen, Saskia. "Towards Post-National and Denationalized Citizenship." In *Handbook of Citizenship Studies*, edited by Engin F. Isin and Bryan S. Turner, 1st edition. London. Thousand Oaks, Calif: SAGE Publications Ltd, 2003.

———. "Denationalization." In *The Blackwell Encyclopedia of Sociology*. American Cancer Society, 2007. https://doi.org/10.1002/9781405165518.wbeosd028.

Sauti, Gloria. "The Limitations of Legalism and Identity Labels in Post-Apartheid South Africa." *Africanus* 49, no. 2 (November 30, 2019): 1–17. https://doi.org/10.25159/2663-6522/6429.

Schabas, William A. "Genocide Trials and Gacaca Courts." *Journal of International Criminal Justice* 3, no. 4 (September 1, 2005): 879–95. https://doi.org/10.1093/jicj/mqi062.

Schenk, Catherine R. *The Decline of Sterling: Managing the Retreat of an International Currency, 1945–1992*. Cambridge: Cambridge University Press, 2010.

Schmid, Alex. "Public Opinion Survey Data to Measure Sympathy and Support for Islamist Terrorism: A Look at Muslim Opinions on Al Qaeda and IS." *Terrorism and Counter-Terrorism Studies*, 2017. https://doi.org/10.19165/2017.1.02.

Scholte, Jan Aart. "Beyond the Buzzwords: Toward a Critical Theory of Globalization." In *Globalization: Theory and Practice*, edited by Eleonore Kofman and Gillian Youngs, 43–57. London: Pinter, 1996.

Searle, Martin Stanley. "Is Use of Cyber-Based Technology in Humanitarian Operations Leading to the Reduction of Humanitarian Independence?" Working Paper. Singapore: S. Rajaratnam School of International Studies, 2021.

Segal, Aaron. "A Look at Books." *Africa Today* 39, no. 3 (Quarter 1992): 121.

Semple, Kirk, and Lydia Polgreen. "Persecuted in Africa, Finding Refuge in New York." *The New York Times*, October 5, 2008, sec. New York. https://www.nytimes.com/2008/10/06/nyregion/06pape.html.

Senegal Criminal Code, 319.3 § (1965).

Serneels, Pieter, and Tomas Lievens. "Microeconomic Institutions and Personnel Economics for Health Care Delivery: A Formal Exploration of What Matters to Health Workers in Rwanda." *Human Resources for Health* 16, no. 7 (January 26, 2018): 1-N.PAG. https://doi.org/10.1186/s12960-017-0261-9.

Serrato, Gabriela. "The Lynching Era: The Tragic Hanging of Laura and L. D. Nelson." *StMU Research Scholars*, February 14, 2017. https://stmuscholars.org/the-lynching-era-the-tragic-hanging-of-laura-and-l-d-nelson/.

———. "The Young and Courageous: Ruby Bridges." *StMU Research Scholars*, October 15, 2017. https://stmuscholars.org/the-young-and-courageous-ruby-bridges/.

Servant, Jean-Christophe. "Homosexuels: Cibles Émouvantes, Boucs Émissaires." *Le Monde Diplomatique* (blog), October 21, 2009. https://blog.mondediplo.net//2009-10-21-Homosexuels-cibles-emouvantes-boucs-emissaires.

Simpson, Andrew. *Language and National Identity in Africa*. [Oxford Linguistics]; Variation: Oxford Linguistics. Oxford; New York: Oxford University Press, 2008.

Small, Melvin, and J. David Singer. *Resort to Arms: International and Civil Wars, 1816-1980*. Beverly Hills, Calif/.: SAGE Publications, Inc, 1982.

Soccio, Douglas J. *Archetypes of Wisdom: An Introduction to Philosophy*. 4th ed. Australia; Belmont, Calif.: Wadsworth, 2001.

Solomon, Ty. "Norms and Human Rights in International Relations." *Political Studies Review* 4, no. 1 (January 2006): 36–47. https://doi.org/10.1111/j.1478-9299.2006.00038.x.

Soriano, Josemaria. "The Power of a Ball: How Soccer Star Didier Drogba Ended the Côte d'Ivoire Civil War." *StMU Research Scholars*, October 24, 2017. https://stmuscholars.org/the-power-of-a-ball-how-soccer-star-didier-drogba-ended-the-cote-divoire-civil-war/.

Spinner, Jackie. "How Morocco Has Weakened Its Press, Pushing Readers to Social Media for News." *Pulitzer Center*, January 2, 2018. https://pulitzercenter.org/stories/how-morocco-has-weakened-its-press-pushing-readers-social-media-news.

Stack, John F. *Ethnic Mobilization in World Politics: The Primordial Perspective*. Greenwood Press, 1986. https://ecollections.law.fiu.edu/faculty_books/247.

Stack, John F., and Christopher L. Warren. "Ethnicity and the Politics of Symbolism in Miami's Cuban Community." *Cuban Studies* 20 (1990): 11–28.

Staub, Ervin. "A World without Genocide: Prevention, Reconciliation, and the Creation of Peaceful Societies." *Journal of Social Issues* 69, no. 1 (March 2013): 180–99. https://doi.org/10.1111/josi.12010.

———. "Building a Peaceful Society: Origins, Prevention, and Reconciliation After Genocide and Other Group Violence." *American Psychologist* 68, no. 7 (October 2013): 576–89. https://doi.org/10.1037/a0032045.

———. *Inclusive Caring, Moral Courage, Altruism Born of Suffering, Active Bystandership, and Heroism*. New York, NY: Oxford University Press, 2016.

———. "Justice, Healing, and Reconciliation: How the People's Courts in Rwanda Can Promote Them." *Peace & Conflict* 10, no. 1 (March 2004): 25–32. https://doi.org/10.1207/s15327949pac1001_2.

———. *Overcoming Evil: Genocide, Violent Conflict, and Terrorism*. Oxford; New York: Oxford University Press, 2011.

———. "Promoting Healing and Reconciliation in Rwanda, and Generating Active Bystandership by Police to Stop Unnecessary Harm by Fellow Officers." *Perspectives on Psychological Science* 14, no. 1 (January 2019): 60–64. https://doi.org/10.1177/1745691618809384.

———. *The Roots of Evil: The Origins of Genocide and Other Group Violence*. Cambridge [England]; New York: Cambridge University Press, 1989.

Staub, Ervin, and Laurie Anne Pearlman. "Reducing Intergroup Prejudice and Conflict: A Commentary." *Journal of Personality & Social Psychology* 96, no. 3 (March 2009): 588–93. https://doi.org/10.1037/a0014045.

Staub, Ervin, Laurie Anne Pearlman, Alexandra Gubin, and Athanase Hagengimana. "Healing, Reconciliation, Forgiving and the Prevention of Violence After Genocide or Mass Killing: An Intervention and Its Experimental Evaluation in Rwanda."

Journal of Social & Clinical Psychology 24, no. 3 (May 2005): 297–334. https://
doi.org/10.1521/jscp.24.3.297.65617.

Staub, Ervin, Laurie Anne Pearlman, and Vachel Miller. "Healing the Roots of
Genocide in Rwanda." *Peace Review* 15, no. 3 (September 2003): 287–94. https://
doi.org/10.1080/1040265032000130878.

"Sterling Devalued against the Nigerian Sterling," *Daily Times of Nigeria.* November
21, 1967.

Stiglitz, Joseph E. *Globalization and Its Discontents.* New York: W.W. Norton, 2003.

Stockwell, Sarah. *The British End of the British Empire.* Cambridge: Cambridge
University Press, 2018.

Straus, Scott. "Background to the Genocide." In *The Order of Genocide: Race,
Power, and War in Rwanda,* 17–40. Ithaca: Cornell University Press, 2006.

———. "Conclusion." In *The Order of Genocide: Race, Power, and War in Rwanda,*
224–26. Ithaca: Cornell University Press, 2006.

———. *The Order of Genocide: Race, Power, and War in Rwanda.* Ithaca: Cornell
University Press, 2006.

———. "Why Perpetrators Say They Committed Genocide." In *The Order of
Genocide: Race, Power, and War in Rwanda,* 122–52. Ithaca: Cornell University
Press, 2006.

Suberu, Rotimi T. "States' Creation and the Political Economy of Nigerian
Federalism." In *Federalism and Political Restructuring in Nigeria,* edited by
Kunle Amuwo, 276–96. Ibadan, Nigeria: Spectrum Books; St. Helier: Safari Books
(Export); Oxford: African Books Collective (distributor), 1998.

Sullivan, Amy. "Rwanda's 'Miracle' of Forgiveness." *USA Today,*
February 15, 2010. https://www.pressreader.com/usa/usa-today-us-edit
ion/20100215/282729108048373.

Sun News Online. "Ex-Commissioner, Don Kick against Pay Rise for Political
Office Holders." *The Sun Nigeria,* February 7, 2020, sec. National. https://www.
sunnewsonline.com/ex-commissioner-don-kick-against-pay-rise-for-political-
office-holders/.

Tar, Usman A., Etham B. Mijah, and Moses E. U. Tedheke, eds. *Globalization in
Africa: Perspectives on Development, Security, and the Environment.* London:
Lexington Books, 2016.

Taras, Ray. *Understanding Ethnic Conflict: The International Dimension/Ganguly,
Rajat.* New York: Longman, 2002.

Tarc, Paul. "The Uses of Globalization in the (Shifting) Landscape of Educational
Studies." *Canadian Journal of Education/Revue Canadienne de l'éducation* 35,
no. 3 (2012): 4–29.

Teeple, Gary. "What Is Globalization?" In *Globalization and Its Discontents,* edited
by Stephen McBride and John Richard Wiseman. Houndmills, Basingstoke,
Hampshire: New York: Macmillan Press; St. Martin's Press, 2000.

Tempels, Placide. *Bantu Philosophy.* Paris: Présence africaine, 1959.

Thamm, Natalie. "Colonialism: Dead or Rebranded? Re-Emerging Patterns of
Destruction in the DRC." *STMU Research Scholars* (blog), April 7, 2019. https://
stmuscholars.org/colonialism-dead-or-rebranded/.

———. "'Doctor Miracle': Denis Mukwege, Healing Women, Children, and Communities." *STMU Research Scholars* (blog), April 7, 2019. https://stmuscholars. org/doctor-miracle-denis-mukwege/.

———. "Kwibuka: Remembering the 1994 Rwandan Genocide." *STMU Research Scholars* (blog), April 8, 2018. https://stmuscholars.org/rwandan-genocide/.

Tharoor, Ishaan. "Gambia's President Threatens to Slit the Throats of Gay Men." *Washington Post*, May 12, 2015. https://www.washingtonpost.com/news/worldviews/wp/2015/05/12/gambias-president-threatens-to-slit-the-throats-of-gay-men/.

"The Implications of Exchange Control." *Financial Times*, July 7, 1961, 5.

"The Proposed Constitution of Ghana," February 1957. British Library Social Science Room.

"They Like the Sterling Area." *The Economist*, March 5, 1960, 929.

Thomas, Charles, and Toyin Falola, eds. *Secession and Separatist Conflicts in Postcolonial Africa*. Calgary, Alberta: University of Calgary Press, 2020.

Thomson, Susan. "The Darker Side of Transitional Justice: The Power Dynamics Behind Rwanda's Gacaca Courts." *Africa* 81, no. 3 (August 2011): 373–90. https://doi.org/10.1017/S0001972011000222.

Thorpe, Earl E. *Black Historians: A Critique*. New York: William Morrow, 1970.

Thuynsma, Heather A., ed. *Political Parties in South Africa: Do They Undermine or Underpin Democracy?* Pretoria: Africa Institute of South Africa, 2017. https://doi.org/10.2307/j.ctvh8r24c.

"Tighter Exchange Control." *Economist*, July 15, 1961, 275.

Tijerina, Roberto. "Black Codes, Jim Crow, and Social Control in the South." *StMU Research Scholars*, March 22, 2017. https://stmuscholars.org/the-south-and-vigilante-justice/.

Tomas, Louisa, Cliff Jackson, and Karen Carlisle. "The Transformative Potential of Engaging in Science Inquiry-Based Challenges." *Teaching Science: The Journal of the Australian Science Teachers Association* 60, no. 2 (June 2014): 48–57.

Tripp, Aili Mari. "New Trends in Women's Political Participation in Africa," 2001. https://citeseerx.ist.psu.edu/viewdoc/download?doi=10.1.1.542.5398&rep=rep1&type=pdf.

Tripp, Aili Mari, Isabel Casimiro, Joy Kwesiga, and Alice Mungwa. "Preface." In *African Women's Movements: Transforming Political Landscapes*, xi–xvi. Cambridge: Cambridge University Press, 2008.

Tsabora, James. "Fighting the 'Resource Wars' in the Democratic Republic of the Congo: An Exploratory Diagnosis of the Legal and Institutional Problems." *The Comparative and International Law Journal of Southern Africa* 47, no. 1 (March 2014): 109–28.

Tunisia Constitution (2014). https://www.constituteproject.org/constitution/Tunisia_2014.pdf.

Tutu, Desmond. *No Future without Forgiveness*. London: Rider, 1999.

Tymoigne, Eric. "Monetary Sovereignty: Nature, Implementation, and Implications." *Public Budgeting & Finance* 40, no. 3 (2020): 49–71. https://doi.org/10.1111/pbaf.12265.

Uche, Maureen Ada. Centuries-old traditional "Song to Welcome the Birth of a Child" lyrics from the oral traditions of the Igbo people, written from memory and translated into English by the author, professor of music and traditional singer, March 2019.

———. Centuries-old traditional "Slay Song" from the oral traditions of the Igbo people, written from memory and translated into English by the author, professor of music and traditional singer, March 2019.

Uchechukwu, P.A., E.U. Ibekwe, N.M. Obi, and C. Okoye, eds. *The Humanities and National Identity*. Awka: Fab Anieh, 2013.

Udoh, Isaac. "The Integrity of Traditional Music in the Nigerian Society': A Case Study of Annang Music." *Nsukka Journal of Musical Arts Research* 1 (2012): 119–30.

Ukpokolo, Chinyere. *Being and Becoming: Gender, Culture and Shifting Identity in Sub-Saharan Africa*. Denver, CO: Spears Media Press, 2016.

Ukpong, Cletus. "Herders Killed More Nigerians in 2018 than Boko Haram—Report." *Premium Times*, November 21, 2019. https://www.premiumtimesng.com/news/headlines/364355-herders-killed-more-nigerians-in-2018-than-boko-haram-report.html.

Umezinwa, E.C., K.L. Nwadialor, and I.L. Umeanolue, eds. *Humanities and African Values*. Awka: Fab Anieh, 2016.

UN Human Rights Council. "Convention on the Elimination of All Forms of Discrimination against Women." Accessed November 8, 2021. https://www.ohchr.org/EN/ProfessionalInterest/Pages/CEDAW.aspx.

———. "OHCHR | UPR Highlights 6 February 2009 Pm," February 6, 2009. https://www.ohchr.org/EN/HRBodies/UPR/Pages/Highlights6February2009pm.aspx.

UN Women. "Facts and Figures: Women's Leadership and Political Participation." UN Women. Accessed December 6, 2021. https://www.unwomen.org/en/what-we-do/leadership-and-political-participation/facts-and-figures.

UNAIDS. "Country Factsheets Senegal 2020." UNAIDS. Accessed July 29, 2021. https://www.unaids.org/en/regionscountries/countries/senegal.

———. "Senegal." UNAIDS, Continually updated. https://www.unaids.org/en/keywords/senegal-0.

UNDP, ed. *Human Development to Eradicate Poverty*. New York: Oxford Univ. Press, 1997.

United Nations Development Programme. "Human Development Indices and Indicators: 2018 Statistical Update." *Human Development Indices and Indicators 2018*. United Nations, 2018. https://www.un-ilibrary.org/content/books/9789210474313c003.

———. "Population with at Least Some Secondary Education, Female (% Ages 25 and Older)." United Nations Development Programme, 2020. http://hdr.undp.org/en/indicators/23906.

United Nations General Assembly. "International Day of Reflection on the 1994 Genocide against the Tutsi in Rwanda." United Nations, December 12, 2017. https://www.undocs.org/A/72/L.31.

United Nations High Commission for Refugees (UNHCR). "The Rwandan Genocide and Its Aftermath." The State of The World's Refugees 2000: Fifty Years of Humanitarian Action, January 1, 2000. https://www.unhcr.org/3ebf9bb60.html.

United Nations Security Council. "Report of the Panel of Experts on the Illegal Exploitation of Natural Resources and Other Forms of Wealth of DR Congo—Democratic Republic of the Congo," April 12, 2001. https://reliefweb.int/report/democratic-republic-congo/report-panel-experts-illegal-exploitation-natural-resources-and.

———. Resolution 1970 (2011), S/RES/1970 § (2011). https://www.nato.int/nato_static_fl2014/assets/pdf/pdf_2011_02/20110927_110226-UNSCR-1970.pdf.

———. Resolution 1973 (2011), S/RES/1973 § (2011). https://www.nato.int/nato_static/assets/pdf/pdf_2011_03/20110927_110311-UNSCR-1973.pdf.

———. Resolution 2009 (2011), S/RES/2009 (2011) § (2011). https://www.nato.int/nato_static_fl2014/assets/pdf/pdf_2011_09/20110927_110916-UNSCR-2009.pdf.

———. Resolution 2150 (2014), S/RES/2150 (2014) § (2014). https://www.securitycouncilreport.org/atf/cf/%7B65BFCF9B-6D27-4E9C-8CD3-CF6E4FF96FF9%7D/s_res_2150.pdf.

United States Central Intelligence Agency. "Nigeria: Adminstrative Divisions." In *The World Factbook*. Central Intelligence Agency, October 19, 2021. https://www.cia.gov/the-world-factbook/countries/nigeria.

United States Department of State. "Country Reports on Terrorism 2012." Washington, D.C. Bureau of Counterterrorism, 2014. //2009-2017.state.gov/j/ct/rls/crt/2012/index.htm.

Usanov, Artur, Marjolein de Ridder, Willem Auping, Stephanie Lingemann, Luis Tercero Espinoza, Magnus Ericsson, Masuma Farooki, Henrike Sievers, and Maren Liedtke. "The Democratic Republic of Congo." Hague Centre for Strategic Studies, 2013.

Uvin, Peter. "The Development/Peacebuilding Nexus: A Typology and History of Changing Paradigms." *Journal of Peacebuilding & Development* 1, no. 1 (September 2002): 5–24. https://doi.org/10.1080/15423166.2002.979203266676.

Uwimbabazi, Penine. "An Analysis of Umuganda: The Policy and Practice of Community Work in Rwanda." Dissertation for the College of Humanities, University of KwaZulu-Natal, 2012.

Uwimbabazi, Penine, and R. Lawrence. "Compelling Factors of Urbanization and Rural-Urban Migration in Rwanda." *Rwanda Journal*, Series B: Social Sciences, 22 (2011): 9–26.

Uya, O., ed. *Perspectives and Methods of Studying African History: Papers Presented at the History Week, University of Calabar, 1976-1979*. Enugu, Nigeria: Fourth Dimension Publishers, 1984.

———, ed. "Trends and Perspectives in African History." In *Perspectives and Methods of Studying African History*, 1–9. Enugu, Nigeria: Fourth Dimension Publishers, 1984.

Van Evera, Stephen. "Primordialism Lives!" *APSA-CP: Newsletter of the Organized Section in Comperative Politics of the American Political Science Association* 12, no. 1 (2001): 20–22.

Vanden-Berger, Pierre L. *Race and Racism: A Comparative Perspective*. New York: John Willey, 1967.

Vanger, Emmanuel Terngu, and Bernard Ugochukwu Nwosu. "Institutional Parameters That Condition Farmer–Herder Conflicts in Tivland of Benue State, Nigeria." *African Security Review* 29, no. 1 (January 2, 2020): 20–40. https://doi.org/10.108 0/10246029.2020.1763413.

Veenhoven, Ruut, ed. *Case Studies on Human Rights and Fundamental Freedoms: A World Survey: 2*. The Hague: Springer, 1975.

Vendatam, Shankar. "Romeo & Juliet in Rwanda | Hidden Brain Media." Hidden Brain. Accessed September 2, 2021. https://hiddenbrain.org/podcast/romeo-juliet-in-rwanda/.

Verwimp, Philip. "An Economic Profile of Peasant Perpetrators of Genocide: Micro-Level Evidence from Rwanda." *Journal of Development Economics* 77, no. 2 (2005): 297–323.

Vinson, Laura Thaut. "Disaggregating Ethnicity and Conflict Patterns: Evidence from Religious and Tribal Violence in Nigeria." *Ethnopolitics* 19, no. 1 (2020): 19–44. https://doi.org/10.1080/17449057.2018.1536376.

Voice of America. "Senegalese Court to Try Teenagers for Homosexuality | Voice of America—English." *Voice of America*, November 2, 2009, sec. Archive. https://www.voanews.com/archive/senegalese-court-try-teenagers-homosexuality.

Volf, Miroslav. "A Vision of Embrace." *Ecumenical Review* 47, no. 2 (April 1995): 195. https://doi.org/10.1111/j.1758-6623.1995.tb03698.x.

Vorster, Nico. "Land, Group Identities and Competing Justice Values in South Africa: Reformed Perspectives on Embracive Justice and Permeable Identity Formation." *In Die Skriflig/In Luce Verbi* 53, no. 1 (January 31, 2019): 1–7. https://doi.org/10.4102/ids.v53i1.2398.

Waas, Laura van. "The Stateless Tebu of Libya?" Tilburg Law School Research Paper. Rochester, NY: Social Science Research Network, May 24, 2013. https://doi.org/10.2139/ssrn.2269569.

Wæver, Ole. "Aberystwyth, Paris, Copenhagen: New Schools in Security Theory and the Origins between Core and Periphery." Montreal, 2004.

Walker, Kathryn. "Resolving Debates over the Status of Ethnic Identities during Transitional Justice." *Contemporary Political Theory* 11, no. 1 (2012): 68–87. https://doi.org/10.1057/cpt.2011.7.

Walker, Tim. "How Uganda Was Seduced by Anti-Gay Conservative Evangelicals." *The Independent*, March 14, 2014. https://www.independent.co.uk/news/world/africa/how-uganda-was-seduced-anti-gay-conservative-evangelicals-9193593.html.

Wan, Enoch, and Mark Vanderwerf. "A Review of the Literature on Ethnicity, National Identity and Related Missiological Studies." *Global Missiology*, 2009, 58.

Watanabe, Lisa. "Libya's Future: Uncertain, Despite a Political Agreement." *Middle East Policy* 23, no. 4 (2016): 114–22. https://doi.org/10.1111/mepo.12237.

Waters-Bayer, Ann, and Wolfgang Bayer. "Coming to Terms: Interactions between Immigrant Fulani Cattle-Keepers and Indigenous Farmers in Nigeria's Subhumid Zone." *Cahiers d'Études Africaines* 34, no. 133/135 (1994): 213–29.

Wehrey, Frederic, and Peter Cole. "Building Libya's Security Sector." Carnegie Endowment for International Peace, August 6, 2013. https://carnegieendowment. org/2013/08/06/building-libya-s-security-sector-pub-52603.

Weingast, Barry R. "The Political Foundations of Democracy and the Rule of Law." *The American Political Science Review* 91, no. 2 (1997): 245–63. https://doi. org/10.2307/2952354.

Weiss, Meredith L., and Michael J. Bosia, eds. *Global Homophobia: States, Movements, and the Politics of Oppression.* Urbana, IL: University of Illinois Press, 2013.

Wendt, Alexander. "Constructing International Politics." *International Security* 20, no. 1 (1995): 71. https://doi.org/10.2307/2539217.

Wikipedia. "Federalism in Nigeria." In *Wikipedia*, June 20, 2021. https://en.wikipedia. org/w/index.php?title=Federalism_in_Nigeria&oldid=1029514291.

World Bank. *Disabled Ex-Combatants in Rwanda Regain Their Independence and Rebuild Their Lives.* YouTube video, 2019. https://www.youtube.com/ watch?v=yU1jywurfZE.

World Vision. *No One To Turn To: Life for Children in Eastern DRC.* Embedded Metadata, 2014. https://www.worldvision.org/about-us/media-center/ no-one-turn-life-children-eastern-drc.

Wright, William D. *Black History and Black Identity: A Call for a New Historiography.* Westport, Conn.: Praeger, 2002.

Yazidi, Ahlem. "The Death of My Cousin and the Birth of a New Tunisia." In *Voices of the Arab Spring: Personal Stories from the Arab Revolutions*, edited by Asaad Alsaleh. New York: Columbia University Press, 2015.

Yeros, P., ed. *Ethnicity and Nationalism in Africa: Constructivist Reflections and Contemporary Politics.* London: Palgrave Macmillan UK, 1999. https://doi. org/10.1007/978-1-349-27155-9.

Young, Crawford. "Evolving Models of Consciousness and Ideology: Nationalism and Ethnicity." In *Political Development and the New Realism in Sub-Saharan Africa*, edited by David E. Apter and Carl Gustav Rosberg, 61–86. Charlottesville: University Press of Virginia, 1994.

Young, Iris Marion. *Inclusion and Democracy.* Repr. Oxford Political Theory. Oxford: Oxford University Press, 2000.

Yurcaba, Jo. "Gay Iranian Man Dead in Alleged 'Honor Killing,' Rights Group Says." *NBC News*, May 11, 2021. https://www.nbcnews.com/feature/nbc-out/ gay-iranian-man-dead-alleged-honor-killing-rights-group-says-n1266995.

Zaid, Bouziane. "Internet and Democracy in Morocco: A Force for Change and an Instrument for Repression." *Global Media and Communication* 12, no. 1 (2016): 49–66. https://doi.org/10.1177/1742766515626826.

Zeleza, Paul Tiyambe. "The Inventions of African Identities and Languages: The Discursive and Developmental Implications," 14–26. Somerville, MA: Cascadilla Proceedings Project, 2006. http://www.lingref.com/cpp/acal/36/www.lingref.com/ cpp/acal/36/abstract1402.html.

Zimmermann, Claus D. *A Contemporary Concept of Monetary Sovereignty.* Oxford: Oxford University Press, 2014.

Zwitter, Andrej. "Constitutional Reform and Emergency Powers in Egypt and Tunisia." *Middle East Law and Governance* 7, no. 2 (August 31, 2015): 257–84. https://doi.org/10.1163/18763375-00702003.

Index

About the Editors and Contributors

EDITORS

Toyin Falola (Ph.D.) is the Jacob and Frances Mossiker Chair in the Humanities at the University of Texas at Austin. Previously he has held teaching positions at the University of Cambridge, York University, and Australian National University. Falola is a Fellow of the Historical Society of Nigeria and Nigerian Academy of Letters. He has also served as the President of African Studies Association, United States. His notable publications include *Colonialism and Violence in Nigeria* (2009); *Nationalism and African Intellectuals* (2001); *Key Events in African History: A Reference Guide* (2002); and *The African Diaspora: Slavery, Modernity, and Globalization* (2013). The University of Michigan Press has published two of his memoirs: *A Mouth Sweeter Than Salt: An African Memoir* (2004) and *Counting the Tiger's Teeth: An African Teenager's Story* (2014). Professor Falola has published many edited books and many articles, for a complete list of his publications and many achievements, visit https://toyinfalolanetwork.org/biography/.

Céline A. Jacquemin (Ph.D.)—Dr. Céline, as she is known by her students—is a Professor of International Relations in the Department of Political Science at St Mary's University in San Antonio. She served as Associate Dean in the School of Humanities and Social Sciences from 2009 to 2019 and as Chair of the Department of Political Science from 2017–2020. Her expertise covers parts of Europe and the Great Lakes of Africa where she more closely studies democratization, human rights, and empowerment, particularly in Rwanda. She also explores the plight of Berbers in North Africa where she examines forms of peaceful political resistance by Kabyles, or Berbers, the indigenous population of North Africa, in the face of oppression resulting from policies of Islamization and Arabization by the Algerian government. She teaches graduate and undergraduate courses on African Security and African Politics respectively, and on Democratization, International Relations Theory, International Political Economy, Political Science Senior Seminars, and on Civic Engagement. She has testified as a pro-bono expert witness for political asylum cases linked to female genital mutilation practices and other human rights violations for several nonprofit organizations. Her recent publications include in 2019 a chapter entitled "Kabyle Resistance and Berber Oppression" in *Oppression and Resistance in Africa and the Diaspora*, edited by Kenneth Kalu & Toyin Falola for the series published by Routledge on Global Africa; in 2016 a chapter on "The Politics of Mixing Evangelizing with Education & Development: Marianist Projects in Kenya" in *Contentious Politics in Africa: Identity, Conflict, and Social Change* edited by Toyin Falola & Wanjala Nasong'o, by Durham: Carolina Academic Press; and in 2015 a chapter on "Hegemony and Counter-Hegemony: Colonial and Post-Colonial Roots of the Rwandan Genocide" in *The Roots of Ethnic Conflict in Africa: From Grievance to Violence* edited by Wanjala S. Nasong'o, Palgrave Macmillan.

Her newest research brings her back to East Africa where she continues assessing democratization through development and through the professionalization of institutions. She focuses on identity politicization, mobilization, and transformation processes that strengthen educational and democratic institutions.

CONTRIBUTORS

Tolulope Adeogun (Ph.D.) is a senior researcher who writes passionately on women's issues, especially in the area of women's inclusion in decision making and peace building in Africa. She has published many articles in reputable journals such as *Women's Studies International Forum, AGENDA, Journal of Gender, Information and Development in Africa (JGIDA)*, among others.

Adeogun received her first, second and third degree In Political Science while her research interests lie at the intersection of politics, gender and peacebuilding, with a particular focus on the roles of women's organizations in peacebuilding.

Victor Adesiyan (Ph.D.) was born at Owobaale, in Ibadan, where he attended elementary and Secondary Schools. He went to The Polytechnic Ibadan, for his Higher National Diploma in Secretarial Administration, and Olabisi Onabanjo University, Ago-Iwoye, for M.Sc in Industrial Relations and Human Resources. He proceeded to Babcock University for M.Phil &

PhD in Political Science with emphasis in Peace and Conflict Studies. He is immediate past Chair, Ogun State Chapter of Society for Peace and Practice. A Senior faculty member in the Department of Political Science and Public Administration, Babcock University, Nigeria, where he has been teaching for more than a decade. He has attended conferences and presented papers within and outside Nigeria and has several publications in reputable local and international journals to his credit.

Bamidele Aly (three M.A.s. plus one M.Phil.) is a French-Nigerian economic historian specializing in the monetary history of anglophone West Africa, the Nigerian diaspora in Europe and West Africa,and African economic development. She holds a Master Degree in Marketing and Management from La Sorbonne Nouvelle (Paris III) in Paris, and a Master in European Business from ESCP Business School, completed in Oxford and Berlin. She also completed an MA in African History at Panthéon-Sorbonne University (Paris I) in 2015, focusing on the introduction of the Sterling in Southern Nigeria (1880–1919). She graduated with an MPhil in Economics on "Monetary Creations in Nigeria as a tool of war and identity (1967–1974)" with a research grant from the Mission Historique de la Banque de France (Historical Mission of the French central Bank). Her published work include: "'Top Up, as You Go!' Mobile Telephony and the Internet Revolution in Sub-Saharan Africa" (2017), "The Status of the West African Sterling in southern Nigeria in 1916." (2018) She held a number of roles analyzing trade finance and derivatives transactions, banks, NBFIs (exchanges, pension funds, mutual funds, private equity funds, securitization vehicles, and structured investment vehicles), hedge funds, supranationals, central banks, countries and sovereigns in a number of organizations.

Patricia Ogugua Anwuluorah (Ph.D.) is currently the Director of Research and Publications, and a Chief Lecturer in Social Ethics in the Department of Religion and Cultural Studies, Nwafor Orizu College of Education, Nsugbe, Anambra State, an Affiliate of the University of Nigeria Nsukka in Enugu State. Dr. Anwuluorah Ogugua Patricia hails from Nkwelle Village Umunachi, Dunukofia Local Government Area of Anambra State. Anwuluorah holds a B.A (Hons.) Religious Studies, University of Leuven, Belgium; M.A and a Ph.D. from University of Ibadan; and a PGDE, Nnamdi Azikiwe University, Awka. She has served the College in various capacities: Head of Department Christian Religious Studies: 2005–2007; Dean School of Arts Social Sciences: (2007–2009); Dean School of General Studies Education (2011–2014); Director, Research and Publications (2018 to date); Chairman and Member of over 30 Committees. She has also attended both National and International Conferences/Workshops including: the University of Ghana,

Boston College U.S.A, Catholic University of America, the University of London, University of Boston, Massachusetts, University of Riverside, California, Catholic University of Australia, and Dubai. She has over sixty publications in journals, book, book chapters; and edited several journals and chapters in books. Currently, she is an external examiner in Federal College of Education Owerri, Imo state, a member of Circle for Concerned African Women Theologians (The Circle) South Africa/Ghana; National Association of Bible Knowledge Teachers of Nigeria (NABKTN); National Association for the Study of Religion and Education (NASRED); National Association for the Advancement of Knowledge (NAFAK); Women in Colleges of Education (WICE); Member, Member of the Research and Development Network.

Jude Chinwuba Asike (Ph.D.) is a lecturer of Philosophy and Africa Studies. He teaches in the Department of Philosophy, Faculty of Humanities, at the University of Port Harcourt, Nigeria. He is also an African Studies scholar and has vested interests in Public Policy and its impact on African Culture, Conflict, Politics and Development. He is currently conducting research on the African Institutional Development Imperatives. His teaching experiences span as a career in the following institutions: Nwafor Orizu College of Education, an Affiliate the University of Nigeria Nsukka (2000–2008); Visiting Research Scholar at the Center for Global Education, Council for Research in Values and Philosophy, Catholic University of America (2009); Research Scholar, Department of African Studies, Howard University, USA (2009–2010); Lecturer, Department of Philosophy, College of Arts and Sciences, Howard University (2010–2014); and a lecturer, Department of Philosophy, University of Port Harcourt (2014–to date). His special core competence is on the politico-logical principles of state and conflicts in Africa, most especially in the Nigeria Federation. He has published and has presented papers at several national and international conferences.

Abidemi Abiola Isola (Ph.D.) is a Senior Lecturer in the Department of Political Science and Public Administration, Babcock University, Nigeria. Her teaching, research interests and area of specialization include: Public administration, sociology, women and gender studies. She has several publications to her credit, some of which have appeared in respected international journals such as the *Journal of Interdisciplinary Feminist Thought,* and the *Journal of Gender, Information, and Development in Africa (JGIDA).*

Auroara Nikkels is pursuing her graduate education at St. Mary's University in the International Relations Master's Program and specializes in Security Studies. Nikkels has published nine articles on the St. Mary's University History Media website (now the StMU Research Scholars online publication https://stmuscholars.org/), including four pieces that focused on the Middle East and North Africa region (MENA). She previously earned her Bachelor's in Political Science-Security Studies with a minor in Sociology during which she also completed an internship with a San Antonio nonprofit organization called *Students of Service*. *SOS* focuses on creating global citizens through local service and education. She has continued volunteering with *SOS* over the past year despite Covid. She currently works with another nonprofit organization in San Antonio called *Culturingua*, which focuses on the language and culture of both the MENA and South Asian regions.

Kialee Nyiayaana (Ph.D.) is a senior lecturer in the Department of Political and Administrative Studies, University of Port Harcourt, Nigeria. He was a research fellow at the Centre of Criminology, University of Cape Town, between January and March 2015. He was also an African Leadership Centre's Peace, Security and Development Fellow at King's College, London, between September 2013 and October 2014. Dr. Nyiayaana was awarded the 2008/2009 Junior Fulbright Fellowship, which was tenable at the Department of Conflict Analysis and Resolution, Graduate School of Humanities and Social Sciences, Nova Southeastern University, Florida. His teaching, research interests and area of specialization include: Ethnic identity politics and conflicts in Nigeria; the United Nations in international peace-building; conflict resolution, armed conflicts and small arms proliferation. He has several publications to his credit, some of which have appeared in respected international journals such as *African Security*.

Soj Ojo (Ph.D.) received his doctorate in Political Science from the University of Benin, Nigeria in 1995. He is a Professor of Political Science in the Department of Political Science, Ambrose Alli University, Ekpoma. His area of specialization, teaching, research interest and publications are majorly in comparative politics, political development, public policy, democratic and election studies, as well as politics of ethno-cultural pluralism and identity. Prof. Ojo has held numerous positions of responsibility within and outside his university. They include, Head, Department of Political Science 1997–1999; Director, University Consultancy Services 1999-2004; Member, University Governing Council 1999-2003; Director, Ford Foundation-supported Institute for Governance and Development 2010-2013 and Dean, Faculty of Social Sciences 2013-2016. Prof. Ojo has also served as Chair of various National Universities Commission (NUC) and accreditation panels for the evaluation of Political Science programs in some Universities in Nigeria. With a sustained academic career of teaching and research spanning over three decades, Prof. Ojo has several journal articles, technical papers and edited books to his credit. Venerable Prof. Ojo who is also an ordained Priest of the

Anglican Communion has just recently retired from the services of Ambrose Alli University, Ekpoma, upon attainment of the mandatory retirement age.

Hon. Olanrewaju Atanda Orija (M.A.) is an independent researcher, an applied social scientist, secretariat administrator, socio-political analysts, and a local government, legislator in Ogun State, Southwest Nigeria. He holds a master's degree from the department of Political Science of the prestigious Obafemi Awolowo University, Ile-Ife, Osun State, Nigeria. His research interests and areas of specialization include Public Management Networks, Politics of Intergovernmental Relations, Local Government Administration, and Collaborative Governance. He has vast skills and capacity in didactic and pedagogical training methods, student-centered and collaborative learning process. He is a professional member of various learned associations, among which include Nigerian Political Science Association (NPSA). He is a German certified Dual Vocational Education Trainer (DVET) in Professional Office Administration, Project Management, and as well recently trained in the art of Competence Based Curriculum Development. He has attended conferences and has to his credit several journal articles in local and international outlets, and chapters in published books.

Meshack Owino (Ph.D.), is an Associate Professor of History at Cleveland State University, Cleveland, Ohio. He earned his B.Ed. and M.A at Kenyatta University, Kenya, and another M.A. and Ph.D. at Rice University, Houston, Texas. As a professor at CSU, Dr. Owino primarily teaches courses on precolonial and modern Africa, Eastern Africa, Kenya, and South Africa. Dr. Owino has written many articles focusing on the social history of African soldiers during the precolonial and colonial periods as well as on Africa and the World Wars in general. His latest article, published online in February 2021, is titled, "Kenya and the Second World War: A Review of the Historiographical Landscape," can be found in *History Compass* journal, at: https://onlinelibrary .wiley.com/doi/10.1111/hic3.12649. Dr. Owino also has interests in the digital media and Africa and has written many articles documenting the intersections between digital humanities and public history in Africa. Dr. Owino has won many grants, including two major Digital Humanities grants with J. Mark Souther from the National Endowment for the Humanities (NEH). The first of these two NEH grants (with J. Mark Souther) focused on "Curating Kisumu: Adapting Mobile Interpretation in East Africa" (2014–15) and the second one dealt with "Curating East Africa: A Platform and Process for Location-based Storytelling in the Developing World" (2017–18). Dr. Owino's research and writing also deals with the origin, nature, and impact of ethnic nationalism on modern African states.

Grayson Michael Posey is currently attending the Master's Program in International Relations at St. Mary's University in San Antonio, Texas. His primary area of research examines the intersectionality of international relations and queer rights and persecution on the African continent. In 2010 he received an internship in Cape Town, South Africa where he studied the long-term effects of apartheid on children versus adults in the Athlone and Khayelitsha townships. This firsthand experience and research project sparked his academic interests. As an undergraduate, Posey was selected to present a study on gender and political theory at the Southwestern Social Science Association in 2010. In 2021, Posey worked with the Tamarindo Foundation to develop a human security plan with the residents of Guarjila township in Chalatenango, El Salvador. He has been selected for scholarships and as a research assistant by two consecutive Graduate Program Directors for his outstanding knowledge, research skills, and writing ability.

J. Mark Souther (Ph.D.) is Professor of History at Cleveland State University, where he directs the Center for Public History + Digital Humanities. Souther directs the Curatescape mobile framework project (curatescape.org), the Cleveland Historical app (clevelandhistorical.org), and the Cleveland Regional Oral History Collection (clevelandvoices.org). He has been awarded numerous grants, including (with Meshack Owino) two National Endowment for the Humanities (NEH) Office of Digital Humanities grants for "Curating Kisumu: Adapting Mobile Interpretation in East Africa" (2014–15) and "Curating East Africa: A Platform and Process for Location-based Storytelling in the Developing World" (2017–18). Souther is also the author of Believing in Cleveland: Managing Decline in "The Best Location in the Nation" (Temple University Press, 2017), New Orleans on Parade: Tourism and the Transformation of the Crescent City (Louisiana State University Press, 2006), and numerous articles and is co-editor of American Tourism: Constructing a National Tradition (University of Chicago Press, 2012). He earned his Ph.D. from Tulane University in 2002

Maureen Ada Uche (Ph.D.) is a senior lecturer and the current head, Department of Performing Arts, University of Delta, Agbor, Nigeria. She is an ethnomusicologist and a researcher especially in African music and cultures. In addition to authoring several chapters to prominent books, Dr. Uche has performed traditional dances of various communities in Nigeria. These dances were choreographed by Dr. Uche, using compositions by some African composers as accompaniment to the dance.

Bradford Whitener (Ph.D.) is a lecturer in the Department of History at St. Mary's University in San Antonio, Texas. He has also taught at the

University of Virginia and the College of William and Mary in Virginia, and at Lewis & Clark College in Portland, Oregon. In 1998, Dr. Whitener was awarded the 1999–2000 Fulbright Fellowship to Munich, Germany, where his research interests focused on the intellectual and cultural history of Europe, and on nineteen-century German Intellectual history in particular. In 2005, Dr. Whitener received his Ph.D. from the University of Virginia in History. He has since taught numerous survey courses in United States history and World History, as well as courses in Modern European History, Modern Germany, the Holocaust in Comparative Perspective, Marx and the Marxist Legacy, and Modern Intellectual History. He is the creator and administrator of an academic website, www.StMUScholars.org featuring the research and scholarly writing of his students and of his colleagues' students at St. Mary's University. He has won two teaching awards at St. Mary's University: the St. Mary's *Provost's Teaching Showcase Prize* (2018), and the St. Mary's *President's Award for Excellence* (2021).

www.ingramcontent.com/pod-product-compliance
Lightning Source LLC
Chambersburg PA
CBHW022301280326

41932CB00010B/935